CW00420137

Normandy 1944

Normandy 1944

1944

German Military Organization, Combat Power and Organizational Effectiveness

Niklas Zetterling

CASEMATE

Philadelphia & Oxford

First edition published by J.J. Fedorowicz Publishing in 2010
This fully revised edition published in 2019

Published in the United States of America and Great Britain in 2019 by
CASEMATE PUBLISHERS
1950 Lawrence Road, Havertown, PA 19083, USA
and
The Old Music Hall, 106–108 Cowley Road, Oxford OX4 1JE, UK

Copyright 2019 © Niklas Zetterling

Hardcover Edition: ISBN 978-1-61200-816-5
Digital Edition: ISBN 978-1-61200-817-2

A CIP record for this book is available from the British Library

Printed and bound in the United States of America

Typeset in India for Casemate Publishing Services. www.casematepublishingservices.com

For a complete list of Casemate titles, please contact:

CASEMATE PUBLISHERS (US)
Telephone (610) 853-9131
Fax (610) 853-9146
Email: casemate@casematepublishers.com
www.casematepublishers.com

CASEMATE PUBLISHERS (UK)
Telephone (01865) 241249
Email: casemate-uk@casematepublishers.co.uk
www.casematepublishers.co.uk

Front cover: *Fallschirmjäger* in Normandy, 1944. (Bundesarchiv, Bild 101I-584-2160-12)

Contents

Introduction

The battle in Normandy during the summer 1944 is among the most well-known events in history. Innumerable books and other publications have been produced on this subject. Given this background it is natural to assume that there is little to add to our knowledge of this battle. A closer scrutiny of the available literature, however, reveals several flaws.

One item that has been lacking is an order of battle for the German forces involved. Most books seem to have a fairly clear picture about the whereabouts of the German divisions. But when it comes to non-divisional combat units, information is much scarcer. This is partly explained by the shortage of suitable order of battle charts in the German documents that have survived. Thus, the researcher is forced to proceed along a much more strenuous path, to scan all available documents for information on unit employment and compile what is found. Also, such a laborious work will uncover more information about the condition of the units that fought in Normandy.

Another imperfection in available publications is the way German casualties are treated. Since no comprehensive compilation has been found among the documents for the units and staffs that were involved in the battle this is understandable. There are, however, ways to make a fairly accurate estimate of German casualties. Given this problem it is hardly surprising that the condition of the German units after the battle is often inaccurately described.

Many myths about how German units were organized are also prolific. This is hardly surprising, since there often existed several different organizations for a given type of unit. Further compounding this difficulty is the fact that German units quite often did not adhere to the proscribed organization. Nevertheless, some of the myths are not excusable despite these circumstances.

These circumstances indicate a need for more research on the German units that fought in Normandy. Hopefully, this book will provide some of the information that can redress the imperfections described above. It is, however, a vast topic and much research remain to be done. Perhaps this work can provide some assistance to such efforts.

One of the protracted discussions of World War II is the relative combat efficiency of the German forces compared to British and US units. Occasionally, the argument that democracies produce better soldiers is encountered. It would certainly be comforting if democracies, almost by default, produce better soldiers than obnoxious regimes like Nazi Germany. Personally I believe that democracies usually do produce better soldiers than dictatorships, but I do not believe that there are no exceptions to this. Rather, it could be dangerous to assume that there are no exceptions, since that could cause complacency. The democracy is too valuable to be jeopardized by such simplifications. The issue of German combat efficiency is discussed further in the book.

When discussing a battle, it might be useful to define the battle. In this book, the battle at Normandy is assumed to last from 6 June to 22 August. Geographically it is delineated by the base of the Brittany peninsula, the Loire, the line Tours–Vendôme–Nogent le Routrou–l'Aigle–Lisieux and the Channel. Obviously, there is information about units outside this area included in the book too. E.g. the units in Brittany often sent elements to Normandy, thus motivating inclusion in this book. Also interesting information about the condition of units is available for dates later than 22 August. Since this information might provide valuable clues to the condition of the units at the end of the battle in Normandy, it is worth including.

In general, the German records are more extensive and reliable in the early part of the campaign, compared to the later part. During the second half of August and early September 1944, German formations were often retreating in a rather chaotic manner, which made it very difficult for the staffs to keep track of them. This has also contributed to the delineation of the battle I have chosen.

A desirable feature would have been a standardized presentation of all units. Unfortunately, the available documents and literature does not allow that. Rather the sources have dictated the disposition for each unit.

The negative side of working on a project like this is the exclusions made. One decision was not to include *Luftwaffe-Flak* units. The only exception is the *III. Flak-Korps*. Most flak units in France were immobile or almost immobile. The major exception was the *III. Flak-Korps*. As argued in the section on the latter unit, *Luftwaffe Flak* units were not a major ground combat system. They did contribute directly to ground combat first and foremost by providing indirect fire. But most important was the indirect contribution by providing air defense. However, an appendix with a list of Flak units in France is included.

Another type of unit that is not included is the coast artillery. Obviously, the principal task for such units is to engage enemy naval vessels. However, when Allied ground units advanced they encountered the coast artillery units' land defenses. Unfortunately, there is precious little information on how these were organized.

When Allied units advanced further from the beaches they occasionally faced German *Sicherungs* (security) or *Landesschützen* units. These were not intended for combat and have been excluded from this book, except *Sicherungs-Regiment 1*. The latter unit was better equipped than most security units and it seems that it was consciously sent from Paris to help stop Patton's spearheads. Again, little information has been available on these units.

The errors on German strength, casualties and organization have also contributed to other errors, since these factors influence for example analyses of combat efficiency. Similarly, errors on the combat readiness, mobility and training of German formations in France affect estimates on the possibility for the Germans to move forces quicker to Normandy than was actually the case. These are some of the main questions this book tries to answer. Another important issue is the effects of Allied air power. These questions, together with the desire to present a description of the German ground combat units that fought in Normandy, are the motivating force behind this work.

This work was originally produced while I worked at the Swedish Defence College. Being a researcher there, I got several opportunities to visit archives and search for relevant documents. I am in particular indebted to Anders Frankson, who has helped me frequently and shared much information he has uncovered from various archives. Richard Anderson provided me with additional information and comments on German casualties and Christopher Lawrence has been a most valuable discussion partner over many years.

This new edition contains additional combat unit information, some corrections, alterations to the appendices and several other updates. Hopefully, it can serve as a reference source to those with an interest in the battle fought in Normandy during the summer months of 1944.

I

The Sources Available

There are several sources for information on the German units that fought in Normandy. They can be divided into three main categories, documents produced during or immediately after the battle, various kinds of attestations given after the war by participants and printed books and articles.

Of these, the first category is usually regarded as most reliable. A problem is that much of the documentation was destroyed during the battle at Falaise and the retreat from Normandy. From the German *7. Armee*, large amounts of documents remain from June 1944. The records for July and August are less complete. The records of *Panzergruppe West*, later renamed *5. Panzerarmee*, contain several interesting documents. They mainly cover July and the first half of August and include almost daily reports on tank strength of attached units.

A large part of the documents produced by *Heeresgruppe B* and *OB West* remain. Among them can be found reports titled *Stand der Bewegungen*, i.e. reports on the transfer of units to Normandy. Several documents found in the records of *OB West* are identical to those found in the files of *Heeresgruppe B*. This is not surprising since all major combat actions within *OB West* area were confined to the area for which *Heeresgruppe B* was responsible, at least before the Allied invasion of Southern France. These two staffs also sent reports to OKH and OKW. However, this material is usually identical to that found in the files of *OB West* and *Heeresgruppe B*.

Another important source is the files of the Inspector-General of Panzer Troops. These contain much valuable information on the organization, equipment, manpower strength and casualties of German mechanized units. Note that reports on the condition of the anti-tank battalions of infantry divisions can often be found in these files.

With few exceptions documents from corps level and below were lost during the retreat from Normandy. There exist valuable records from *58. Panzer-Korps* and also from *25., 81.* and *84. Panzer-Korps*.

German war time records are today located at *Bundesarchiv–Militärarchiv* (*BA-MA*) in Freiburg. Most of these documents can also be studied on microfilm at the National Archives and Records Administration (NARA) at Washington D.C. In this book references to both these archives appear. If a document has been found in Freiburg this is indicated by "BA-MA" followed by the code for the specific file where the document is located. If the document has been found in Washington this can be indicated by e.g. "T312, R1569, F000172". The digits following the T indicate the microfilm publication series, those following the R indicate the particular microfilm roll and the number following the F indicate the frame on the roll. An example is file BA-MA RH 21-5/50 at *Bundesarchiv-Militärarchiv*, which contains reports on tank strength for units subordinated to *Panzergruppe West*. The same documents can be found in T313, R420 at National Archives in Washington.

A problem that may be encountered when using archival documents is that information may be coded. This need not be for security reasons. Rather, it is often caused by the desire to keep reports to be transmitted as short as possible. An example of this is the reports on tank strength discussed above. In these reports a letter, or a letter and a digit indicate types of tanks. *Tigers* are represented by an E, *Panthers* by a D, *Panzer IV* with L43 or L48 gun by C2, *StuG* (*Sturmgeschütze*) by Gl, *JagdPz* (*Jagdpanzer*) *IV* by G2, *Marder* by H1 and *StuPz* (*Sturmpanzer*) *IV*. Similarly, 7.5 cm AT guns are represented by the letter P and 8.8 cm AT guns by Q.

Another problem is the need for understanding the circumstances prevailing when the document was produced. This does, for example, apply to casualty reports. Occasionally compilations were made before all subordinate units had yet sent in complete reports. Also, there were delays in the reporting, which can cause errors.[1]

Sometimes the staff members were too sloppy when writing the documents. An example is the coding of the *Panzer IV* with long 7.5 cm gun described above. Sometimes the code CL was used rather than C2. The L probably stands for "*Lang*" or long-barreled gun. However, this is sometimes written in the reports by using lower-case "*l*". This is very confusing since it looks almost identical to C1 (C-one). The latter is the code for the old *Panzer IV* with the short-barreled 7.5 cm gun.

The overall impression of the German documents is that they are reliable. Incorrect information appears mainly when circumstances were chaotic, but most commonly, such conditions cause information not to be recorded at all.

Usually German records consist of two parts, the war diary and the "*Anlagen*". The war diary is usually a written narrative of the events in a chronological order. It rarely contains hard data on individual combat units. The "*Anlagen*" are more useful for this purpose. They contain most of the reports, compilations and documents produced at the time of battle.

A German staff was divided into several sections. Perhaps the most important was the operations section, headed by the Ia. Most of the documents used for this book was produced by the *Ia* sections of the various staffs. Other important sections are the *IIa/b*, which dealt with personnel matters, and the quarter master section, *O.Qu*. The general impression is that most documents that have survived originate from the *Ia* section.

As mentioned above either the original documents or microfilm copies can be studied. The original documents, of course, have advantages. This is especially true for maps and charts that employ color coding. Also, if the original document had poor contrast, the microfilm copy is often difficult to read.

Despite everything, the volume of documents available is still considerable. Exactly how many that remains is unclear, but the files and microfilm rolls consulted for this book encompass well over 100,000 pages. Obviously, it is beyond the capacity of one man to carefully read, digest, analyze, summarize and evaluate all that information in the limited time available for a book project. There is most likely much information that still can be extracted from the archives. Hopefully the references in this book may provide some help for future researchers.

Another important source is the manuscripts written by German officers after the war. This was done upon request from the US Army Historical Division. Usually commanders at division level or above, or their chiefs of staff, wrote the manuscripts. Since they often had nothing but their memory to rely upon, they are, of course, not free from errors. Occasionally, they may have had a personal diary to support their writing. The German officers often emphasized that they wrote from memory and that they were not positive about specific details. My impression is that they declined from stating anything when they were uncertain, rather than giving information that might be false. Consequently, the main problem with the manuscripts is not that they are wrong, but that they do not provide enough information. These manuscripts are available today at the NARA and copies of them can be ordered.

The character of these manuscripts can vary considerably. Perhaps the most extensive is the series of manuscripts on *352. Infanterie-Division*. These were produced by the chief of staff (or *Ia*) Lieutenant-Colonel Ziegelmann.[2] They comprise about 200 pages, plus maps. I have been able to check some of his information against archival documents and generally found Ziegelmann to be quite reliable. The errors found are of minor importance. For example, he states that the *621. Ost-Bataillon* was located near Isigny on D-Day, while in fact it was the *439. Ost-Bataillon*. Similarly, he has mixed up some of the 10.5 cm howitzer battalion locations on D-Day. However, when Ziegelmann indicates an artillery battalion in a specific location, the records I have found also shows an artillery battalion in that location, but perhaps another battalion. The 15 cm howitzer battalion is correctly located by Ziegelmann. Similar errors can be found in many other manuscripts.

The third source is, of course, the books and articles published. Generally, I have endeavored to use such sources as little as possible, since many of them are of poor quality and contain many errors. Some of these errors concern hard data, e.g. Stephen Badsey writes that more than a million German soldiers fought in Normandy.[3] Such statements are clear and accordingly it is quite easy to show that they are wrong. In other cases, the errors are subtler. An example of this is the British official history of the campaign in Normandy.[4] On page 316 the casualties suffered by both sides during Operation *Charnwood* 8–9 July are discussed. First the British losses, 3,500 men, are given. This is followed by:

> According to the German war diaries all the battalion commanders of the 16th G.A.F. Division's regiment west of Orne had either been killed or wounded and it had lost 75% of its strength; the total infantry strength of the 12th SS Panzer Division had been reduced to the equivalent of one battalion.

While these statements are close to the truth, important facts are concealed. First of all, since this is part of a section where the losses suffered during *Charnwood* are discussed, it is easy for the reader to assume that the poor state of the infantry of *12. SS-Panzerdivision* is, at least mainly, the result of *Charnwood*. However, this is far from the reality. During *Charnwood*, the losses suffered by *12. SS-Panzerdivision* amounted to about 600 men.[5] The vast majority of the losses that had diminished the infantry strength of the *12. SS-Panzerdivision* had been inflicted well before *Charnwood*.

The infantry of the "16th G.A.F. Division" was probably far below full strength before *Charnwood* and from the war diaries it is also explicit that the 75% losses refer to riflemen only.[6] Finally the figure of 75% may seem very high, but probably this meant that casualties numbered less than 1,000. Together with the losses suffered by *12. SS-Panzerdivision*, the German forces lost less than half compared to the British. This is not really the impression given by the description in the official British history.

Several similar cases exist in the official British history. Generally, its information on the German forces is very unreliable. In fact, many of the errors are of such nature that it must be doubted if the book was actually written as an honest attempt at disclosing the truth.

Unsurprisingly, the literature that has been of greatest value to this book is the unit histories. Probably the best of them is the history of *12. SS-Panzerdivision*, written by Hubert Meyer who was *Ia* during the battles in Normandy. Generally, the books on *Waffen-SS* divisions are very comprehensive.[7] Those on army panzer divisions are more brief. Relatively few histories of German infantry divisions have been written. It should, of course, be held in mind that many books written by veterans are apologetic.

Occasionally, authors of unit histories have been able to locate records that are private property. Thus, they may include information not otherwise available. See also the appendix on unit histories.

---

1 This problem is discussed in more detail in N. Zetterling & A. Frankson, Analyzing WWII East Front Battles (article in *Journal of Slavic Military Studies,* Frank Cass London, Vol 11, No 1, March 1998) pp. 176–203. Even though the examples concern the Eastern Front, the basic problems are the same.

2 These are MS # B-432, B-433, B-434, B-435, B-436, B-437, B-438, B-439, B-455, B-489, B-741, B-490.

3   S. Badsey, *Normandy 1944* (Osprey, London 1990) p. 85. Also, the information on German casualties given on this page is completely wrong.

4   L. F. Ellis, *Victory in the West, Vol I, The Battle of Normandy* (HMSO, London 1962).

5   H. Meyer, *Kriegsgeschichte der 12. SS-Panzerdivision "Hitlerjugend", vol I* (Munin, Osnabrück 1982) pp. 264–7. Meyer uses the casualty reports for the battalions engaged in Operation *Charnwood*. However, the reports for *III./SS-Panzergrenadier-Regiment 25* are missing and it is assumed that this battalion suffered casualties similar to its nearest neighbour, the II./SS-Pz.Gren.Rgt. 25.

6   See the narrative for this division.

7   There exist histories by Lehmann & Tiemann (*1. SS-Panzerdivision*), Weidinger (*2. SS-Panzerdivision*), Fürbringer (*9. SS-Panzerdivision*), Meyer (*12. SS-Panzerdivision*) and Stöber (*17. SS-Panzergrenadier Division*).

2

German Terminology

Needless to say, a good understanding of the terminology used by the *Wehrmacht* during the war is a prerequisite for using archival documents. Generally, the terminology is rather straight-forward, but there are some intricacies that have to be careful with. One of them is the way the Germans reported manpower strength. The following terms were used[1]:

Verpflegungsstärke: Ration strength, i. e. the number of men the unit was ordered to provide with necessary substance. Thus, it could include sick, wounded, prisoners of war, non-military manpower and manpower from other military organizations.

Kopfstärke: This is a rather unusual term but it seems to be used to depict the same kind of strength as *Verpflegungsstärke*.

Iststärke: Actual strength, includes all men that are part of the unit's composition. Men on leave or temporarily detached to other units are included. Also, men sick or wounded are included if they are assumed to return to service within eight weeks. Thus, despite its name, this strength category does not give the actual number of men available for service with the unit at the given time.

Tagesstärke: Daily strength, this includes all men momentarily available for service with the unit. Temporarily attached personnel is included too.

Gefechtstärke: Combat strength, i.e. the number of fit men in units of combat type, e.g. armor, infantry, combat engineer reckon etc.

Kampfstärke: Front strength, i. e. those men in units of combat type who were up front, e.g. tank crews, rifle men, anti-tank gun crews, etc.

An example of how much the manpower strength could vary is given by Table 2.1. Note that Table 2.1 does not include non-combat GHQ units and units directly under command of *OKH* (which were quite few[3]). If these are included, the *Iststärke* for the army groups were 550,000 (AG South Ukraine), 597,000 (AG North Ukraine), 849,000 (AG Centre) and 561,000 (AG North)[4].

Table 2.1 German strength on the Eastern Front 1 June 1944[2]

Army Group	Iststärke	Tagesstärke	Gefechtstärke	Kampfstärke
South Ukraine				
Divisions & Brigades	418,984	360,562	198,510	140,320
GHQ Combat Troops	58,692	47,913	33,169	19,346
Total:	477,676	408,475	231,679	159,666
North Ukraine				
Divisions & Brigades	475,347	367,266	235,649	175,229
GHQ Combat Troops	57,391	40,398	27,840	18,587
Total:	532,738	407,664	263,489	193,816
Centre				
Divisions & Brigades	578,225	442,053	283,543	214,164
GHQ Combat Troops	66,171	44,440	32,657	22,608
Total:	644,396	486,493	316,200	236,772
North				
Divisions & Brigades	376,268	287,078	180,001	138,373
GHQ Combat Troops	58,481	43,947	31,967	19,924
Total:	434,749	331,025	211,968	158,297
Total for Eastern Front:	**2,089,559**	**1,633,657**	**1,023,336**	**748,551**

Verpflegungsstärke–ration strength–often shows an inflated manpower strength, at least at army and army group level. No compilation comparable to that presented in Table 2.1 has been found, but an example is given by a document discussing the ration strength of Army Group North.[5] Here it is reported that the ration strength of the army group was 1,012,000 men on 1 June 1944. However, the main message of the document is the inaccuracy of the ration strength reports and the fact that so much manpower is included in them that has nothing to do with the combat efforts of the army group. According to the document only 550,200 men can be included in the *Iststärke*. According to the listing, this includes Divisions, Brigades, GHQ combat units, security units, rear supply services and men serving with intelligence, construction, army justice, propaganda, map production, railways and various technical units. Even including all German personnel (thus also civilians) the strength of the army group amounts to 670,000 men. Evidently ration strength, at least as the Germans calculated it, can give a very inflated and inaccurate picture. Indeed, it is explicitly stated in the document that this was a well-known problem. However, this seems mainly to be the case for units above division level. Divisions and lower level units seldom had large numbers of men to feed except their own men, or attached GHQ units.[6]

German casualties are usually given as *Gefallen*, *Verwundet* and *Vermißt*. These terms refer to killed, wounded and missing *in action*. Note that *Gefallen* include those who died before arriving at dressing stations. Sometimes the term *Verstorbene* is used, to include also those who died after receiving medical care.

When the word casualties is used in this book it invariably refer to the sum of *Gefallen*, *Verwundet* and *Vermißt*. In German, this is sometimes referred to as *personelle blutige Verluste*. These losses can be regarded as losses due to enemy action. In addition, soldiers fell ill or got injured in accidents, but such losses were reported separately. When a unit was engaged in heavy combat, such losses were usually small compared to losses due to enemy action.

Also, equipment losses can be tricky. Usually German reports use the words *Ausfälle* and *Totalausfälle*. The former term refers to equipment that has been rendered unserviceable while the latter term refers to equipment that has been permanently lost. Thus, *Ausfälle* include equipment that can be recovered and repaired while *Totalausfälle* does not. When it comes to tanks this is a very important distinction, since the majority of the German tanks that were rendered inoperable could be repaired.[7]

Reports on the condition of units can include terms that warrant explanation. The strength of battalions is often given by using the following terms[8]:

Starkes Bataillon	*Kampfstärke* more than 400 men
Mittelstarkes Bataillon	*Kampfstärke* 300–400 men
Durchschnittliches Bataillon	*Kampfstärke* 200–300 men
Schwaches Bataillon	*Kampfstärke* 100–200 men
Abgekäpftes Bataillon	*Kampfstärke* less than 100 men

These terms were used for infantry, engineer, reckon and field replacement battalions. For divisions, another system was used. They were assigned a *Kampfwert* (combat value) ranging from I to V, where I was the highest. These were not connected to particular strength levels. Rather they were a judgement based on the unit's capabilities, taking into account manpower strength, combat fatigue, equipment status, training levels and perhaps supply situation.[9] A unit assigned *Kampfwert I* was considered fit for any mission.

It is worth noting the Germans sometimes used the word *Vernichtet*, i.e. destroyed or eliminated, even when a unit still had considerable strength. An example of this is the *Panzer-Lehr-Division* which on 28 July was reported to be *Vernichtet*.[10] Four days later it had over 11,000 men and was still in action.[11]

German units are numbered using either roman or Arabic numerals. Corps were given Roman numbers, while divisions were indicated by Arabic numerals. Regiments were invariably indicated by Arabic numerals, but battalions could be indicated by both Arabic and Roman numerals. A non-divisional battalion had its number written by Arabic digits. Battalions belonging to a division, but not part of a regiment, were also given Arabic numbers, often the same number as the division. Battalions that were part of a regiment were given Roman numbers, I, II, III, etc.

Companies were indicated by Arabic numbers. If the companies were part of a battalion that in turn was part of a regiment the companies were numbered consequently. If the *I. Battalion* of a regiment had four companies, they were given numbers 1–4. The companies of *II. Battalion* were given numbers 5–8 etc. At the beginning of the war the German infantry regiments had three infantry battalions, each with four companies, and also an infantry howitzer company and an AT company. The infantry companies were number 1–4 in *I. Battalion*, 5–8 in *II. Battalion* and 9–12 in *III. Battalion*. The howitzer and AT companies had number 13 and 14. When the *III. Battalion* was removed from the infantry regiments the numbers for the howitzer and AT companies were retained, despite the fact that companies 9–12 no longer existed.

There are two words in German for battalion. *Bataillon* was used for infantry, mortar and engineer units while *Abteilung* was used with tank, anti-tank, artillery, rocket artillery and recon units.

Reports on tank status often give the number of operational tanks. Quite often they also give the number of tanks in workshops. Tanks in workshops were divided into two categories, short-term repair and long-term repair. Sometimes the distinction between the two categories is time. In some cases, tanks scheduled to be operational within three weeks are considered in short-term repair, while the limit in other cases seems to have been two weeks. In reality it must often have been difficult to make such predictions and it seems that vehicles that remained with repair facilities at the front-line units were labeled as short-term repair and those vehicles sent to army level workshops or other rear facilities were classified as long-term.

Often terminology develops without any real intention. Probably an example of this is the German distinction between medium and heavy AT guns. The latter category includes 7.5 cm *Pak* 40 and 8.8 cm AT guns plus captured Soviet 7.62 cm guns. Medium AT guns refer mainly to 5 cm guns but also to the French 7.5 cm gun on the chassis of 5 cm *Pak* 38 (7.5 cm *Pak* 97/38) and other captured weapons of similar size.

These comments should, however, not obscure the fact that the German terminology usually is quite easy to understand. The reader will probably not find it a hindrance to his understanding of the issues discussed later.

---

1 OKH GenStdH/Org.Abt. Nr. I/2000/44 geh. H.Qu., den 25.4.44. Betr,: Festlegung der Stärkebegriffe, BA-MA RH 2/60. See also N. Zetterling & A. Frankson, Analyzing WWII Eastern Front Battles (Article in *Journal of Slavic Military Studies*). This article contain a fuller description of the intricacies of terminology.

2 OKH Org. Abt. I, H.Qu., den 26.7.1944, Verbände Stand 1.6. and Fechtende Heerestruppen Stand 1.6. (BA-MA RH 2/1341).

3 According to OKH. Org.Abt. (I) Nr. I/20,737/44 g,Kdos, Betr: Iststärken, Fehlstellen und Ersatzzuführungen des Ostheeres von Januar bis Oktober 1944, 24. November 1944 (BA-MA

RH 2/1341) the Iststärke on the Eastern Front amounted to 2,620,000 men on 1 June, this is only 63,000 more than the combined total for the army groups.

4   Notiz Betr.: Iststärken und Tagesstärken des Feldheeres aufgegliedert nach Kriegsschauplätzen, Stand 1.6.44. (BA-MA RH 2/1339).

5   OKH Org.Abt. I Nr. I/18280/44 g.Kdos H.Qu., den 23. Juli 1944 (BA-MA RH 2/1341).

6   The document from which the definitions of strength given insist that ration strength should not be used for analyses of combat capabilities, because it simply is not relevant. The document (issued by OKH) orders the use of ration strength to discontinue, except in reports pertaining to supply matters.

7   See N. Zetterling & A. Frankson, Analyzing WWII Eastern Front Battles (Article in *Journal of Slavic Military Studies*) for a more complete discussion on this subject.

8   OKH GenStdH/Org Abt Nr. IZ/45,100/44 geh., 15 Juni 1944, T78, R421, R6390282.

9   An example of this is the *Panzer-Lehr-Division*, which on 30 July was rated at "barely IV", despite the fact that the division had a strength of over 11000 men and 77 tanks and assault guns.

10   OB West Ia Nr. 6091/44 g.Kdos, 28.7.44, T311, R28, F7034840.

11   See narrative for *Panzer-Lehr-Division*.

3

German Combat Unit Organization

Since the beginning of the war, many German combat units had undergone important changes in organization. Furthermore, German units in the field often did not correspond to the tables of organization and equipment (T/O&E). Since each German combat unit is presented later in the book this chapter will focus on various aspects of how German units were organized, rather than exact data on specific types of units.

Infantry Divisions

Since October 1943 a new T/O&E had applied to the German infantry divisions. This called for three infantry regiments, each with two infantry battalions, one *Fusilier-Bataillon*, an antitank battalion, an engineer battalion and an artillery regiment with three artillery battalions plus various services. However, few German divisions in Normandy corresponded exactly to that structure.

Several of the German infantry formations were so-called *bodenständige Divisionen*, or static divisions. Sometimes it has been believed that this category only included the divisions numbered 700–719, but there existed static divisions with much lower numbers.

Occasionally, divisions that had initially been classified as static were upgraded in mobility. One example was the *243. Infanterie-Division* on the Cotentin. It was not an immediate process to upgrade the mobility. Just issuing or commandeering vehicles could usually not motorize a division. In those days, quite few men could drive a motor vehicle and it required training to get drivers to the vehicles. Fuel shortages, of course, hampered training.

The static infantry divisions exhibited greater variation in organization and it is quite simply not any point in trying to describe a general T/O&E for these units. In some cases, like *265.* and *266. Infanterie-Divisionen*, a large part of the divisions were static, while a smaller *Kampfgruppe* was more mobile (though it could not be considered motorized). Often in these cases, the *Kampfgruppe* was sent to Normandy, while most of the division remained in its original position.

Usually a *Feldersatz-Bataillon*, i.e. a field replacement battalion, was included in the infantry divisions. This was intended to give the replacements their final training and to give them acquaintance with the personnel of the division before going into combat. Accordingly, the battalion was not committed to combat except in emergencies. Thus, the *Feldersatz-Bataillon* did generally not contribute to the combat power of the division,[1] but to its staying power.

One of the most important components of the infantry divisions was the anti-tank battalion, the *Panzerjäger-Abteilung*. At the beginning of the war this was equipped with towed 3,7 cm AT guns. Experience in Russia showed that this was not an effective weapon and more powerful guns were introduced. In Normandy, almost all anti-tank guns among infantry divisions were of the type 7.5 cm *Pak 40*.

Some of the infantry divisions in Normandy had their *Panzerjäger-Abteilung* equipped with *Marder* SP AT guns and *Sturmgeschütz III* assault guns. This, of course, provided more powerful and flexible anti-tank defense, but there was one further advantage. A problem for the infantry divisions was the low mobility. If the *Panzerjäger-Abteilung* was equipped with *Marders* and *Sturmgeschütz III* it had tracked mobility and could also serve as a highly mobile reserve available to the commander of the division.

The age of the men in the infantry divisions could vary considerably. The soldiers of *352. Infanterie-Division* were 18–19 years old, while those of *709. Infanterie-Division* were about 36 years old. Similarly, the proportion of officers with combat experience could vary considerably.

Panzer-Divisionen

Two different types of panzer divisions took part in the fighting in Normandy. These were the army and the *Waffen-SS-Panzer-Divisionen*. The differences between these have often been described incorrectly. Among other things it has been said that the following number of tanks were included in these types of divisions in 1944:

	Panzer IV	*Panther*
Wehrmacht Panzer-Division	52	51
Waffen-SS-Panzer-Division	64	62

These figures are, however, completely wrong. No such T/O&E ever existed for either type of division. In reality the number of tanks according to establishment strengths were identical in the two types of divisions. Both had, at full strength, 101 *Panzer IVs* and 79 *Panthers*.

Other errors are the inclusion of a *Sturmgeschütz* battalion, a 17 cm gun battalion and a rocket artillery battalion in the organization for *SS-Panzer-Divisionen*. All of this is wrong.

Some *SS-Panzer-Divisionen* had an assault gun battalion in 1944, but that was as a substitute for the missing *Panzerjäger-Abteilung*. It was not part of any general T/O&E for *SS-Panzer Divisionen* in 1944. How the myth of 17 cm guns has appeared is difficult to understand, since this kind of gun was only issued to GHQ artillery units. It is easier to understand why the rocket artillery battalion has been included, since a few of the *SS-Panzer-Divisionen* had such a battalion in their established organization. This was, however, not a standard organization applying to all *SS-Panzer Divisionen*.

Even though there indeed existed established organizations for army and *SS-Panzer Divisionen* many of them deviated in various aspects. Occasionally, these alterations made the unit stronger, e.g. both *2.* and *21. Panzer-Divisionen* had two infantry battalions carried by armored half-tracks rather than only one as the official organization called for. In other cases, the deviations could make the unit weaker, like the *10. SS-Panzer-Division*, which only had one tank battalion and no anti-tank battalion and no assault gun battalion.

In 1943, panzer divisions began to have one battalion equipped with *Panthers* and one with the older *Panzer IV*. Usually the *I. Abteilung* was given *Panthers* and *II. Abteilung* was equipped with the lighter *Panzer IV*. In Normandy, all *Panzer* divisions had a *Panther* battalion except *21. Panzer-Division* and 10. *SS-Panzer-Divisionen*. The *9. Panzer-Division* was the only division in Normandy to have its *Panthers* in *II. Abteilung*. However, during the Normandy battle, this *Panther* battalion did not fight together with its parent division.

It has often been argued that the *Waffen-SS* units had priority over *Wehrmacht* units when it came to receive new equipment to replace losses in battle. This does, however, not find much support in the deliveries of new tanks to the divisions. Perhaps statements made by German army officers after the war have fostered this perception. No analyses concerning the relative deliveries of equipment to army and *Waffen-SS-Panzer-Divisionen* have been found. Neither has any analysis comparing such data to casualties or any other factor.

For tanks useful data is available for such analyses. During the period May 1943 to August 1944, the following number of *Panzer IV*s were delivered[2]:

	Unspecified Replacements	SS Tank Units	Army Tank Units	HG Panzer-Division	Other
5/43	162	0	133	20	19
6/43	0	16	201	20	17
7/43	72	53	72	0	15
8/43	30	10	137	0	74
9/43	20	25	193	0	30
10/43	35	58	146	0	26
11/43	0	60	232	0	4
12/43	0	89	143	0	111
1/44	0	77	211	13	19
2/44	35	0	258	0	2
3/44	0	77	133	20	115
4/44	0	24	181	34	98
5/44	15	11	202	0	42
6/44	0	77	168	0	45
7/44	0	34	223	40	37
8/44	8	12	152	0	124

For *Panthers*, the following deliveries took place[3]:

	Unspecified Replacements	SS Tank Units	Army Tank Units	HG Panzer Division	Other
5/43	0	0	192	0	65
6/43	0	0	0	0	0
7/43	0	142	108	0	0
8/43	0	0	169	0	6
9/43	0	3	7	0	17
10/43	0	96	76	0	0
11/43	0	2	264	0	0
12/43	0	70	359	0	0
1/44	0	49	228	0	0
2/44	65	15	175	0	31
3/44	0	74	195	0	52
4/44	0	8	227	0	10
5/44	0	160	175	0	15
6/44	0	56	325	0	0
7/44	0	64	242	6	23
8/44	24	0	367	0	6

Unspecified replacements include those vehicles sent to a particular army group, but whose further whereabouts are unknown.[4] The category "Other" for *Panzer IV* includes vehicles exported to other countries (278), tanks sent to training and testing facilities (137), vehicles delivered to army reserve units (252) and a few other categories. Of the 252 *Panzer IV* sent to reserve units probably all eventually ended up with army *Panzer-Divisionen*. Almost all *Panthers* under the "Other" category went to training facilities.

It should be emphasized that a tank may very well have been issued in the month indicated in the table, but still it may have been dispatched the following month.

The situation is pretty clear for the *Panthers*. During the period 736 vehicles went to *SS-Panzer-Divisionen* and 3,104 to army *Panzer-Divisionen*. There existed seven *SS-Panzer-Divisionen*[5] and on average about 25 army panzer divisions.[6] This means that 124 *Panthers* were delivered per army panzer division and 106 per SS-Panzer division.[7] This hardly indicates that the *SS* divisions had priority. The main reason for this is that rather few of the *SS-Panzer-Divisionen* had any *Panther* battalion in action. Before 1944, only *1.* and *2. SS-Panzer-Divisionen* had any *Panthers* in action. In March 1944, the *Panther* battalion of SS-Wiking went into action, and during June both *9.* and *12. SS-Panzer-Divisionen* went into action with *Panthers*. The *10. SS-Panzer-Division* did not get its *Panthers* until 1945, while the *Panther* battalion of *3. SS-Panzer-Division* went into action in July 1944.

For the deliveries of *Panzer IV*, the *Wehrmacht* divisions received an even greater share. On average, each *SS-Panzer-Division* received only 89 during the period, while the Wehrmacht divisions received 121.[8] Partly this greater share for the Army *Panzer-Divisionen* is explained by the fact that some of the *Panzer-Divisionen* had assault guns in a few of their tank companies instead of *Panzer IV*.[9]

From these basic calculations, it is not possible to conclude conclusively that the *Wehrmacht Panzer-Divisionen* had priority over the *Waffen-SS*, but it can certainly be doubted if the allegation that the *Waffen-SS* had priority is anything more than one of the many myths and clichés prevalent in the literature on World War II.[10]

Wehrmacht Panzer-Divisionen had four infantry battalions. Of these three were transported by trucks and the fourth by armored half-tracks. The *SS-Panzer-Divisionen* had six infantry battalions of which five were truck borne and one was carried in lightly armored half-tracks. In practise, there were deviations from these prescribed organizations. Two of the *SS-Panzer-Divisionen*, *Leibstandarte* and *Das Reich*, did not have enough motor vehicles to fully motorize all their infantry battalions. On the other hand, the *Panzer-Lehr-Division* division had all four of its infantry battalions in armored half-tracks and *2.* and *21. Panzer-Divisionen* had two of their four infantry battalions carried by *SPW*s. Again, it cannot be concluded that the *SS-Panzer-Divisionen* had priority.

GHQ Units

Among British and US forces non-divisional artillery was very prevalent. This was found in independent battalions in the US Army and in regiments in the Commonwealth Armies.[11] In Normandy about half the Allied artillery pieces of caliber 85 mm and above were found in such units.[12] In the German army, such units were much less common. In fact, only seventeen German independent artillery battalions participated in the campaign. Also, one independent long-range gun battery participated. Accordingly, only about one German battery of seven were in GHQ units, a vast difference between the German Army and the Allied forces in Normandy.

However, there was one arm that did redress the imbalance somewhat. The Germans had several rocket artillery units, something that the Allies lacked. Except for a few rocket artillery units in *1.* and *12. SS-Panzer-Divisionen* and *21. Panzer-Division*, all *Nebelwerfers*, as they were called, were in non-divisional units. Three *Werfer* brigades and one *Werfer* regiment participated. Together, these comprised 21 battalions plus a few extra batteries. Thus, they more than doubled the German non-divisional artillery.

It is difficult to evaluate the rocket artillery. Compared to conventional artillery it had much shorter range and was less accurate. The two advantages were the vast instant firepower and the low cost to produce these weapons. A battalion with 15 cm *Nebelwerfers* had 18 launchers, each with six barrels. Within seconds a battalion could fire 108 15 cm rockets. To fire a similar number of 15 cm shells, a howitzer battalion would have to fire for about two minutes.

On the other hand, to take advantage of that instant firepower large quantities of ammunition were required. Added to this was the inferior accuracy of the rockets, which further increased ammunition expenditure. Given the general German difficulties with supply of ammunition this was not a desirable feature.

The cost for a 15 cm *Nebelwerfer 41* was only 3,350 *Reichsmark*, which can be compared to 38,500 *Reichsmark* for a 15 cm *schwere Feld-Haubitze 18*.[13] However, the cost of the gun is only part of the cost for an artillery unit. A motorized artillery battalion requires about eight motor vehicles for each gun.[14] Also, there are further vehicles needed for artillery observers, supply units to bring up the ammunition, etc. When all such costs are added together it is doubtful if the rocket artillery units really were much cheaper. It is even more doubtful whether the cost is so much lower that it compensates for the shorter range and inferior accuracy.

Tanks, assault guns and tank destroyers could also be found in independent units and again the British and American forces were much more lavishly furnished with such units. Only nine German non-divisional tank or assault guns participated in the campaign.[15] Together these had a T/O&E strength of 363 tanks and assault guns.

Thus, less than one sixth of all German tanks, assault guns and tank destroyers in Normandy belonged to non-divisional units. The Allied forces were quite different.

Among the Commonwealth forces five armored divisions figured.[16] Most British non-divisional armor was found in independent brigades, almost always containing three battalions each. Eleven Commonwealth brigades participated.[17] Since the number of tanks of an armored division was about 1.5 times the number of tanks in an armored brigade[18] the armored brigades actually contributed with more tanks than the armored divisions.

Similarly, the US forces had an abundance of non-divisional armor. The seven armored divisions[19] that participated in Normandy had 1 394 medium tanks and 647 light tanks according to T/O&E. The fifteen independent tank battalions had a T/O&E strength of 767 medium tanks and 339 light tanks.[20] Also twenty battalions with self-propelled AT guns (M-10) participated with a total of 720 vehicles.[21] Thus about half the US tanks and tank destroyers were found outside divisions.

According to T/O&E, the Allied non-divisional units participating in Normandy had about ten times more tanks and tank destroyers than German non-divisional tank, tank destroyer and assault gun units. If replacement vehicles are considered too, the difference will become even greater.

As shown by the two cases described above a very large and important part of the Allied forces were found outside the divisions. Consequently, a cursory counting of divisions when comparing forces may result in a grossly distorted picture.

Another important type of non-divisional German unit was the *Flak*. These have often been depicted as an important anti-tank asset, but this is highly questionable. See the section on *III. Flak-Korps* for a fuller description on how AA units were used.

Other shortcomings

France had long been an area for German units to rest, refit, form and train. This meant that many units were not combat ready when the Allied forces assaulted the beaches in Normandy. But perhaps an even greater weakness was the shortage of vehicles. During the war, the German industry never came close to satisfying the demand for trucks and other vehicles. Since France had been a backwater for years, while violent battles were fought on the Eastern Front, few vehicles were sent to Western Europe.

Some units, like the static infantry divisions, were, of course, not supposed to have much transport, but also those infantry divisions that were "regular" had a low motorization level. Even many of the mechanized divisions suffered from serious shortages of motor vehicles. Lack of motor transport forced the Germans to rely on railroads, but since these where a suitable target for Allied bombers, it was almost inevitable that the Germans would suffer from shortages of ammunition, fuel, spare parts and other items indispensable to World War II warfare.[22] But it must also be said that had the Germans had more motor vehicles, shortages of fuel would probably have prevented them from making much use of them.

----

1   Of course, there may have been cases where divisional commanders found themselves able to commit a larger part of their assets since the field replacement battalion could serve as an emergency reserve.

2   Derived from Lieferungen der Pz.Fahrzeuge, Bd. Ab Mai 1943, BA-MA RH 10/349.

3   Ibid.

4   Often the replacements were sent to a particular army group. Sometimes they were sent to an army group which had no *Waffen-SS* units subordinated. In those cases the tanks have been included in the "Army Tank Units" category. If replacements were sent to an army group which had both *Waffen-SS* and Army tank units subordinated the tanks have been included in the category "Unspecified Replacements".

5   The SS-Panzer Divisions were 1., 2., 3., 5., 9., 10. and 12.

6   Army Panzer Divisions initially included numbers 1-9, 11-14, 16-21, 23-26 and also the Grossdeutschland division. During the period the 18. was disbanded, but also the 116. was raised, as was the Pz-Lehr.

7   Exept for a few *Panthers* sent to s.Pz.Jäg.Abt. 654 all *Panthers* were sent to panzer divisions or battalions temporarily dispatched from panzer divisions.

8   This includes the 252 *Panzer IV* sent to reserve units.

9   In fact there were some panzer divisions of the army that had assault guns in their tank regiments. The *14., 16.* and *24.* had a nominal organization of three battalions in the tank regiment, one battalion with *Panthers*, one with Pz IV and one with StuG. However, in these three divisions the assault guns did not replace tanks, rather they were an extra asset.

10 It is certainly possible that a decision was taken that the *Waffen-SS* divisions should receive priority. When it came to the real actions taken, it seems, however, that they did not receive priority, at least not from the spring 1943 to the summer 1944.

11 British artillery regiments had 24 or 16 guns, making them the equivalent of one and a half or two US battalions.

12 See e.g. S. L. Stanton, *Order of Battle U.S. Army World War II* (Presidio, Novato 1984).

13 K. R. Pawlas, *Datenblätter für Heereswaffen, Fahrzeuge und Gerät*, pages 82 &105, Publizistisches Archiv für Militär- und Waffenwesen, Nürnberg 1976.

14 See for example the situation report for s.Art.Abt. (mot.) 460, LXXXII. A.K. Ia, Anlagen zum KTB 6, Artillerie-Kommandeur 141 Nr. 306/44 g.K., 2.3.44, T314, R1602, F000327.

15 These were the 101. s.SS-Pz.Abt., 102. s.SS-Pz.Abt., 503. s.Pz.Abt., 217. Stu.Pz.Abt., 654. s.Pz. Jäg.Abt., 341. StuG.Brig., 394. StuG.Brig., 902. StuG.Abt. and 12. Fallsch.StuG.Brig. The 100. Pz.Ers. u. Ausb.Abt. and 206. Pz.Abt. has been excluded since these units, equipped with obsolete tanks, were never intended for real combat.

16 These were 7th, 11th and Guards Armoured Divisions plus 1st Polish and 4th Canadian Armoured Divisions.

17 These were the *1st Tank Brigade, 1st Assault Brigade Royal Engineers*, 4th Armoured Brigade, 6th Guards Tank Brigade, 8th Armoured Brigade, 27th Armoured Brigade, 30th Armoured Brigade, 31st Tank Brigade, 33rd Armoured Brigade, 34th Tank Brigade and 2nd Canadian Armoured Brigade. Those units italicized were nominally part of 79th Armoured Division, but this formation

never fought as a division, rather its units were temporarily parcelled out to divisions according to the needs of the situation.

18   There were several different organizations for armored divisions and brigades, see H. F. Joslen, *Orders of Battle, Second World War 1939–1945* (London Stamp Exchange 1990).

19   This include the 2nd Free French Division and US Armored Divisions 2–7.

20   There were 13 battalions with 59 medium tanks and 17 light, while two had 59 light tanks, see Stanton, op. cit.

21   Derived from Stanton, op.cit.

22   R. A. Hart, "Feeding Mars: The Role of Logistics in the German Defeat in Normandy, 1944", *War in History*, 1996 3 (4).

4

Number of Soldiers Employed in Normandy

The number of German soldiers that fought in Normandy has never really been properly established. Neither have strength ratios between Allied and German forces been reliably presented. This applies both to the overall situation and to individual battles fought in Normandy. Despite the paucity of this kind of information explanations for the German defeat has been numerous. Clearly this is not satisfying. To try to analyze the factors for the outcome of an operation without establishing the relative force strength seems hazardous.

A few authors have bothered to give the number of German soldiers that fought in Normandy. One of them is Stephen Badsey who claims that over a million men fought under Rommel, von Kluge and Model in Normandy.[1] This is a gross exaggeration and the sources for the statement are obscure. Another figure is presented by Hans Stöber, who contends that until about 10 August, 540,000 Germans had been sent to the Normandy battlefield.[2] Even though he does not give his sources for this, it is clearly much closer to the truth than Badsey's figure.

Unlike ancient armies, World War II forces did not deploy on a well-defined piece of territory and clash for a day. Naturally, this means that the forces committed can vary considerably from day to day. Also, the large logistical tail typical for 20th century forces poses additional problems. Furthermore, units may have more than one mission. In the case of the Germans in Normandy, this is especially true for the rear services.

Fortunately, the divisions and other combat units were usually not split in this way and in those cases where they were, it is often possible to see how they were split. Another fortunate circumstance is that most of the available German manpower was employed in divisions.

On 1 June 1944, the German ground forces (including *Waffen-SS* and *Luftwaffe* ground combat units) in the Netherlands, Belgium and France numbered 880,000 men.[3] As shown in Table 4.1 the divisions in the same area mustered about 680,000 men. This means that about 77% of all men were found in divisions.

Table 4.1 Strength of German divisions in OB West area at the beginning of June.[4]

Division	Manpower Strength	Division	Manpower Strength
3. Fallschirmjäger-Division	17420	346. Infanterie-Division	9816
5. Fallschirmjäger-Division	12253	347. Infanterie-Division[5]	10604
16. Luftwaffenfelddivision	9354	348. Infanterie-Division	10000
17. Luftwaffenfelddivision	9543	352. Infanterie-Division	12734
18. Luftwaffenfelddivision	9400	353. Infanterie-Division	13330
19. Luftwaffenfelddivision	9400	363. Infanterie-Division	11000
47. Infanterie-Division[6]	10513	708. Infanterie-Division	8123
48. Infanterie-Division	10500	709. Infanterie-Division	12320
49. Infanterie-Division[7]	10627	711. Infanterie-Division	7242
77. Infanterie-Division	9095	712. Infanterie-Division	9000
84. Infanterie-Division	8437	716. Infanterie-Division	7771
85. Infanterie-Division	8393	719. Infanterie-Division[8]	9029
91. Luftlande-Division	7500	148. Reserve-Division[9]	14612
242. Infanterie-Division[10]	11306	157. Reserve-Division	10000
243. Infanterie-Division	11529	158. Reserve-Division	10000
244. Infanterie-Division[11]	13107	159. Reserve-Division	10000
245. Infanterie-Division[12]	11432	165. Reserve-Division[13]	8216
265. Infanterie-Division	9726	182. Reserve-Division[14]	11918
266. Infanterie-Division	8852	189. Reserve-Division	10000
271. Infanterie-Division	11617	Panzer-Lehr-Division	14699
272. Infanterie-Division	11211	2. Panzer-Division	16762
275. Infanterie-Division	10768	9. Panzer-Division[15]	14459
276. Infanterie-Division	11658	11. Panzer-Division[16]	14431
277. Infanterie-Division	9136	21. Panzer-Division	16297
319. Infanterie-Division[17]	12276	116. Panzer-Division	13621
326. Infanterie-Division	11533	1. SS-Panzer-Division	19618
331. Infanterie-Division	10543	2. SS-Panzer-Division[18]	18108
338. Infanterie-Division[19]	9312	12. SS-Panzer-Division	20516
343. Infanterie-Division	11021	17. SS-Panzer-Grenadier-Division	17321
344. Infanterie-Division	10000 EST.		

There were, of course, also non-divisional combat units, such as artillery battalions, anti-tank battalions, coast artillery units etc. The strength of these amounted to 58,047 men on 1 June.[20] Consequently, it seems that about 16% of the manpower employed in Western Europe were not included in divisions or other combat units. Note that this applies to army units, *Waffen-SS* and those units of the *Luftwaffe* that were ground combat units. It does not include navy units, nor does it include *Luftwaffe Flak* and air units and their supporting organization.

No compilations of the number of soldiers committed to the fighting in Normandy have been found in the documents. Rather, we are forced to resort to another approach to obtain an estimate as accurate as possible.

Since divisions and non-divisional combat units account for such a large share of the total manpower strength we can calculate the total manpower strength by adding together the strength of the units that arrived in Normandy and then multiply it with 1.19 (the inverse of 0.84).

Appendix 1 gives the arrival and strength of the units that took part in Normandy. This data has been compiled and is shown in Diagram 4.1.

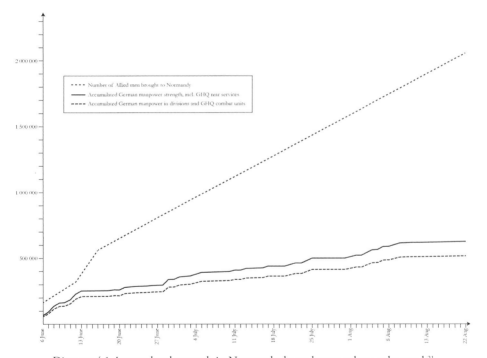

Diagram 4.1 Accumulated strength in Normandy, losses have not been subtracted.[21]

The use of a factor 1.19 to represent the services supporting the combat units may of course be subject to argument. Let us, however, remember that over 80% of the German manpower strength in Western Europe were employed in divisions and non-divisional combat units. Consequently, this factor cannot cause a major change in total strength. There are however two factors that may introduce a systematic error in the calculations.

First of all, theater supply services were probably mainly focusing on supporting the units fighting in Normandy. Similarly, railroad repair efforts were also focusing on keeping lines to Normandy open. This may result in the factor 1.19 being slightly too low.

Secondly, there were several security units that were employed over France to keep the area under control. These units did not have anything to do with the combat efforts against the Allied forces (unless the French resistance movement is included in the Allied forces). This may result in the factor 1.19 being slightly too high.

The German strength given in Diagram 4.1 does not include replacements. Given the German paucity of replacements this is not a major issue. Until 23 July, only 10,078 replacements had arrived in Normandy.[22] Later the rate was speeded up somewhat but by 13 August no more than 30,069 had arrived, while another 9433 were on their way.[23]

It seems that the Allied numerical superiority in Normandy has not been clear to all authors. Indeed, some have not even observed it at all. Stephen E. Ambrose has even written:

> Soviet dictator Joseph Stalin relied on overwhelming numbers, and to some extent American-supplied equipment, to fight the Wehrmacht.
>
> The British and Americans were going to have to rely on their soldiers outfighting Nazi soldiers, because the numbers of troops on the opposing sides were roughly equal.[24]

This is entirely wrong. When Operation *Cobra* was launched, the Germans had brought to Normandy about 410,000 men in divisions and non-divisional combat units.[25] If this is multiplied with 1.19 we arrive at approximately 490,000. However, until 23 July, casualties amounted to 116,863, while only 10,078 replacements had arrived.[26] This means that no more than about 380,000 soldiers remained in Normandy or supported the fighting in Normandy.

On 25 July, there were 812,000 US soldiers and 640,000 British in Normandy.[27] This means that the Allies had a 3.8:1 superiority in manpower. This was better than the superiority enjoyed by the Red Army on the Eastern Front. On 1 June 1944, the Soviets pitted 7.25 million men against 2.62 million Germans.[28]

It is also clear from Diagram 4.1 that the Allies constantly enjoyed a considerable numerical superiority. Casualties magnified this. Even though German casualties for most of the campaign were slightly smaller, relative to the numbers employed they were greater.

Probably the main reason for the assumption that the Allies did not enjoy a considerable manpower advantage is the fact that they did not employ an appreciably greater number of divisions than the Germans. This illuminates the usefulness of the term "divisional slice".[29] The German divisional slice in Western Europe on

1 June was 14,900 men. Allied divisional slices were slightly greater than 40,000.[30] This means that when the number of divisions on both sides were roughly equal, the Allies had a manpower superiority of between 2:1 and 3:1.

It would be a mistake to believe that the larger Allied divisional slices were the result of unnecessary organizational "fat". As shown in Chapter 3, the Allied armies had a much greater number of non-divisional combat units. These units actually doubled the number of combat units of several vital types like tank, antitank, artillery, AA and engineer. Since these types consumed large quantities of ammunition and fuel they also necessitated larger supply services, but they also contributed with more combat power than for example ordinary rifle battalions.

Overall the Allies probably had a better balance between combat units and supply services than the Germans. Even though the Allies occasionally suffered from various shortages of fuel, ammunition or spare parts, these problems were nowhere as chronic as they were for the Germans.[31] It seems that the Germans had based their plans for the defense of France on the assumption that the railroads would be capable of handling all supply necessary for the operations. Hence, the supply services were rather small. When Allied air power effectively targeted the French rail net this presupposition quickly became fallacious and the German supply services were overtaxed.

The Allies on the other hand planned an invasion over sea and they also planned to destroy the French rail net. Consequently, they had to assume that supplies had to be transported by ship and then reloaded to trucks. This, by its very nature, required more men than the German solution, but it also resulted in an organization better capable of standing up to the demands. This is illustrated by the fact that US artillery consumed on average about 1500 tons of ammunition per day during July.[32] It can be contrasted to the fact that on average only 480 tons per day was sent to *7. Armee* 3–27 July.[33] Note that this latter figure refer ammunition sent, not ammunition that arrived and it included all types of ammunition, not only artillery ammunition. Thus, it seems that US expenditure of artillery ammunition may have been about four times greater than German consumption.[34]

As mentioned above, there has been a widespread perception of approximately numerical equality in Normandy, at least concerning manpower. However, the Allied superiority in materiel has never been challenged. Simultaneously, it has been argued that the Germans had a greater share of their manpower directly involved in manning and operating weapons. These views are irreconcilable unless it is assumed that Allied equipment was far more effective. The arguments in favour of that assumption seem slim though.

It would have been quite strange if the manpower strength had been equal in Normandy. After all, the combined population of the United States and Great Britain was much greater than German population. The Pacific theater did, of course, tie up Allied manpower, but this drain was almost insignificant compared to the German commitment on the Eastern Front. Also, until 31 May 1944 German casualties in Russia amounted to 751,237 killed in action, 2,824,807 wounded and 541,043 missing.[35] This level of casualties would constitute a severe strain on any army. Given these circumstances it would indeed have been remarkable if the Allies had not succeeded in outnumbering the Germans in Normandy.

It is not only the overall German manpower strength that has been exaggerated. Also, descriptions of individual actions sometimes include statements on German strength or force ratios. Almost never do they rely on proper sources or analysis. It must be advised that unless force ratios given in the literature are accompanied by information on how they have been obtained and which sources that have been used, the force ratios must be regarded with suspicion. Also, the information on German strength must be derived from German sources, or preferably German archival records, to be considered reliable. Allied intelligence estimates seem not to be reliable enough.

Clearly, the method used here to calculate German overall strength in Normandy is approximate. However, since the vast majority of German soldiers were employed in divisions and GHQ combat units, there is no room for significant errors. Thus, it seems safe to conclude that not many more than 640,000 Germans may have fought in Normandy or supported those operations.

---

1 S. Badsey, *Normandy 1944* (Osprey, London 1990) p. 85.

2 H. Stöber, *Die Sturmflut und das Ende, Geschichte der 17. SS-Panzergrenadierdivision "Götz von Berlichingen"* (Munin, Osnabrück 1976) p. 314.

3 OKH/Gen.St.d.H./Org.Abt. Nr. I/18941/44 g.Kdos. v. 7.9.44, T78, R414, F6383114.

4 See narratives of the divisions for the sources, except those specifically given. Those figures in the table that are in *italic* type are estimates.

5 Der Kommandierende General und Befehlshaber der Truppen des Heeres in den Niederlanden (Generalkommando LXXXVIII A.K.) Abt. Ia, Az: K95 Nr. 1495/44 g.Kdos, den 1.6.44, T314, R1622, F000651-678.

6 Anlagen zum KTB LXXXI. A.K. Ia, Verpflegungs- und Gefechtsstärken, Stand 20.6.44, T314, R1602, F000459.

7 Anlagen zum KTB LXXXI. A.K. Ia, Verpflegungs- und Gefechtsstärken, Stand 20.6.44, T314, R1602, F000459.

8 Der Kommandierende General und Befehlshaber der Truppen des Heeres in den Niederlanden (Generalkommando LXXXVIII A.K.) Abt. Ia, Az: K95 Nr. 1495/44 g.Kdos, den 1.6.44, T314, R1622, F000651-678.

9 AOK 19 Ia, Br.Nr. 7194/44 geh., 19.7.44, BA-MA RH 20-19/76.

10 AOK 19 Ia, Br.Nr. 7194/44 geh., 19.7.44, BA-MA RH 20-19/76.

11 AOK 19 Ia, Br.Nr. 7194/44 geh., 19.7.44, BA-MA RH 20-19/76.

12 Anlage zu Gen.Kdo. LXXXI. A.K. Iib, Nr. 272/44 geh. 1.3.44, T314, R1590, F000826. Strength refer to authorized strength, but the division was already close to authorized strength on 1 March.

13 OB West Ia Nr. 4754/44 g.Kdos, 20.6.44.

14 LXXXII. A.K. Ia Anlagen zum KTB Nr. 6, Verpflegungs- und Gefechtsstärken, Stand 20.5.1944, T314, R1602, F000462.

15 BA-MA RH 10/148.

16 Pz.Gr. West Ia Nr, 2592/44 g.Kdos., Meldung über Stand der Neuaufstellung (Stand 15.6), H.Qu., den 21. Juni 1944 (T311, R25, F7029882.

17 Gliederungen AOK 7, BA-MA RH 20-7/136.

18 BA-MA RH 10/313.

19 AOK 19 Ia, Br.Nr. 7194/44 geh., 19.7.44, BA-MA RH 20-19/76.

20 OKH Org.Abt. I, Notiz <u>Betr.:</u> Auswertung der Stärkemeldungen des Feldheeres Stand 1.6.44, BA-MA RH 2/1341. In this file there is also a report giving the total strength of all divisions in western Europe. However, the figure given is too low. There are several possible reasons for this. The figure may exclude SS and *Luftwaffe* divisions and it may also exclude units that were still forming or divisions that were under direct OKW control, even though they were located in France. It is of course possible that this also applies to the figures for *Fechtende Heerestruppen* but it can be assumed that the differences are smaller. First of all, there were much fewer GHQ troops belonging to the *Waffen-SS* and the *Luftwaffe* compared to the number of divisions. Also, it seems that a lower share of the GHQ troops were directly subordinated to OKW. Finally most of the GHQ troops that were still forming on 1 June seems to have been located in Germany, not France, Belgium or the Netherlands. It must also be remembered that if the true strength of GHQ units were greater the error in the calculations will be that German strength in Normandy as given in this chapter is exaggerated.

21 German data has been taken from Appendix 1, while Allied strength has been taken from the British and US official histories.

22 HGr B Ia Nr 5110/44 g.Kdos, Wochenmeldung 17.7–23.7, 23.7.44, T311, R3, F7002204.

23 HGr B Ia Nr 6070/44 g.Kdos, Wochenmeldung 14.8.44, T311, R3, F7002225.

24 S. E. Ambrose, Why We Won the War: The Politics of WWII (*Army*, June 1994) p. 15. The article is exceedingly poor in other respects too. E.g. The author states that the German panzer divisions, if used properly, would have made the difference, since "the Allies would not be able to bring even a single tank regiment ashore on D-Day" (p. 16). This is one of the most absurd statements ever made. The US army did not have tank regiments at all (except in the 2nd and 3rd Amroured Divisions) but tank battalions. On D-Day the following were landed: 70, 741, 743, 745, 746, 749 plus the 899 TD Bn (See S. L. Stanton, *Order of Battle: US Army in World War II*, Presidio Press, Novato, California 1984.) Also the British forces landed on D-Day included about 900 tanks and armored vehicles (See L. F. Ellis, *Victory in the West, Vol I*, Her Majesty's Stationery Office, London 1962, p. 217). This can be contrasted to the fact that only four German tank battalions equipped with *Panzer IV* or better tanks were theoretically within distance to attack on D-Day (these were the two battalions of *12. SS-Panzer-Division*, the *Panzer IV* battalion of *Panzer-Lehr* [the *Panther* battalion of this division was on its way to the Eastern Front] and one of the battalions of *21. Panzer-Division*. [the other was mainly equipped with obsolete or captured vehicles]).

25 See Appendix 1.

26 HGr B Ia Nr 5110/44 g.Kdos, Wochenmeldung 17.7–23.7, 23.7.44, T311, R3, F7002204.

27 R. G. Ruppental, *Logistical Support of the Armies vol I* (Office of the Chief of Military History, Dept of the Army, Washington D. C. 1953) p. 457.

28 N. Zetterling, Loss Rates on the Eastern Front during WWII (*Journal of Slavic Military Studies*, Vol 9, No 4, Dec 1996) p. 902.

29 The divisional slice is the average division in a theater plus a share of non-divisional units. The share is obtained by assuming that all non-divisional units and manpower is allocated evenly among the divisions in the theater.

30 See Ruppental, op. cit. p 458 (note 82) and Ellis, op. cit. p. 536 and 541.

31 A very good account of the German supply problems is provided by R. A. Hart, Feeding mars: The Role of Logistics in the German Defeat in Normandy, 1944, *War in History* 1996 3 (4).

32 Derived from table on page 528 in Ruppental, op. cit.

33 Anlagen zum KTB O.Qu. West (O.B. West), 1.6.-17.8.44, Versorgungsübersichten AOK 7, T311, R15, F7015377-5472.

34 It could of course be argued that the Germans could use stockpiled ammunition and this is of course true. However during June the German supply deliveries were much smaller than in July and those stocks available in Normandy were largely consumed. Also, even if supplies had arrived in Normandy, they were sometimes destroyed by air attacks on depots (see Hart, op. cit.). Hence it seems that German ammunition consumption could not have been appreciably greater than deliveries.

35 Der Heeresarzt im OKH Gen.St.d.H/Gen Qu Az 1335 c/d (IIb), Personelle blutige Verluste des Feldheeres, T78, R414, F6383234f.

5

The Effects of Allied Air Power

Usually Allied air power is considered a decisive factor for the Allied victory in Normandy, sometimes it is even regarded as *the* decisive factor. Unfortunately, the descriptions of the effects of Allied air power are often superficial at best. A problem is that air power can affect operations in many different ways. There are direct effects, such as casualties and bridges destroyed. However, there are also many other factors, such as delays and influence on enemy decision-making, effects that are best described as indirect. This does not mean that those effects are of less importance. To the contrary, they are probably of greater importance than the casualties inflicted and destruction of military hardware caused. Unfortunately, the indirect effects are far more difficult to assess than the direct effects, which, however, should not be taken to mean that they are less important.

Another problem with air power is that its effectiveness can vary greatly with different types of targets. Also, given the great effects of weather and visibility on air operations, the effectiveness of air power used against a particular target can be very different from time to time.

All of this makes it complicated to describe Allied air power and how it affects operations where all arms are involved.

Attacks on German ground combat units in Normandy

Occasionally attacks on German combat units in the battle zone are emphasized. Often the attacks on German tanks by Allied fighter-bombers that are put forward as examples on the great effectiveness of Allied air power. This is actually quite strange, since the weapons carried by aircraft were unsuitable for attacking tanks. The image of Allied fighter-bombers as effective tank killers is probably the result of claims by the pilots themselves. However, it is hard to conceive a less reliable source for information on the effectiveness of the attacks. Such claims are notoriously exaggerated.

Often the German attack at Mortain is used as an example to show the effectiveness of the fighter-bombers as tank killers. But in fact this engagement is rather an example of vastly exaggerated claims. The British 2nd TAF claimed to have destroyed or damaged 140 German tanks in the Mortain area 7–10 August, while 9th US Air Force claimed 112.[1] This actually exceeded the number of German tanks employed in the operation.[2] In fact no more than 46 tanks were lost in the operation and of these only nine had been hit by air weapons.[3]

Actually, it seems that very few German tanks were lost due to hits from weapons carried by aircraft. Probably no more than about 100 tanks were lost due to hits from air weapons during the entire campaign. Rather it seems that air attacks on tank formations protected by AA units were more dangerous to the aircraft than to the tanks. Allied losses of aircraft were considerable, the 2nd TAF (including elements of Air Defence of Britain that took part in the Normandy campaign) lost 829 aircraft, while US 9th Air Force lost 897.[4]

The main reason for the poor results of air attack on tanks was lack of suitable armament. Machine guns and cannons had fairly good accuracy, but lacked the power necessary to produce more than superficial damage. Heavy bombs could destroy a tank, but it took a direct hit, which was very difficult to achieve. The vaunted rockets had sufficient penetration capabilities. Trials against captured German *Panther* tanks showed that the rockets could penetrate the armor except on the front of the tank.[5] The accuracy of the rockets was, however, alarmingly poor, even when fired in salvos of eight. At trials on training ground in England, the probability of achieving a hit on a tank was at most 4%.[6] On operations, when the aircraft was subjected to AA fire and the targets were not stationary on an open field, hit rates must have been even lower.

Probably tanks were among the most difficult targets for aircraft to attack. Non-armored targets were more lucrative. But even among such targets it seems that losses inflicted by air power were comparatively small compared to Allied artillery, mortars, machine guns etc. Deployed German ground combat units were not easy targets for Allied air power.

No statistics on causes of casualties among the German units has been found in the documents. An alternative approach would be too see to what extent German daily casualties vary in correlation to the weather.

An example is the *12. SS-Panzer-Division* during June. The worst day for the division was 26 June, when it suffered 730 casualties.[7] During this day it rained. In fact, on the six most casualty-intensive days during June the weather either prevented or seriously hampered air operations.[8] If anything the correlation between air operations and casualties seem to be inverse in this case.

A similar case can be made for the *II. SS-Panzer-Korps*. The costliest actions for this corps were fought during the British Operation *Epsom*. In a report the effects of the enormous Allied artillery fire are described. It is said that this was the main cause of German losses. It is also explicitly stated that the effects of the numerous attacks by Allied air units were of "secondary importance".[9]

Another example is the initial actions fought by the *346. Infanterie-Division.* Until 10 June the casualties suffered by the infantry regiments amounted to 916. Simultaneously, the elements of the division that were not involved in direct combat with enemy ground forces suffered only ten casualties.[10] If Allied air power had been a significant cause of casualties, the losses would not have been as concentrated to the units directly engaged with enemy ground combat units as they were in this case. Neither does this appear to be an isolated example. On 13 July, it was reported that the *Panzergrenadiere* suffered 90% of all casualties among panzer divisions.[11]

In the German war diaries, it seems that losses due to enemy air power could be exaggerated. An example is the description of the German attack at Mortain on 7 August as it is given by the war diary of Army Group B[12]:

> In the early morning, the 7th Army, with its left wing consisting of four panzer divisions, thrust towards Avranches … Mist during the morning favoured the attack, which by noon had gained 10 km of ground … As the weather cleared, hundreds of enemy aircraft attacked the assaulting forces, which brought them to standstill, and heavy losses of men and equipment occurred.

Even though it is not explicitly stated that it was the aircraft themselves that inflicted the "heavy" losses, it is quite easy to interpret the citation that way. Actually, the German losses to air were modest as is shown above.

Another example is a report conceived by Rommel on 3 July where he states that 12. SS-*Panzer-Division* suffered considerable losses during the march to Normandy.[13] This is, however, hardly in line with the fact that the division lost 83 men during that period.[14]

It is not only in war diaries and other documents that losses due to air power are exaggerated. In his post-war manuscript about the attack at Mortain, von Gersdorff, the chief of staff of *7. Armee*, wrote that the majority of the equipment losses had been caused by enemy air power.[15]

This statement can be compared with the true causes[16]:

	Hit by Air Weapons	Hit by Ground Weapons	Abandoned or Destroyed by Crew	Unknown Cause	Total
Tanks & SP Guns	9	20	11	6	46
Other Combat Vehicles	12	9	2	9	32
Towed guns	0	2	1	1	4
Cars	4	4	0	3	11
Lorries	6	2	2	20	30
Ambulances	2	0	2	1	5
Motorcycles	0	1	1	2	4
Total:	33	38	19	42	132

Evidently it was only about a quarter of the German equipment lost that had been hit by weapons carried by aircraft. This does not support von Gersdorff's statement. It should be emphasized that it is not likely that many of the unknown causes were due to enemy air power. The sources make it clear that losses due to air attacks were among the easiest to identify.[17]

Neither is the Mortain attack an example of unusually low efficiency for the Allied air forces. It is interesting to see the causes for losses of *Panther* tanks. Three British studies of captured *Panther* tanks (or wrecks of *Panther* tanks), two of them during Normandy and one during the Ardennes battle gave the following results[18]:

	Armor-Piercing Shot	Hollow Charge Projectiles	HE Shells	Aircraft Rockets	Aircraft Cannon	Destroyed by crew	Aban-doned	Un-known
6 June–7 Aug	36	7	7	6	2	6	3	13
8 Aug–31 Aug	11	1	1	2	1	44	30	6
17 Dec–16 Jan	16	0	3	3	0	10	10	5
Total	63	8	11	11	3	60	43	24

Evidently two of the main causes for losing *Panthers* were abandonment and destruction by the crews. These two categories accounted for nearly half the *Panthers* lost and during the period in August they constituted 80% of all the *Panthers* lost. Air power only accounted for about 6% of all the investigated *Panthers*. Those investigations showed above also included other types of tanks. Of 40 *Tigers* only one was hit by air weapons, of *121 Panzer IV* nine were hit by air weapons. Evidently Allied air power was not really capable of destroying large numbers of German tanks.[19]

It should be noted that it seems that air power was an even less important cause of tank losses on the Eastern Front. At the Kursk battle in 1943 air power probably accounted for 2–5% of Soviet tanks lost.[20]

As shown above, there are examples of German officers who after the war stated that the Allied air forces to a large extent caused the German losses. Some authors, like John Ellis,[21] largely bases conclusions on such statements. Probably no German studies were made on the causes of their losses. No such studies have been found among the archival documents that have survived. On the other hand, studies showing the causes of enemy losses have been found. It is not likely that the estimates given by German officers after the war are based on anything more than general impressions. Hence, it is important to consider the circumstances shaping their impressions.

Most of the officers who have given their views held higher positions. Even in the German army, despite its emphasis on commanding from the front, such persons were behind the front line to a much greater extent than riflemen and tankers. For men who spent much of the time in rear areas Allied air power naturally made a greater impact compared to enemy ground forces. The men who served in the combat units probably had a different view.

To this must be added the fact that the extent of Allied air superiority was a completely new experience for most German soldiers. It is quite natural that new threats are magnified compared to those experienced previously. Those officers and men who had served on the Eastern Front seem to have regarded the Allied ground forces as less terrifying than the fighting against the Red Army.

Finally, it cannot be excluded that many of the German army officers had a certain "bias" when they presented their views after the war. The *Luftwaffe* was responsible for stopping the Allied air forces. If Allied air power was the main cause of defeat, the responsibility for the failure did not fall on the shoulders of the army officers. Even if such thinking were not explicit, it can very well have clouded judgement unconsciously. There are also examples of documents produced by army staffs during the campaign in Normandy that explicitly state that the lack of German air power was the main cause of enemy success.[22]

With this in mind, it is not advisable to uncritically accept the statements of German officers concerning this issue. An example of this is Ellis' assertion that

> [heavy bombers] … were not especially useful in attacks on static defenses – a saturation bombing of Caen prior to Operation *Charnwood* was as counter-productive as the flattening of Cassino monastery and town a few months earlier. Against armoured formations out in the open, however, even working with broad tolerances, the bombers often wreaked havoc.[23]

Ellis goes on by citing a report by von Kluge to Hitler on 22 July that concern Operation *Goodwood*:

> Whole armoured formations, allotted to the counter-attack, were caught in bomb-carpets of the greatest intensity, so that they could be extricated from the torn-up ground only by prolonged effort and in some cases only by dragging them out. The result was that they arrived too late. It is immaterial whether such a bomb carpet catches good troops or bad, they are more or less annihilated.[24]

A few points must be noted here. First, there are in fact very few occasions when heavy bombers hit armored formations. Probably Operation *Goodwood* and Operation *Cobra* are the only real examples. Thus, it cannot be said that bombers "*often* wreaked havoc". Second, during the example given by Ellis, Operation *Goodwood*, the bombers hit one armored formation, the *503. schwere Panzer-Abteilung*. This unit suffered losses, but it was far from annihilated, since most of it remained fighting in Normandy until the end of the campaign.[25] It seems that von Kluge was exaggerating grossly. It is clear that the carpet-bombing prevented the battalion from immediately intervening in strength, but the bombers did not annihilate it, rather it was temporarily incapacitated.

Another example is *Panzer-Lehr* during Operation *Cobra*. Ellis cited Bayerlein who has stated that all his forward tanks were knocked out.[26] Either a large part of his tanks were not in forward positions or he was simply exaggerating. On 1 August, *Panzer-Lehr* reported that it had 67 tanks and at least 10 assault guns, if vehicles in workshops are included.[27] The number of operational tanks had shrunk from 31 on 23 July to 27 on 1 August.[28]

Unfortunately, there is no information found in the archival records on the number of tanks in workshops during July. It must be emphasized that between 23 July and 1 August, several tanks must have been lost to American ground forces or abandoned during the retreat after 25 July. Whatever the case, the available evidence does not indicate that large parts of the division had been annihilated, even though parts of it had been severely hit. Also, the division reported that it had a manpower strength of 11,018 men on 1 August, which is quite impressive for a division that was supposed to be destroyed.[29] For more information on the Carpet bombing of *Panzer-Lehr* before Operation *Cobra* see the narrative for the division.

A result of attacks by heavy bombers, both during *Goodwood* and *Cobra*, was the disabling of tanks, rather than destruction. Often the tanks were disabled due to the need to dig them out after the air attack. Thus, it was absolutely necessary to follow up the air attack by ground forces advancing immediately. Otherwise the aerial bombardment would have little lasting effect.

This was also the conclusion by Allied operations research teams, which investigated areas where Allied heavy bombers had been used.[30]

An example of the swift recovery that was possible occurred on 29 June. Late in the afternoon the *SPW* battalion (*III./SS-Panzergrenadier-Regiment 20*) of the *Hohenstaufen* division had assembled for an attack together with *Panther* tanks from the *Panzer* regiment. About 100 Lancaster planes bombed the assembly area. A huge dust cloud covered the area and those who observed the event were convinced that all units in the area must have been destroyed. However, by the evening 80% of the armored vehicles were operational again. About twenty men had died during the bombing attack.[31]

This unit was not dug in for defense, but rather deployed in a forest, which hardly provided any cover against this kind of enemy attack.

This took place during Operation *Epsom* and there is another effort by heavy bombers that warrant discussion. During the night between 29 and 30 June about 1,000 tons of bombs were dropped on Villers-Bocage and its immediate surroundings. It has been said that this prevented units, mainly from *9. SS-Panzer-Division*, to attack since they had to approach through Villers-Bocage. This view is, however, very peculiar, since the combat units of *9. SS-Panzer-Division* were already north of Villers-Bocage. Possibly the Allied bombing may have caused difficulties for supply transports to the division and it may also have hampered movements by tanks that had been repaired in workshops and were to re-join their units. In fact, the unit histories of the German formations involved do not mention this bombing at all.[32]

According to the *OB West* war diary the attacks by *II. SS-Panzer-Korps* were halted by the very intensive enemy artillery fire. The bombing of Villers-Bocage is not mentioned at all.[33] This entire story seems to be the result of faulty Allied intelligence. Unfortunately, it has been reiterated after the war.[34]

What is presented here are examples of data on German losses inflicted by air power and also examples of statements by German officers that do not stand up to the hard facts available. Of course, it can be argued that the number of cases presented here are too few. There is some merit to that. But it must also be emphasized that not a single example supporting the image of extensive losses being inflicted by Allied air forces on German combat units in Normandy has been found. In every case where reliable data has been found, losses by enemy air are not great. Also in every single case where data found has been possible to compare with German officer's statements of high losses due to enemy air power, these statements have been found exaggerated.

However, it must be made clear that it was usually not necessary to inflict losses to affect ground operations. An air attack almost invariably caused ground units to take cover. Air attacks on German artillery, even if not causing losses, could very well mean that German infantry was left without valuable artillery support at critical moments. Also, even if Allied air units did not cause significant tank losses at Mortain, the air attacks caused German tanks to take cover rather than continue thrusting forward. Air power was probably not capable of inflicting significant physical losses on ground units. Its effect on the morale could, however, be much greater, though these effects might be transitory.

There were other effects of Allied air superiority. German units had to spend much more time to conceal than Allied units. Another vital factor was the contribution Allied air superiority made to intelligence. This included both immediately used information, such as artillery fire directed from the air as well as important information on German reserves moving just behind the front line.

Allied air attacks could also cause units not to be sent to Normandy. An example of this is the engineer battalion of *17. SS-Panzergrenadier-Division* which remained in the Saumur area for almost a month to ensure that the crossing over the Loire was operable.[35] Also the divisional *Flak* battalion remained in this area due to the Allied air attacks on the Loire crossings.

Attacks on ground combat units moving to Normandy

Attacks on German ground units moving to Normandy seem to have caused insignificant losses. During its march to Normandy, the *12. SS-Panzer-Division* lost 83 men due to all causes.[36] Compared to the losses the division suffered when fighting in Normandy these casualties are irrelevant.

Quite often the march to Normandy by *Panzer-Lehr* is used as an example of losses inflicted by Allied air power. These allegations are based on information provided by the division commander, Fritz Bayerlein, after the war. He seems to have had no other source than his memory. There exist, however, a report dated 10 June where it is said that the *Panzer-Lehr* did not have any significant losses even though losses had been inflicted by enemy air power during the march to Normandy.[37]

There are other descriptions of Allied air attacks on units moving towards Normandy. The commander of *9. Panzer-Division*, Erwin Jolasse, stated after the was that his division suffered no significant losses, neither of men nor of equipment, during its march to Normandy.[38]

The general impression is that losses of men and equipment were not significant during the movement of combat units towards Normandy. There is no case where there are indications that losses during the march to Normandy affected the combat value of the unit.

Delays were the important cost for the Germans when they moved units in face of Allied air power. One reason for this was of course the direct attacks on the units. Another was the destruction of bridges. For example, Allied air units destroyed all bridges over the Seine from Paris to the coast. This forced the *2. Panzer-Division* to make a long detour when it moved from Amiens to Normandy. Rather than moving by Rouen, it had to travel via Paris, which increased the distance by more than 150 km.

The *2. Panzer-Division* moved mainly by road and by using nights and periods of poor weather, it managed to cover about 400 km in two days, an impressive marching performance.[39]

The destroyed Seine bridges also caused delays later. When the *116. Panzer-Division* moved to Normandy it had to cross the Seine by ferries.[40]

Another example of fast moving units is the *17. SS-Aufklärungs-Abteilung* which covered more than 200 km on one day when moving to Normandy, despite being subjected to several air attacks[41]

As long as motorized units had ample fuel and were not hampered by conflicting orders, they could move quite rapidly over France, despite Allied air power. Furthermore, they did that without undue losses.

Shortages of vehicles and fuel were a much greater hindrance to rapid movements of German units than attacks on the moving units. Often the units arrived low on fuel.[42] The *2. Panzer-Division* is an example of this. Another is the *Panther* battalion of *12. SS-Panzer-Division*, which had arrived on 7 June but was prevented from being sent into battle because the tanks were out of fuel. Also the *II./Panzer-Artillerie-Lehr-Regiment* 130 had to wait in Chartres for fuel to continue its journey to Normandy.[43]

Proponents of air power could of course argue that the fuel shortages were the result of Allied air activity. It certainly contributed, but it must be made clear that the Allied air forces did not create these problems, rather they aggravated an already serious situation. The German production of fuel was simply too low. This is particularly true if compared to US production[44]:

	1942	1943	1944
United States	183.9	199.6	222.5
Germany	7.7	8.9	6.4

Figures include imports and production by synthetic fuel plants and refer to million metric tons.

The low German fuel production created shortages already in 1942, when fuel was not even targeted by Allied air power. During the offensive towards the Soviet oil fields in the Caucasus, shortages of fuel seriously hampered German operations.[45]

Lack of fuel also restricted training for the units in France. Furthermore, since units on the Eastern Front had priority, there was no significant stockpiling of fuel in Normandy. The depot closest to the Allied beachhead was located in Domfront, about 70 km from Caen. This depot contained about 960 m³ fuel, which was more than one quarter of the fuel available in Normandy. Since a *Panther* tank had a fuel capacity of 0.7 m³ it clear that stockpiling in Normandy was insufficient. Tanks, despite their great fuel consumption per kilometre moved, were too few to burn up more than a small fraction of the fuel consumed by the German forces.[46]

To compound the situation the Germans had too few trucks. The Quartermaster of *7. Armee* had only 248 trucks available with a total payload of about 500 tons. These few trucks were required to move fuel, munitions and rations and they could even be called upon to assist poorly motorized units to move to Normandy.[47]

The effect of these small stocks in Normandy and the limited capacity to move supplies within Normandy meant that units could not necessarily be committed to combat immediately upon arrival in Normandy simply because of lack of fuel.

One of the factors that limited the possibilities for Allied air power to delay the German units moving to Normandy was the considerable periods of poor weather and darkness. Probably these conditions made more than half the time available safe for German movements.

Attacks on railways

Given the German shortages of petrol and vehicles, rail transports were vital, both for the movement of supply to the German units engaged in Normandy and for bringing up fresh combat formations to the front.

Rail transport was a much more profitable target for Allied air power than the combat units themselves. Attacks on units moving along a road have to take place at the very moment they move, but railways can be attacked in advance and still affect movements considerably. Also, the location of railways, vital bridges and marshalling yards are well known in advance. Finally, rail transport is inherently less flexible than road transport.

All of this made the railroads a suitable target for Allied air power and the efforts paid off. The railroads were not paralysed but the capacity declined seriously. Also, the time needed to complete movements rose alarmingly. Above the *2. Panzer-Division* was mentioned as an example of fast movements by road, moving from Amiens to Normandy in about two days. But some parts of the division were transported by rail and these elements arrived about a week later.[48]

Another example of the slow rail movements is the two battalions formed at the *Artillerie Schule* in Suippes-Mourmelon. One battalion was motorized and the other horse-drawn. Both battalions received orders to move to Normandy on 10 June. The motorized battalion moved by its own means, while the other battalion used rail transport. Exactly when the motorized battalion arrived is unclear, but it is known that it had arrived by 15 June. The battalion that moved by rail did not arrive until the beginning of July. Thus, it took at least four times longer for the non-motorized battalion, which moved by rail, to reach its destination.[49]

But even if Allied air power had not seriously reduced the capacity of the French rail net it would have been impossible to quickly gather the German forces in Western Europe for defending Normandy. A *Panzer-Division* usually required about 60–80 trains to move the entire division, while a full-strength *Infanterie-Division* required about 50.[50] This meant that a force of five panzer divisions and five infantry divisions would have required about 600 trains.

Outside Normandy, *OB West* had some 34 infantry divisions (excluding divisions not intended for combat, like the reserve divisions) and nine *Panzer-* and *Panzergrenadier-Divisionen*. If all of these would have been moved by rail, close to 2500 trains would have been required. To move that number of trains into Normandy would have taken several weeks. Again, it must be concluded that the Allied air forces did not really create a problem. Rather they aggravated a difficult situation. It must be said, however, that generally Allied air power was much more effective in strangling German rail movements than road movements.

Attacks on German supply movements

It has been argued above that the Allied air forces had little ability to destroy German tanks. However, according to the presented statistics on causes of German tank losses during August 1944, the majority of German tanks lost were either destroyed by the crews or simply abandoned. Probably some of these had been abandoned due to lack of fuel. An important cause for this shortage may clearly have been Allied air attacks on supply transports. It is quite possible that the Allied air forces caused more tank losses in this way than through direct attacks on the tanks.

It must be emphasized that these tanks losses cannot be regarded as caused by air power alone. Had not Allied ground forces advanced, the Germans could have recovered these tanks. Hence, it is not reasonable to regard them as losses due to Allied air power only, but as losses due to the combined efforts of Allied air and ground units.

Nevertheless, supply was one of the weakest cogs in the German war machine. As mentioned above stockpiling of fuel in Normandy was wholly insufficient. The ammunition situation was not much better. The depots in Normandy only contained 7,172 tons of ammunition.[51] This was sufficient for only a few days of combat even if only modest reinforcements were sent to Normandy. A further 11,576 tons were available in Brittany[52] but, as shown above, the 7. Armee possessed very limited means to move these stocks without resort to rail transport.

Similarly, only small amounts of supplies could be transported into the 7. Armee area, except by rail. When the bridges over Seine and Loire were destroyed, rail movement of supplies were crippled. By concentrating the repair efforts on two lines the Germans were able to reopen the routes Paris–Versailles–Dreux–Surdon and Tours–Le Mans–Alençon–Sees–Surdon. The latter line could not be used to its maximum capacity since the Loire bridge at Tours was damaged and could not take fully loaded trains.[53]

Up to 15 June, the Germans consumed 5,000 tons of ammunition.[54] This corresponds to a daily average consumption of 500 tons. This was a load that could be carried by one train only.[55] For the entire Army Group Center in Russia during the great summer offensives in 1941 it was sufficient with 24 supply trains a day.[56] Had the Germans not used most of the rail capacity to move combat units the rail net could probably have coped with the supply needs. But in June the number of troop trains exceeded supply trains four times.[57] A balanced conclusion seems to be that the Allied air attacks could inflict sufficient damage on the rail net to seriously curtail large-scale troop movements. But to do the same to supply movements was much more difficult, since it required an almost complete shutdown of the rail net. This could only be achieved by destroying bridges over large rivers. This was indeed also accomplished by the destruction of the Tours bridges on 15 July.[58] This led to an increasingly difficult supply situation for 7. Armee, which seems to have culminated when US forces launched Operation Cobra ten days later. When this operation began, fuel shortages prevented German reserves from acting quickly enough.[59]

It seems that German losses of trucks due to air attacks were not very great. During the first ten days of the battle in Normandy 20% of the strategic transport vehicles were disabled by air attack, accidents and breakdowns.[60] This can be compared to the fact that during the first 27 days of Operation Barbarossa fully 50% of the supply trucks been disabled.[61] It would be premature to conclude that poor roads were as severe a threat to supply trucks as air attacks. After all, an important explanation for the fact that losses to air attack were limited is the German reluctance to move on the roads except during nights and when the weather was poor.

Conclusions

Allied air power caused serious damage to the French rail net. Similarly, destruction of bridges over Loire and Seine also was a great hindrance to road movements. Otherwise it seems that the destruction caused by air power was modest. Even in August, when the Germans were forced to move in the open, losses to air attacks remained limited. The item most vulnerable to air attack was probably trucks without cross-country capabilities. But even during the Falaise pocket no more than about 1100–1200 cars and trucks were destroyed by aircraft.[62] This might at first seem to be a considerable total but it means that only 2.5–8.9% of all sorties flown resulted in a motor vehicle being hit.[63] Claims were *at least* 5 times greater.[64] Also it can be compared to the large number of motor vehicles employed by the Germans. The *9., 10.* and *12. SS-Panzer-Divisionen* had 7,783 cars and trucks operational or in short term repair on 1 June.[65] The Allied operations research teams estimated that the Germans had about 30,000 cars and trucks when the Falaise battle began. If anything, this number seems to be on the low side.[66] This means that about 3% of the cars and trucks were hit by air weapons during this period when Allied air forces had the best opportunities imaginable.[67]

Except for railroads, the destructive power of aircraft seems not to have been considerable. Rather the main effects were indirect. The reluctance to move when weather permitted air operations resulted in reductions of transport capacity. Since the Germans were critically short of transport this was serious.

Even though the amount of equipment destroyed usually was very small when fighter-bombers attacked German ground combat units the effects on the behaviour of the soldiers were usually greater. During the Mortain battle, German tanks took cover when attacked by fighter-bombers and often crews bailed out when subject to air attack, despite the fact that the inside of a tank was probably the safest place during an air attack.[68] This effectively halted German attacks and could also cause reserves to be delayed when they were about to counterattack against Allied attacks.

Similarly, the most important effect of carpet bombings by heavy bombers was the disruption caused. If exploited immediately this was of great value to the attacking ground units, but if there was a delay the Germans could soon recover.

This chapter does not argue that air power was ineffective. Rather it must be understood that physical destruction was, with the exception of railroads and bridges, not a very important result of air attacks. Allied air power was decisive in another respect. Had they not enjoyed air supremacy, or at least air superiority, it is very unlikely that the Allies would have proceed with Operation *Overlord* at all.

The main point in this chapter is that the effects of air power were the less tangible factors. The enemy's decision making was affected as well as his behaviour and morale. Furthermore, air power contributed to the Allied information advantage. Hence, it is necessary to look at the indirect factors. These are probably more difficult to analyse, but the results would probably be more rewarding.

1   I. Gooderson, Allied Fighter-Bombers Versus German Armour in North-West Europe 1944–1945: Myths and Realities (*Journal of Strategic Studies*, vol 14, No 2 June 1991) p. 221. The basic sources for the data on destruction of German tanks and other equipment used by Gooderson are the reports of the operations research teams that investigated the battlefields after the end of the battles and examined the wrecks found. These are probably the most reliable sources for such information available today.

2   The Germans employed 75 Pz IV, 70 Pz V and 32 StuG for the attack towards Avranches (OBW Ia, Notiz 19.00 Uhr Anruf Gen.Oberst Jodl bei Ia/OB West, 6.8.44, T311, R28, F7035209). Other German sources gives other figures, but not greater than these.

3   Gooderson, op. cit. p. 222

4   L. F. Ellis, Victory in the West, vol I (HMSO, London 1962) p. 488.

5   Gooderson, op. cit. p. 212.

6   Gooderson, op. cit. p. 212.

7   H. Meyer, *Kriegsgeschichte der 12. SS-Panzerdivision "Hitlerjugend", vol I* (Munin Verlag, Osnabrück 1982) p 198.

8   Losses have been compiled from Meyer, op. cit. while the weather is taken from KTB AOK 7 Ia, T312, R1564.

9   OB West Ia Nr. 5223/44 geh.Kdos, 2.7.44, T311, R28, F7034140f.

10   See narrative for 346. Inf.Div.

11   HGr B Ia Nr. 4646/44 g.Kdos., 13.7.44, T311, R4, F7003797.

12   KTB HGr B, 7.8.44, BA-MA RH 19 IX/87.

13   See HGr B Ia Nr. 4257/44 g.Kdos.Chefs. p. 6, 3.7.44, T311, R4, F7003769. Rommel uses the word "erhebliche" to decribe the losses.

14   H. Meyer, *Kriegsgeschichte der 12. SS-Panzerdivision "Hitlerjugend"* (Munin Verlag, Osnabrück 1982) p. 68.

15   Von Gersdorff, *Der Gegenangriff auf Avranches*, MS # A-921, p. 37.

16   Gooderson, op. cit. p. 222.

17   For a fuller discussion on this see Goodersons article, in particular p. 229.

18   Jentz, op. cit. p. 147 & 153.

19   See also The International TNDM Newsletter, vol 1, No 6 (June 1997) p. 28.

20   Tank Forces in Defence of the Kursk Bridgehead (*Journal of Slavic Military Studies*, vol 7, no 1, March 1994) p. 114.

21   See J. Ellis, *Brute Force* (Andre Deutsch, London 1990) pp. 364ff.

22   See e.g. Besprächung Generalfeldmarschall v. Kluge mit OB Pz.Gr. West, OB AOK 7, Komm. Gen. I. SS-Pz.Korps, Komm.Gen. LXXXVI. A.K., 20.7.44, T311, R4, F7003821.

23   Ellis, op. cit. p. 365.

24   Ibid.

25 See narrative for 503. s.Pz.Abt. In particular, note the table on the number of tanks available to the unit.

26 Ellis, op. cit. p. 366.

27 See narrative for Pz.Lehr.

28 Ibid.

29 Status report to the Inspector-General of Panzer Troops, Stand 1.8.44, BA-MA RH 10/172.

30 See I. Gooderson, Heavy and Medium Bombers: How Successful Were They in Tactical Close Air Support During World War II? (*Journal of Strategic Studies*, September 1992, vol 15, no 3) pp. 367–9.

31 H. Fürbringer, *9. SS-Panzer-Division Hohenstufen* (Heimdal, 1984) p. 282.

32 See Fürbringer, op. cit. Also it seems that the 2. SS-Pz.Div. was allegedly affected by the bombing, but the bombing is not mentioned at all in O. Weidinger, *Division Das Reich 1943-45* (Munin Verlag, Osnabrück 1982). From the descriptions of the intended actions and the actual actions there is nothing that supports the thesis that this division was hampered.

33 KTB OB West Ia entry 30.6, T311, R24, F7029309-13.

34 It has been written that "Bombing was more successful in causing obstruction. On 30 June 1944, for example, 266 aircraft of Bomber Command delivered 1,100 tons of bombs on a road junction at Villers-Bocage in Normandy through which tanks of the German *2.* and *9. Panzer Divisionen* would have to pass in order to counter-attack the Allied beachhead. The resulting obstruction ensured that no such attack took place. This was an example of what heavy bombing alone could achieve but in close support of the causing of such obstruction also hindered the progress of Allied troops."(I. Gooderson: *Air Power at the Battlefront. Allied Close Air Support in Europe 1943-1945* (Frank Cass, London 1998) p. 158; Gooderson refer to Middlebrook and Everitt: *The Bomber Command War Diaries* p. 536)

Arthur Harris wrote: "On June 30th it was learned that the 2nd and 9th Panzer division were moving up through Villers Bocage to make an attack that night; there was a network of roads here which it would be almost impossible for the enemy to by-pass and it was therefore the obvious place in which to bomb the *Panzer* divisions and their equipment – the enemy had also established a supply point there. This time Bomber Command attacked in daylight and dropped 1,100 tons of bombs; the Panzer divisions had to call off the planned attack." (A. Harris, *Bomber Offensive*, Greenhill Books, London 1990, p. 210).

From the passages above, it is not clear that the bombing took place during the night between 29 and 30 June. It may have occurred somewhat later. However this would just have given the German panzer divisions even more time to pass through Villers-Bocage. Also the bombing is still not mentioned by the German sources given here.

35 See narrative for *17. SS-Panzer-Grenadier-Division*.

36 See Meyer, op.cit.

37 Reisebericht Hauptmann Pickardt, 10.6.44, T311, R25, F7029430.

38 E. Jolasse, *Einsatz der 9. Panz.Division vom 24.7.–4.9.1944.*, MS # B-837, p. 4.

39 See narrative for *2. Panzer-Division*.

40 See narrative for *116. Panzer-Division*.

41 See narrative for *17. SS-Panzer-Grenadier-Division*.

42 Der Gen.Insp.d.Pz.Truppen Nr. 1710/44 g.Kdos 19.6.44, T78, R623, F000175.

43 KTB HGr B Abt Qu., entry 10.6, T311, R1, F7000077.

44 J. Ellis, *Brute Force* (André Deutsch, London 1990) table 50.

45 See E. F. Ziemke & M. E. Bauer, *Moscow to Stalingrad* (Military Heritage Press, New York 1988) p 359ff.

46 R. A. Hart, Feeding mars: The Role of Logistics in the German Defeat in Normandy, 1944, *War in History* 1996 3 (4), p. 423f.

47 Ibid, see also note 10 on page 425.

48 See narrative for 2. Pz.Div.

49 See narrative for Artillerie Schule Suippes.

50 The 277. Inf. Div. was moved by 52 trains (OB West Ia Nr. 5027/44 g.Kdos, 26.6.44, T311, R25, F7029913), while the 10. SS-Pz.Div travelled by 67 trains (OB West Ia Nr. 4879/44 g.Kdos. 23.6.44, T311, R25, F7029779).

51 Hart, op. cit. p. 423.

52 Ibid.

53 Ibid, p. 426f.

54 Ibid. p. 426, note 12.

55 According to the document OB West Ia Nr. 4858/44 geh.Kdos, 22.6.44 (T311, Roll 25, Frame 7029750) a tank battalion with 79 *Panther* tanks, each weighing 45 tons, could be transported on six trains. These tanks weighed 3,555 tons together or 592 tons per train. To this should be added other vehicles and equipment included in the battalion.

56 F. Halder, Kriegstagebuch, Bd. III (Kohlhammer Verlag, Stuttgart 1964) p. 178.

57 Hart, op. cit. p. 425, note 11.

58 Ibid, p. 430.

59 Ibid, pp. 431–3.

60 Ibid, p. 427.

61 M. Van Creveld, *Supplying War – Logistics from Wallenstein to Patton* (Cambridge University Press, New York 1977) p. 163.

62 In the so called "Pocket" area 701 cars and trucks were found. Of these 325 had been hit by air weapons. In the "Shambles" area 2,447 cars and lorries were found. Of these 330 were examined and it was found that 110 had been hit by air weapons. If this percentage is representative for all the 2,447 motor vehicles 816 would have been hit by air weapons. These figures do not include armored vehicles (of which very few had been hit by air weapons). All data from I. Gooderson, Allied Fighter-Bombers Versus German Armour in North-West Europe 1944–1945: Myths and Realities (*Journal of Strategic Studies*, vol 14, No 2 June 1991) p. 223–5.

63 According to Gooderson op. cit. the US 9th Air Force and the British 2 TAF flew 12,787 sorties to the "Pocket" area. This would indicate that 325 trucks and cars were destroyed during those sorties, giving a percentage of 2.4%. However it is not completely clear that the sortie total apply only to the "Pocket" area, but possibly it could also include the area classified as "Shambles". Hence the larger percentage.

64 Gooderson, op. cit. p. 224.

65 See files BA-MA RH 10/318, RH 10/319 and RH 10/321 for the status reports for the three divisions on 1 June 1944.

66 The Panzer divisions alone must have brought about 25,000 cars and trucks into Normandy. Losses seems not to have been excessive previously. During June 3,186 cars, trucks and towing vehicles were complete write-offs (HGr. B Ia, 1. Anlage zu Tgb Nr. 1281/44 geh. O.U. den 29. Juli 1944, BA-MA RH 19 IX/46).

67 German losses of vehicles were by no means over when the Falaise battle ended on 22 August. In the so called "Chase area", west of the Seine another 3,178 cars and trucks were found. See Gooderson, op.cit. p. 227.

68 Gooderson, op. cit. p 223.

6

German Tanks Employed in Normandy

Several types of tanks were used in Normandy by the Germans. For various reasons their characteristics varied considerably. The extremely rapid development of new types during the war quickly made designs obsolete. For example, the difference between the *Panzer IV*, which entered production in 1938, and the *Panther*, which entered production in 1943, was considerable.

Another factor was the thicker armor carried on the newer tanks. This necessitated bigger anti-tank guns, which were heavier than their predecessors. Consequently, it became desirable to mount these guns on AFV chassis. Thereby a new type of AFV was created. Finally, obsolete models were often developed into specialized types.

There were three main categories of German "tanks":

1. Main Battle Tanks. These were designed to be as versatile as possible. Their armament was mainly designed to be effective against other tanks, but did also have good effect on unarmored targets. The main gun was mounted in a revolving turret.
2. Assault guns. Originally this type was created to provide the infantry with mobile HE fire support. It was mainly supposed to be used as an offensive weapon. As the German infantry was gradually forced to take a defensive posture this type was rather used in an AT role, since it was more mobile than towed AT guns and had better survivability.
3. Tank destroyers. These were called *Panzerjäger* by the Germans and were initially constructed by mounting an AT gun on the chassis of an obsolete tank and providing the gun crew compartment with thin armor. Usually, there was no roof armor and often no rear armor either. This type was a direct response to the increasing weight of AT guns. Later during the war the emphasis was shifted to more heavily armored vehicles with low silhouette and armor on all surfaces. This tended to make the distinction between tank destroyers and assault guns quite vague and this is also reflected in some of the inconsistencies in the documents.

Often the quality of German tanks has been regarded as an advantage over their adversaries. And to some extent this is true. The *Panther* and *Tiger* tanks were superior to most Allied tanks in several important aspects. However, the most common German tank was the *Panzer IV* and it can hardly be said to have been superior The third most common German "tank" was the *Sturmgeschütz III*, which was not superior to Allied tanks. These two vehicles had no better armor than the Sherman tanks, were inferior in terms of mobility and mechanical reliability. The only significant advantage these two German types had was the main armament, which was more powerful than the 75 mm gun of the Sherman, though not better than the 76 mm gun mounted in some of the Shermans.

There were, however, some advantages enjoyed by the Germans that do not show up in data sheets. One important advantage was the powder used by German guns. When firing, it produced less flash and smoke than Allied powder. This made it easier for German tankers to spot their adversaries. This was a factor that Allied tankers realized too.[1]

This chapter does not contain as many references to sources as other chapters. The main reason for this is that some of the technical data is ambiguous, even if primary sources are used. An example of this is the armor-piercing capabilities. Test firing can be done under many different conditions. Variations can occur due to differences in firing distance and angle of target plate. Even in primary documents these factors can be confused. Finally, there are always variations in armor plate. Different types of plates, produced with different hardening techniques, can be used. This will make it difficult to compare the results from test firing. There are inevitably variations within armor plates of a specific type, which will make it even more difficult to compare the results from test firing.

Fortunately, there are ways to cope with this problem. Most tank and antitank guns of World War II vintage had muzzle velocities of 600–1000 m/s. In this velocity range the capabilities are usually possible to calculate with sufficient precision and reliability. Many of the figures presented here are the results of such calculations or else calculations have been used to verify figures found in the literature.

Measurements Used in Charts

Metric units have been used for the data presented here:

- Weight is measured in metric tons
- Horsepower is, as far as has been possible to ascertain, measured according to DIN
- Road speed is given in km/h
- Range is given in km
- Ground pressure is given in kg/cm^2
- Ammo carried is the number of complete main gun rounds carried
- Armor is given as thickness/angle, where thickness is given in mm and angle in degrees from vertical (R means rounded)

- Caliber is given in mm
- Length of bore is given in m
- Shell weight is given in kg
- Muzzle velocity is given in m/s
- Armor penetration is given in mm against homogenous armor set at an angle of 30° from vertical

German tanks mainly employed two types of ammunition. High explosive, HE, was used against non-armored targets. The other main type was APCBC (Armored Piercing, Capped, Ballistically Capped), i e. an AP round with a cap to improve penetration (especially against face-hardened armor and at oblique angles) and also a soft pointed cap outside the first cap to reduce air resistance. There also existed other types, like smoke rounds.

There existed another type of AP round, the AP40. This had a tungsten carbide core enclosed in a light alloy body. When the target was hit, only the very hard core penetrated, while the surrounding body disintegrated. Since the total weight of the projectile was lower, it achieved higher muzzle velocity. This, together with the fact that the ratio between weight and cross-section area of the core was usually rather similar to conventional AP shot, resulted in considerable increases in penetration. However, since the ratio between weight and cross-section area for the *entire* projectile was much less than for conventional shot, it lost more velocity with range due to air drag. Consequently, the improvement in penetration was confined to short and medium ranges.

The AP 40 round seems to have been relatively scarce. Given the power of the German guns and the relatively weak armor of most Allied tanks, this was not a major problem. Older weapons, like the 5 cm Pak 39, may have been in greater need of the AP 40 ammunition.

Tiger II

This vehicle, which was also called *Königstiger* (King Tiger) or Tiger B, was the newest of the German tanks. The first *Tiger II* produced left the assembly lines in the Henschel factory in January 1944[2]. Only the 503. *schwere Panzer-Abteilung* was with certainty equipped with *Tiger II*. The 1. *Kompanie* had twelve *Tiger II*.[3]

Thus it seems that only 12 *Tiger II* participated in Normandy. Powerful as the *Tiger II* may have been, the numbers employed nevertheless precluded it from playing a major role in the Normandy campaign.

Why the Germans actually developed the *Tiger II* may appear strange. They already had tanks like the *Panther*, which was superior to the adversaries in terms of fire power and armor protection. It is possible that the Germans, due to the shock of meeting superior Soviet tanks in 1941, were determined never again to fall behind in the race for more powerful guns and better armor protection.

Tiger II data

Weight	Horse-Power	Road Speed	Range	Ground Pressure	Ammo carried
68	700	35	170	1.03	72

	Chassis armor			Turret armor		
Front	Side	Rear	Front	Side	Rear	Main Armament
150/50	80/25	80/30	185/9	80/21	80/21	8.8 cm KwK 43

Main gun, 8.8 cm KwK 43, data

Caliber	Length in calibers	Length of bore	Shell weight HE	Muzzle velocity HE
88	71	6.25	9.4	750

Shell weight	Muzzle velocity		APCBC Armor pen at distance		
APCBC	APCBC	500	1000	1500	2000
10.2	1000	185	165	148	132

Shell weight	Muzzle velocity		APCR Armor pen at distance			
APCR	APCR	100	500	1000	1500	2000
7.3	1180	237	217	193	171	151

Tiger I

This model had entered production in 1942 and was at that time the most powerful tank in the world. But development of new tanks continued rapidly. In 1944 the *Panther* and the *Tiger II* surpassed it in most respects, and also some enemy tanks, like the Soviet IS-2. Compared to the *Panther* it had only one advantage, the thicker side and rear armor. The frontal armor of the Tiger I was much inferior to the *Panther*'s front armor. Also, the 8.8 cm KwK 36 gun of the Tiger had much less penetration than the 7.5 cm KwK 42 of the *Panther*.[4] If to this is added the superior mobility of the *Panther* it is quite clear which of the tanks that was the better.

However, there were certain circumstances that favoured the *Tiger*. Except for the most thickly armored Churchill tanks, the gun of the *Tiger* was sufficient to penetrate the frontal armor of all Allied tanks, save for very long distances. Similarly, most Allied guns were not powerful enough to penetrate the frontal armor of the *Tiger*. Given the deficiencies of the opposition it can be said that the penetration capabilities of the *Panther* and the excellent frontal armor protection were usually "overkill".

The *Tiger* tanks were employed in independent tank battalions, each of which were supposed to have 45 *Tiger*. The *Schwere SS-Panzer-Abteilungen 101* and *102* had 45 *Tigers* each, while the *schwere Panzer-Abteilung 503* had 33 *Tiger I*.[5] Also it seems that the *316. Panzer-Kompanie (Funklenk)*, which was subordinated to the *Panzer Lehr* division, had three *Tiger I* when it went to Normandy. Thus, it seems that 126 *Tiger I* participated in the battle of Normandy.

Tiger I data

Weight	Horse-power	Road Speed	Range	Ground Pressure	Ammo carried
57	700	38	140	1.04	92

Chassis armor			Turret armor			
Front	Side	Rear	Front	Side	Rear	Main Armament
100/10	80/0	80/8	100/8	80/80	80/0	8.8 cm KwK 36

Main gun, 8.8 cm KwK 36, data

Caliber	Length in calibers	Length of bore	Shell weight HE	Muzzle velocity HE
88	56	4.93	9.0	600

Shell weight APCBC	Muzzle velocity APCBC		APCBC Armor pen at distance			
		500	1000	1500	2000
10.2	780	110	100	90	82

Shell weight APCBC	Muzzle velocity APCBC			APCR Armor pen at distance			
		100	500	1000	1500	2000
7.3	930	171	156	138	123	110

Panther

The *Panther* was a very successful combination of fire power, protection and mobility. The frontal armor protection surpassed most heavy tanks during the war. The 7.5 cm gun had, due to the very high muzzle velocity, good accuracy at longer distances and excellent armor-penetration capabilities.

Most of the teething troubles plaguing the *Panther* at the battle at Kursk had been corrected on the G-model which entered production during March 1944,[6] even though the *Panther* did not match the mechanical dependability of the US Sherman tank. But in combat few tankers would have traded the protection and firepower of the *Panther* for the mechanical reliability of the Sherman.

Altogether, the *Panzer-Divisionen* brought 623 *Panther* tanks to Normandy.[7] Additionally, 13 were sent to the 12. *SS-Panzer-Division* and eight to the *Panzer-Lehr-Division* during June. Finally, another 24 were sent to *OB West* as replacements. Of these, eight reached *OB West* on 8 August. These probably reached the combat area, but the rest most likely did not.[8] Finally the *schwere Panzerjäger-Abteilung* 654 brought command versions of the *Panther* to Normandy, most likely two or three. The total number of *Panthers* in Normandy would then amount to 654 or 655.

It is sometimes said that the Sherman had an advantage over the *Panther* due to its powered turret traverse. It is questionable if this really was much of an advantage. First of all, the *Panther* had powered traverse, not electric but hydraulic. This meant that the speed with which the turret could be traversed depended on the engine speed. If the driver, gunner and commander of the tank were trained together this was not much of a problem. The driver could select a suitable gear to ensure quick traverse of the turret. If this was done the turret could be rotated 360° in 15 to 18 seconds. This corresponds to an angular velocity of 20–24°/sec, which was only marginally slower than the Sherman.[9]

To put this into perspective it can be compared to the mobility of a tank. Assume that a vehicle is at a distance of 200 m and moves with a speed of 30 km/h perpendicular to the line of sight from the tank. This corresponds to an angular velocity of 2.4°/sec, or only a tenth of the speed that the *Panther* turret could traverse. Except at extremely short distances it seems not very likely that the "slow" turret traverse of the *Panther* enabled Allied tanks to "outmanoeuvre" the opponent.

The main advantage with a rapidly traversing turret is the ability to quickly bring fire to bear upon a target suddenly discovered. This can make it possible to hit the enemy before being hit and it is possible that Sherman tanks occasionally hit the enemy before as a result of the slightly faster turret traverse. However, such situations could also be caused by the poor visibility plaguing all tanks. It is certainly conceivable that at least occasionally the slowly traversing turret of a German tank may have been the result of the crew scanning the terrain for a target they were not certain where it is located.

Panther data

	Weight	Horse-Power	Road Speed	Range	Ground Pressure	Ammo carried
Panther D	43	700	46	200	0.83	79
Panther A	44.8	700	46	200	0.86	79
Panther G	45.5	700	46	200	0.87	81

	Chassis armor			Turret armor			
	Front	Side	Rear	Front	Side	Rear	Main Armament
Panther D	80/55	40/40	40/30	120/R	45/25	45/25	7.5 cm KwK 42
Panther A	80/55	40/40	40/30	120/R	45/25	45/25	7.5 cm KwK 42
Panther G	80/55	50/30	40/30	120/R	45/25	45/25	7.5 cm KwK 42

Main gun, 7.5 cm KwK 42, data

Caliber	Length in calibers	Length of bore	Shell weight HE	Muzzle velocity HE
75	70	5.25	5.74	700

Shell weight APCBC	Muzzle velocity APCBC		APCBC Armor pen at distance		
		500	1000	1500	2000
6.8	935	141	126	112	101

Shell weight APCR	Muzzle velocity APCR			APCR Armor pen at distance		
		100	500	1000	1500	2000
4.75	1120	194	174	149	127	106

Panzer IV

Introduced in mid-thirties, the *Panzer IV* was the oldest of the German tanks still in production. In Normandy, it was the most numerous German tank. The panzer divisions that fought in Normandy brought 841 *Panzer IV* to the battlefield. Also, between 6 July and 2 August, the following number of *Panzer IV* (*Panzerbefehlswagen*) were sent: three each to *21. Panzer-Division* and *17. SS-Panzergrenadier-Division* and five to *2. SS-Panzer-Division*. Finally, on 8 July, 11 *Panzer IV* were sent to *Panzer*

Lehr, seventeen to *12. SS-Panzer-Division* and seventeen to *21. Panzer-Division*. This brought the total number of *Panzer IV* that participated in the campaign in Normandy to 897.

At the time of its introduction, the *Panzer IV* was among the very best in the world, but development of new models proceeded rapidly during the war. In most respects the *Panzer IV* was much inferior to the *Panther*. There were, however, a few advantages that the older tank enjoyed. One was the electrical power traverse of the turret. In the section on the *Panther* it has been argued that that it was not such a great advantage from a tactical point of view. But hydraulic systems present a fire hazard if the armor is penetrated. The *Panther*, with its heavy frontal armor, could be expected to keep the majority of hits out. For the *Panzer IV*, a hit was much more likely to penetrate and then the value of not having a hydraulic system in the fighting compartment was certainly welcome to the crews.

On the J-model of the *Panzer IV*, the electrical traverse was deleted to make room for additional fuel. This model must have been very rare in Normandy since it entered production in June 1944.

But even though the *Panzer IV* was ageing it was still a useful vehicle. With the L48-gun, it had much better penetration capabilities than the Sherman with 75 mm gun. Protection and mobility though was slightly inferior to the Sherman tank.

Panzer IV data

	Weight	Horse-Power	Road Speed	Range	Ground Pressure	Ammo carried
Pz IV E	21	300	42	200	0.79	80
Pz IV F1	22.3	300	40	200	0.84	80
Pz IV F2	23	300	40	200	0.87	80
Pz IV G	24	300	38	210	0.90	80
Pz IV H	25	300	38	210	0.94	80
Pz IV J	25	300	38	320	0.94	80

	Chassis armor			Turret armor			
	Front	Side	Rear	Front	Side	Rear	Main Armament
Pz IV E	60/10	40/0	20/10	30/11	20/24	20/14	7.5 cm KwK 37
Pz IV F1	50/10	30/0	20/10	50/11	30/26	30/16	7.5 cm KwK 40 L43
Pz IV F2	50/10	30/0	20/10	50/11	30/26	30/16	7.5 cm KwK 40 L43
Pz IV G	80/10	30/0	20/10	50/11	30/26	30/16	7.5 cm KwK 40 L43
Pz IV H	80/10	30/0	20/10	50/11	30/26	30/16	7.5 cm KwK 40 L48
Pz IV J	80/10	30/0	20/10	50/11	30/26	30/16	7.5 cm KwK 40 L48

Main gun data

	Caliber	Length in calibers	Length of bore	Shell weight HE	Muzzle velocity HE
7.5 cm KwK 37	75	24	1.8	5.74	420
7.5 cm KwK 40 L43	75	43	3.22	5.74	550
7.5 cm KwK 40 L48	75	48	3.60	5.74	550

	Shell weight APCBC	Muzzle velocity APCBC	500	APCBC Armor pen at distance		
				1000	1500	2000
7.5 cm KwK 37	6.8	385	39	35	32	29
7.5 cm KwK 40 L43	6.8	740	89	78	68	60
7.5 cm KwK 40 L48	6.8	770	96	84	74	65

	Shell weight APCR	Muzzle velocity APCR	100	APCR Armor pen at distance			
				500	1000	1500	2000
7.5 cm KwK 37	-	-	-	-	-	-	-
7.5 cm KwK 40 L43	4.10	920	126	108	87	69	-
7.5 cm KwK 40 L48	4.10	990	143	120	97	77	-

Panzer III

Production of the *Panzer III* had ceased in the summer 1943[10], but a few nevertheless remained with the forces in *OB West*. Including command tanks, the *21. Panzer-Division* had five *Panzer III* on 1 June 1944, while the *116. Panzer-Division* reported eleven *Panzer III* of various models on 8 June. The *Panzer-Ersatz-und Ausbildungs-Abteilung 100* had one Panzer III. The *Hohenstaufen* division had six *Befehlspanzer III*, while *Frundsberg* had three and *Hitlerjugend* two. Also the *4./Panzer-Abteilung 301 (Fkl)* had two Panzer III. This gives a total of 30 *Panzer III*.

It is possible that further *Panzer III* may have participated in the battle. At this stage of the war, the model was regarded to have little combat value and it was perhaps not always reported if the type was present with a unit. Also command vehicles were not necessarily reported. Since the *Panzer III* had been out of production for a year when the Allied forces landed in Normandy it is not very likely that further vehicles of the type was sent to the units.

Panzer III data

	Weight	Horse-Power	Road Speed	Range	Ground Pressure	Ammo carried
Pz III H	21.8	300	40	165	0.94	99
Pz III L-M	22.7	300	40	155	0.95	92
Pz III N	23	300	40	155	0.96	64

	Chassis armor			Turret armor			
	Front	Side	Rear	Front	Side	Rear	Main Armament
Pz III H	60/9	30/0	60/10	35/R	30/25	30/12	5 cm KwK L42
Pz III L-M	70/9	30/0	50/10	77/R	30/25	30/12	5 cm KwK 39
Pz III N	70/9	30/0	50/10	77/R	30/25	30/12	7.5 cm KwK 37

Main gun data

	Caliber	Length in calibers	Length of bore	Shell weight HE	Muzzle velocity HE
5 cm KwK L42	50	42	2.1	1.82	?
5 cm KwK 39	50	60	3.0	1.82	550
7.5 cm KwK 37	75	24	1.8	5.74	420

	Shell weight APC	Muzzle velocity APC	APC Armor pen at distance			
			500	1000	1500	2000
5 cm KwK L42	2.06	685	45	35	27	21
5 cm KwK 39	2.06	835	67	52	40	31
7.5 cm KwK 37	6.8	385	39	35	32	29

	Shell weight APCR	Muzzle velocity APCR	APCR Armor pen at distance				
			100	500	1000	1500	2000
5 cm KwK L42	0.925	1060	96	58	-	-	-
5 cm KwK 39	0.925	1180	130	72	38	-	-
7.5 cm KwK 37	-	-	-	-	-	-	-

Sturmgeschütz III and *Sturmhaubitze III*

The main disadvantage with the *Panzer III* was that it could not mount a longer 7.5 cm gun than the short 7.5 cm KwK 37. But by discarding the revolving turret, the longer 7.5 cm *Sturmkanone 40 L 48* could be fitted. This made it possible to use the *Sturmgeschütz III* as an effective anti-tank weapon. This was a departure from the original role of the assault guns, to provide fire support for attacking infantry units. The first *Sturmgeschütz III* models had been armed with the short 7.5 cm *Sturmkanone 37*, which could perform that task. The superiority of Soviet tanks forced the Germans to adopt the longer gun to provide the infantry with effective and mobile AT capabilities. From March 1942, the *Sturmgeschütz III* was produced with the longer gun.[11]

There was still a need for fire support for the infantry. To provide this a new version of the *Sturmgeschütz III* was designed. It was armed with a 10.5 cm howitzer and called *Sturmhaubitze 42* or *Sturmhaubitze III*. Production was initiated in October 1942.[12] Still the 7.5 cm variant was much more common. Production of the latter type was about seven times greater than production of the *Sturmhaubitze III*.[13]

There were three main categories of units that used the assault guns. These were independent assault gun battalions (or brigades), infantry divisions and panzer divisions. Three army assault gun battalions, 341, 394 and 902 and one from the air force, the *12. Fallschirm-Sturmgeschütz-Brigade*, participated in Normandy. All these had an authorized strength of 31 assault guns, except the 341, which had 45. The three army units were all at full strength when they were sent to Normandy. The actual strength of the *12. Fallschirm-Sturmgeschütz-Brigade* is more uncertain, but probably it was at full strength when it moved to Normandy.

Some of the infantry divisions had one of the companies in the *Panzerjäger* battalion equipped with ten *Sturmgeschütz IIIs*. Six of the infantry divisions had such a company[14]. Also eight *Sturmgeschütz IIIs* were sent to the *16. Luftwaffenfeldivision* on 9 July.[15]

Panzer divisions were not supposed to be equipped with *Sturmgeschütz III*, but some of the divisions in Normandy nevertheless were. In both *1.* and *2. SS-Panzer-Divisionen* the *Panzerjäger* battalion was equipped with *Sturmgeschütz III* rather than tank destroyers. Each division had 45 *Sturmgeschütze*. The *9.* and *10. SS-Panzer-Divisionen* had no *Panzerjäger* battalion, but two of the tank companies were equipped with *Sturmgeschütz III* rather than *Panzer IV*. The *9. SS-Panzer-Division* had 40 *Sturmgeschütze* and the *10. SS-Panzer-Division* had 38.[16] Also the *9. Panzer-Division* had six *Sturmgeschütz III* while the *116. Panzer-Division* had five.[17] As could be expected the *17. SS-Panzergrenadier-Division* had a battalion equipped with *Sturmgeschütz III*. It had 42 assault guns.

Assault guns were also found among the *Funklenk* units (units operating remote controlled vehicles). The *4./Panzer-Abteilung 301 (Fkl)* had six *Sturmgeschütz III* while the *316. Panzer-Kompanie (Fkl)* had ten.

Also, on 30 July the ten *Sturmgeschütz III* of *348. Infanterie-Division* were sent to Normandy.[18]

Altogether this means that 453 *Sturmgeschütz III* and *Sturmhaubitze III* went to Normandy with the combat sent there (assuming that the *12. Fallschirm-Sturmgeschütz-Brigade* received its authorized number of *Sturmgeschütz*). It is much more difficult to establish how many *Sturmgeschütz* were sent to Normandy to replace losses. Among the files of the Inspector-General of Panzer Troops there are lists of the deliveries of tanks and assault guns.[19] However, these lists do not cover deliveries to GHQ assault gun units before July 1944, probably because those units were considered part of the artillery. Similarly, these lists do not include deliveries to *Luftwaffe* units.[20]

The available lists show that 17 *Sturmgeschütz III* and 10 *Sturmhaubitze III* were sent to the west on 31 July. But further deliveries may have occurred, at least to *12. Fallschirm-Sturmgeschütz-Brigade* and *902. Sturmgeschütz-Brigade* since these units saw action during June. The *341. and 394. Sturmgeschütz-Brigaden* were not committed to combat before August and replacements to those units would have been included in the lists.

Also, there is another possible source for replacements. There were schools, like the assault gun training area at Tours, which may have sent some of their guns to the front in Normandy. However, such deliveries could not have been considerable. Weighing in all factors it seems safe to assume that less than 100 *Sturmgeschütze* were sent to Normandy to replace losses.

There also existed a third assault gun model, the *Sturmgeschütz IV*. Firepower, armor and mobility were almost identical to the *Sturmgeschütz III* but as the name implies it was built on the *Panzer IV* chassis rather than the *Panzer III* chassis. Usually no distinction is made between *Sturmgeschütz III* and *Sturmgeschütz IV* in the reports. The *Sturmgeschütz IV* was produced in much smaller numbers than the *Sturmgeschütz III*.

The ratio between *Sturmgeschütz III* and *Sturmhaubitze III* among the assault guns sent to Normandy is unclear. Probably only the GHQ assault gun units were given *Sturmhaubitze III*.[21]

Sturmgeschütz and *Sturmhaubitze* data

	Weight	Horse-Power	Road Speed	Range	Ground Pressure	Ammo carried
StuG III	23.9	300	40	155	1.00	54
StuH III	24.0	300	40	155	1.00	36

	Chassis armor			Superstructure armor			
	Front	Side	Rear	Front	Side	Rear	Main Armament
StuG III	80/21	30/0	50/10	80/10	30/11	30/0	7.5 cm StuK 40
StuH III	80/21	30/0	50/10	80/10	30/11	30/0	10.5 cm StuH 42

Main armament data

	Caliber	Length in calibers	Length of bore	Shell weight HE	Muzzle velocity HE
7.5 cm StuK 40 L48	75	48	3.60	5.74	550
10.5 cm StuH 42	105	28	2.94	14.8	470

	Shell weight APC	Muzzle velocity APC		APCBC Armor pen at distance			
			500	1000	1500	2000
7.5 cm StuK 40 L48	6.8	770	96	84	74	65
10.5 cm StuH 42	14.0	470	59	54	50	46

	Shell weight APCR	Muzzle velocity APCR		APCR Armor pen at distance				
			100	500	1000	1500	2000
7.5 cm StuK 40 L48	4.10	990	143	120	97	77	-
10.5 cm StuH 42	-	-	-	-	-	-	-

Sturmpanzer IV

This was one of the more specialized German AFV and only 306 vehicles of this type were manufactured during the war.[22]

From the beginning of the war, German infantry regiments had an infantry gun company to provide fire support. There were two types of infantry guns, the 7.5 cm *leichtes Infanterie-Geschutz* and the 15 cm *schweres Infanterie-Geschutz* (*s.IG*). The larger of these was difficult to handle in the terrain and this problem was of course even more serious for the infantry units among the panzer divisions. To remedy this problem the Germans introduced a succession of lightly armored vehicles carrying the 15 cm *s.IG*. These were built on the chassis of the *Panzer I*, *Panzer II* and the *Panzer 38*(t). The thin armor and open top made it impossible to use these vehicles in close quarters or expose them to enemy AT guns.

The *Sturmpanzer IV* was a departure from this line of vehicles. It was built on the *Panzer IV* chassis and the armor was thick.

During the battle at Kursk in July 1943 the vehicle made its combat debut, when the *216. Sturmpanzer-Abteilung* fought with the *9. Armee*. The only unit equipped with the *Sturmpanzer IV* in Normandy was the *217. Sturmpanzer-Abteilung*. It employed between 16 and 28 *Sturmpanzer IV*.[23]

Sturmpanzer IV data

Weight	Horse-Power	Road Speed	Range	Ground Pressure	Ammo carried
28.2	300	40	210	1.06	38

Chassis armor			Superstructure armor			
Front	Side	Rear	Front	Side	Rear	Main Armament
80/12	30/0	20/10	100/40	50/15	30/25	15 cm StuH 43

Main gun data

	Caliber	Length in calibers	Length of bore	Shell weight HE	Muzzle velocity HE
15 cm StuH 43	150	12	1,80	38	240

	Shell weight APC	Muzzle velocity APC		APC Armor pen at distance		
			500	1000	1500	2000
15 cm StuH 43	-	-	-	-	-	-

	Shell weight APCR	Muzzle velocity APCR			APCR Armor pen at distance		
			100	500	1000	1500	2000
15 cm StuH 43	-	-	-	-	-	-	-

The main advantage the model enjoyed was of course the large high explosive shell that was very effective against infantry targets. On the other hand, the very low muzzle velocity made it almost useless against enemy tanks.

Marder

As the war progressed it became increasingly clear that the heavy anti-tank guns required to deal wth tanks that became better and better protected had to be mounted on tracked chassis to provide sufficient mobility. The Germans used obsolete tank chassis like the *Panzer II* and *Panzer 38(t)* for this purpose.[24] The light chassis did

Marder data

	Weight	Horse-Power	Road Speed	Range	Ground Pressure	Ammo carried
Marder II	10.8	140	40	190	?	37
Marder 38	10.5	160	42	190	?	27

	Chassis armor			Superstructure armor			
	Front	Side	Rear	Front	Side	Rear	Main Armament
Marder II	35/13	15/0	15/7	30/10	10/8	Open	7.5 cm PaK 40
Marder 38	15/15	15/0	10/41	10/30	10/15	Open	7.5 cm PaK 40

Main gun data

	Caliber	Length in calibers	Length of bore	Shell weight HE	Muzzle velocity HE
7.5 cm PaK 40 L48	75	48	3,60	5.74	550

	Shell weight APC	Muzzle velocity APC	APCBC Armor pen at distance			
			500	1000	1500	2000
7.5 cm PaK 40 L48	6.8	770	96	84	74	65

	Shell weight APCR	Muzzle velocity APCR	APCR Armor pen at distance				
			100	500	1000	1500	2000
7.5 cm PaK 40 L48	4.10	990	143	120	97	77	-

not make it possible to use heavy armor. The tactical employment of these vehicles focused largely on finding good concealed fire positions to alternate between.

In Normandy, this kind of vehicle was mainly used by infantry divisions. Often one of the companies in the *Panzerjäger* battalion had fourteen vehicles of this type. Few of the infantry division had one such company.[25]

At this stage of the war the *Panzer-Divisionen* were not supposed to be equipped with *Marders*, but it seems that the *9. Panzer-Division* had nine of them. These were supposed to be replaced by *Jagdpanzer IV*, but these did not arrive before the division went to Normandy and probably it had to retain the *Marders*.[26]

Jagdpanzer IV

Since the *Marders* had poor armor protection they lacked the ability to counterattack against enemy tanks. Rather they had to rely on firing from concealed positions. The *Jagdpanzer IV* had much more effective protection. The sloped frontal armor was as efficient as the thicker, but vertical, armor of the *Tiger I*. In May 1944, the armor was improved by increasing the thickness of the frontal plates to 80 mm.[27] This made its armor almost as good as the frontal armor of the *Panther*. It also meant that the weight went up by a ton and this extra weight was concentrated at the front of the vehicle, making it nose heavy. This problem was later compounded by mounting the more powerful gun of the *Panther* in the *Jagdpanzer IV*. No such vehicles were, however, produced in time for the battle in Normandy.

The *Jagdpanzer IV* equipped the panzer *Panzerjäger* battlions of the panzer divisions. Since *1.* and *2. SS-Panzer-Divisionen* had *Sturmgeschütz III* for their *Panzerjäger* battalions they had no *Jagdpanzer IV*. Neither the 9. and 10. SS-Pz. Div. had any panzerjäger battalion in Normandy. These battalions were forming but they did not receive any *Jagdpanzer IV* before August 1944. Neither had the 21. *Panzer-Division* any *Jagdpanzer IV*.

Two divisions that had *Jagdpanzer IV* when they went to Normandy were the *Panzer Lehr* and *2. Panzer-Division*. They had 31 and 21 respectively. The *12 SS-Panzerjäger-Abteilung* of the *Hitlerjugend* division was forming when the Allies landed in Normandy. It seems that one its companies arrived in Normandy equipped with ten *Jagdpanzer IV*. All these vehicles had been manufactured before May and probably had the thinner armor.

On 10 July 21 *Jagdpanzer IV* were sent to *116. Panzer-Division*. These participated in Normandy and may very well have had the thicker frontal armor. Also the 21 sent to *9. Panzer-Division* on 20 July may have had the thicker armor, but they did not see action in Normandy. Finally 31 *Jagdpanzer IV* were sent to *17. SS-Panzergrenadier-Division* on 30 June. These saw action in the Laval area during August. No *Jagdpanzer IV* were sent to Normandy to replace losses.[28]

Altogether 114 *Jagdpanzer IV* were sent to Normandy.

Jagdpanzer IV data

Weight	Horse-Power	Road Speed	Range	Ground Pressure	Ammo carried
24	300	40	210	0.90	79

Chassis armor			Superstructure armor			
Front	Side	Rear	Front	Side	Rear	Main Armament
60/45	30/0	20/11	60/50	30/30	20/35	7.5 cm Pak 39

Main gun data

	Caliber	Length in calibers	Length of bore	Shell weight HE	Muzzle velocity HE
7.5 cm Pak 39 L48	75	48	3.60	5.74	550

	Shell weight APC	Muzzle velocity APC		APCBC Armor pen at distance		
			500	1000	1500	2000
7.5 cm Pak 39 L48	6.8	770	96	84	74	65

	Shell weight APCR	Muzzle velocity APCR		APCR Armor pen at distance			
			100	500	1000	1500	2000
7.5 cm Pak 39 L48	4.10	990	143	120	97	77	-

Jagdpanther

Only one unit in Normandy was equipped with *Jagdpanthers*, the *654. schwere Panzerjäger-Abteilung.* It seems that this unit employed 26 *Jagdpanthers* in Normandy. Thus, this vehicle was quite rare in Normandy and since the battalion also arrived quite late, the *Jagdpanther* had little impact on the overall operations.

This should not distract from the fact that the *Jagdpanther* was an excellent vehicle, with a superb gun, very well armored and with good automotive characteristics. However, given the fact that very few Allied tanks presented any problem for the 7.5 cm gun of the *Panther*, the *Jagdpanther* was probably an inferior vehicle compared to the *Panther*. The value of a revolving turret was usually a greater advantage than the more powerful 8.8 cm gun.

Jagdpanther data

Weight	Horse-Power	Road Speed	Range	Ground Pressure	Ammo carried
46	700	46	200	0.88	57

Chassis armor			Superstructure armor			Main Armament
Front	Side	Rear	Front	Side	Rear	
80/55	50/30	40/30	80/55	50/30	40/35	8.8 cm Pak 43

Main gun data

	Caliber	Length in calibers	Length of bore	Shell weight HE	Muzzle velocity HE
8.8 cm Pak 43	88	71	6.25	9.4	700

	Shell weight APC	Muzzle velocity APC	APC Armor pen at distance			
			500	1000	1500	2000
8.8 cm Pak 43	10.2	1000	185	165	148	132

	Shell weight APCR	Muzzle velocity APCR	APCR Armor pen at distance				
			100	500	1000	1500	2000
8.8 cm Pak 43	7.3	1180	237	217	193	171	151

According to the British official history of the campaign in Normandy most British tanks knocked out fell victim to the German "long-range anti-tank guns, particularly 88s".[29] This seems to be a statement made without any thorough research.[30] Rather, the available evidence suggests that German tanks, assault guns and tank destroyers were the main killers of Allied tanks.

The vast majority of German tanks mounted a 7.5 cm gun and also most German AT guns had that caliber. The shells that were fired by these guns were almost identical (even though the propellant charges could be quite different). Hence it was impossible to tell by examination of a wreck if it had been hit by fire from a 7.5 cm Pak 40 anti-tank gun or a 7.5 cm KwK 40 gun of a *Panzer IV*. Similarly. it seems that tank crews being hit by enemy fire are not perfectly objective observers.

Probably the best source for establishing the proportion between various causes for Allied tank losses is to look at German claims. A report dated 29 June showed the following causes of tank kills among enemy units[31]:

17. SS-Panzergrenadier-Division:	*Sturmgeschütz*	7
	Towed AT guns	5
	Close Combat	5
352. Infanterie-Division:	*Panzerjäger*	21
	Flak	21
	Artillery	25
	Close Combat	30
2. Panzer-Division:	Towed AT guns	15
	Artillery	4
	Close Combat	5
Panzer-Lehr:	Tanks	85
	Jagdpanzer IV	18
	Towed AT guns	7
	Artillery	4
	Close Combat	40
12. SS-Panzer-Division:	Tanks	105
	Towed AT guns	16
	Close Combat	23
21. Panzer-Division:	Tanks	37
	8.8 cm AT guns (towed)	41
	7.5 cm AT guns (SP)	15
	Artillery	3
	Close Combat	5

This warrants some comments. First, even though the document is dated 29 June it cannot include data for all days preceding that day. During the last four days of June the *Panther* battalion of *2. Panzer-Division* was credited with the destruction of 89 enemy tanks.[32] Second, close combat includes vehicles destroyed by *Panzerschreck* and *Panzerfaust*. Third, the claims for artillery are probably more likely to be exaggerated than the other causes. Fourth, the category *Panzerjäger* in *352. Infanterie-Division* must include *Sturmgeschütz IIIs* too.

According to this data tanks, assault guns and tank destroyers accounted for slightly more than half the tanks knocked out. The second most common cause was close combat, which accounted for 20%. But among the three divisions that fought exclusively against British units during June, tanks and *Jagdpanzer IV*s accounted for nearly two thirds of all tanks destroyed. Again, close combat weapons accounted for more tanks than towed AT guns.

Finally, it is worth noting that these figures are claims, not actual losses, even though the Germans may well have assumed that the figures were true. However, it seems that the German claims were not very exaggerated.[33]

But what is of interest here is not the absolute numbers of tanks destroyed, rather the focus is on the ratio between various categories. There is no reason to believe that any category systematically exaggerated claims compared to the other categories. Hence, even though absolute numbers were exaggerated in claims, the proportions between the various causes of tank losses need not be wrong.

---

1   See e.g. T. Jentz, *Germany's Panther Tank* (Schiffer, Atglen 1995) p. 155.

2   Chamberlain & Doyle, *Encyclopedia of German Tanks of WWII* (Arms and Armour Press, London 1978) p. 142.

3   Ferngespräche und Besprächungen AOK 7 Ia, Besprächung mit Gen.Maj. Tomale 22.6.44, T312, R1566, F000313.

4   The 8.8 cm shell may, however, have caused more damage if it penetrated, compared to what a 7.5 cm shell would have done.

5   See the narratives for the respective units for details.

6   Chamberlain & Doyle, op. cit. p. 124. The A-model, which preceded the G-model, seems to have been quite reliable too. A report dated 22 February 1944 stated:
"The Panther is in its present shape mature for combat. It is much superior to the T-34. Almost all tething troubles are gone. Much superior to the Pz IV in terms of armament, armour, terrain mobility and speed. The engine has a lifespan of 700–1000 km." See Der Gen.Insp.d.Pz.Truppen Nr. 510/44 g.Kdos, 4.3.44, T78, R623, F000290.

7   See the narratives for the respective divisions for details.

8   Lieferungen der Pz.-Fahrzeuge, Bd. ab Mai 1943.

9   T. Jentz, *Germany's Panther Tank* (Schiffer, Atglen 1995) p. 126.

10 Chamberlain & Doyle, op. cit. p. 68.

11 Chamberlain & Doyle, op. cit. p. 82.

12 Ibid, p. 85.

13 Ibid, p. 82–85.

14 These were the 243., 326., 331., 346. 352. and 353.

15 Lieferungen der Pz.-Fahrzeuge, Bd. ab Mai 1943.

16 See the narratives for the respective divisions for details.

17 See the narratives for the respective divisions for details.

18 BA-MA RH 10/242.

19 See files BA-MA RH 10/349 and RH 10/350.

20 There are exceptions. Deliveries to the *Luftwaffe Feld Divisionen* are included, as are deliveries to the *Hermann Göring* division.

21 At this stage of the war, the most important task for the assault guns in the infantry divisions was to fight enemy tanks. For this purpose, the 10,5 cm howitzer was decidedly inferior to the 7.5 cm gun. Similarly, when the assault guns were present in the panzer divisions, they usually replaced

tanks or antitank weapons, which again were roles that favoured the assault guns equipped with the 7.5 cm gun rather than the 10.5 cm howitzer.

22 Chamberlain & Doyle, op. cit. p. 101. The figure given include eight converted from Panzer IV in addition to the 298 produced by Deutsche Eisenwerke.

23 Derived from data presented in the narrative on 217. Stu.Pz.Abt.

24 A vehicle built according to the same philosophy was the Nashorn, also called Hornisse. It was, however, built on a chassis that had not ceased to be utilized for tanks, the Panzer IV. This vehicle did, however, mount the more powerful 8.8 cm Pak 43. No unit employed in Normandy was equipped with such vehicles.

25 These were the 243., 326., 346. 352. and 353.

26 See narrative for 9. Pz.Div.

27 Chamberlain & Doyle, op. cit. p. 102.

28 Lieferungen der Pz.-Fahrzeuge, Bd. ab Mai 1943.

29 L. F. Ellis, *Victory in the West, vol I*, Her Majesty's Stationery Office, London 1962, p. 492.

30 There is nothing in Ellis' book that backs up this statement.

31 Anlage 3 zu HGr. B/Stoart Nr. 630/44 g.Kdos, Panzerabschussliste, 29.6.44, BA-MA RH 19 IX/3.

32 See BA-MA RH 10/141.

33 According to R. G. Ruppental, *Logistical Support of the Armies vol I* (Office of the Chief of Military History, Dept of the Army, Washington D. C. 1953) p. 522f, US forces lost 187 Shermans in June, 280 in July and 432 in August as total write offs. According to a British document (WO 165/136, 'Half Yearly Report on the Progress of the Royal Armoured Corps' No. 10, 1 July to 31 December 1944) British tank losses (write offs) amounted to 146 in June, 231 in July and 834 in August. The figures in this document are, however, suspicious. It does not seem resonable that losses should be that high in August compared to the previous months. German claims on the entire front in Normandy 6 June–3 July were 1,059 enemy tanks, 4 July–30 July 1,300 enemy tanks and 31 July–21 August 1,304. For the first period this means that the claims were 38 tanks/day, during the second period 48 tanks/day and during the third 59 tanks/day. To me this seems like a reasonable distribution over the three periods given the size of forces engaged and intensity of combat. If we would accept the British figures given above it would mean that German claims were about 124% too high during June, 129% too high in July and 16% too *low* in August. I have assumed that Shermans constituted two thirds of all US tanks and tank destroyers lost and I have also assumed that Allied tank losses in the last ten days of August were insignificant (given the fact that the Germans had lost most of their heavy weapons and were quite dispirited this seems not like a bold assumption).

My explanation for the strange figures in the British document is as yet not fully substantiated, but I believe that the British practise was to classify knocked-out tanks in either of two categories, repairable within 24 hours or not. Whether the more serious damages would eventually be repaired or not was left open until later. Hence the large number of tanks classified as destroyed in August. It should also be noted that the document indicates a loss of 731 tanks in October, a figure that also seem unreasonable.

The Germans on the other hand made the initial classification into three categories: beyond economical repair (Totalausfälle), Long Term Repair (Langfristig) or Short Term Repair (Kurzfristig). It seems that the major difference between the latter two was that the long term objects were sent to rear facilities while the short term objects remained with the formation and were repaired with the units own means. According to research made on Kursk (See N. Zetterling & A. Frankson, *Kursk July 1943: A statistical analysis*, Frank Cass, London 2000) this system was adhered to and it was accurate. Of course there were cases when damaged tanks were cannibalized or not repaired, but such cases were few and it seems that a more important source of deviations were tanks captured by the enemy when overrunning field workshops.

Another British document (Appendix A to 21 AGp/2870/RAC dated 21 Jul 44, PRO WO 205/112) states that write offs until 20 July were 609, while 667 had been damaged but were repairable (of these 379 had been repaired). The figure on write offs include 213 tanks lost 17–20 July that were presumed write offs.

If we accept the total of 1,211 British tanks and 1,350 US tanks for the entire campaign it would mean that German claims on average have to be reduced by 30% to get the true losses (complete write offs).

7

German Losses in Normandy

In British literature on the battle in Normandy, it is often stated that Germans casualties amounted to 450,000 men. Sometimes this is given as 210,000 prisoners and 240,000 killed and wounded. These figures seem to originate from Montgomery and his book *From Normandy to the Baltic*.[1] Probably they are nothing more than wartime estimates, a notoriously unreliable source.

There are, however, German documents that provide a better picture. For *OB West*, the following casualties were recorded during the summer 1944[2]:

Date	Killed in Action	Wounded	Missing
June	4975	14,631	15,848
July	10,839	38,824	55,135
August	7205	13,605	127,633
Total:	23,019	67,060	198,616

These figures have been compared to by-name lists of killed soldiers and found to be very reliable.[3] The proportion between killed, wounded and missing is remarkable. Missing soldiers constituted 69% of all casualties. On the Eastern Front during the period 22 June 1941–31 December 1944 casualties amounted to 885,802 killed in action, 3,448,180 wounded and 1,105,197 missing.[4] Thus, missing only constituted 20% of total casualties. Admittedly the proportion of missing was higher on the Eastern Front during the summer 1944,[5] but it is difficult to escape the conclusion that German soldiers facing British and American troops were more willing to surrender than those fighting the Red Army. Another explanation is that the German shortages of fuel and motor transport were greater in the west, which made it more difficult to retreat.

The figures presented above refer to the entire western theater until 31 August. Thus they include losses suffered in southern France and during the retreat from

France. Casualties in Normandy were smaller. Losses are also given by the weekly reports of *Heeresgruppe B*:

6 June–25 June[6]	43,070
6 June–1 July[7]	62,603
6 June–7 July[8]	80,783
6 June–16 July[9]	100,089
6 June–23 July[10]	116,863
6 June–30 July[11]	127,247
6 June–6 August[12]	148,075
6 June–13 August[13]	158,930

These include killed, wounded and missing. The figure for 1 July is somewhat uncertain due to losses at Cherbourg. According to the report they were estimated at 15,500. This estimate was probably too low.

Usually German casualties in the Falaise pocket are estimated at about 50,000. If these losses were incurred 14–22 August it would mean that total German casualties in Normandy 6 June–22 August would have amounted to 210,000. Hence, losses sustained in southern France 15–31 August and in northern France 23–31 August should have amounted to about 79,000.

This seems fairly reasonable. In Marseille and Toulon 31,000 soldiers were left behind when the Germans retreated from the Mediterranean coast.[14] These were lost when these two cities surrendered late in August. Another 27,000 soldiers did not succeed to retreat from south-western France.[15] It seems fully reasonable that 17,000 casualties would have been incurred during the retreat by *19. Armee* and during the fighting in northern France after 22 August.

Table 7.1 gives the losses for each division involved in the fighting in Normandy 6 June–22 August. In some cases, the figures presented are data directly from archival documents, in other cases they are calculations based on several documents and also some of the figures are mere judgements.

Total losses suffered by the divisions as given by Table 7.1 are 206,000. Since non-divisional units also must have suffered losses the figures in the table are perhaps somewhat too high. However, the overwhelming majority of all casualties were incurred by the divisions, and in particular the riflemen, which means that the figures in Table 7.1 cannot be far off the mark.

Note that we are discussing losses suffered among army units, *Waffen-SS* units and *Luftwaffe* units employed in ground fighting. The Germans most likely suffered further manpower losses when air fields or naval bases were overrun. On this no figures have been available for this study.

Table 7.1 Casualties suffered by German divisions in Normandy.[16]

Division	Casualties	Division (6·6/ 22-8)	Casualties
3. Fallschirmjäger-Division	11,000	352. Infanterie-Division	9000
5. Fallschirmjäger-Division	8000	353. Infanterie-Division	7000
16. Luftwaffenfelddivision	2500	363. Infanterie-Division	7000
77. Infanterie-Division	5000	708. Infanterie-Division	4000
84. Infanterie-Division	5500	709. Infanterie-Division	12,320
85. Infanterie-Division	3000	711. Infanterie-Division	1500
89. Infanterie-Division	4000	716. Infanterie-Division	6261
91. Luftlande-Division	5000	Panzer-Lehr	7000
243. Infanterie-Division	10,000	2. Panzer-Division	6000
265. Infanterie-Division	3000	9. Panzer-Division	3500
266. Infanterie-Division	5500	21. Panzer-Division	7500
271. Infanterie-Division	3000	116. Panzer-Division	3800
272. Infanterie-Division	3000	1. SS-Panzer-Division	5000
275. Infanterie-Division	9000	2. SS-Panzer-Division	4000
276. Infanterie-Division	5000	9. SS-Panzer-Division	4000
277. Infanterie-Division	4000	10. SS-Panzer-Division	5000
326. Infanterie-Division	6000	12. SS-Panzer-Division	8000
331. Infanterie-Division	1500	17. SS-Panzer-Grenadier-Division	8000
346. Infanterie-Division	3500		

There are also reports that have been interpreted to show that the German panzer divisions were almost wiped out. For example Max Hastings wrote that the German panzer divisions had the following strengths 22/23 August[17]:

2. Panzer-Division: 1 infantry battalion, no tanks, no artillery
21. Panzer-Division: 4 weak infantry battalions, 10 tanks, artillery unknown
116. Panzer-Division: 1 infantry battalion, 12 tanks, approx. two artillery batteries
1. SS-*Panzer-Division*: weak infantry elements, no tanks, no artillery
2. SS-*Panzer-Division*: 450 men, 15 tanks, 6 guns
9. SS-*Panzer-Division*: 460 men, 20–25 tanks, 20 artillery
10. SS-*Panzer-Division*: 4 weak infantry battalions, no tanks, no artillery
12. SS-*Panzer-Division*: 300 men, 10 tanks, no artillery

It must be remembered that the number of soldiers given refer to rifle men, not the total manpower strength of the divisions. Thus, the *12. SS-Panzer-Division* had more than 12,000 men on 22 August, not 300, which is a considerable difference. But there is a further problem with these figures. Actually there is no report with exactly those figures, but two reports. The first of these is dated 21 August, 8 pm and gives the following figures[18]:

10. SS-Panzer-Division: weak leg elements, no tanks, no artillery
12. SS-Panzer-Division: 300 men, 10 tanks, no artillery
1. SS-Panzer-Division: at the moment no report
2. Panzer-Division: infantry strength unknown, no tanks, no artillery
2. SS-Panzer-Division: 450 men, 15 tanks, 6 artillery pieces
9. SS-Panzer-Division: 460 men, 20–25 tanks, 20 artillery pieces
116. Panzer-Division: 1 battalion, 12 tanks, no artillery

It is explicitly stated that the report was preliminary. The second report is dated 23 August but concern the situation on 22 August for units intended for an attack[19]:

1. SS-Panzer-Division: weak infantry elements, no tanks, no artillery
2. Panzer-Division: approximately one battalion, no tank, no artillery
12. SS-Panzer-Division: 300 men, 10 tanks
116. Panzer-Division: 2 battalions., 12 tanks, 2 artillery batteries.
21. Panzer-Division: 4 weak battalions, 10 tanks, artillery unknown

Evidently, Hasting's figures are a mixture from the two reports. But in either case the reports may very well be incomplete. The first report is explicitly stated to be preliminary and the second gives elements assembled for a specific task. Also at this stage the picture was probably very confused for the German staffs and it is possible that units whose location and strength were unknown were assumed to be destroyed. As shown in the narratives for the respective panzer divisions they were in better shape than these reports indicate.

Similar errors are found in several other books. Authors have often used German reports without fully understanding their content.[20]

The German defeat in Normandy has been compared to the simultaneous defeat in Belorussia. John Keegan has compared the two battles and arrived at the conclusion that the defeat in Normandy was greater.[21] However, his comparison is fundamentally flawed by the fact that his figures are completely wrong, e.g. he writes that almost a quarter of a million German soldiers had died during the fighting in Normandy.[22]

The battle in White Russia cost the Germans 26,361 killed in action, 109,776 wounded and 262,959 missing.[23] This was greater than the losses suffered in the west during the summer 1944. Also, to a much greater extent entire divisions were destroyed in Belorussia. In the west, losses were largely confined to the infantry, which was easier to replace than many of the specialists lost in the east.

Keegan also argues that the Allies achieved their victory with much less effort than did the Russians, since they employed much smaller forces. This is not true. The Allies employed 2,052,299 men in Normandy, while the Red Army amassed

2,411,600 for its offensive operation.[24] The German Army Group Center mustered 849,000 men when the Soviet offensive was launched.[25] Thus, in terms of manpower the western Allies faced better odds.

In one very important aspect the Allies fared far better than the Red Army. Soviet casualties in the Belorussian operation were 180,040 killed and missing and 590,848 wounded,[26] a cost that far surpassed British and American losses.

German equipment losses were perhaps more significant than the manpower losses, even though they were easier to make up for. Until 25 August the Germans lost, in the *OB West* area, 164 captured artillery pieces and 437 of German design.[27] Losses of tanks were very severe. On all fronts the Germans lost 2366 tanks and 1684 assault guns 1 June–31 August 1944.[28] How many of these that were lost in Normandy is impossible to tell. Even though many tank units had perhaps less than 10% of their original tanks still operational at the end of the Falaise battle, this does not necessarily mean that the rest had been lost.

Until 27 July, 224 *Panzer IV*, 131 *Panther* and 33 *Tiger* tanks were reported to have been irrevocably lost.[29] Also three command tanks, 60 assault guns and 45 self-propelled anti-tank guns had been written off.[30] According to the *OKW* War Diary 406 tanks of types *Panzer IV, V* and *VI* plus 75 assault guns had been irretrievably lost 6 June to 31 July in Normandy.[31] On 31 July, there were also 353 tanks and 117 assault guns in workshops.[32] This means that less than half of the original tanks were still operational.

It is much more difficult to establish tank losses during August. No documents giving such information have been found. A possible solution would be to check the tank strength situation in September and compare with the situation on 31 July to see the change. This would of course have to be balanced with replacements sent to the units in the west.

The problem with such an approach is that tanks requiring major repairs could be sent to facilities far from the front or even back to the manufacturer. Such tanks were regarded as lost to the original unit and could, when repaired, be sent to any unit. It is known that during the period 1 October 1943 to 31 January 1944 complete losses of tanks amounted to 2945 on all fronts. Simultaneously 453 were repaired in the zone of interior.[33] According to Lefèvre half the *Panzer* regiments in Normandy lacked their repair company.[34] This would of course to a greater extent make it necessary to send damaged tanks to rear facilities for repairs.

Another example concern *Panther* tanks on the Eastern Front during the summer 1943. After Zitadelle, the units on the Eastern Front possessed 135 *Panthers*. Of these only 19 were operational, while 74 were at workshops belonging to the units. Another 15 had been sent to Germany for repairs and the remaining 27 had been sent to a repair facility at Dnepropetrovsk[35] (located about 250 km from the units, thus exceeding the distance between Caen and Paris).

It is possible that there were comparatively fewer facilities capable of taking care of severely damaged vehicles in the west.[36] This would suggest that a larger percentage of seriously damaged tanks were sent to the zone of interior for repairs.

Another approach is to see what Allied operations research teams found when they investigated the battlefields after the Allied forces had advanced further to the east. At Mortain, 46 destroyed or captured German tanks and assault guns were found. In the Falaise pocket area, 320 tanks and assault guns were found. Of these 80% had been abandoned or destroyed by their crews. A further 150 were found in the area west of Seine, which the German forces retreated through.[37] This means that at least 516 were lost west of Seine. However, this is clearly not the complete tally of losses. Possibly another 500 were lost in Normandy during August. This would mean that of the 2336 tanks, tank destroyers and assault guns sent to Normandy[38], around 1500 were lost. Of these, probably no more than half fell victim to Allied fire.[39]

1   B. L. Montgomery, *Normandy to the Baltic* (Houghton Mifflin, Boston 1948) p. 180.

2   Der Heeresarzt om OKH GenSt d H/GenQu Az 1335 c/d (IIb), Personelle blutige Verluste des Feldheeres, Berichtigte Meldung für die Zeit vom 1.6.1944 bis 10.1.1945, T78, R414, F6383234.

3   N. Zetterling & A. Frankson, Analyzing WWII Eastern Front Battles (*Journal of Slavic Military Studies*, Vol 11, No 1, March 1998) p 186f. According to H. Stöber, *Die Sturmflut und das Ende, Bd. I* (Munin Verlag, Osnabrück 1976) p. 376 the number of German soldiers buried in France is 42,000, a figure considerably higher than that given in this chapter. Note that the figure 23,019 does not include soldiers who died of wounds. Usually this category constitute about 20% of all who die. This percentage may well have been higher in Normandy due to lack of medical equipment. Also some of the missing soldiers may have been killed.

4   Der Heeresarzt om OKH GenSt d H/GenQu Az 1335 c/d (IIb), Personelle blutige Verluste des Feldheeres, Berichtigte Meldung für die Zeit vom 1.6.1944 bis 10.1.1945, T78, R414, F6383234. Usually losses were reported by the *Heeresarzt* in ten-day periods. The problem with these reports is that if there are delays in the reporting from the field armies to the *Heeresarzt*, casualties were not placed in the period when they were incurred, but when they were reported to the *Heeresarzt*. Usually this was not a problem, but on the Eastern Front there were times, e.g. during Operation Bagration, when the ten day reports were completely unreliable. For that operation there are *Nachmeldungen* that can give a complete picture (see N. Zetterling & A. Frankson, Analyzing WWII Eastern Front Battles (*Journal of Slavic Military Studies*, vol 11, No 1, March 1998) page 181f.), but that is rare. For Normandy too the ten day reports are incomplete. However, the report used here is a compilation made four months after the end of the Falaise battle. It raises the casualties suffered in the West 1 June–31 August by a factor of 2.4 compared to the initial ten day reports. I have much more confidence in this report.

5   During this period casualties on the Eastern Front amounted to 71,685 killed in action, 325,380 wounded and 503,564 missing. Der Heeresarzt om OKH GenSt d H/GenQu Az 1335 c/d (IIb), Personelle blutige Verluste des Feldheeres, Berichtigte Meldung für die Zeit vom 1.6.1944 bis 10.1.1945, T78, R414, F6383234.

6   HGr B Ia Nr 4043/44 g.Kdos, Wochenmeldung 19.6 – 26.6, 26.6.44, T311, R3, F7002166.

7   HGr B Ia Nr 4320/44 g.Kdos, Wochenmeldung 27.6 – 2.7, 3.7.44, T311, R3, F7002175.

8   HGr B Ia Nr 4595/44 g.Kdos, Wochenmeldung 3.7 – 9.7, 10.7.44, T311, R3, F7002183.

9   HGr B Ia Nr 4860/44 g.Kdos, Wochenmeldung 10.7 – 16.7, 17.7.44, T311, R3, F7002194.

10 HGr B Ia Nr 5110/44 g.Kdos, Wochenmeldung 17.7 – 23.7, 23.7.44, T311, R3, F7002204.

11 HGr B Ia Nr 5360/44 g.Kdos, Wochenmeldung 24.7 – 30.7, 31.7.44, T311, R3, F7002214.

12 HGr B Ia Nr 5690/44 g.Kdos, Wochenmeldung 7.8.44, T311, R3, F7002223.

13 HGr B Ia Nr 6070/44 g.Kdos, Wochenmeldung 14.8.44, T311, R3, F7002225.

14 J. Ludewig, *Der deutsche Rückzug aus Frankreich 1944* (Rombach, Freiburg 1995) p. 128.

15 Some 87,000 soldiers tried to retreat from the area held by AOK 1 in mid-August. Of these 60 000 eventually joined up with AOK 19. Ludewig, op. cit p. 124f & 211.

16 See narratives of the divisions for the sources, except those specifically given. Those figures in the table that are in *italic* type are estimates.

17 M. Hastings, *Overlord* (Guild, London 1984) p. 313.

18 HGr B Ia Nr. 6388/44 g.Kdos. 21.8.44., T311, R4, F7004565. The exact formulation in German is:

10. SS-Panzer-Division: schwache Fußteile, keine Panzer, keine Artl.

12. SS-Panzer-Division: 300 Mann, 10 Panzer, keine Artl.

1. SS-Panzer-Division: Vorläufig, noch keine Meldung

2. Panzer-Division: infanteristische Stärke nicht bekannt, keine Panzer, keine Artl.

2. SS-Panzer-Division: 450 Mann, 15 Panzer, 6 Rohre

9. SS-Panzer-Division: 460 Mann, 20-25 Panzer, 20 Rohre

116. Panzer-Division: 1 Btl.., 12 Panzer, keine Artl.

19 HGr B Ia Nr 6457/44, Tagesmeldung 22.8.44, 23.8.44, T311, R3, F7002806. The exact formulation in German is:

1. SS-Panzer-Division. "LAH": Schwache Inf.Teile, keine Panzer, keine Artl.

2. Panzer-Division: Etwa 1 Btl., keine Panzer, keine Artl.

12. SS-Panzer-Division: 300 Mann, 10 Panzer

116. Panzer-Division: 2 Btle., 12 Panzer, 2 Battrn.

21. Panzer-Division: 4 schwache Btle., 10 Panzer, Artl. Unbekannt

20 See e.g. M. Blumenson, *Breakout and Pursuit* (Washington D.C. 1961) p. 516. The author states that the 9. Pz.Div. had 260 men on 13 August. This is clearly implausible. Compare with the fact that the Gefechtstärke was reported to be 2 214 (excluding the Panzer Regiment) on 22 August. Blumenson's figure refer to a period when important parts of the division were detached. Also it was spread over a large area, making it difficult to obtain a correct picture of its component units. Blumenson also states that 2. Pz.Div. had 2 220 men on 13 August. This is the strength of the two panzer grenadier regiments, the engineer battalion and the reckon battalion. Also the report does not specifiy if it is Kampfstärke, Gefechtstärke, Tagesstärke, Iststärke or Verpflegungsstärke. Probably it is Gefechtstärke, since reports for such units usually give Gefechtstärke.

21 J. Keegan, *Six Armies in Normandy* (Penguin, London 1988) pp. 314–16.

22 Ibid, p. 316.

23 For a detailed description of the German casualties in Belorussia during the summer 1944 see N. Zetterling, Loss Rates on the Eastern Front during WWII (*Journal of Slavic Military Studies*, Vol 9, No 4, December 1996) p 902 and N. Zetterling & A. Frankson, Analyzing WWII Eastern Front Battles (*Journal of Slavic Military Studies*, Vol 11, No 1, March 1998) p 181f.

24 G. F. Krivosheev, *Grif Sekretnosti Sniat* (Voenizdat, Moscow 1993) p. 203.

25 N. Zetterling, Loss Rates on the Eastern Front during WWII (*Journal of Slavic Military Studies*, Vol 9, No 4, December 1996) p 898.

26 Krivosheev, op. cit. p. 203.

27 Gen. Der Artillerie beim Chef Gen.St.d.Heeres Ib Nr. 2610/44 g.Kdos, 27.8.44, BA-MA RH 11 II/v. 4.

28 B. Müller-Hildebrand, *Das Heer 1933–1945 vol III* (Mittler & Sohn, Frankfurt am Main 1956) Anhang B.

29 HGr B Ia Anlagen, Totalausfälle an Panzern, Sturmgeschützen und Sf.-Pak in der Zeit vom 6.6. - 27.744, BA-MA RH 19 IX/46. In the report, it is actually said that 23 Tigers had been lost, but I strongly suspect this is a typo and that the correct figure is 33.

30 Ibid.

31 P. E. Schramm, *KTB des OKW (Wehrmachtführungsstab) Bd. IV: 1.1.1944 – 22.5.1945* (Bernard & Graefe, Frankfurt am Main 1961) p. 330.

32 Ibid.

33 N. Zetterling & A. Frankson, Analyzing WWII Eastern Front Battles (*Journal of Slavic Military Studies*, Vol 11, No 1, March 1998) p 191.

34 E. Lefèvre, *Panzers in Normandy* (Battle of Britain Prints, London 1983) p. 6.

35 Entwicklung der Panzerlage bei Pz.Abt. 51 und 52 (Panther, 18.8.43, BA-MA RH 10/60.

36 The Germans seem to have relied heavily on the rail net in western Europe which could have made it possible to move damaged vehicles to Germany for repair. This appears to have been the case with supply at least. Also, during operations, many trains go with load to the front but empty in the other direction. Thus the Germans may have expected that there would be plenty of transport capacity available.

37 Figures obtained from I. Gooderson, Allied Fighter-Bombers Versus German Armour in North-West Europe 1944–1945: Myths and Realities (*Journal of Strategic Studies*, Vol 14, No 2 June 1991) p. 223–5.

38 Derived from Chapter 6.

39 According to data presented in chapter five, of 129 *Panthers* investigated by Allied operations research teams in August (this includes 33 at Mortain), only 36 had been hit by enemy fire (including 20 at Mortain). Possibly a larger percentage of the *Panzer IV* that were lost had been hit by enemy fire, but it still seems unlikely that more than half the tanks and SP guns would have been destroyed by enemy fire, since the majority of them were lost in August.

8

German Combat Efficiency

The efficiency of German combat units compared to their Allied adversaries is a topic that occasionally has caused heated debate. Most publications that have at least partially discussed the subject seem to agree that the Germans were more efficient, at least as long as combat units are analyzed. But there are also authors who disagree.

For example, it has been argued that the bocage terrain made the German defense very effective, thus giving the impression of German combat effectiveness superiority. Certainly the bocage aided the defender in certain aspects. But there were also disadvantages for the defender in the bocage. One of the greatest was that it limited observation. This meant that the Germans had to have many men in front line, just to ensure observation. This was very troublesome since casualties quickly drained the infantry strength of a division. Also, the terrain made it difficult to concentrate indirect fire. The latter was a greater problem for the defender who had to rely on flexibility to meet attacks, while the attacker could, to a greater extent, rely on preplanned fires.[1]

It is a very common assumption that it is more costly, to attack than defend. Charles B. MacDonald has even written on the fighting by the US 110th Infantry Regiment in the Ardennes, 16–19 December 1944:

> To those casualties in the race for Bastogne would have to be added those incurred by the 28th Division's 110th Infantry and its attached and supporting units. The 110th Infantry lost 2,750 officers and men wounded, captured and killed … It was impossible to ascertain with accuracy what the fight cost the Germans, but losses of forces on the attack almost always exceeded those of forces on the defence.[2]

Let us first note that contrary to MacDonalds assumption, US losses were markedly higher than German losses during the action MacDonald describes.[3] But it is highly dubious if losses of forces on the attack almost always exceeded those of forces on the defense. On the Eastern Front German and Soviet casualties per year was:[4]

Year	German losses	Soviet losses	Ratio Soviet: German losses
1941	831,050	4,473,820	5.38
1942	1,080,950	7,369,278	6.82
1943	1,601,445	7,857,503	4.91
1944	1,947,106	6,878,600	3.53

These figures warrant a few comments. First of all, figures include killed, wounded and missing in action. Secondly, Soviet casualties during 1941 may actually have been higher than indicated. It seems that Soviet records for the period are not completely reliable.[5] But the main point with these figures is that during the two years when the Red Army was predominantly on the offensive, the casualty rates were more favourable than during the two years when the Germans were mainly the attackers. What we have here is not some obscure little example, but the costliest campaign ever in the history of land warfare.

It is also illuminating to study the German attack at Kursk 1943. During the German offensive German casualties were 55,261 killed, wounded and missing, while the Red Army lost 177,847 officers and men.[6] Thus, during this offensive German operation, which failed, the Red Army's casualties were 3.2 times greater than German losses. The Germans achieved this despite considerable Soviet numerical superiority, well prepared defenses and revealed attack plan.

Possibly the notion that attack is costlier than defense originate from Clausewitz statement that "defence is the stronger form of combat". Probably this is true if the two opposing forces are identical in all respects. Such a situation seems quite rare, however. In reality, the relative losses depend on a number of factors: relative combat efficiency, force ratios, equipment characteristics, tactics, surprise, terrain, posture, missions, firepower, air superiority, weather, naval fire support, ammunition supply, motorization levels etc. The data from the Eastern Front suggest that the advantage of defensive posture can easily be—and usually is—cancelled by other factors.

But it seems that many US operations in the Pacific also contradict this statement. Despite usually being on the offensive, US forces seem to have inflicted more casualties on their adversaries than they incurred.

The two examples above, the German advance towards Bastogne and the fighting around Bastogne 21–26 December, indicate that the Germans could inflict greater casualties than they incurred even when they attacked US forces. Unfortunately, the data available on German casualties during Normandy rarely allow similar analyses.

There are however a few situations with ample data. When *SS-Panzergrenadier-Regiment 25*, supported by *Panzer IV* tanks of *II./SS-Panzer Regiment 12*, counterattacked Canadian forces on 7 June, the Germans lost 205 men, compared to 308 Canadian soldiers.[7]

Another way to look at combat capabilities is to focus on the ability to gain ground. In Normandy, there were few sincere German attempts to advance. One attempt was the counterattack by *Panzer-Lehr* at Le Désert on 11 July. This attack was made despite considerable numerical inferiority.[8] Against the odds the Germans managed to thrust several kilometres into the American defenses, but when the real force ratio began to dawn upon them, they clearly had to withdraw. As such the attack was a failure, which is hardly surprising given the force ratio, what is surprising is that it did gain ground at all.

Something that does not come as a surprise is that the claims of German tanks destroyed in this engagement were grossly inflated. US ground forces claimed to have destroyed about 50 tanks,[9] while the air force claimed to have destroyed 22.[10] The latter figure is even said to be fully substantiated.[11] Actually the *Panzer-Lehr-Division* lost 22 tanks due to all causes from 1 July to 15 July.[12] That all these should have been destroyed by air power on 11 July only seems very unrealistic, especially since there are several German reports and participants stating that tanks have been knocked out by gun fire, but none has been found saying that a tank was hit by aircraft. The "substantiating" methods of the Allied air forces must certainly be called into question. Also, it seems wholly unlikely that all claims by ground forces should have been wrong and all claims by air forces should have been correct.

The most well-known German offensive action was of course the Mortain attack. Indeed, one author has even claimed that the best answer to the perception of German combat effectiveness superiority is given by the 30th US Infantry Division during its heroic performance at Mortain.[13] However, a closer look at the author's sources shows that they are interviews of US veterans 45 years after the battle and also some after action reports by US units. To make statements about relative combat performance or force ratios by only consulting one side is a flagrant mistake. Also, had he not had such one-sided sources he might have avoided errors like stating that Tiger tanks participated in the attack.[14] The author also uses expressions like terrible odds and similar formulations.[15]

However, it seems that the odds were not very unfavourable. It seems that in terms of manpower the Germans had an advantage of about 2:1 when they began the offensive.[16] Of course the Germans had a substantial superiority in tanks,[17] but on the other hand the US defenders had considerably more artillery available.[18] The latter was a consequence of the fact that the Germans had no GHQ artillery units available,[19] while the US 30th Division was supported by twelve artillery battalions, divisional and GHQ.[20]

.jermans seem not at all have had a tremendous numerical superiority at
.n. Rather the numerical superiority was markedly less than average Allied
numerical superiority over the entire front. In fact, it seems that the Allies would
have been extremely reluctant to attack at all with such slender numerical superiority.
The remarkable thing is not that the Germans were stopped by the 30th Division,
supported by air power and aided by reinforcements. What is remarkable is that
the Germans were able to advance 8 km before being stopped.[21]

Before continuing the discussion on relative combat effectiveness, it must be
emphasized that neither for the Germans nor for the Allies were units uniformly

Table 8.1 German Casualties on Eastern and Western Fronts 1 June to 31 December 1944

Eastern Front

	Killed in action	Wounded	Missing	Percentage Missing
June	10,629	41,165	73,723	58.7
July	30,420	131,732	238,284	59.5
August	30,636	152,484	191,557	51.1
September	18,159	87,284	15,581	12.9
October	21,620	100,549	26,691	17.9
November	10,703	52,883	7,856	11.0
December	11,866	55,125	10,489	13.5

Western Front

	Killed in action	Wounded	Missing	Percentage Missing
June	4,975	14,631	15,848	44.7
July	10,839	38,824	55,135	52.6
August	7,205	13,605	127,633	86.0
September	9,418	30,558	86,131	68.3
October	7,238	28,143	33,559	48.7
November	8,182	30,712	44,645	53.4
December	9,268	31,909	25,996	38.7

Comments: The figures include casualties suffered by Army, *Waffen-SS* and *Luftwaffe* units in ground
combat. Probably the casualties suffered at Cherbourg are placed in July.

From 22 June 1941 to 31 May 1944 German casualties on the Eastern Front amounted to
751,769 killed in action, 2,826,958 wounded and 541,505 missing. Thus, before the summer 1944
missing only constituted 13.1% of all casualties on the Eastern Front.

*Source: Der Heeresarzt im Oberkommando des Heeres, GenStdH/Gen Qu, Az 1335 c/d (IIb), Personelle
blutige Verluste des Feldheeres, Berichtigte Meldung für die Zeit vom 1.6.1944 bis 10.1.1945, T78,
R414, F6383234f.*

skilled. It seems that the Germans in particular varied considerably from unit to unit on the Western Front. In the west were committed top quality units like *Panzer-Lehr* and *2. Panzer-Division*. Simultaneously there were units composed of older men and "volunteers" from eastern Europe. There were even peculiar units like the *70. Infanterie-Division*, which was composed of soldiers with various stomach diseases, thus requiring special food. These men had previously been rejected for service with combat units, but by 1944 the shortage of men for service was grave. Clearly many of these soldiers knew that they were regarded as stop-gap units, a knowledge that hardly contributed to high morale. Of course, there were variations in the quality of the units on the Eastern Front too. But the low-quality units were far fewer and to a larger extent used against partisans rather than as regular combat units.

This is also evident from the statistics on casualties shown in Table 8.1.
On the Eastern Front, the Germans were usually well motivated and also fearful that surrender might very well lead to death anyway. Consequently, the percentage of missing was very low before the summer 1944 (only 13.1%).[22] During June–August 1944, substantial German units were surrounded in Belorussia and Romania, causing the percentage of missing to rise alarmingly, but it returned to normal levels after the summer.

On the Western Front the picture is quite different. It is understandable that the percentage missing is high during August, but it is more remarkable that there were more missing than wounded in every month except December. Since there were very few Allied encirclements on the Western Front it is hard to escape the conclusion that there were many German soldiers who were not very reluctant to surrender to the Allies.

Among the casualties suffered by the Allies missing only constituted 9.2%.[23] This can be seen as a relatively normal percentage for forces on the offensive. From 22 June to 30 November 1941 the Germans suffered 753,193 casualties, of which only 31,338, or 4.2%, were missing.[24] The latter is a very low percentage even for offensive operations.

Clearly high quality German units did not report many missing in action unless they were cut off. During the period 3–10 July 1944 Das Reich lost 119 men killed, 457 wounded and only three missing.[25] The *Hitlerjugend* division lost 405 men killed, 847 wounded and 165 missing 6-16 June 1944.[26] The Götz von Berlichingen division lost 233 killed in action, 777 wounded and 86 missing 6–30 June 1944.[27] It should be noted that during this period neither Das Reich nor Götz von Berlichingen could be regarded as elite formations.[28] The *Hitlerjugend* on the other hand was probably one of the best divisions the Germans had.[29]

These three examples show that at least some German units did not suffer undue losses of missing. However, during very adverse situations like the Falaise pocket, the percentage of missing could be considerably higher even for an elite division like *12. SS-Panzer-Division*. It lost 45 killed, 248 wounded and 655 missing 15–22 August.[30]

The problem of relative efficiency is actually a quantitative problem[31]. To make a thorough analysis on this issue it is necessary to resort to mathematics. The best known in this respect is probably Trevor N. Dupuy and his successors. They have not used their mathematical methods on the actions in Normandy, but their analyses of combat between German and Allied units in action in Italy and during the Ardennes show a consistent German efficiency superiority. Their methods are quite complicated and time consuming and another method will be used here.

The relative casualty inflicting efficiency of the attacker to the defender (Eff_{aci}) can be defined as:[32]

$$Eff_{aci} = F_{dp} \frac{N_d C_d}{N_a C_a} \qquad (1)$$

where

F_{dp} is A factor to compensate for defensive posture.
N_d is The number of defending soldiers committed.
C_d is The number of casualties of the defender.
N_a is The number of attacking soldiers committed.
C_a is The number of casualties of the attacker.

The relative efficiency of the defender is the inverse of the attacker's efficiency. Of course the formula can be written either as:

$$Eff_G = F_{dp} \frac{N_A C_A}{N_G C_G} \qquad (2)$$

or

$$Eff_G = \frac{1}{F_{dp}} \frac{N_A C_A}{N_G C_G} \qquad (3)$$

depending on whether the Germans attack (formula 2) or defend (formula 3), where

Eff_G is the German casualty inflicting efficiency superiority relative to the Allies. Note that a value less than one means that the Allies were actually superior to the Germans.

F_{dp} is A factor to compensate for defensive posture.
N_G is the number of German soldiers committed.
C_G is the number of German casualties.
N_A is the number of Allied soldiers committed.
C_A is the number of Allied casualties.

It should be noted that we need not have absolute values on casualties and strengths to use formula 2 or 3. Rather it is sufficient to have the force ratio and the casualty ratio.

The value of F_{dp} is of course very important. Data from the Eastern Front in 1943 suggest a value of about 1.4.[33] This is quite close to the factor 1.3 used by T. N. Dupuy.[34]

If formula 3 is applied to the overall situation in Normandy until 13 August we have a casualty ratio of 1.13.[35] The Allied numerical superiority grew gradually over the time but here we assume that it on average was 3:1.[36] This would suggest a German casualty inflicting efficiency superiority of 2.4.

There are some comments that have to be made both concerning this particular case and the method in general. Those factors that would tend to raise the German efficiency superiority are marked with >>, while those factors that tend to produce a lower value are marked with <<. They are listed in arbitrary order.

>>The less reliable units that fought on the German side seem to have suffered a disproportionate part of the missing incurred by the Germans. Given the methodology they will have greater weight in the final figure calculated than their actual combat effort would suggest.

>>Due to Allied air supremacy and the French resistance the Germans seems to have had more supply difficulties than the Allied ground forces.

>>The method assumes that there is a linear relation between enemy casualties and own strength and efficiency. This is usually a reasonable approximation, but when the attackers force superiority or relative efficiency (or the combination of the two) becomes large, it seems that the defender's casualties increase disproportionally, usually in the form of prisoners. Exactly when this point is reached can vary considerably, but it seems that during the Falaise battle and also the fall of Cherbourg this was the case.

<<Compared to the conditions in Russia, the battlefield in Normandy was quite small compared to the forces committed. This usually favors the defender since the attacker can find it difficult to use all his forces effectively and concentrate formidable superiority at the main effort.

>>Some German equipment, like tanks and anti-tank weapons were often better than Allied weapons. Also, some German small arms, like machine guns, were better. On the other hand, since the method only consider personnel casualties, quality of artillery equipment is probably more important. Allied artillery weapons were not generally inferior to German equipment. Since the Germans operated many captured guns, the opposite might in fact be true.

>>Superior mobility may affect the efficiency. Since the Allies both were more lavishly equipped with vehicles and had much more fuel available they could achieve greater mobility. However, during June and July this probably had little effect on the outcome. In August it may have been more important.

>>The Allied air supremacy and naval fire support contributed both directly to German casualties and also indirectly these factors increased German casualties and reduced Allied casualties.

These factors may of course affect the value on German casualty inflicting efficiency superiority. The reader may judge how they influence this issue. My opinion is that it seems wholly unlikely that they would indicate that there was no German efficiency superiority.

It must not be concluded that the German efficiency superiority of 2.4 calculated above means that 100 German soldiers would make an even fight with 240 Allied men. Rather the square root of the casualty inflicting efficiency gives that kind of relationship.[37] Since the square root of 2.4 is approximately 1.5 it could be concluded that 100 Germans would make an even fight against about 150 Allied soldiers.

For those who are not impressed by this kind of mathematics it can be reiterated from chapter 4 that during the summer 1944 the Allies actually had a greater numerical superiority in Normandy than the Red Army had on the Eastern Front. Despite this the Allies did not really make better progress than the Red Army. Few have questioned the superior combat effectiveness of the Germans over the Red Army.

Finally let's caution that the methodology described above should not be used if one sides casualties constitute a considerable percentage of the total numbers committed. In such cases, some of the assumptions the methodology makes will not be valid.[38]

---

1   See also P. Mahlmann, *353. Inf.Div.*, MS # A-983, p. 12.

2   C. B. MacDonald, *The Battle of the Bulge* (Weidenfeld and Nicholson, London 1984) pp. 296–7.

3   The US units in the example given by MacDonald faced elements from three German divisions, the 26th, the 2nd Panzer and Panzer-Lehr. These three divisions suffered losses of 1,012,255 and 329 respectively during the period 16–23 December, giving a total of 1,596. Note that these losses refer to a period twice as long as that given by MacDonald. Also these three divisions only committed elements against 110th Infantry Regiment. In reality, German casualties were therefore lower. Figures are taken from most reliable source available in print, T. N. Dupuy, *Hitler's Last*

Gamble (Airlife, Shrewsbury 1995) pp. 473 and 475. It should be noted that principally all statements on German losses given in MacDonalds book are based on US after action reports and witnesses, two sources of very low reliability for such information. MacDonalds book may have a value as a source for the actions by US units. It is however utterly unreliable when it comes to information on strength and losses of German units.

4   G. F. Krivosheyev, *Grif Sekretnosti Sniat* (Voenizdat, Moscow 1993) page 147, BA-MA RW 6/v.552, BA-MA RW 6/v.553, BA-MA RH 2/1343 and Der Heeresarzt im Oberkommando des Heeres, GenStdH/Gen Qu, Az 1335 c/d (IIb), Personelle blutige Verluste des Feldheeres, Berichtigte Meldung für die Zeit vom 1.6.1944 bis 10.1.1945, T78, R414, F6383234f.

5   See N. Zetterling & A. Frankson, Analyzing World War II East Front Battles (article in *Journal of Slavic Military Studies*, March 1998). See also B. Kavalerchik & L. Lopukhovsky, *The Price of Victory: The Red Army's Casualties in the Great Patriotic War*, Pen & Sword, 2017.

6   N. Zetterling, Loss Rates on the Eastern Front during World War II (article in *Journal of Slavic Military Studies*, December 1996) p. 899f.

7   H. Meyer, *Kriegsgeschichte der 12. SS-Panzerdivision "Hitlerjugend", vol I* (Munin Verlag, Osnabrück 1982) p 84f. Note that the author has not used German estimates for Canadian losses, rather he has used war diaries of the involved Canadian units for Canadian losses and German documents for German losses. The Germans had no numerical superiority in this engagement.

8   The attacking force consisted of four depleted panzer grenadier battalions and elements of two tank battalions. Also four other battalions, three of them weak, covered the attacking forces. Against this force there were deployed 21 US infantry battalions and nine tank and anti-tank battalions. All data according to H. Ritgen, *Die Gechichte der Panzer-Lehr-Division im Westen 1944–1945* (Motorbuch Verlag, Stuttgart 1979) pp. 150–3 and M. Blumenson, *Breakout and Pursuit* (Office of the Chief of the Army, Washington D.C. 1961) pp. 107–116.

9   Blumenson, op. cit. p. 138.

10   W. F. Craven & J. L. Cate, *The Army Air Forces in World War II, Vol 3* (University of Chicago Press, 1951). p. 206.

11   Ibid.

12   Compare figures on page 147 with diagram on page 159 in Ritgen, op. cit.

13   A. Featherston, *Saving the Breakout, The 30th Division's Heroic Stand at Mortain, August 7–12, 1944* (Presidio, Novato 1993) p. xv.

14   Ibid, p. 50. All Tiger tanks were found in 101. and 102. SS-Pz.Abt. and 503. s.Pz.Abt. None of these units were employed on the American sector.

15   Featherston, op. cit. p. xv. Also on the dust cover one can read that the 30th division held on for five days against overwhelming odds.

16   R. C. Anderson, *New Engagement Data for the Breakpoints Data Base* (a report from Historical Evaluation and Research Organization to US Army Concepts Analysis Agency dated 30 September 1988) pp. 31–35. Given the fact that many German records did not survive the data must partly be estimates though the researchers have used both US and German records. However, since only two divisions actually took part in the initial attack this seems quite reasonable (even though elements of five division took part the actual attacking force was much smaller since 116. Pz.Div. only contributed with one battalion, the 17. SS-Pz.Gren.Div. committed a regimental sized Kampfgruppe and also from 1. SS-Pz.Div. only elements participated; if it is also taken into account that all formations were more or less depleted it seems unlikely that the attacking force was much larger than two divisions).

17   It is difficult to produce a meaningful ratio on tanks since the defender need not face tanks with tanks, but can also use anti-tank weapons, like the 3" guns of 823rd antitank battalion that was attached to 30th Division.

18 Anderson, op.cit.

19 KTB AOK 7 Ia, entry 7.8.44, T312, R1569, F000205.

20 Featherston, op. cit. p. 133.

21 This advance is evident also in American sources like Blumenson, op. cit. map XI at the rear folder of the book.

22 See Table 8.1.

23 L. F. Ellis, *Victory in the West, vol I, The Battle of Normandy* (HMSO, London 1962) p. 493.

24 Derived from tables compiled by Wehrmacht Verlustwesen, found in file BA-MA RW 6/v. 552.

25 O. Weidinger, *Division Das Reich 1943–45* (Munin Verlag, Osnabrück 1982) p. 217. The figures does not include Kampfgruppe Wisliceny, since information is not available for this unit.

26 Anlage zu HGr. B Ia Nr. 3725/44 g.K. O.U 16.6.44, BA-MA RH 19 IX/2.

27 KTB HGr B Ia Anlagen, BA-MA RH 19 IX/3, frame 15 on Mikrofiche 1

28 Both divisions contained many so called "Volksdeutsche" (i.e. men who had been recruited from areas that were not part of Germany, but still considered to be of "German race").

29 Though it seems that when the division was rebuilt before the Ardennes offensive it received replacements inferior to the soldiers who fought with the division in Normandy.

30 Meyer, op. cit. p. 354.

31 The outcome in combat is strongly affected by factors such as numbers of men, tanks and guns, ammunition supply. Also the results of combat, like advances made and casualties inflicted are quantitative data.

32 This is a deduction from the Lanchester square law. It is formulated:

$$dN_A/dt = F_I k_D N_D$$
$$dN_D/dt = F_I k_A N_A$$

dN_A/dt is the loss rate of the attacker; dN_D/dt is the loss rate for the defender; F_I is a factor for the intensity of the combat; k_D is a coefficient which is proportional to the efficiency of the defender def; N_D is the number of defending soldiers; k_A is a coefficient which is proportional to the efficiency of the defender def; N_A is the number of defending soldiers.

k_A/ k_D is the relative efficiency of the attacker compared to the defender.

If it is assumed that the loss rate is relatively constant and proportional to the total casualties suffered the equations can be written:

$$Cas_A = F_I k_D N_D$$
$$Cas_D = F_I k_A N_A$$

Note that the value of F_I need not be identical to F_I in the original equations, since it now also takes into account the duration of the combat.

$Cas_A = F_I k_D N_D$ can be written $F_I = Cas_A/(k_D N_D)$. If we combine this with $Cas_D = F_I k_A N_A$ we get $Cas_D/Cas_A = (k_A N_A)/ (k_D N_D)$. This is equivalent to $k_A/ k_D =(Cas_D Cas_A)$ If we include the factor F_{dp} we have the expression in the text.

33 See N. Zetterling, Loss Rates on the Eastern Front during World War II (article in *Journal of Slavic Military Studies*, December 1996) p. 899f. During the German offensive action at Kursk the superiority was 6.2 while it was 12.1 during the defensive battles later during the autumn. Both these figures are calculated without consideration of advantages of defensive posture. A factor 1,4 for defensive posture would give a German superiority corresponds to a casualty inflicting efficiency of 8,66 in either case.

34 T. N. Dupuy, *Numbers, Predictions and War* (Hero Books, Fairfax, Virginia 1985) p. 99.

35 HGr B Ia Nr 6070/44 g.Kdos, Wochenmeldung 14.8.44, T311, R3, F7002225 and Blumenson, op. cit. p. 516.

36 See chapter 4.

37 A mathematical proof of this is found in N. Zetterling, Loss Rates on the Eastern Front during World War II (article in *Journal of Slavic Military Studies*, December 1996) page 905, note 30.

38 Mainly it is questionable that the assumption that the loss rate is relatively constant and proportional to the total casualties suffered is true in such cases. The original Lanchester equations are differential equations and take into account the changes in force strength. The methodology described here does not. As long as losses do not significantly reduce force size this will only produce insignificant errors. Note that if both sides suffer considerable casualties but relative to the respective force strengths similar, the problem is negated.

9

Movements to Normandy

At the beginning of June 1944, there were 880,000 German soldiers in France, Belgium and the Netherlands.[1] Superficially it may seem strange that these did not succeed in throwing back the Allied invaders, who only put 156,000 men ashore on D-Day.[2] Three explanations for this are the most common:

1. Allied air superiority hampered German movements.
2. Allied deception operations made the Germans hesitant to send their forces to Normandy.
3. The static divisions did not have sufficient mobility.

These three explanations are of course all to some extent valid. But the first limitation for the Germans was the fact that many of their units were simply not yet combat ready. Ever since Operation *Barbarossa* was launched, Western Europe had been a calm backwater where new units could be raised and where formations depleted on the Eastern Front could refit. Consequently, a significant number of formations in the west were not combat ready. This was true even at the beginning of June 1944, especially for the mechanized formations.

Of the ten mechanized divisions in Western Europe only one was complete and fully combat ready. This was the *2. Panzer-Division*. It was up to strength and had had sufficient time to train. The *21. Panzer-Division* was also up to strength and had even had more time to train, but its modified captured vehicles were poor substitute for a *Panther* battalion. Nevertheless, the components the division possessed were combat ready and consequently the division went into action on D-Day.

Two other mechanized divisions also had high combat readiness, the *Panzer Lehr* and the *12. SS-Panzer-Division*. They lacked certain components, but those available were fit for action. Also, they had sufficient motorization.[3]

Most of the other mechanized divisions were not fit for moving to Normandy. The *9.*, *11.* and *116. Panzer-Divisionen.* had recently arrived from the Eastern Front and badly needed time to rest, refit and train replacements.[4] Neither of these was capable of making a major combat effort on D-Day. Possibly they could have formed small *Kampfgruppen* but not anything more.[5]

The *1.* and *2. SS-Panzer-Divisionen* had recently received large numbers of replacements and were desperately short of transport. They were not ready for combat and even less capable of swiftly moving all their units to Normandy. The *17. SS-Panzergrenadier-Division* had reached a relatively uniform level of training but was in effect only partially motorized and also incompletely equipped in certain important aspects, such as anti-tank weapons.

With this in mind it is not surprising that the German mechanized divisions were scattered over France and Belgium. Their primary task was to train and suitable training facilities largely governed their location.

The Germans saw two principal areas were the Allies were likely to land. The first was the Pas-de-Calais area and the second was Normandy. The coast of the Bay of Biscay was regarded as a very unlikely target for an Allied invasion. The Mediterranean coast was not ruled out, but since the area north of the coast is mountainous, an Allied invasion of southern France was not regarded as a serious threat.

Of the four German mechanized divisions that had a high combat readiness one (*2. Panzer-Division*) was located near Pas-de-Calais, while another (*21. Panzer-Division*) was located in Normandy. The other two were placed further from the coast to constitute a reserve possible to commit against either sector.

The six mechanized divisions that were not immediately fit for combat were, except for the *1. SS-Panzer-Division*, located in less threatened areas.

While the main reason for not moving certain units to Normandy was lack of combat readiness, another important factor was lack of mobility. Many of the infantry divisions in Western Europe had very limited mobility, even if they were not considered static. Not only were motor vehicles fewer in Western Europe than on the Eastern Front. Often the quality of them was inferior. Greater use was made of commandeered civilian vehicles.

But even those divisions often depicted as elite mechanized formations suffered from serious shortages of vehicles. A striking example is the *2. SS-Panzer-Division*, which only had 617 operational trucks on 1 June 1944.[6]

Shortages of motor vehicles and fuel made it imperative that the vast majority of German troop movements had to be made by rail. To move an infantry division required about 50 trains[7] and to move a *Panzer-Division* required approximately 70 trains[8]. If we assume that the Germans on D-Day had decided to move five *Panzer-Divisionen* and ten *Infanterie-Divisionen* by rail to Normandy this would have required about 850 trains. Even if Allied air power had not targeted the French rail net this would probably have taken more than a week to accomplish.

This can be compared to the fact that he Allies landed 326,000 men during the first week of the invasion. The forces landed included 23 British and Canadian tank battalions and eleven US medium tank battalions plus two M10 tank destroyer and two light tank battalions.[9] The T/O&E strength of these battalions exceeded

2000 tanks. It is clear that even with an undamaged rail net and fully combat ready divisions the Germans could not have matched the build-up of the Allies.[10]

If the Germans had moved all the 34 divisions that were in *OB West* area but not under control of *7. Armee* on D-Day to Normandy, it would have required almost 2,500 trains. Several weeks would have passed before all these trains had unloaded in Normandy, even if the rail network were still intact. The Germans had a strength of about 880,000 men in France, Belgium and the Netherlands on 1 June.[11] This can be compared to the fact that during June 850,279 Allied soldiers went ashore from ships. Simultaneously about 25,000 men were brought in by air.[12] Clearly, even if it is assumed that the Germans had assumed that *Overlord* was the only invasion, had had an undamaged rail network and no interference from Allied air power during the march to Normandy, they would still not have been able to outnumber the Allies in Normandy.

Again, it must be concluded that the Allied air forces did not really create a problem. Rather they aggravated an already difficult situation. It must be said however that generally Allied air power was much more effective in strangling German rail movements than road movements.

The only mechanized division that may have been delayed mainly due to Allied deceptions is the *2. Panzer-Division*. The *1.* and *2. SS-Panzer-Divisionen*, the *9.* and *116. Panzer-Divisionen* were mainly delayed by their low combat readiness and lack of transport, not Allied air power, deception or the French Resistance.

Even if the Allies had not made considerable efforts to deceive the Germans as to where the actual landing was to take place and even if the Allies had not enjoyed air superiority, it is hard to conceive that the Germans could have outnumbered the Allies on the ground. Had the Germans known, or correctly guessed, where the invasion was to take place, they could of course have concentrated their combat ready units there and achieved numerical superiority. It is however unlikely that such a concentration would have passed unnoticed by their enemies. Rather it would have been detected and prompted a revision of Allied plans.

This does not mean that Allied deception and interdiction efforts were wasted. Because the Germans were seriously short of motor transport and fuel, the attacks on the French rail net hit a very critical link in the German defenses in the West. Also, the deception efforts did not only cause the Germans to make faulty dispositions. They contributed to the surprise attained on D-Day. Furthermore, they contributed to delays in moving some of the (almost) fully combat ready German panzer divisions to Normandy. For the *12. SS-Panzer-Division* and *Lehr*, the delay amounted to a few hours. The *2. Panzer-Division* did however not receive orders to move to Normandy until three days after the invasion.

Also, the most effective effort by the French resistance was probably the demolition of railroads. Attempts to attack or ambush regular German combat units moving by road seem to have met with very little success. Another worthwhile effort seems to have been cutting of telephone lines. The German forces in Western Europe appear to have had relatively few radios, thus making them more dependent on telecommunications. Generally, it is necessary to identify bottlenecks and attack them if irregular forces, with their limited capabilities, are to make an important contribution.

---

1   OKH/Gen.St.d.H./Org.Abt. Nr. I/18941/44 g.Kdos. v. 7.9.44, T78, R414, F6383114. This does not include men navy and air force units (except those that were part of ground combat units).

2   L. F. Ellis, *Victory in the West, Vol I*, Her Majesty's Stationery Office, London 1962, p. 223.

3   See narratives for the units. Note that the SS-Werfer-Abteilung 12 lacked motorization and was consequently not combat ready on 6 June 1944.

4   The *116. Panzer-Division* was actually a new unit, but it was built around the depleted *16. Panzer-Grenadier-Division* that had been fighting on the Eastern Front.

5   See also Panzergruppe West Ia Nr. 2205/44 g.Kdos, 17.5.44, found among OB West Ia Anlagen, T311, R24, F7028691ff.

6   See narrative for *2. SS-Panzer-Division*.

7   See narratives for *271.* and *272. Infanterie-Division*.

8   See narrative for *10. SS-Panzer-Division*.

9   Derived from H. F. Joslen, *Orders of Battle Second World War, 1939–1945* (The London Stamp Exchange Ltd, London 1990), M. A. Bellis, 21st Army Group Order of Battle, Malcolm A. Bellis (Cheshire 1991) and S. L. Stanton, *Order of Battle: US Army in World War II* (Presidio Press, Novato, California 1984).

10 At the end of May 1944 there were1244 operational tanks and 318 assault guns in Western Europe, also there were 222 tanks and 27 assault guns in workshops (See Gen.Insp.d.Pz.Truppen records, Anlage zu Gen.Qu. Nr. III/012075/44 g.Kdos, 15.6.44, T78, R623, F000487). Similarly, given the size of the German divisional slice the fifteen divisions suggested in the example represented a force of less than 200 000 men.

11 OKH/Gen.St.d.H./Org.Abt. Nr. I/18941/44 g.Kdos. v. 7.9.44, T78, R414, F6383114.

12 L. F. Ellis, Victory in the West, vol I, *The Battle of Normandy* (HMSO, London 1962) p. 303.

Conclusion

Unfortunately, there are no quick ways to answer the questions outlined in the introduction. No suitable compilations on overall German casualties for the campaign in Normandy have been found in the archival documents. Similarly, there are no compilations for German overall strength.[1] To establish overall German strength and losses it is necessary to check with each unit that participated in the battle. This is, of course, a much more tedious procedure. And despite this there is a need for estimates since there is a lack of data on certain units, or for certain periods of the battle. This may, of course, appear disappointing, but it is comforting that there are certain confines to the estimates, which set the upper and lower limits for casualties and other hard data.

Thus, despite the fact that many of the figures on German strength and casualties in this book are approximations, they are far from arbitrary. German casualties and forces committed are possible to estimate with little room for error. Also, other questions can be given satisfactory answers.

The image of the German forces in the west as combat ready units eagerly awaiting an Allied invasion, but hampered by ambiguous, divided and hesitant command does not stand up to closer scrutiny. While the description of the German higher command certainly has some merit, it is not true that the German ground forces in general could have intervened swiftly on any of the possible invasion sites. The main reason for this was the lack of mobility and incomplete training among several units. Insufficient mobility was caused by shortages of vehicles, spare parts and fuel. These factors, together with shortages of ammunition also hampered training. Another important factor was, of course, the fact that many of the panzer formations in the west were units depleted after sustained combat on the Eastern Front. The replacements fed into these units needed training and since important units had arrived during the spring 1944, they were not yet fully trained when the Allies invaded. These factors, together with limited stockpiling of fuel and ammunition were the main reasons for the slow German commitment of units to Normandy.

Of course, it is possible that even if the German units had had sufficient mobility and combat readiness dilatory command would have delayed their commitment.

The fact that many German units arrived late in Normandy can, however, not be taken as proof that German command was ineffective, or that Allied air power was effective. Rather a careful analysis is required for each unit separately, weighing in factors like motor vehicles, fuel and spare parts available, orders issued, air attacks conducted, training of the unit and presence of important specialists[2].

Allied air power seems to have been misrepresented quite often. The casualties and equipment losses caused by Allied air units appear to have been quite limited. What is more important to study is the effects on German decision making, morale and delays and disruption caused. On this, the present volume, does not pretend to give a definitive answer. Rather this is a field were current research is insufficient. And this does not only apply to air operations in Normandy, but to air operations in general.

The available information suggests that the most important part of the Allied air campaign was the attacks on the French rail net. Since the Germans suffered from poor mobility this had important effects on the defenders.

Given the Allied numerical preponderance and air superiority it seems hard to avoid the conclusion that the German ground units on average were more efficient in combat than their adversaries. Of course, there were variations in performance among the units of both sides, but probably the Germans showed greater variation than their adversaries.

Other authors have claimed that the fact that the Germans predominantly were on the defensive is the main explanation for their apparent combat effectiveness superiority. The available data on engagements were the Germans were on the offensive suggest that this claim is untenable.

Perhaps the most important conclusion of this study is that the sources on the German side are diverse. Much important information is scattered among various documents, but if pieced together it is possible to answer several important questions. Such a procedure naturally requires great effort and the present work is certainly not the final publication on this issue. Hopefully it will be an assistance to future writers on this topic.

---

1   There is one document showing the ration strength of 7. Armee on 1 June 1944 (Armeeintendent der 7. Armee S I, 2 Nr. 245/44 g.Kdos, 5. Juni 1944, T312, R1571, F000614f). The ration strength was 311,117 men and 41,114 horses. However, it is also clear from the document that army personnel constituted 169,344, *Luftwaffe* 39,827 and Navy 4900. The rest of the ration strength was forced labour of Organization Todt, prisoners of war, personnel for administration of occupied areas and other categories, which did not contribute to the military power when operations began. Rather they were a logistical burden. This is an example of how ration strength can present an inflated impression of strength.

    The *7. Armee* controlled not only Normandy, but also Brittany. Thus the document is even less relevant for the strength in Normandy.

2   For example, many of the tank drivers in *1. SS-Panzer-Division* were in Germany for training. Obviously, a tank without driver is not very combat effective.

PART 2

German Combat Formations

General Headquarters Artillery Formations

Artillerie-Brigade 704

With very few exceptions, German GHQ artillery was available as battalions. Higher units were generally only command and control headquarters that were assigned GHQ artillery battalions according to the requirements of the situation. Artillerie-Brigade 704 was no exception. When it was activated on 28 September 1939 it was called *Artillerie-Regiments-Stab zur besonderen Verfügüng 704* (Artillery Regiment Staff for Special Employment 704)[1]. After the defeat at Sevastopol in May 1944, the staff was transferred to the west for refitting and it was redesignated as "leichte Heeres-Artillerie-Brigade 704" on 11 June 1944[2].

This brigade has perhaps caused some confusion over which artillery units were or were not transferred to Normandy. On 24 June the brigade was ordered to transfer to Normandy. It had the following units attached to it[3]:

Artillerie-Abteilung 628 (21 cm *Mörser* 18)
Kanonen-Batterie 625 (17 cm K 18 Gun)
Artillerie-Abteilung 861 (10.5 cm *IFH*)
Artillerie-Abteilung 934 (10.5 cm *IFH*)

On 28 June it was on its way to *Panzergruppe West*[4]. One day later the brigade was designated as an Army Group reserve. The composition of the brigade had also changed; it now consisted of:

Artillerie-Abteilung 628 (21 cm *Mörser* 18)
Kanonen-Batterie 625 (17 cm K 18 Gun)
Artillerie-Abteilung 861 (10.5 cm *IFH*)
Artillerie-Abteilung 934 (10.5 cm *IFH*)

Artillerie-Abteilung 151 (10 cm *K18* gun)
Sturmpanzer-Abteilung 217 (Sturmpanzer IV with the 15 cm very short-barreled howitzer; it was still forming at the time.)

However, on 8 July the brigade staff was ordered to leave Western Europe[6] (eventually it went to the Eastern Front). The battalions that had not yet arrived in Normandy discontinued their movements and turned east instead. Thus the following battalions never arrived in Normandy[7]:

Artillerie-Abteilung 151 (10 cm *K18* gun)
Artillerie-Abteilung 861 (10.5 cm *lFH*)
Artillerie-Abteilung 934 (10.5 cm *lFH*)

In some instances these battalions are credited with having taken part in the battle, but this is wrong. If the researcher did not know about the existence of the 8 July orders countermanding the transfer to Normandy, then he probably assumed the units completed the movements they were initially ordered to make.

---

1   Georg Tessin, *Verbände und Truppen der deutschen Wehrmacht und Waffen-SS* (Mittler & Sohn, Frankfurt am Main (vol 1-5), Biblio Verlag, Osnabrück (vol 6–14) 1966–75), entry for units with number 704).

2   Ibid.

3   Ob.West Ia Nr. 4927/44 geh. Kdos. 24.6.44, T311, R25, F7029822. The equipment of the battalions is taken from Anlage 1 & 2 zu Okdo.d.H.Gr.B. Ib/Stoart/Ia Nr. 3748/44 g.K.Chefs v.21.6.44, T312, R1563, F000589f.

4   Pz.Gr. West Ia, Nr 24/44 g.Kdos, Nachtrag zur Tagesmeldung 29.6.44, BA-MA RH 21-5/50.

5   AOK 7 Ia Kriegsgliederungen zum KTB der Führungsabteilung ab 6.6.44 bis 30.6.44, T312, R1566, F000023.

6   OB West Ia, Anruf OKW/WFSt. Major d.g. Friedei 8.7.44, T311, R28, F7034297.

7   Ibid.

SS-Artillerie-Abteilung 101

Originally it was intended to raise a unit named *SS-Werfer-Abteilung 101*. The activation commenced in October 1943. This was never completed; instead, it was decided to organize the unit as *SS-Artillerie-Abteilung 101*.[1]

The forming of the unit seems to have taken some time, since it was reported only conditionally combat ready on 1 June.[2] The battalion had the following equipment[3]:

1. Batterie: Four 21 cm *Mörser 18's*
2. Batterie: Three 17 cm *K 18's*
3. Batterie: Three 17 cm *K 18's*

After the Allied landings, it was decided to send the battalion to Normandy. It arrived at *I. SS-Panzer-Korps* from 10-12 June, having traveled from its original location at Beauvais via Paris.[4]

The battalion was intended to be a permanent component of *I. SS-Panzer-Korps,* and it seems to have remained with the corps during the entire campaign.

The battalion had three artillery pieces combat ready on 25 August.[5]

---

1   G. Tessin, *Verbände und Truppen der deutschen Wehrmacht und Waffen-SS* (Mittler & Sohn, Frankfurt am Main and Biblio Verlag, Osnabrück 1966–1975).

2   Report from *I. SS-Panzer-Korps* to the Inspector-General of Panzer Troops, 1.6.44, BA-MA RH 10/309.

3   Ibid.

4   H. Meyer, *Kriegsgeschichte der 12. SS-Panzerdivision "Hitlerjugend", Vol I* (Munin Verlag, Osnabrück 1982) p. 115f.

5   Anlage 1 zum Gen der Art beim Chef Ge,St.d.Heeres Ib Nr. 2610/44 g.Kdos, 27.8.44, BA-MA RH 11 II/v. 4.

Artillerie-Abteilung 456

The battalion was formed in France in January 1943.[1] It was soon moved to the Cotentin peninsula, where it was located when US air-borne forces landed in the area around Ste-Mère-Église. In January 1944 the battalion possessed four 12.2 cm guns and eight 15.2 cm gun-howitzers.[2] It was motorized.[3] On 11 April the battalion was deployed as follows[4]:

1. Batterie: Magneville (9 kilometers southwest of Valognes)
2. Batterie: l'Etang-Bertrand (7 kilometers southwest of Valognes)
3. Batterie: l'Etang-Bertrand (7 kilometers southwest of Valognes)

It remained west of Valognes on 18 May[5] and on 5 June it was located southwest of Valognes.[6] After ten days of fighting on the Cotentin, US units threatened to reach the western coast of the peninsula, thus isolating the German forces in the Cherbourg area. For this reason it was suggested on 17 June that *Artillerie-Abteilung 456* should move south to avoid encirclement.[7] It seems that the battalion succeeded in withdrawing in time, since it was reported to be in the area of the *353. Infanterie-Division* and the *17. SS-Panzergrenadier-Division "Götz von Berlichingen"* on 22 June.[8]

The battalion's organization was slightly altered one month later. On 21 July it had the following structure[9]:

1. Batterie: Four 12.2 cm guns
2. Batterie: Four 8,8 cm guns
3. Batterie: Four 15.2 cm gun-howitzers

At that time it was in the area of the *LXXXIV. Korps,* tactically it was in support of the *17. SS-Panzergrenadier-Division "Götz von Berlichingen"*.[10]

On 1 September the battalion had one 15.2 cm gun-howitzer and two 15 cm *sFH* operational.[11] At that time it was with the *7. Armee.*

---

1   G. Tessin, *Verbände und Truppen der deutschen Wehrmacht und Waffen-SS* (Mittler & Sohn, Frankfurt am Main and Biblio Verlag, Osnabrück 1966–1975).
2   BA-MA RHD 18/69.
3   Ibid.
4   AOK 7 Ia Nr. 2152/44 g.Kdos 11.4.44, T312 R1565, F000467.
5   Anlage zu HGr D Ia Nr. 315/44 g.Kdos, 18.5.44, T312, R1563, F000613.
6   Lagekarte AOK 7 5.6.1944, BA-MA RH 20-7/138K.
7   KTB AOK 7 Ia, T312, R1569, F000052.
8   AOK 7 Ia Kriegsgliederungen zum KTB der Führungsabteilung ab 6.6.44 bis 30.6.44, T312, R1566, F000013.
9   Gen.Kdo. LXXXIV A.K. Ia Nr. 035/44g.Kdos 22.7.44, Taktische Gliederung der Artillerie, Stand 21.7.44, T314, R1604, F001388
10 Ibid.
11 Vorläufige Zustandsmeldung der Heeresartillerie beim OB West, Stand 1.9.44, BA-MA RH 11 II/v. 4.

Artillerie-Abteilung 457

The battalion was formed in France in January 1943.[1] It was soon moved to the Cotentin peninsula, where it was located when the US airborne forces landed in the area around Ste-Mère-Église. In January 1944 the battalion possessed four 12.2 cm guns and eight 15.2 cm gun-howitzers.[2] It was motorized.[3]

On 11 April it was reported that the battalion was deployed as follows[4]:

1. Batterie: Grosville (19 kilometers west of Valognes)
2. Batterie: Rauville (15 kilometers west of Valognes)
3. Batterie: Couville (16 kilometers west-northwest of Valognes)

It remained west of Valognes on 18 May[5] and, on 5 June, it was still located in the same area.[6] After 10 days of fighting on the Cotentin peninsula, US units threatened to reach the western coast, thus isolating the German forces in the Cherbourg area. For this reason it was suggested on 17 June that *Artillerie-Abteilung 457* move south to avoid encirclement.[7] It seems that the battalion succeeded in withdrawing in time, since it was reported to be in the area of the *353. Infanterie-Division* and the *17. SS-Panzergrenadier-Division "Götz von Berlichingen"* on 22 June.[8]

On 1 September the battalion was in relatively good condition, having five 15.2 cm gun-howitzers and one 15 cm *sFH* operational.[9] At that time it was with 5. *Panzer-Armee.*

---

1   G. Tessin, *Verbände und Truppen der deutschen Wehrmacht und Waffen-SS* (Mittler & Sohn, Frankfurt am Main and Biblio Verlag, Osnabrück 1966–1975).
2   BA-MA RHD 18/69.
3   Ibid.
4   AOK 7 Ia Nr. 2152/44 g.Kdos 11.4.44, T312 R1565, F000467.
5   Anlage zu HGr D Ia Nr. 315/44 g.Kdos, 18.5.44, T312, R1563, F000613.
6   Lagekarte AOK 7 5.6.1944, BA-MA RH 20-7/138K.
7   KTB AOK 7 Ia, T312, R1569, F000052.
8   AOK 7 Ia Kriegsgliederungen zum KTB der Führungsabteilung ab 6.6.44 bis 30.6.44, T312, R1566, F000013.
9   Vorläufige Zustandsmeldung der Heeresartillerie beim OB West, Stand 1.9.44, BA-MA RH 11 II/v. 4.

Artillerie-Abteilung 460

The battalion was formed in Oppeln in eastern Germany in February 1943.[1] It was moved to France to be a reserve in the *OB West* area.[2] On 1 March the battalion had a strength of 508 men.[3] This was five men more than its authorized strength.[4] The battalion had its full complement of 12 artillery pieces.[5]

The unit was located near Tours en Vimen in the area of the *15. Armee* on 18 May 1944.[6] There is, however, conflicting information concerning its equipment. All sources agree that the battalion had three batteries with four guns each, but the type of guns in the batteries vary with the sources, even though in every case the equipment was captured Russian. One source indicates that all three batteries had 12.2 cm guns[7]. This is, however, most likely only a printing error.[8] All other sources indicate the battalion had only one battery with 12.2 cm guns.[9] When explicitly mentioned, it is invariably the *3. Batterie* that has 12.2 cm guns.[10] The equipment of the other two batteries is said to be either 15.2 cm guns or 15.2 cm howitzers or, in one case, 15.2 cm gun-howitzers.

On 10 June the battalion received the order to road march to St. Lô as soon as possible.[11] The march began one day later. The unit was located at Brienne, 20 kilometers west of Argentan, on the morning of 17 June.[12] Two days later it had arrived within the area of operations for the *II. Fallschirm-Korps*.[13]

On 1 September the battalion was reported to have three 15.2 cm gun-howitzers available.[14] At that time it was in support of the 7. Armee.[15] One month later the battalion had eight operational guns and one undergoing repair.[16] It had 475 men (actually 25 more than its TOE requirement) and during the period from 7–30 September casualties amounted to only one man. No replacements arrived.[17] Thus it seems likely that the battalion suffered insignificant losses in Normandy.

---

1   G. Tessin, *Verbände und Truppen der deutschen Wehrmacht und Waffen-SS* (Mittler & Sohn, Frankfurt am Main and Biblio Verlag, Osnabrück 1966–1975).

2   Ibid.

3   LXXXII. A.K. Ia, Anlagen zum KTB 6, Artillerie-Kommandeur 141 Nr. 306/44 g.K., 2.3.44, T314, R1602, F000327.

4   Ibid.

5   Ibid.

6   Anlage zu HGr D Ia Nr. 315/44 g.Kdos, 18.5.44, T312, R1563, F000613.

7   Stoart AOK 15 Nr. 629/44 g.Kdos, Art. Gliederung der 15. Armee, Stand 1.6.44 T312, R516, F8115288.

8   The file also contain information applying to 1 May and 30 May which states that the battalion had eight 15.2 cm guns and four 12.2 cm guns. This fits better with the avilable documents pertaining to the period when the battalion was in Normandy.

9   See e.g. Stoart AOK 15 Nr. 584/44 g.Kdos, Landzielgliederung der 15. Armee, Stand vom 30.5.44, T312, R516, F8115285ff.

10   Ibid.

11   AOK 7 Ia Tagesmeldung 10.6.44, BA-MA RH 20-7/135.
12   OB West Ia Nr. (unreadable)/44 g.Kdos, 17.6.44, T311, R25, F7029619.
13   OB West Ia Nr. 4739/44 g.Kdos, 19.6.44, T311, R25, F7029652.
14   Vorläufige Zustandsmeldung der Heeresartillerie beim OB West, Stand 1.9.44, BA-MA RH 11 II/v. 4.
15   Ibid.
16   Gen.Kdo. LXXXI. A.K. Ia, Zustandberichte 1.10.44 - 17.12.44, T314, R1597, F000076.
17   Ibid.

Artillerie-Abteilung 555

The battalion was formed in the Netherlands in March 1943 from three separate coast artillery batteries.[1] It was located near den Haag.[2] On 1 June 1944 it had three motorized batteries, each with four captured Russian 12.2 cm howitzers.[3]

On 10 June it was decided to move the battalion to Normandy.[4] The following day all trains carrying the unit had departed.[5] When the battalion left the Netherlands it had a strength of 473 men.[6] The battalion traveled to Chartres, where it unloaded on 13 June and had to move by its own means.[7]

One week after it was ordered to leave the Netherlands, the battalion entered the area of operations of the 7. *Armee*.[8] It was deployed in support of the *LXXXVI. Korps* on 18 June.[9] The battalion probably remained with the corps for most of the campaign. It has been documented with that corps as late as 18 July.[10]

It was reported that the battalion had 10 combat-ready howitzers on 25 August.[11] Thus it seems that the battalion came out of the Normandy battles relatively unscathed. However, one week later, the battalion was regarded as *zerschlagen* (combat ineffective).[12] There are at least three possible explanations for this sudden change. Parts of the battalion may have been cut off during the retreat from France, but another possible explanation is that either of the reports are mistaken. Also, the term *zerschlagen* is rather vague. It is known from other cases that *zerschlagene* units have remained fighting for quite a long time after receiving such a verdict. Since the battalion was located in the area of *LXXXVI. Korps* it had a better chance to escape relatively unscathed than most German units.

1   G. Tessin, *Verbände und Truppen der deutschen Wehrmacht und Waffen-SS* (Mittler & Sohn, Frankfurt am Main and Biblio Verlag, Osnabrück 1966–1975).

2   Anlage zu HGr D Ia Nr. 315/44 g.Kdos, 18.5.44, T312, R1563, F000614.

3   Anlagen zum KTB LXXXVIII. A.K Ia, Gliederungen Stand 1.6.44, T314, R1622, F653.

4   AOK 7 Ia Tagesmeldung 10.6.44, BA-MA RH 20-7/135.

5   OB West Ia 4487/44 g.Kdos., 11.6.44, T311, R25, F7029461.

6   Der Kommandierende General und Befehlshaber der Truppen des Heeres in den Niederlanden (Gen.Kdo. LXXXVIII. A.K.) Ia Nr. 2467/44 g.Kdos, den T314, R1626, F000481.

7   HGr B Ia Nr. 3440/44 g,Kdos, Tagesmeldung 13.6, T311, R3, F7002386.

8   OB West Ia Nr. illegible/44 g.Kdos, 17.6.44, T311, R25, F7029619.

9   AOK 7 Stoart/Ia Nr. 3193/44 g.Kdos. A.H.Qu 18.6.44, Befehl für Einsatz von Heeres-Art.Abt., BA-MA RH 20-7/135.

10   Pz.Gr. West Ia, Nr 24/44 g.Kdos, Nachtrag zur Tagesmeldung 29.6.44, BA-MA RH 21-5/50.

11   Anlage 1 zum Gen der Art beim Chef Gen.St.d.Heeres Ib Nr. 2610/44 g.Kdos, BA-MA RH 11 II/v. 4.

12   Vorläufige Zustandsmeldung der Heeresartillerie beim OB West, Stand 1.9.44, BA-MA RH 11 II/v. 4.

Artillerie-Batterie 625

This unit, formed in June 1940, had originally been a battalion equipped with 15 cm guns. It had fought on the Eastern Front and been reduced to one battery, equipped with 17 cm guns.[1] The battery was motorized[2] and had three 17 cm guns.[3] Orders for the transfer to Normandy were issued 17 June, when the unit was still in Germany.[4]

The battery was located 30 kilometers southeast of Paris on 30 June.[5] Five days later, the battery was near Vimont, south east of Caen, with two guns ready to fire.[6] On 7 July the entire battery was ready for action. On 18 July the battery was directed to support the *LXXXVI. Korps*.[8] Due to the longer-range of the guns of this battery, it did not need to deploy as close to the enemy as weapons of lesser caliber. This seems to have been an advantage during the hasty retreat, since this battery still had all three guns operational on 25 August.[9] On 1 September it still had three guns and was in the area of operations of the *15. Armee*.[10] The battery presumably came out of the battle in Normandy relatively intact.

---

1   G. Tessin, *Verbände und Truppen der deutschen Wehrmacht und Waffen-SS* (Mittler & Sohn, Frankfurt am Main and Biblio Verlag, Osnabrück 1966–1975) and also BA-MA RHD 18/69.

2   Gliederung Pz.Gr. West 18.7.44, BA-MA RH 21-5/50.

3   BA-MA RHD 18/69.

4   OB West Ia Nr. 412/44 g.K. Ch., 17.6.44, T311, R25, F7029628.

5   AOK 7 Ia 30.6.44 BA-MA RH 20-7/135.

6   Pz.Gr. West Ia, Nr. 197/44 geh. von 7.7.1944., Nachtrag zur Tagesmeldung., BA-MA RH 21-5/50.

7   Pz.Gr. West Ia, Nr. 197/44 geh. von 7.7.1944., Nachtrag zur Tagesmeldung., BA-MA RH 21-5/50.

8   Gliederung Pz.Gr. West 18.7.44, BA-MA RH 21-5/50.

9   Anlage 1 zum Gen der Art beim Chef Ge,St.d.Heeres lb Nr. 2610/44 g.Kdos, 27.8.44, BA-MA RH 11 II/v. 4.

10 Vorläufige Zustandsmeldung der Heeresartillerie beim OB West, Stand 1.9.44, BA-MA RH 11 II/v. 4.

Artillerie-Abteilung 628

The battalion was formed in May 1943 and organized into two batteries with the Karl 040 mortar.[1] This was one of the types of heavy guns used during the siege of Sevastopol in 1942. In September 1943 it was reorganized into two batteries equipped with 21 cm *Morser 18*.[2] During May 1944 it was reorganized and received a third battery.[3] This brought the TOE of the battalion to nine 21 cm howitzers. It seems that the battalion had its authorized strength of nine 21 cm *Mörser 18* since this is mentioned in a document concerning the planned employment of artillery in Normandy.[4]

On 17 June, the battalion was ordered to be transferred from Germany to Normandy.[5] Exactly when the battalion arrived is not known, but by 6 July it was located near Condé-sur-Noireau, on its way to the *II. Fallschirm-Korps*.[6] The battalion seems to have made its escape from the Normandy battle in pretty good order, since it was reported on 1 September that it had six howitzers in operational condition.[7]

1   G. Tessin, *Verbände und Truppen der deutschen Wehrmacht und Waffen-SS* (Mittler & Sohn, Frankfurt am Main and Biblio Verlag, Osnabrück 1966–1975).

2   Ibid.

3   Ibid.

4   Anlage 1 & 2 zu Okdo.d.H.Gr.B. Ib/Stoart/Ia Nr. 3748/44 g.K.Chefs v.21.6.44, T312, R1563, F000589f.

5   OB West Ia Nr. 412/44 g.K. Ch., 17.6.44, T311, R25, F7029628.

6   OB West Ia Nr. 5323/44 g.Kdos. 6.7.44, T311, R28, F7034234.

7   Vorläufige Zustandsmeldung der Heeresartillerie beim OB West, Stand 1.9.44, BA-MA RH 11 II/v. 4.

Artillerie-Abteilung 763

The battalion was formed in January 1943 and organized into three batteries with 17 cm guns.[1] Thirteen months later it gave up two of its batteries. They were sent to Italy but replaced later.[2] The unit was motorized and had three guns in each battery.

At the time of the Allied invasion, the battalion was in support of the *1. Armee* and located near La Rochelle on the Atlantic coast south of Brittany.[3] The battalion was transferred to Normandy, but initially only the headquarters, the headquarters battery and the *1.* and *3. Batterien* were sent.[4] These units left the area of the *1. Armee* during the night of 14/15 June[5] and, on 22 June, they were deployed east of the British bridgehead over the Orne.[6] The *2. Batterie* was sent to Normandy on 29 June.[7] During June and at least as late as 18 July, the battalion remained in the area of the *LXXXVI. Korps.*[8]

On 25 August the battalion was reported as having nine guns[9], its full complement. This had shrunk to five operational guns on 1 September.[10] At that time, it was detailed to support the *15. Armee.*[11]

---

1   G. Tessin, *Verbände und Truppen der deutschen Wehrmacht und Waffen-SS* (Mittler & Sohn, Frankfurt am Main and Biblio Verlag, Osnabrück 1966-1975).

2   Ibid.

3   Anlage zu HGr D Ia Nr. 315/44 g.Kdos, 18.5.44, T312, R1563, F000613.

4   AOK 1 Ia Nr. 3156/44 g.Kdos, 15.6.44, T312, R28, F7535502.

5   Ibid.

6   OB West Ia Nr. 4858/44 geh.Kdos, den 22.6.44., T311, R25, F7029750.

7   AOK 1 Ia Nr. 3562/44 g.Kdos, 29.6.44, T312, R28, F7535524.

8   Gliederung AOK 7 26.6.44, T312, R1566, F000018, Pz.Gr. West Ia, Nr 24/44 g.Kdos, Nachtrag zur Tagesmeldung 29.6.44, BA-MA RH 21-5/50, Gliederung Pz.Gr. West 18.7.44, BA-MA RH 21-5/50.

9   Anlage 1 zum Gen der Art beim Chef Gen.St.d.Heeres Ib Nr. 2610/44 g.Kdos, 27.8.44, BA-MA RH 11 II/v. 4.

10 Vorläufige Zustandsmeldung der Heeresartillerie beim OB West, Stand 1.9.44, BA-MA RH 11 II/v. 4.

11 Ibid.

Artillerie Abteilung 937

See *Artillerie-Schule Suippes.*

Artillerie-Abteilung 989

The battalion was formed in France during November 1943.[1] It had three batteries, of which the *2. Batterie* was motorized. The other two were partly motorized.[2] Each battery had four captured Russian 12.2 cm howitzers.[3] When the Allied forced assaulted the beaches in Normandy, the battalion was located south of Courseulles.[4] The battalion was probably destroyed during the first days of the campaign, since it does not appear on any of the charts showing the organization of the *7. Armee* starting 12 June.

---

1   G. Tessin, *Verbände und Truppen der deutschen Wehrmacht und Waffen-SS* (Mittler & Sohn, Frankfurt am Main and Biblio Verlag, Osnabrück 1966–1975).

2   Gliederung der 716. Inf.Div., Stand 1.5.44., T312, R1566, F000215.

3   Ibid.

4   Lagekarte AOK 7 5.6.1944, BA-MA RH 20-7/138K.

Artillerie-Abteilung 992

The battalion was formed in southern France during November 1943 in the area of *19. Armee*.[1] It was ordered to be completely motorized by 18 December.[2] It is unclear when this was accomplished, since the battalion was equipped with captured Russian 15.2 cm gun-howitzers and still listed as partly motorized in January 1944.[3]

The unit was quickly sent to Normandy. On 11 June it was supporting the *Panzer-Lehr-Division*.[4] One week later it was detailed to support the *I. SS-Panzer-Korps*.[5] On 28 June it was still attached to the *I. SS-Panzer-Korps*.[6] On 18 July it had the mission to support the *XLVII. Panzer-Karps*.[7] It probably remained in the sector facing the British forces until 9 August, when it was ordered to be transferred to the jurisdiction of the *7. Armee*.[8]

It seems that the battalion escaped from Falaise in relatively good order, since it still had seven howitzers on 25 August.[9] One week later it had four howitzers remaining.[10]

On 1 October the battalion had an authorized strength of 450 men and was only short one man; it also had 12 guns.[11] During September the battalion had suffered 34 casualties, while 46 men left the battalion for other reasons. During the same period, it had received 202 replacements. Thus, it must have had a strength of about 327 men on 1 September.

1   G. Tessin, *Verbände und Truppen der deutschen Wehrmacht und Waffen-SS* (Mittler & Sohn, Frankfurt am Main and Biblio Verlag, Osnabrück 1966–1975).

2   Ibid.

3   BA-MA RHD 18/69

4   H. Ritgen, *Die Gechichte der Panzer-Lehr-Division im Westen 1944-1945* (Motorbuch Verlag, Stuttgart 1979) p. 134.

5   AOK 7 Stoart/Ia Nr. 3193/44 g.Kdos. A.H.Qu 18.6.44, Befehl für Einsatz von Heeres-Art.Abt., BA-MA RH 20-7/135.

6   Pz.Gr. West Ia, Nr 24/44 g.Kdos, Nachtrag zur Tagesmeldung 29.6.44, BA-MA RH 21-5/50.

7   Gliederung Pz.Gr. West 18.7.44, BA-MA RH 21-5/50.

8   HGr B Ia Tagesmeldung 9.8.44, BA-MA RH 19 IX/9b.

9   Anlage 1 zum Gen der Art beim Chef Ge,St.d.Heeres lb Nr. 2610/44 g.Kdos, 27.8.44, BA-MA RH 11 II/v. 4.

10 Vorläufige Zustandsmeldung der Heeresartillerie beim OB West, Stand 1.9.44, BA-MA RH 11 II/v. 4.

11 Gen.Kdo LXXXI. A.K., Zustandberichte T314, R1597, F000076.

Artillerie-Abteilung-1151

The battalion was formed in northern France, in the area of the *15. Armee* during December 1943.[1] It remained in that area until the Allied invasion. On 15 May 1944 it was located near St. Valery en Caux.[2] At the beginning of June the battalion was attached to the *245. Infanterie-Division* and had three batteries, each with four captured Russian 12.2 cm howitzers.[3] The battalion was motorized.[4]

Except for one battery, the battalion was attached to the *346. Infanterie-Division* on 8 June and ordered to join the division in its attacks on the British bridgehead over the Orne.[5] It seems to have remained in the area east of the Orne for much of the campaign.[6] On 1 September the battalion had four howitzers remaining.[7]

---

1   G. Tessin, *Verbände und Truppen der deutschen Wehrmacht und Waffen-SS* (Mittler & Sohn, Frankfurt am Main and Biblio Verlag, Osnabrück 1966–1975).

2   Anlage zu HGr D Ia Nr. 315/44 g.Kdos, 18.5.44, T312, R1563, F000613.

3   Stoart AOK 15 Nr. 629/44 g.Kdos, Art.Gliederung der 15. Armee, Stand vom 1.6.44, T312, R516, F8115287ff.

4   Ibid.

5   AOK 15 Ia Nr. 5635/44 g.Kdos. II. Ang, 8.6.44, T312, R516, F8114849

6   See e.g. Pz.Gr. West Ia, Nr 24/44 g.Kdos, Nachtrag zur Tagesmeldung 29.6.44, BA-MA RH 21-5/50 and Gliederung Pz.Gr. West 18.7.44, BA-MA RH 21-5/50.

7   Vorläufige Zustandsmeldung der Heeresartillerie beim OB West, Stand 1.9.44, BA-MA RH 11 II/v. 4.

Artillerie-Abteilung-1192

The battalion was formed in southern France, in the area of the *19. Armee* during December 1943.[1] It had twelve captured Italian 14.9 cm howitzers.[2]. It is unclear to what extent the unit was motorized, since it is referred to as partly motorized in some documents,[3] while another document says it was fully motorized.[4]

On 18 May the battalion was located at St. Raphael on the French Riviera.[5] In June the unit was ordered to Normandy and, on 19 June, the first train had arrived at Tours.[6] It was intended to send the battalion to the *XLVII Panzer-Korps*.[7] The first train unloaded at Le Mans on 21 June,[8] while the remaining two had unloaded by 23 June.[9]

Parts of the battalion had arrived at *XXXXVII. Panzer-Korps* on 24 June[10] and the battalion was still attached to that corps on 18 July.[11]

On 25 August, the battalion had 300 men and no guns in operational order.[12] One week later it was deemed to be *zerschlagen* (combat ineffective).[13]

---

1 G. Tessin, *Verbände und Truppen der deutschen Wehrmacht und Waffen-SS* (Mittler & Sohn, Frankfurt am Main and Biblio Verlag, Osnabrück 1966–1975).

2 Anlage 1 & 2 zu Okdo.d.H.Gr.B. Ib/Stoart/Ia Nr. 3748/44 g.K.Chefs v.21.6.44, T312, R1563, F000589f and also BA-MA RHD 18/69.

3 See e.g. Pz.Gr. West Ia, Nr 24/44 g.Kdos, Nachtrag zur Tagesmeldung 29.6.44, BA-MA RH 21-5/50.

4 See e.g. Anlage zu HGr D Ia Nr. 315/44 g.Kdos, 18.5.44, T312, R1563, F000613.

5 Anlage zu HGr D Ia Nr. 315/44 g.Kdos, 18.5.44, T312, R1563, F000613.

6 OB West Ia Nr. 4739/44 g.Kdos, 19.6.44, T311, R25, F7029652.

7 AOK 7 Stoart/Ia Nr. 3193/44 g.Kdos. A.H.Qu 18.6.44, Befehl für Einsatz von Heeres-Art.Abt., BA-MA RH 20-7/135.

8 OB West Ia Nr. 4818/44 g.Kdos, 21.6.44, T311, R25, F7029728.

9 OB West Ia Nr. 4879/44 g.Kdos. 23.6.44, T311, R25, F7029779.

10 KTB AOK 7 Ia Anlagen 24.6.44, Stand der Aufmarschbewegungen (24.6), T312, R1565, F001297.

11 Gliederung Pz.Gr. West 18.7.44, BA-MA RH 21-5/50.

12 Anlage 1 zum Gen der Art beim Chef Ge,St.d.Heeres Ib Nr. 2610/44 g.Kdos, BA-MA RH 11 II/v. 4.

13 Vorläufige Zustandsmeldung der Heeresartillerie beim OB West, Stand 1.9.44, BA-MA RH 11 II/v. 4.

Artillerie-Abteilung 1193

The battalion was formed in southern France, in the area of the *19. Armee* during December 1943. It was motorized during 1944.[1] It had twelve captured Italian 14.9 cm howitzers.[2]

On 18 may the battalion was located at St. Tropez on the French Riviera.[3] In June, the battalion was ordered to Normandy, and it arrived at Tours on 20 June. Four days later it was found north of Le Mans, after unloading from trains in that town.[4] The battalion was committed in the area of the *LXXXVI. Korps*.[5] It took some time for the complete battalion to arrive. By 1 July only one battery had arrived, while the remaining two were still located ten kilometers west of Falaise.[6]

The battalion seems to have lost most of its guns during the fighting in Normandy. It was reported that the unit had only one howitzer remaining in operational condition on 1 September. On that day, the battalion was attached to the *7. Armee*.[7]

---

1   G. Tessin, *Verbände und Truppen der deutschen Wehrmacht und Waffen-SS* (Mittler & Sohn, Frankfurt am Main and Biblio Verlag, Osnabrück 1966–1975).

2   BA-MA RHD 18/69.

3   Anlage zu HGr D Ia Nr. 315/44 g.Kdos, 18.5.44, T312, R1563, F000613.

4   KTB AOK 7 Ia Anlagen 24.6.44, Stand der Aufmarschbewegungen (24.6), T312, R1565, F001297 and OB West Ia Nr. 4858/44 geh.Kdos, den 22.6.44., T311, R25, F7029750.

5   Pz.Gr. West Ia, Nr 24/44 g.Kdos, Nachtrag zur Tagesmeldung 29.6.44, BA-MA RH 21-5/50.

6   OB West Ia Nr. 5157/44 g.Kdos. 23.6.44, T311, R25, F7030016.

7   Vorläufige Zustandsmeldung der Heeresartillerie beim OB West, Stand 1.9.44, BA-MA RH 11 II/v. 4.

Artillerie-Abteilung 1194

The battalion was formed in southern France, in the area of the *19. Armee* during December 1943. It was motorized during 1944.[1] It had twelve captured Italian 14.9 cm howitzers.[2]

On 16 June, the battalion was ordered from southern France to Normandy by rail.[3] Two days later it had begun its rail movement. It was intended to send it to the *II. Fallschirm-Korps*.[4] It had reached the area south of Angers by 21 June.[5] The following day, the battalion had unloaded in Angers and was marching north.[6] Two days later it was found east of Rennes.[7] On 30 June, it was reported that the battalion had recently arrived at the *II. Fallschirm-Korps* area.[8]

The battalion evidently suffered badly during the Normandy campaign, since it was classified as *zerschlagen* (combat ineffective) on 1 September.[9] It was officially disbanded in October 1944.[10]

---

1   G. Tessin, *Verbände und Truppen der deutschen Wehrmacht und Waffen-SS* (Mittler & Sohn, Frankfurt am Main and Biblio Verlag, Osnabrück 1966–1975).

2   Ibid and Anlage 1 & 2 zu Okdo.d.H.Gr.B. Ib/Stoart/Ia Nr. 3748/44 g.K.Chefs v.21.6.44, T312, R1563, F000589f.

3   OB West Ia/Gen.d.Art (V.O.Art) Nr. 1248/44 g.Kdos, 16.6.44, T311, R25, F7029602.

4   AOK 7 Stoart/Ia Nr. 3193/44 g.Kdos. A.H.Qu 18.6.44, Befehl für Einsatz von Heeres-Art.Abt., BA-MA RH 20-7/135.

5   OB West Ia Nr. 4818/44 g.Kdos, 21.6.44, T311, R25, F7029728.

6   OB West Ia Nr. 4858/44 geh.Kdos, den 22.6.44., T311, R25, F7029750.

7   KTB AOK 7 Ia Anlagen 24.6.44, Stand der Aufmarschbewegungen (24.6), T312, R1565, F001297.

8   AOK 7 Ia 30.6.44 BA-MA RH 20-7/135.

9   Vorläufige Zustandsmeldung der Heeresartillerie beim OB West, Stand 1.9.44, BA-MA RH 11 II/v. 4.

10 Tessin, op. cit.

Artillerie-Abteilung 1198

The battalion was formed in southern France in the area of the *19. Armee* during March 1944. *Artillerie-Abteilungen 1191, 1196* and *1197* each gave up elements to form the new battalion, which consisted of three batteries.[1] The battalion was partly motorized,[2] and had twelve captured Italian 14.9 cm howitzers.[3]

On 16 June, the battalion was ordered from southern France to Normandy by rail.[4] Two days later, it had begun its rail movement. It was intended for it to support the *LXXXIV. Karps*.[5] It had reached the area south of Angers by **22** June;[6] one day later the first train had unloaded at Angers.[7] The battalion remained south of Angers to refit on 24 June.[8] Five days later it was attached to the 7. *Armee*, but it was still not combat ready.[9] Nothing further is known about the unit's activities in Normandy.

---

1   G. Tessin, *Verbände und Truppen der deutschen Wehrmacht und Waffen-SS* (Mittler & Sohn, Frankfurt am Main and Biblio Verlag, Osnabrück 1966–1975).
2   OB West Ia/Gen.d.Art (V.O.Art) Nr. 1248/44 g.Kdos, 16.6.44, T311, R25, F7029602.
3   Anlage 1 & 2 zu Okdo.d.H.Gr.B. Ib/Stoart/Ia Nr. 3748/44 g.K.Chefs v.21.6.44, T312, R1563, F000589f.
4   OB West Ia/Gen.d.Art (V.O.Art) Nr. 1248/44 g.Kdos, 16.6.44, T311, R25, F7029602.
5   AOK 7 Stoart/Ia Nr. 3193/44 g.Kdos. A.H.Qu 18.6.44, Befehl für Einsatz von Heeres-Art.Abt., BA-MA RH 20-7/135.
6   OB West Ia Nr. 4858/44 geh.Kdos, den 22.6.44., T311, R25, F7029750.
7   OB West Ia Nr. 4879/44 g.Kdos. 23.6.44, T311, R25, F7029779.
8   KTB AOK 7 Ia Anlagen 24.6.44, Stand der Aufmarschbewegungen (24.6), T312, R1565, F001297.
9   AOK 7 Ia Kriegsgliederungen zum KTB der Führungsabteilung ab 6.6.44 bis 30.6.44, T312, R1566, F000023.

Artillerie-Schule Autun

This was a training facility located at Autun, southwest of Dijon. In case of emergency, it was to provide one horse-drawn artillery battalion with three batteries. Additionally, the school was supposed to establish one motorized artillery battery.[1]

On 10 June *Artillerie-Schule Autun* was ordered to send an artillery battalion to Normandy.[2] It was to be transported by rail.[3] Six days later, the battalion had two batteries 60 kilometers southeast of Le Mans; one battery was located 80 kilometers east of these.[4] It was intended that the battalion would be sent to the *II. Fallschirm-Korps.* According to the organizational lists for the *7. Armee,* the battalion had arrived by 22 June. Two days earlier it was still in transit.[5]

In most documents referring to the battalion during its transfer to Normandy, the unit is referred to as motorized. The *7. Armee* also listed it as motorized. Possibly the school found additional means to motorize this unit when it was dispatched.

The school also fielded an artillery regiment staff, which was sent to Normandy. It was found in the area of *LXXXVI. Korps* on 28 June.[6] Twenty days later it was still with the *LXXXVI. Korps.*[7] This unit was used for command and control purposes only, it had no guns or howitzers.

---

1   Anlage zu HGr D Ia Nr. 315/44 g.Kdos, 18.5.44, T312, R1563, F000613.

2   AOK 7 Ia Tagesmeldung 10.6.44, BA-MA RH 20-7/135.

3   Ibid.

4   OB West Ia Nr. 4648/44 g.Kdos, 16.6.44, T311, R25, F7029598.

5   AOK 7 Ia Kriegsgliederung zum KTB 20.6.44, T312, R1566, F000010 and AOK 7 Ia Kriegsgliederung zum KTB 22.6.44, T312, R1566, F000013.

6   Pz.Gr. West Ia, Nr 24/44 g.Kdos, Nachtrag zur Tagesmeldung 29.6.44, BA-MA RH 21-5/50.

7   Gliederung Pz.Gr. West 18.7.44, BA-MA RH 21-5/50.

Artillerie-Schule Suippes

This was a training facility located at Suippes-Mourmelon southeast of Reims. In case of emergency, it was designated to establish two artillery battalions. One was to be motorized and consist of two batteries, while the other was horse-drawn and had three batteries.[1] The horse-drawn battalion was also known as *Artillerie-Abteilung 937*.[2] This has perhaps been a source of confusion, since it is easy to assume that an extra battalion existed.

It is possible that a third battery was added to the motorized battalion (which was usually referred to as *I./Artillerie-Schule Suippes (mot.)*. One document states that *3. Batterie* had arrived in the area of operations of the *II. Fallschirm-Korps* by 19 June.[3]

The motorized battalion was ordered to road march to Normandy as quickly as possible on 10 June.[4] Exactly when it arrived is not clear, but it was within the area of operations of the *II. Fallschirm-Korps* on 15 June.[5]

On 10 June the horse-drawn battalion *(Artillerie-Abteilung 937)* was ordered to move by rail to Normandy.[6] It is interesting to see how much slower the rail net was after the Allied air attacks. One week after it was ordered to transfer to Normandy, the battalion had unloaded at Versailles.[7] Seven days later, on 24 June, the battalion was at Breteuil (southwest of Evreux).[8] Thus it still was about 100 kilometers from Caen. Finally, on 30 June, the battalion was located seven kilometers northeast of Argentan,[9] where it was on its way to join the *II. Fallschirm-Korps*.[10]

On 1 September 1944, after the Normandy campaign, both battalions were assessed as *zerschlagen* (combat ineffective).[11] The horse-drawn battalion was disbanded after the campaign.[12] It is most likely that the motorized battalion was disbanded as well. Any remnants of the battalions might have been used to replenish other battalions.

---

1 Anlage zu HGr D Ia Nr. 315/44 g.Kdos, 18.5.44, T312, R1563, F000613.

2 See G. Tessin, *Verbände und Truppen der deutschen Wehrmacht und Waffen-SS* (Mittler & Sohn, Frankfurt am Main and Biblio Verlag, Osnabrück 1966–1975) and also Gliederungen AOK 7 18.6.44 - 28.6.44, T312, R1566, F000009-000021. Especially the latter frame is evident on this issue.

3 OB West Ia Nr. 4739/44 g.Kdos, 19.6.44, T311, R25, F7029652.

4 AOK 7 Ia Tagesmeldung 10.6.44, BA-MA RH 20-7/135.

5 AOK 7 Ia Kriegsgliederung zum KTB 15.6.44, T312, R1566, F000006.

6 AOK 7 Ia Tagesmeldung 10.6.44, BA-MA RH 20-7/135.

7 OB West Ia Nr. unreadable/44 g.Kdos, 17.6.44, T311, R25, F7029619.

8 KTB AOK 7 Ia Anlagen 24.6.44, Stand der Aufmarschbewegungen (24.6), T312, R1565, F001298.

9 AOK 7 Ia 30.6.44 BA-MA RH 20-7/135.

10 Gliederung AOK 7 27.6.44, T312, R1566, F000019.

11 Vorläufige Zustandsmeldung der Heeresartillerie beim OB West, Stand 1.9.44, BA-MA RH 11 II/v. 4.

12 Tessin, op. cit., entry for units with number 937.

Werfer-Brigade 7

The brigade was formed in March 1944 and had two regiments, *Werfer-Regiment 83* and *Werfer-Regiment 84*.[1] It was deployed in France and on 18 May it was located near Beauvais.[2]

It was ordered to Normandy after the Allied landings and, by 10 June, it had reached Falaise.[3] In the night from 10/11 June, the headquarters of the brigade was located **10** kilometers south of Caen.[4] The brigade was used to support an attack on the British bridgehead over the Orne on 16 June.[5] On **1** July the strength of the brigade was[6]:

Formation	Manpower Strength	Number of combat-ready Werfer
Stab, Werfer-Regiment 83	68	
I./Werfer-Regiment 83	622	22
II./Werfer-Regiment 83	620	22
III./Werfer-Regiment 83	622	17
Stab, Werfer-Regiment 84	66	
I./Werfer-Regiment 84	577	16
II./Werfer-Regiment 84	621	18
III./Werfer-Regiment 84	589	15

Formation	Number of Werfer in workshops	Casualties during June	Mobility
Stab, Werfer-Regiment 83			
I./Werfer-Regiment 83	2	37	100%
II./Werfer-Regiment 83	4	18	80%
III./Werfer-Regiment 83	1	20	90%
Stab, Werfer-Regiment 84			
I./Werfer-Regiment 84	0	34	90%
II./Werfer-Regiment 84	0	26	90%
III./Werfer-Regiment 84	3	10	73%

The *I./Werfer-Regiment 84* had seven *Panzerwerfer*, while the *II./Werfer-Regiment 84* also had seven plus one in maintenance facilities.[7]

According to a situation map, two of the *Werfer* battalions in *Werfer-Regiment 83* had 15 cm *Werfer*, while the third battalion had 21 cm *Werfer*. *Werfer-Regiment 84* had two 15 cm battalions and one 30 cm battalion.[8] On 18 July the regiment was in the sector of the *1. SS-Panzer-Korps.*[9]

---

1   G. Tessin, *Verbände und Truppen der deutschen Wehrmacht und Waffen-SS* (Mittler & Sohn, Frankfurt am Main and Biblio Verlag, Osnabrück 1966–1975).

2   Anlage zu HGr D Ia Nr. 315/44 g.Kdos, 18.5.44, T312, R1563, F000613.

3   OB West Ia 4463/44 g.Kdos., den 10.6.44., T 311, R25, F7029425.

4   Lagekarte AOK 7 11.6.44,22.00, BA-MA RH 20-7/139K.

5   Gen.Kdo. LXXXI. A.K. Ia Nr. 1419/44 g.Kdos., 15.6.44, T314, R1590, 000241.

6   Status report to Inspector-General of Panzer Troops, Stand 1.7.44, BA-MA RH 10/300.

7   Ibid.

8   Lagekarten 81. A.K., Lage am 17.6.44,24.00, T314, R1590, F0003000.

9   Gliederung Pz.Gr. West 18.7.44, BA-MA RH 21-5/50.

Werfer-Brigade 8

Werfer-Brigade 8 was formed by using two regiments, *Werfer-Lehr-Regiment 1* and *schweres Werfer-Regiment 2*. The latter regiment had been destroyed at Stalingrad, but was subsequently rebuilt. Each regiment had three battalions with three batteries each. In addition, *Werfer-Lehr-Regiment 1* had two batteries with the *Panzerwerfer*, while *schweres Werfer-Regiment 2* had one such battery.[1]

When the Allied forces struck Normandy, the brigade was still in Germany. On 8 June it was ordered to move to Normandy.[2] Three days later, 11 trains transporting the brigade had arrived in France, with two of them having reached Chartres.[3] It was reported the brigade was on its way to the *II. Fallschirm-Korps* on 18 June.[4] On that day the most advanced elements had reached Vire.[5] On 28 June the brigade was assembling in the area of the *II. SS-Panzer-Korps*, presumably to support the planned counterattack by that corps against the British Epson offensive.[6] It was still reported to be with *II. SS-Panzer-Korps* on 18 July.[7] On 30 August, *Werfer-Brigade 8* had 5 30 cm *Werfer*, 5 21 cm *Werfer* and 14 15 cm *Werfer*. It had suffered 15% casualties.[8]

---

1 G. Tessin, *Verbände und Truppen der deutschen Wehrmacht und Waffen-SS* (Mittler & Sohn, Frankfurt am Main and Biblio Verlag, Osnabrück 1966–1975).
2 OB West Ia 4484/44 g.Kdos v. 8.6.44., T311, R25, F7029384.
3 OB West Ia 4487/44 g.Kdos., 11.6.44, T311, R25, F7029461.
4 AOK 7 Stoart/Ia Nr. 3193/44 g.Kdos. A.H.Qu 18.6.44, Befehl für Einsatz von Heeres-Art.Abt., BA-MA RH 20-7/135.
5 Lagekarte OB West 18.6.44, T311, R15, F7015216.
6 Pz.Gr. West Ia, Nr 24/44 g.Kdos, Nachtrag zur Tagesmeldung 29.6.44, BA-MA RH 21-5/50.
7 Gliederung Pz.Gr. West 18.7.44, BA-MA RH 21-5/50.
8 OKH Org.Abt. Nr. 1/19 102/44, 1.9.44, Zustand der Werfer-Brigaden bei OB West, T78, F6387501-3.

Werfer-Brigade 9

Werfer-Regiment 54 had been raised before the German invasion of the Soviet Union and had been fighting on the Eastern Front. *Werfer-Regiment 14* was a newly activated formation, but it had received batteries from other regiments when it was formed. These two regiments were combined into *Werfer-Brigade 9*. Both regiments had three battalions with three batteries each. In addition, each regiment had one battery equipped with *Panzerwerfer*. *Werfer-Regiment 54* also had one additional battery with self-propelled, but non-armored *Werfers*.[1]

On 12 June *OB West* was informed that *Werfer-Brigade 9* would be transferred to Normandy from Germany.[2] It was still reported to be in transit on 24 June,[3] but two days later it was with the *LXXXVI. Korps*[4].

It was still in support of the *LXXXVI. Korps* on 18 July.[5] It was badly shaken by the British Operation *Goodwood* and lost 47 *Nebelwerfers* during 18 July.[6] On 9 August the brigade was ordered to march from the area around Caen to the *7. Armee*.[7]

1   G. Tessin, *Verbände und Truppen der deutschen Wehrmacht und Waffen-SS* (Mittler & Sohn, Frankfurt am Main and Biblio Verlag, Osnabrück 1966–1975).
2   OB West Ia Nr 4521/44 g.Kdos, 12.6.44, T311, R25, F7029499.
3   AOK 7 Ia Kriegsgliederungen zum KTB der Führungsabteilung ab 6.6.44 bis 30.6.44, T312, R1566, F000016.
4   AOK 7 Ia Kriegsgliederungen zum KTB der Führungsabteilung ab 6.6.44 bis 30.6.44, T312, R1566, F000018.
5   Gliederung Pz.Gr. West 18.7.44, BA-MA RH 21-5/50.
6   HGr B Ib/Br. B Nr. 01087/44 geh 20.7.44, T311, Rl, F7000812. Losses refer to total write-offs.
7   HGr B Ia Tagesmeldung, BA-MA RH 19 IX/9b.

Stellungs-Werfer-Regiment 101

In January 1944 the regiment was formed from three separate battalions (101, 102 and 103). The battalions had been raised in October 1943.[1]

Each of the three battalions had three batteries. All batteries were equipped with six rocket launchers for a total of 54 launchers in the regiment.[2] Despite the name of the unit, its batteries were motorized.[3]

On 5 June the *I. Abteilung* was located east of Valognes, near the coast, while the other two battalions were found west-south-west of Cherbourg.[4]

The regiment was among the units surrounded in Cherbourg.[5] It was destroyed when Cherbourg fell and was never rebuilt.

---

1   G. Tessin, *Verbände und Truppen der deutschen Wehrmacht und Waffen-SS* (Mittler & Sohn, Frankfurt am Main and Biblio Verlag, Osnabrück 1966–1975).

2   Gliederungen der AOK 7, Kleinere Verbande im Bereich LXXXIV. A.K., T312, R1566, F000214.

3   Ibid.

4   Lagekarte AOK 7 5.6.1944, BA-MA RH 20-7/138K.

5   See Kriegsgliederungen zum KTB der Fuhrungs abteilung AOK 7 6.6.44 – 30.6.44, T312, R1566, F000002ff.

SS-Werfer-Abteilung 102

This unit was intended to be a corps unit for the *II. SS-Panzer-Korps*, but on 1 March 1944 it was with *2. SS-Panzer-Division "Das Reich"*. It had an authorized strength of three batteries, each with six 15 cm *Nebelwerfer*.[1]

On 1 July it had 24 *Werfer*. This had shrunk to 10 *Werfer* on 1 August and increased to 16 on 11 September.[2]

The battalion remained with the *2. SS-Panzer-Division "Das Reich"* and was committed in July with that division. However, its support relationship to the division appears to have been severed not later than 20 July.[3] According to Tieke, the battalion joined *II. SS-Panzer-Korps* late in July.[4] From that point on, it stayed with the corps for the remainder of the battle in Normandy.

When the *II. SS-Panzer-Korps* was moved to Vimoutiers before the Falaise pocket was closed, *SS-Werfer-Abteilung 102* was with it.[5]

The battalion had a ration strength of 645 on 1 July 1944 and 537 on 11 September.[6] Casualties from 1 February 1944 to 11 September 1944 included eight killed in action, **88** wounded and 96 missing.[7]

---

1   See Gliederung II. SS-Panzer-Korps 1.3.44 (BA-MA RH 20-7/136).

2   W. Tieke, *Im Feuersturm letzter Kriegsjahre* (Munin, Osnabrück 1975) p. 626.

3   It is not mentioned by Gen.Kdo. LXXXIV A.K. Ia Nr. 035/44g.Kdos 22.7.44, Taktische Gliederung der Artillerie, Stand 21.7.44, T314, R1604, F001388. Neither is it mentioned by Gen.Kdo. LXXXIV. A.K. Ia 048/44 g.Kdos. T314, R1604, F001373 which gives the condition of Das Reich on 23 July.

4   W. Tieke, *Im Feuersturm letzter Kriegsjahre* (Munin, Osnabrück 1975) p. 186.

5   Ibid, p. 268.

6   Ibid, p. 626.

7   Ibid.

Miscellaneous General
Headquarters Formations

II. Fallschirm-Korps

Usually German corps organizations were command and control headquarters with no combat units assigned on a permanent basis. However, this corps was an exception. The authorized organization called for the following combat units:[1]

Fallschirm-Aufklärungs-Abteilung 12
Fallschirm-Sturmgeschütz-Abteilung 12
Fallschirm-Artillerie-Regiment 12 (I. - III. Abteilungen)
Fallschirm-Flak-Regiment 12 (I. - III. Abteilungen)

At the beginning of June, this organization was far from complete. *Fallschirm-Artillerie-Regiment 12* had just begun forming. *Fallschirm-Artillerie-Ausbildungs-Regiment Luneville* in northeastern France was ordered to set up the regiment's first two battalions. It was instructed to accomplish this by 25 August.[2] The *III./Fallschirm-Artillerie-Regiment 12* had not even begun forming by 7 August.[3] The *I.* and *II./Fallschirm-Artillerie-Regiment 12* were still at Luneville on 18 August.[4] *Fallschirm-Flak-Regiment 12* was not with the corps on 17 May.[5] It was in Germany on 10 July[6] but, according to Meindl, the corps commander, the regiment arrived on 25 July.[7] On the other hand, Blauensteiner, the corps chief of staff, stated that the regiment did not join the corps before the end of the war.[8] Blauensteiner is probably correct in this instance. The regiment was previously designated *Fallschirm-Flak-Regiment 2*. It was not until June 1944 that it received number 12.[9] *Fallschirm-Flak-Abteilung 2* was present in Normandy and it is possible that Meindl, two years after the battle in Normandy, had confused the battalion with the regiment.

The fact that these units were missing is also reflected in the manpower situation for the corps. Its authorized strength, excluding attached divisions, was 8,951 men, but it only had 3,363.[10]

The corps also had a training unit for parachute infantry, *Fallschirm-Jäger-Ersatz-und Ausbildungs-Regiment 2,* with three battalions.[11] Two of the battalions were located in Brittany and one just south of Cherbourg. According to Blauensteiner, this regiment had about 1,000–2,000 men but no equipment.[12] The clothing situation was poor and the men were not trained.[13]

Both *Fallschirm-Aufklärungs-Abteilung 12* and *Fallschirm-Sturmgeschutz-Brigade 12* were sent to Normandy. For more information on these units, see the respective sections.

The losses suffered by the corps units during June are not known, but from 1 July–10 September casualties amounted to 176 killed in action, 776 wounded and 577 missing.[14] According to Meindl, the corps troops arrived in the Cologne (Wahn) area on 28 August for refitting.[15]

---

1   Gliederung II. Fs.Korps, Stand 17.5.44, BA-MA RH 20-7/136.

2   KTB des höherer Artilleriekommandeurs der Fallschirmtruppe KTB Nr. 1, Höherer Art. Kommandeur Abt. Ia Az 11 5.6.44, BA-MA RL 33/3.

3   Übersicht über den Stand der Art. Einh., Anlage 33 zum KTB des höheren Artilleriekommandeurs der Fallschirmtruppe, KTN Nr. 1, BA-MA RL 33/3.

4   Höh. Art. Kommandeur Abt Ia, Az 11 Br. B. Nr. 797/44 geh. 18.8.44, BA-MA RL 33/3.

5   Gliederung II. Fs.Korps, Stand 17.5.44, BA-MA RH 20-7/136.

6   KTB des höherer Artilleriekommandeurs der Fallschirmtruppe KTB Nr. 1, BA-MA RL 33/3.

7   E. Meindl, II. Fallschirm-Korps 25 Juli - 5 Augusti, MS # A-969.

8   E. Blauensteiner, *Normandie: Vorgeschichte II. Fallschirmkorps Anfang Mai 1944 - 6. Juni 1944,* MS # B-240, p. 3.

9   G. Tessin, *Verbände und Truppen der deutschen Wehrmacht und Waffen-SS* (Mittler & Sohn, Frankfurt am Main and Biblio Verlag, Osnabrück 1966–1975).

10 Gliederung II. Fs.Korps, Stand 17.5.44, BA-MA RH 20-7/136.

11 Ibid.

12 E. Blauensteiner, *Normandie: Vorgeschichte II. Fallschirmkorps Anfang Mai 1944 - 6. Juni 1944*, MS # B-240, p. 2.

13 Ibid.

14 Anlage I zu Korpsarzt II. Fallsch.Korps B Nr. 65050/45 g.Kdos vom 27.1.45, Berichtzeit 1.7 - 4.9.44, BA-MA RL 33/5.

15 E. Meindl, II. Fallschirm-Korps 21 August - 3 September, MS # A-859, p. 1.

III. Flak-Korps

The *III. Flak-Korps* was a rather unique unit. There existed other *Flak-Korps* on the Eastern Front, but they were only partly composed of motorized units. The *III. Flak-Korps* was made up of motorized units exclusively,[1] even though there were shortages of vehicles.

It is common to emphasize the antitank role of the 8.8 cm *Flak*. However, this does not seem consistent with the employment of the *III. Flak-Korps*.[2] The major reason is that the 8.8 cm *Flak* gun was not very suitable for antitank missions. Consider the following:

1. The 8.8 cm *Flak* had a high silhouette. This made it difficult to dig in and thereby provide protection against enemy artillery fire. The overwhelming Allied artillery fire often destroyed the 8.8 cm guns before they got a chance to open fire. The AT guns were not as vulnerable as the AA guns.[3]

2. The high silhouette also made it easy for the enemy to spot the gun once it had opened fire.[4]

3. The armor penetration capabilities of the 8.8 cm *Flak* 36 were only about 15% better than those of the 7.5 cm *Pak* 40, which was the standard German antitank gun. Given the fact that the vast majority of the Allied tanks were Shermans, or vehicles with even weaker armor, the 7.5 cm *Pak* 40 was quite sufficient to deal with most enemy tanks. Only the frontal armor of the Churchill tanks — equipped with 6-inches of armor — was proof against the 7.5 cm AT gun, but that armor was also sufficient to keep out hits from the 8.8 cm *Flak* 36.[5]

4. The longer range of the 8.8 cm *Flak* compared to the 7.5 cm AT gun was, of course, an advantage, but, at longer range, accuracy declines for all guns, even the 8.8 cm gun. Thus, the chances of hitting with the first round were lower. Since the 8.8 cm AA gun was difficult to conceal and easy to spot when it fired, it was likely that the enemy tanks could respond with HE fire or calls for indirect artillery on the *Flak* positions before they themselves were knocked out.

5. The much greater weight of the 8.8 cm gun compared to the 7.5 cm AT gun made it difficult to move. This was compounded by the fact that the gun had to be limbered for movement. Thus, it was much more difficult to withdraw the 8.8 cm gun out of the enemy's reach if a position had to be abandoned.

This actually made the 7.5 cm *Pak* 40 a better AT weapon than the 8.8 cm *Flak* 36. It must also be remembered that a German infantry division had 20–40 7.5 cm antitank guns, either towed or self-propelled (including *Sturmgeschütze*). Of course, the armor divisions, with their *Panzer IV* and *Panther* tanks, had an unparalleled ability to combat enemy tanks.

The fact that the 8.8 cm *Flak* was not suitable for antitank missions was also clearly recognized by the commanders and men serving in the *III. Flak-Korps*. This is clear both in the post-war manuscript produced by the corps commander, Wolfgang Pickert,[6] and in a report dated 20 September 1944, discussing the experiences of the corps during the fighting in Normandy.[7]

First and foremost, the corps was employed in the air defense role.[8] This was its main mission and it extended initially from the front to a line from Falaise to Le Beny Bocage.[9] The second important mission of the corps was to provide indirect fire to support the ground combat units.[10] The chief reason for this was the shortage of GHQ artillery. Due to the range of the 8.8 cm guns, this could often be provided from the same positions where they provided air defensive protection.

If enemy tanks had broken through, the *Flak* units were expected to engage them if they had advanced as far as the *Flak* positions. The corps also had *Flakkampfgruppen (Flak* sections) at its disposal. These were created for ground combat. However, they did not arrive at the corps until it was already in Normandy. When the *Flakkampfgruppen* arrived, they were deemed to be insufficiently trained. Consequently, they were placed in the Trun area to train and were not sent into combat until Operation *Goodwood*, the British offensive, was launched in July. Each *Flakkampfgruppe* consisted of four *Flakkampftrupps,* which each had two 8.8 cm *Flak*. Three such *Flakkamfgruppen* were created.[11] Two of them had the numbers 11,700 and 13,300.[12] The third one probably had number 12,400.[13]

The *Flakkampfgruppen* were not very successful in combat. The results achieved were not in proportion to the casualties sustained.[14] They lost about 55 8.8 cm guns and 70 light *Flak*, while the number of tanks they knocked out were assessed to be 20.[15]

The main components of the corps were the four *Flak-Sturm-Regimenter.* These were numbered 1–4. These had been formed by using the regimental staffs — numbered 32, 36, 37 and 79, respectively.[16] It seems that these numbers were occasionally used too, which may have caused some confusion as to which *Flak* units actually participated in the battle.[17] The regiments had only recently received their *Flak-Sturm* designation when the Allied forces landed.

Nominally, each regiment was supposed to have three battalions with five batteries each. Three of the batteries were authorized to have 8.8 cm guns and two were to be equipped with light AA guns. Altogether this meant that the corps was intended to have 36 batteries with heavy guns and 24 with light guns.

In reality, the organization of the corps did not correspond exactly to the authorized amounts. On 23 June, it had 27 heavy batteries and 26 light batteries.[18] This had increased to 29 heavy and 40 light batteries by 8 August.[19] Since a heavy battery had four 8.8 cm guns, the authorized strength of the corps included 108 such guns on 23 June and 116 on 8 August. Three of the heavy batteries had the more powerful 8.8 cm *Flak* 41.[20] With its higher muzzle velocity, it also had much better armor penetration capabilities than the 8.8 cm *Flak* 18/36/37 which made up the vast majority of the heavy batteries.

According to Pickert, the corps had an authorized strength of about 12,000 men at the beginning of June.[21] This estimate seems reasonable, since the authorized strength for 27 heavy batteries, 26 light batteries, twelve battalion staffs and three regiment staffs was 12,027 men.[22] To this should be added the corps staff and its support elements. The corps did not have any means to repair vehicles and other heavy equipment.[23] Since the corps was close to full strength, it probably had a strength of about 12,000 men when it was ordered to move to Normandy.

On D-Day *Flak-Sturm-Regimenter 2, 3* and *4* were located around the Somme Estuary, while *Flak-Sturm-Regiment 1* was deployed between Isigny and Bayeux.[24] The latter regiment had recently been redeployed to that area.[25]

The corps (minus *Flak-Sturm-Regiment 1*) received orders on the afternoon of D-Day to move to Normandy as rapidly as possible.[26] During the night from 6–7 June, the corps reached Paris.[27] Most of the corps had reached positions southwest of Caen on the evening of 8 June.[28]

During the march to Normandy the corps suffered greater casualties than most German units shifted into to Normandy. In his post-war manuscript Pickert estimated casualties at 100 killed, 200 wounded and about 100 vehicles.[29] According to the 20 September 1944 after-action report, losses during the march included 20 guns, 110 trucks and towing vehicles and 100 motorcycles, passenger cars and trailers.[30] In the report the term *Ausfälle* is used, which means that both permanently destroyed equipment and such equipment that could be repaired is included. It also includes equipment which has suffered mechanical breakdown or which had been involved in traffic accidents. The march to Normandy did not only result in losses for the corps. It also claimed to have shot down about 35 aircraft during the movement.[31]

Ammunition supply was a problem for most German units in Normandy, and the *III. Flak-Korps* was no exception. Since no ammunition had been stored in advance in Normandy, the distances to haul the ammunition to the corps were long.[32] Despite these difficulties the *III. Flak-Korps* was probably better off than the army formations. The following amounts of ammunition were delivered to the corps during its operations in Normandy:[33]

2,716,313 rounds for 2 cm guns
272,057 rounds for 3.7 cm guns
209,946 rounds for 8.8 cm guns

Also the corps received the following number of new guns during its actions in Normandy[34]:

53 8.8 cm guns
36 3.7 cm guns
72 2.0 cm guns
12 2.0 cm guns (4-barreled)

As has been emphasized above, the corps was mainly employed in the air defense role, not in the antitank role. This is also reflected in the claims by the corps during the Normandy battle[35]:

Aircraft shot down: 462
Tanks destroyed: 92
Armored cars destroyed: 14

Of the tanks destroyed, about 12 fell victims to the hand-held *Panzerfaust* close-range antitank weapon.[36]

It is important to emphasize that the effectiveness of AA guns in the air defense role cannot only be measured in numbers of aircraft shot down. Equally important is the effect on how the enemy conducts his air operations. A very important effect of the German air defenses was that it forced Allied air units to operate at higher altitude,[37] thus reducing the accuracy of Allied air units when they attacked ground targets. Similarly, the main effect of Allied air power was not the casualties and equipment losses inflicted, but the indirect effects, such as the German reluctance to move during daylight.[38]

The number of tanks claimed is quite small. Given the fact that Army and *Waffen-SS* units claimed to have destroyed 3,663 enemy tanks from 6 June to 21 August,[39] the *III Flak-Korps* cannot be regarded as a very important part of German antitank defenses.

The achievements of the corps did not come without cost. In Pickert's post-war manuscript, he estimated that the corps casualties amounted to about 800 killed and 1,500 wounded. He did not know how many missing there were. Fortunately, there exists more precise information:[40]

Killed in Action	Wounded	Missing	Total
662	1,658	3,457	5,777

These figures include casualties from D-Day to the corps retreat into Germany. Evidently Pickert's memory was pretty close to the mark for killed and wounded.

According to Pickert, the casualties were mainly caused by artillery. Air attacks on AA units in firing positions had relatively little effect.[41] Given the large number of missing, it is clear that another major cause was the Allied ground units succeeding in cutting off possible retreat paths for the corps units.

The corps was employed in the eastern half of the German front in Normandy against the British units. Its participation in halting Operation *Goodwood* warrants certain comments. In several publications, it is stated that this corps employed "144 AT/AA guns". This probably refers to the 8.8 cm guns, but the number 144 seem to have been derived by assuming that the corps had four regiments with three battalions each and that each battalion had 12 8.8 cm guns. However, each battalion did not have 12 8.8 cm guns. As shown above, the corps had fewer than 144 8.8 cm guns. Further, the guns were not "AT/AA guns" but AA guns.

The *Flak-Sturm-Regimenter* were employed so far to the rear that the British armor units did not encounter them during the operation.[42] The three *Flakkampfgruppen*, however, were deployed further forward, and they did become involved in combat. Since they only had a TOE strength of eight 8.8 cm *Flak* each these units were hardly significant.

Finally, it is worth discussing why the 8.8 cm *Flak* has received such a reputation in the history of Operation *Overlord*. In 1940 and 1941, when the German antitank defenses mainly consisted of the 3.7 cm AT gun, the 8.8 cm *Flak* 36 was significantly superior in terms of armor penetration and range. With the introduction of the 7.5 cm *Pak* 40, the superiority of the 8.8 cm *Flak* 36 was relatively marginal. However, it seems that the image of the all-pervasive 8.8 cm *Flak* was created in the early years of the war, largely in North Africa. During much of the fighting in North Africa, British tank units were equipped with tanks armed with guns that had no HE ammunition. The cooperation between British tanks and artillery was often abysmal. In Normandy the behavior of British forces was quite different however. Hence, the drawbacks of the 8.8 cm *Flak* described above were much more pronounced. Nonetheless, the image of the "88 mm *Flak*" seems to have been vivid.

Another factor to consider is the fact that there existed several different 8.8 cm guns. At the beginning of the war, there were three 8.8 cm AA guns, the *Flak* 18, *Flak* 36 and *Flak* 37. These were very similar and used the same Ammunition. Their ballistic performance was identical. During the war, new 8.8 cm guns were introduced. First came the *Flak* 41, which had much higher muzzle velocity, thus improving armor penetration by about 60%. This gun also had a much lower profile, making it easier to dig in and conceal. Weighing all factors together, it was a much better AT weapon than the *Flak* 18/36/37. But the *Flak* 41 was a very rare gun, produced in much smaller numbers than the older types.

There also existed an 8.8 cm AT gun, the *Pak* 43. This weapon was more powerful than the *Flak* 41, though only marginally. The gun was mounted on a very low cruciform carriage of excellent design. Due to lack of carriages, the gun barrel was also mounted on a howitzer carriage. This configuration was called the *Pak* 43/41. It was higher and clumsier. The *Pak* 43/41 and, in particular, the *Pak* 43 were very good AT guns. They were, however, generally only issued to *Panzerjäger* units and, occasionally, artillery units. They were not used by *Flak* units.

Another factor which may have contributed to the image of the 8.8 cm *Flak* gun is the many false identifications in after-action reports by Allied units. It is a well known fact that German tanks were quite often identified as *Tigers* by Allied soldiers, even in situations where no *Tigers* participated. Probably the same phenomenon appears with these guns. To Allied soldiers, German AT fire was, almost by default, from 8.8 cm guns. Also, if a tank was knocked out, it is not easy to see if it was hit by a 8.8 cm round or one of 7.5 cm caliber. Quite possibly, to many Allied tank crews, the first assumption was that their tank was destroyed by an "88".[43]

1   W. Pickert, *Das III. Flakkorps in der Normandie-Schlacht*, MS # B-597, p. 4.

2   See also H. Meyer, *Kriegsgeschichte der 12. SS-Panzer-Division "Hitlerjugend", Vol I* (Munin Verlag, Osnabrück 1982) p. 203.

3   Gen.Kdo. III. Flakkorps, Br.B.Nr. (Ia op 2) 163/44 g.Kdos, 20.9.44., p. 9, BA-MA RL 11/114.

4   Ibid.

5   A British survey of 53 hits on Shermans showed that only three had failed to penetrate. This survey was made when few *Panthers* had reached the front, therefore most of the 75 mm hits must have been from either *Panzer IV* or 75 mm *PAK* (PRO WO 291/1331, Operational Research in NW Europe, Chapter 10, Tank casualties, Report No. 12, Analysis of 75 mm Sherman Casualties 6 June–10 June, pp. 199–201).

6   Pickert, op.cit.

7   See note 3.

8   See note 3, p. 5.

9   Pickert, op.cit., p. 14.

10   See note 3, p. 7. See also Pickert, op.cit., p. 19.

11   See Pickert, op.cit., p. 17 and Anlage 1.

12   Luftflotten-Kommando 3 Ia/Flak Nr. 11457/44 g.Kdos 17.7.44, Gliederung der Flakartillerie, Stand 15.7.44, BA-MA RL 7/58

13   See G. Tessin, *Verbände und Truppen der deutschen Wehrmacht und Waffen-SS* (Mittler & Sohn, Frankfurt am Main and Biblio Verlag, Osnabrück 1966–1975). According to Tessin, the *Flakkampfgruppen* had six *Flakkampftrupps* each. It is possible that they were expanded after a while. It is also possible that they were intended to have six *Flakkampftrupps* each (Tessin has used the field post numbers to establish the organization), but this may not have been carried out. Finally, of course, it is possible that Pickert is simply wrong.

14   Pickert, op.cit., p. 20.

15   See note 3, p. 10.

16   W. Dierich, *Die Verbände der Luftwaffe 1935 - 1945* (Motorbuch Verlag, Stuttgart 1976) p. 351–3.

17   These numbers were used during a conversation between the *AOK 7 Ia* and the general staff officer of the *III. Flak-Korps* at 1830 hours on 11 June 1944. See Anlagen zum KTB AOK 7 Ia, Ferngesprache und Besprachungen, T312, R1566, F000275.

18   H. A. Koch, *Flak* (Podzun, Bad Nauheim 1954) p. 443.

19   Ibid.

20   Ibid, p. 139.

21   Pickert, op.cit., p. 38.

22   Authorised strength: 167 men for a heavy battery; 210 men for a light battery; 130 men for a battalion staff; and, 166 men for a regimental staff. See H. A. Koch, *Flak* (Podzun, Bad Nauheim 1954) p. 657.

23   See note 3, p. 18.

24   See note 3, p. 4.

25   Pickert, op.cit., p. 6.

26   Pickert, op.cit., p. 8.

27   Pickert, op.cit., p. 9.

28   Pickert, op.cit., p. 11.

29   Pickert, op.cit., p. 10.

30 See note 3, p. 4.

31 Pickert, op.cit., p. 10.

32 Pickert, op.cit., p. 13.

33 See note 3, p. 16.

34 See note 3, p. 16.

35 See note 3, p. 19.

36 See note 3, p. 17.

37 Pickert, op.cit., p. 15.

38 Pickert, op.cit., p. 36.

39 HGr B Ia Nr. 6375/44 g.Kdos., 21.8.44, T311, R3, F7002227.

40 See note 3, p. 20.

41 Pickert, op.cit., p. 16.

42 Pickert, op.cit., p. 24f and also map in Anlage. Note that the author has got the dates wrong. The British offensive was launched on 18 July, not 19 July.

43 This was also recognized by British operations research teams investigating the battlefields immediately after operations. They found that estimates by fighting soldiers were unreliable since many reported that they had been knocked out by 88 mm guns when, in fact, it had been 75 mm rounds. The reverse had not been discovered. (PRO WO 291/1331, Operational Research in NW Europe, Chapter 10, Tank casualties, Report No. 12, Analysis of 75 mm Sherman Casualties 6 June–10 June, pp. 199–201)

Sicherungs-Regiment 1

Security units were not intended for regular combat. Rather, they were supposed to keep occupied areas under control and perhaps participate in anti-partisan operations. *Sicherungs-Regiment 1* did, however, find it self in the path of Patton's troops advancing eastwards. Hence it became involved in serious combat operations.

The regiment had been created in 1942 by renaming *Wach-Regiment Paris 1*.[1] It seems to have remained in the Paris area until August 1944, when it was sent to the west. The regiment consisted of three battalions, each with four companies.[2] According to the organization chart, two of the battalions were motorized and one was equipped with bicycles.[3] What vehicles the battalions were equipped with is unknown, but it may well have been commandeered buses or other civilian vehicles. The regiment had an antitank company with twelve 3.7 cm AT guns, and it also had a company with twelve French Panhard armored cars.[4] Thus it was very well equipped for being a security unit.

On 5 August the regiment was located at Le Mans.[5] Eight days later the regiment was attached to the *352. Infanterie-Division* and fighting in the La Loupe area.[6] At that time, the regiment was also known as *Sperrgruppe von Krawel* (Blocking Group von Krawel). The II./*Sicherungs-Regiment 1* was located near Rambouillet on 17 August.[7]

It seems that the *I.* and *II./Sicherungs-Regiment 1* remained attached to the *352. Infanterie-Division* until the retreat across the Seine.[8] The remaining battalion seems to have been employed further to the west, under the *LXXXI. Korps*.[9] The regiment was disbanded on 2 October 1944.[10] Other units had probably already absorbed most of its remaining personnel by that date.

---

1   G. Tessin, *Verbände und Truppen der deutschen Wehrmacht und Waffen-SS* (Mittler & Sohn, Frankfurt am Main and Biblio Verlag, Osnabrück 1966–1975).
2   LXXXI. A.K. Ia, Anlagen, Gliederung Sich.Rgt. 1, T314, R1593, F000970.
3   Ibid.
4   Ibid.
5   LXXXI. A.K., Lagekarte 5.8.44, T314, R1594, F000005.
6   Ziegelmann, MS # B-741, p. 8.
7   Ibid, p. 9.
8   Ibid, pp. 10–13.
9   See Lagekarten 81. A.K., T314, R1594, F000005ff.
10 Tessin, op. cit.

Schnelle Brigade 30

The brigade had been raised in February 1943 as *Reserve-Rad-Regiment 30* (reserve bicycle regiment). A few weeks later it was reorganized as *Schnelle Brigade 30*.[1]

On 1 April 1944 it was organized as follows:[2]

Schnelle Abteilung 513 with

1. *Kompanie:* 14 machine guns, 3 mortars
2. *Kompanie:* 17 machine guns, 3 mortars
3. *Kompanie:* 22 machine guns, 3 mortars

Schnelle Abteilung 517 with

1. *Kompanie:* 18 machine guns, 5 mortars
2. *Kompanie:* 17 machine guns, 4 mortars
3. *Kompanie:* 9 machine guns, 4 mortars, 2 towed antitank guns, 5 self-propelled 4.7 cm antitank Guns

Schnelle Abteilung 518 with

1. *Kompanie:* 11 machine guns, 3 mortars
2. *Kompanie:* 11 machine guns, 3 mortars
3. *Kompanie:* 8 machine guns, 3 mortars

The brigade had a total strength of 1,878 men.[3]

On the eve of the Allied invasion the brigade was deployed in the Coutances — Granville area.[4] It was ordered to move to the Bayeux area on 6 June. The following day, two battalions were committed in the sector of *Grenadier-Regiment 915* and one battalion — *Schnelle Abteilung 517* — reinforced *Grenadier-Regiment 916*.[5]

Schnelle Brigade 30 remained with the *352. Infanterie-Division* and it seems that its men were subsequently absorbed by that division. This makes it impossible to estimate the casualties suffered by this unit. It was formally disbanded on 5 September 1944.[6]

---

1   G. Tessin, *Verbände und Truppen der deutschen Wehrmacht und Waffen-SS* (Mittler & Sohn, Frankfurt am Main and Biblio Verlag, Osnabrück 1966–1975).
2   Kriegsgliederung der 7. Armee, Stand 18.5.44, T312, R1566, F000219.
3   Ibid.
4   Lagekarte AOK 7 5.6.1944, BA-MA RH 20-7/138K.
5   Ziegelmann, *Die Geschichte der 352. Infanterie-Division*, MS # B-433, p. 2.
6   Tessin, op. cit.

Fallschirmjäger-Regiment 6

The original *Fallschirmjäger-Regiment 6* had been used to raise new parachute units. In November 1943 it was decided to form a new *Fallschirmjäger-Regiment 6*, which was intended to be part of the *2. Fallschirm-Division.*[1] This unit was ordered to move to France on 1 May 1944.[2]

Its organization on 19 May 1944 included three parachute battalions. Each battalion had three companies with 18 machine guns and 3 8 cm mortars. The battalions also had a heavy company with 12 heavy machine guns, 4 8 cm mortars and 2 howitzers. This gave the battalion a strength of 70 machine guns (including four with the headquarters platoon), 13 mortars and 2 howitzers.[3]

In addition to its three battalions, the regiment had three supporting companies. They were outfitted as follows:[4]

13. Kompanie (schwerer Granatwerfer): Nine 12 cm mortars, eight machine guns

14. Kompanie (Panzerjäger): Four 7.5 cm AT guns, 34 *Panzerschrecks*, six machine guns

15. Kompanie (Pionier): Two 8 cm mortars, six machine guns (two of them heavy)

Total strength of the regiment amounted to 3,457 men on 19 May.[5] According to von der Heydte, the regiment was further strengthened during June 1944. Its bicycle reconnaissance platoon was expanded into a company and became the *16. Kompanie.*[6] During the summer, further companies were added: *17. Kompanie (Fliegerabwehr), 18. Kompanie (Kraftfahr), 19. Kompanie (Versorgung und Instandsetzung)* and *20. Kompanie (Feldersatz).*[7] With these additions, the regiment had a strength of about 4,500 men.[8]

About a third of the officers and a fifth of the noncommissioned officers were veterans, while the men were, on average, 17.5 years old.[9] The regiment had about 70 trucks. These were of more than 50 different types.[10] For such a large regiment this was not sufficient to provide more than modest mobility.

Shortly after the Allied landings, *Fallschirmjäger-Regiment 6* was engaged in the Carentan area. It was involved in prolonged fighting and, on 27 June, it was reported that the regiment had three *mittelstarke Bataillone* (battalions of medium strength)[11]. This included 1,000 replacements that had recently arrived, poorly armed and equipped.[12]

When US forces launched Operation *Cobra*, *Fallschirmjäger-Regiment 6* was attached to the *2. SS-Panzer-Division "Das Reich"* and, together with this division, it broke out of the La Baleine pocket.[13] The regiment was almost surrounded again in the Villedieu pocket but, acting on his own initiative, von der Heydte led his regiment out of the pocket.[14] Subsequently, the regiment was attached to the *353. Infanterie-Division.*[15]

On 10 August the regiment received orders to disengage and move to Nancy for refitting. Altogether 1,007 men left for this new task.[16] The regiment suffered about 3,000 casualties during its operations in Normandy.

1   von der Heydte, *Das Fallschirmjägerregiment 6 in der Normadie*, MS # B-839, p. 2f.
2   Ibid, p. 7.
3   Gliederungen der AOK 7, Kleinere Verbände im Ber. LXXXIV. A.K., T312, R1566, F000214.
4   Ibid.
5   Ibid.
6   Heydte, op. cit. p. 3.
7   Ibid.
8   Ibid, p. 4.
9   Ibid.
10   Ibid, p. 6.
11   AOK 7 Ia Nr. 3454/44 g.Kdos., 27.6.44., T312, R1565, F001375.
12   Ibid, see also Heydte, op. cit. p. 50.
13   See Gen.Kdo. LXXXIV. A.K. Ia 048/44 g.Kdos. T314, R1604, F001373. and Heydte, op.cit. pp. 59–73. The La Balaine pocket was also known as the Roncey pocket and the Coutances pocket.
14   Heydte, op.cit. pp. 73–76.
15   Ibid.
16   Ibid. p. 77.

Fallschirm-Aufklärungs-Abteilung 12

This battalion was raised in January 1944 to be a permanent component of the *II. Fallschirm-Korps*.[1] It had the following authorized organization:[2]

1. Kompanie: *Panzerspähwagen* (armored cars)

2. Kompanie: *Schützenpanzerwagen (SPW)* (armored personnel carriers) (with 47 machine guns and 2 8 cm mortars)

3. Kompanie: *SPW* (with 47 MG and 2 8 cm mortars)

4. schwere Kompanie: 15 machine guns; 4 2 cm *Flak*; 9 7.5 cm antitank guns; 2 infantry howitzers

5. Versorgungskompanie (supply company)

By 17 May, however, it was far from attaining that status. It had not received any of its armored cars and only half of its mortars.[3] Many of the units of the *II. Fallschirm-Korps* were only partially equipped, manned and trained. It is possible that during the three weeks between 17 May and D-Day the battalion received equipment to bring it up to strength, but that would still leave the training of the unit in a less than satisfactory state.

According to Blauensteiner, the chief of staff of the *II. Fallschirm-Korps,* the battalion was equipped with *Volkswagen* passenger cars and trucks not capable of cross-country movement.[4] He estimated that it had a manpower strength of 900 men.[5] Effectively, the battalion seems to have been a motorized infantry unit.

On 10 June the battalion had reached Pont Brocard (east-southeast of Coutances).[6] It was with the *II. Fallschirm-Korps* on 1 July[7], and it seems to have remained with the corps for the remainder of the campaign. On 29 July, the battalion was considered to be *schwach* (weak) — meaning the battalion had a combat strength (*Kampfstärke*) of 100–200 men.[8] The battalion was among those surrounded in the Falaise pocket and, on 19 August, it was just west of the Dives river.[9]

---

1   G. Tessin, *Verbände und Truppen der deutschen Wehrmacht und Waffen-SS* (Mittler & Sohn, Frankfurt am Main and Biblio Verlag, Osnabrück 1966–1975).

2   BA-MA RH 2/1594.

3   Gliederung II. Fs.Korps 17.5.44, BA-MA RH 20-7/136.

4   E. Blauensteiner, *Normandie: Vorgeschichte II. Fallschirmkorps Anfang Mai 1944 - 6. Juni 1944,* MS # B-240, p. 2.

5   Ibid.

6   E. Blauensteiner, *Normandie: 6. Juni 1944 - 24. Juli 1944,* MS # B-261, p. 2.

7   Anlage I zu Korpsarzt II. Fallsch.Korps B Nr. 65050/45 g.Kdos vom 27.1.45, Berichtzeit 1.7 - 4.9.44, BA-MA RL 33/5.

8   AOK 7 Ia Nr. 4174/44 g.Kdos. den 2.8.44, T312, R1569, F000358.

9   E. Blauensteiner, *Einsatz des II. Fallsch.Korps in Nordfrankreich 25.7.1944 - 25.8.44,* MS # B-346, p. 11.

Maschinengewehr-Bataillon 17

This unit had been raised in 1940, but it had not seen any action before the Allied invasion. It had spent all its time in Western Europe.[1] It had three companies with twelve heavy machine guns each. There was also an AT platoon with three 5 cm Pak, a platoon with six 8 cm mortars and an engineer platoon. The engineer and AT platoons were motorized. Total strength of the battalion was 632 men.[2]

When the Allies landed, *Maschinengewehr-Bataillon 17* was located west of Cherbourg.[3] It remained on the northwestern tip of the Cotentin peninsula until 11 June, but on the 12 it was moved to the defensive perimeter around Cherbourg. The battalion remained there until Cherbourg fell.[4] *Maschinengewehr-Bataillon 17* was destroyed at Cherbourg and was not rebuilt.[5]

---

1   G. Tessin, *Verbände und Truppen der deutschen Wehrmacht und Waffen-SS* (Mittler & Sohn, Frankfurt am Main and Biblio Verlag, Osnabrück 1966–1975).
2   Gliederungen der AOK 7, Gliederung der 709.I.D. Stand 1.5.44., T312, R1566, F000217.
3   Lagekarte AOK 7 5.6.1944, BA-MA RH 20-7/138K.
4   Lagekarten AOK 7, 6.6.44 - 30.6.44, T312, R1570, F000014 - 000039.
5   Tessin, op. cit.

Pionier-Bataillon 600

This unit had recently been formed in Bitsch in Lorraine.[1] It was probably formed on an ad hoc basis. On 24 June it was decided that the unit should be committed in the area around Condé-sur-Noireau.[2] It was reported on 13 July that the battalion had arrived.[3] One day later the unit was near Canteloup, about 15 kilometers east of Caen.[4] The battalion (minus one company) was attached to the *LXXIV Korps* on 11 August.[5] No further information about the unit has been found.

1   G. Tessin, *Verbände und Truppen der deutschen Wehrmacht und Waffen-SS* (Mittler & Sohn, Frankfurt am Main and Biblio Verlag, Osnabrück 1966–1975).
2   Ob.West Ia Nr. 4927/44 geh.Kdos. 24.6.44, T311, R25, F7029822.
3   KTB OB West Ia, entry 14.7.44, T311, R16, F7016800.
4   Pz.Gr. West Ia Nr. Unreadable, v. 15.7.44, Nachtrag zur Tagesmeldung 14.7, T313, R420, F8713914.
5   PzAOK 5 Ia Nr 899/44 g.Kdos vom 12.8.44, T313, R420, F8714187.

Festungs-Stamm-Truppen

Some of the more important cities had permanent garrisons to man the prepared defenses. These were called *Festungs-Stamm-Truppen* (Fortress Garrison Troops). The following cities had such units:[1]

Cherbourg	1,355 men
Dinard	900 men
Lorient	953 men
Plouhinec	172 men
Ause de Pouldu	395 men
Brest	2,001 men
St. Nazaire	761 men
St. Michel	109 men
Vannes	305 men
Guerrance	501 men

Of these, Cherbourg was located in the area of operations of the *LXXXIV. Korps,* while Dinard was within the area of operations of the *LXXIV. Korps.* The remaining cities were in the area of the *XXV. Korps.*

---

1   Kriegsgliederung der 7. Armee, Stand 18.5.44, T312, R1566, F000212.

Ost-Bataillon Huber

This was an ad hoc formation. It was composed of various eastern volunteer units from the training facility at Quetquidan on the Brittany peninsula. On 11 June it was reported that the unit was to be sent to the St. Saveur le Vicomte area to guard against potential Allied air landing operations.[1]

It is not clear when and if the battalion actually arrived in Normandy. On the order-of-battle chart for 29 June, it was still indicated as being in transit to the front. The original reason for moving it had largely been rendered superfluous, since US forces had occupied St. Saveur le Vicomte two weeks earlier. Of course, it is possible that the battalion was sent to Normandy anyway, but it could not have had high priority for transport assets.

---

1   KTB AOK 7 Ia, entry 11 June 1944, T312, R1568, F000747.

Pionier-Bataillon Angers

An engineer school was located at Angers. It formed an emergency unit — *Pionier-Bataillon Angers* — that could be employed in case of an Allied invasion. On 6 June 1944 this battalion had a strength of 433 men.[1]

It is not clear exactly when the battalion arrived in Normandy, but it is known that it was located close to St. Lô on 11 June.[2] Two days later it was attached to the *352. Infanterie-Division*.[3] It remained with the *352. Infanterie-Division* until 28 June.[4] It remained physically close to that division, since it was collocated with the *Panzer-Lehr-Division* on 16 July, which was to the left of the *352. Infanterie-Division* at that point in the battle.[5] It has not been possible to establish the fate of the unit.

---

1   AOK 7 Ia KTB Anlagen, 6.6.44, T312, R1565, F000865.
2   OB West Ia 4487/44 g.Kdos., 11.6.44, T311, R25, F7029460.
3   Kriegsgliederungen zum KTB der Führungsabteilung AOK 7 ab 6.6.44 bis 30.6.44, T312, R1566, F000005.
4   Ibid, frames until 000021.
5   OB West Ia Nr. 5779/44 geh.Kdos, 18.7.44, T311, R28, F7034580.

Sturm-Bataillon AOK 7

The battalion was raised in May 1943.[1] It was a permanent component of the 7. *Armee*. The organization of the battalion on 5 April 1944 was:[2]

Three infantry companies, each with 12 machine guns, 3 *Panzerschrecks* and 2 8 cm mortars
One heavy company with 8 heavy machine guns and 2 7.5 cm infantry howitzers
One artillery battery with 4 French howitzers
One headquarters company with 4 light *Flak,* 2 5 cm *Pak,* 1 7.5 cm *Pak,* 4 12 cm mortars and 5 machine guns.
One engineer platoon 3 machine guns, 2 flame throwers and 1 *Panzerschreck*.

The battalion had an engineer platoon at Angers. This was comprised of 58 men. The total strength of the unit was 1,106 men. It was commanded by a *Major* Messerschmidt.[3]

On 5 June the battalion was located east of Cherbourg.[4] It counterattacked US forces in the Ste. Mère-Église area on D-Day. The battalion remained north of the US forces on the Cotentin and was among the units surrounded in Cherbourg.[5] It should be noted that the artillery battery was not available to the battalion on D-Day. It was located southeast of Ste. Mère-Église and was committed to support *Fallschirmjäger-Regiment 6* on D-Day.[6]

Sturm-Bataillon AOK 7 was destroyed at Cherbourg and was not rebuilt.[7]

---

1   G. Tessin, *Verbände und Truppen der deutschen Wehrmacht und Waffen-SS* (Mittler & Sohn, Frankfurt am Main and Biblio Verlag, Osnabrück 1966–1975).
2   Gliederungen der AOK 7, Kleinere Verbände im Ber. LXXXIV. A.K., T312, R1566, F000214.
3   Ibid.
4   Lagekarte AOK 7 5.6.1944, BA-MA RH 20-7/138K.
5   Kriegsgliederungen zum KTB der Führungsabteilung AOK 7 ab 6.6.44 bis 30.6.44, T312, R1566, F000003 - 000025.
6   K.-W. Von Schlieben, *Die deutsche 709. Infanterie-Division vor und während der anglo-amerikanischen Invasion vom 6. Juni 1944*, MS # B-845, p. 25.
7   Tessin, op. cit.

General Headquarters *Panzer* Formations

Panzer-Ausbildungs-und Ersatz-Abteilung 100

As the name implies, this was not a regular combat unit, but a training unit. The unit had been raised in April 1941 in Germany. One year later it moved to France.[1] On 18 May 1944 it was with the *91. Division* on the Cotentin Peninsula. At that time, it had the following tanks:[2] 14 R 35; 8 Hotchkiss; 1 Somua; 1 Char B2; and, 1 *Panzer III*. In addition, there were five light French tanks whose type it is not possible to discern from the document. It is clear, however, that they were equipped with short 3.7 cm guns.[3] They were probably FT 17's.[4] The manpower strength of the unit was 664 men.[5]

The unit was committed in Normandy with the *91. Division*. On the organizational chart for the 7. *Armee,* it is listed as attached to the *91. Division* as late as 22 June. From 23 June onwards, it does not appear at all on the charts.[6] The battalion was probably destroyed, since it was officially disbanded on 1 July.[7]

---

1   G. Tessin, *Verbände und Truppen der deutschen Wehrmacht und Waffen-SS* (Mittler & Sohn, Frankfurt am Main and Biblio Verlag, Osnabrück 1966–1975).

2   Kriegsgliederungen der AOK 7, Kleinere Verbände im Bereich LXXXIV. A.K., T312, R1566, F000214.

3   Ibid.

4   Bob Mackenzie has provided the following argument: Given that R 35s and Hotchkiss' are already mentioned, those remaining with the short 37 mm gun must have been either the FCM 36 or the FT 17. Only 100 FCM 36's were built and the Germans converted 96 to SP guns. I've never seen a picture of an FCM in German service. Plenty of pictures of FT 17's exist, so I would assume the remaining tanks were FT 17's.

5   Ibid.

6   Kriegsgliederungen zum KTB der Führungsabteilung AOK 7 ab 6.6 bis 30.6.44, T312, R1566, F000002 - 000024.

7   Tessin, op. cit.

schwere SS-Panzer-Abteilung 101

This unit was formed on 22 October 1943 from a *Tiger* battalion that was intended for the *I. SS-Panzer-Korps*[1]. It was initially located at Mailly-le-Camp.[2] Later, elements from *Waffen-SS Tiger* companies on the Eastern Front were included in the battalion. On 16 April, the battalion had *19 Tiger I's,* but during the period from 17–20 April another 26 were sent by rail to the battalion. No further tanks were sent to the battalion until 28 July, when five *Tiger II's* were sent, followed by another nine *Tiger II's* from 31 July–1 August.[3] It seems doubtful that these saw any action with the unit. They were probably sent to Mailly-le-Camp, where surplus crews from the battalion would arrive. They would train with the new vehicles there and rejoin the battalion later.[4]

On 1 June 1944 the battalion had 37 operational *Tigers* and eight in maintenance facilities, and it was located near Beauvais.[5] The first operation in Normandy for the battalion was the well-known engagement around Villers-Bocage. The casualties from 13–16 June amounted to 16 killed in action and 22 wounded.[6] As of 16 June, nine *Tigers* had been lost.[7]

The battalion remained attached to the *I. SS-Panzer Korps* for the battle in Normandy. By 5 July, 15 *Tigers* were lost.[8] From the end of July until the beginning of August the battalion was included in *Kampfgruppe Wünsche*. This was an ad hoc formation which also consisted of *SS-Panzer-Regiment 12* (except the *II. Abteilung),* the *III./SS-Panzergrenadier-Regiment 26* (the armored infantry battalion of the *12. SS-Panzer-Division*) and the *I./SS-Panzer-Regiment 1.*[9]

The battalion had at least 25 *Tigers* on 1 August, but most of them were probably lost during the Falaise battle and the subsequent retreats.

Date	Number of tanks operational	Tanks in short-term repair	Tanks in long-term repair
1 June[10]	37	8	0
16 June[11]	15	15	6
1 July[12]	11	19	?
4 July[13]	0	25	?
6 July[14]	0	25	5
7 July[15]	5	?	?
8 July[16]	20	?	?
9 July[17]	18	9	?
10 July[18]	15	13	?
11 July[19]	13	15	?

Date	Number of tanks operational	Tanks in short-term repair	Tanks in long-term repair
15 July[20]	17	8	?
16 July[21]	16	?	?
17 July[22]	1	6	?
21 July[23]	6	?	?
22 July[24]	7	18	?
24 July[25]	13	11	?
25 July[26]	13	?	?
27 July[27]	13	11	?
28 July[28]	20	4	?
29 July[29]	21	4	?
30 July[30]	20	?	?
31 July[31]	19	?	?
1 August[32]	20	5	?
2 August[33]	19	?	?
3 August[34]	20	?	?
4 August[35]	20	?	?
9 August[36]	8	?	?

1   Georg Tessin, *Verbände und Truppen der deutschen Wehrmacht und Waffen-SS* (Mittler & Sohn, Frankfurt am Main (vol 1-5), Biblio Verlag, Osnabrück (vol 6–14) 1966–75), entry for units with number 102).

2   Ibid.

3   See Verteilung der Panzer Fahrzeuge, Band ab Mai 1943, BA-MA RH 10/349.

4   If this assumption is true it would be a procedure analogous to schwere Panzer-Abteilung 503.

5   *I. SS-Panzer-Korps'* monthly reports to the Inspector-General of Panzer Troops, BA-MA RH 10/309.

6   H. Meyer, *Kriegsgeschichte der 12. SS-Panzerdivision "Hitlerjugend"*, Vol I (Munin Verlag, Osnabrück 1982) p 132.

7   H.Gr. B Ia Nr. 3725/44 g.K. 17.6.44, BA-MA RH 19 IX/2.

8   Pz.Gr. West Ia Nr.268/44 geh. v. 9.7, Nachtrag zur Tagesmeldung 8.7, BA-MA RH 21-5/50.

9   H. Meyer, *Kriegsgeschichte der 12. SS-Panzerdivision "Hitlerjugend"*, *Vol I* (Munin Verlag, Osnabrück 1982) p. 287.

10   *I. SS-Panzer-Korps'* monthly reports to the Inspector-General of Panzer Troops, BA-MA RH 10/309.

11   H.Gr. B Ia Nr. 3725/44 g.K. 17.6.44, BA-MA RH 19 IX/2.

12 *I. SS-Panzer-Korps'* monthly reports to the Inspector-General of Panzer Troops, BA-MA RH 10/309.

13 Pz.Gr. West Ia, Nr. 197/44 geh. von 7.7.1944., Nachtrag zur Tagesmeldung, BA-MA RH 21-5/50.

14 Pz.Gr. West Ia, Nr. 217/44 geh. von 7.7.1944., Nachtrag zur Tagesmeldung BA-MA RH 21-5/50.

15 Pz.Gr. West Ia, Nr. 258/44 geh. von 8.7.1944., Nachtrag zur Tagesmeldung BA-MA RH 21-5/50.

16 Pz.Gr. West Ia Nr.268/44 geh. v. 9.7, Nachtrag zur Tagesmeldung 8.7, BA-MA RH 21-5/50.

17 Pz.Gr. West Ia, Nr. 306/44 geh. von 10.7.1944., Nachtrag zur Tagesmeldung BA-MA RH 21-5/50.

18 Pz.Gr. West Ia, Nr. 287/44 geh. von 11.7.1944., Nachtrag zur Tagesmeldung T313, R420, F8713880.

19 Pz.Gr. West Ia, Nr. 361/44 geh. von 12.7.1944., Nachtrag zur Tagesmeldung T313, R420, F8713889.

20 Pz.Gr. West Ia Nr. 388/44 g.Kdos 16.7.44, Nachtrag zur Tagesmeldung 15.7, T313, R420, F8713921.

21 Pz.Gr. West Ia, Nr. 424/44 geh. von 17.7.1944., Nachtrag zur Tagesmeldung BA-MA RH 21-5/50.

22 Pz.Gr. West Ia Nr. 479/44 geheim von 18.7.44, Nachtrag zur Tagesmeldung 17.7.44, BA-MA RH 21-5/50.

23 Pz.Gr. West Ia, Nr. 517/44 geh. von 21.7.1944., Nachtrag zur Tagesmeldung BA-MA RH 21-5/50.

24 Pz.Gr. West Ia, Nr. 535/44 geh. von 23.7.1944, Nachtrag zur Tagesmeldung BA-MA RH 21-5/50.

25 Pz.Gr. West Ia, Nr. 557/44 geh. von 25.7.1944, Nachtrag zur Tagesmeldung BA-MA RH 21-5/50.

26 Pz.Gr. West Ia, Nr. 572/44 geh. von 26.7.1944, Nachtrag zur Tagesmeldung BA-MA RH 21-5/50.

27 Pz.Gr. West Ia, Nr. 605/44 geh. von 27.7.1944, Nachtrag zur Tagesmeldung BA-MA RH 21-5/50.

28 Pz.Gr. West Ia Nr. 633/44 g.Kdos, 29.7.44, Nachtrag zur Tagesmeldung 28.7, T313, R420, F8714036.

29 Pz.Gr. West Ia Nr. 647/44 g.Kdos, 30.7.44, Nachtrag zur Tagesmeldung 29.7, T313, R420, F8714042.

30 Pz.Gr. West Ia Nr. 665/44 g.Kdos, 31.7.44, Nachtrag zur Tagesmeldung 30.7, T313, R420, F8714049.

31 Pz.Gr. West Ia, Nr. 678/44 geh. von 1.8.1944, Nachtrag zur Tagesmeldung BA-MA RH 21-5/50.

32 *I. SS-Panzer-Korps'* monthly reports to the Inspector-General of Panzer Troops, BA-MA RH 10/309.

33 Pz.Gr. West Ia Nr. 725/44 g.Kdos. 3.8.44, Nachtrag zur Tagesmeldung 2.8, T313, R420, F8714075.

34 Pz.Gr. West Ia, Nr. 734/44 geh. von 4.8.1944, Nachtrag zur Tagesmeldung 3.8, BA-MA RH 21-5/50.

35 Pz.Gr. West Ia Nr. 758/44 g.Kdos. 5.8.44, Nachtrag zur Tagesmeldung 4.8, T313, R420, F8714097.

36 Pz.Gr. West Ia Nr. 853/44 g.Kdos. 10.8.44, Nachtrag zur Tagesmeldung 9.8, T313, R420, F87141177. Note that the battalion was attached to the *12. SS-Panzer-Division* and the strength is found among the figures for that division.

schwere SS-Panzer-Abteilung 102

This unit was formed 22 October 1943 from a *Tiger* battalion that was intended for the *II. SS-Panzer-Korps*.[1] The latter unit had been forming during the summer 1943, but scheduled deliveries of *Tigers* had been diverted to the Eastern Front as replacements.[2] The first delivery of tanks to the battalion did not take place until 21 April 1944, when 6 *Tigers* were shipped.[3]

At the beginning of June, the unit was in Oldebroek in Holland.[4] It was not ready for combat since many men were detached from the unit. The majority of the tank drivers had been sent to Paderborn in Germany for training. Similarly, the majority of the radio operators had been sent away. Finally, 70 technicians had also been sent away for training. They were all scheduled to return to the battalion on 15 June. After that date exercises in platoon and company formations could be initiated. The battalion commander estimated that his unit would be combat ready on 15 July.[5]

In terms of manpower, the unit was almost at full strength on 1 June,[6] even though many of them had been sent away, as indicated above. The availability of tanks was not as bright. Between 20 and 29 May 39 *Tigers* were shipped to the battalion,[7] bringing it up to its authorized strength of 45. On 11 June it was reported to be at full strength.[8] The battalion received no tank replacements during the campaign[9].

Despite the battalion commander's estimate that the battalion would not be combat ready until mid-July, it was ordered to transfer to Normandy in June. On 22 June, eight trains had departed; six of them had reached the area around Paris.[10] One day later, three trains had unloaded west of Paris.[11] The rail transport took several days, and it was not until 2 July that the last train was unloaded (at Versailles).[12] This extended rail transport resulted in the battalion being committed piecemeal which is shown by the battalion's tank strength at various dates:

Date	Number of operational tanks	Tanks in short-term repair	Tanks in long-term repair	On approach march
1 June[13]	28	1	?	?
9 July[14]	25	?	?	10
11 July[15]	14	12	1	11
13 July[16]	10	14	2	11
14 July[17]	19	7	3	10
15 July[18]	19	8	2	?
20 July[19]	17	11	3	10
30 July[20]	30	?	?	?
5 August[21]	20	?	?	?

Date	Number of operational tanks	Tanks in short-term repair	Tanks in long-term repair	On approach march
8 August[22]	21	?	?	?
11 August[23]	7	7	2	?
13 August[24]	15	19	8	?
14 August[25]	14	16	12	?
15 August[26]	7	20	12	?
16 August[27]	5	21	12	?
17 August[28]	5	21	12	?

After having unloaded from the trains at Paris, the battalion had to move the *Tigers* to Normandy.[29] During July, the battalion was with the *II. SS-Panzer-Korps,* usually employed as a substitute for the missing *Panther* battalion in the *10. SS-Panzer-Division "Frundsberg".* It seems that the battalion first went into action on 9 July.[30]

Through 31 July the battalion lost three *Tigers* (complete writeoffs).[31] At the beginning of August the battalion was still with the *II. SS-Panzer-Korps* but, on 9 August, it was sent to the area north of Falaise.[32] It fought successive actions at Espins, Martainville, Falaise and Necy until 18 August.[33] During the retreat from the Falaise pocket the battalion seems to have lost most of its tanks. Several damaged *Tigers* were lost when they had to be blown up on 24 August during the retreat to the Seine.[34] According to a report from the battalion that fell into British hands, the battalion had lost seven Tigers up to 17 August.[35]

---

1   Georg Tessin, *Verbände und Truppen der deutschen Wehrmacht und Waffen-SS* (Mittler & Sohn, Frankfurt am Main (vol 1–5), Biblio Verlag, Osnabrück (vol 6–14) 1966–75), entry for units with number 102).

2   See Verteilung der Panzer-Fahrzeuge, Band ab Mai 1943, BA-MA RH 10/349.

3   Verteilung der Panzer-Fahrzeuge, Band ab Mai 1943, BA-MA RH 10/349.

4   Der Generalinpekteur der Panzertruppen Nr. 032/44 g.Kdos, 3.6.44, T78, R623, F000201.

5   BA-MA RH 10/334.

6   The battalion had an authorized strength of 1,036 men and reported a shortage of 43 men on 1 June 1944 (BA-MA RH 10/334).

7   On 20 May, 18 *Tigers* were sent by rail; on 22 May 6; on 26 May 12; and, on 29 May 3. See Verteilung der Panzer-Fahrzeuge, Band ab Mai 1943, BA-MA RH 10/349.

8   HGr B Ia Entwurf 11.6.44 (OB West Ia, Nr 4470/44 g.Kdos. 11.6.44, T311, R25, F7029465.

9   Verteilung der Panzer-Fahrzeuge, Band ab Mai 1943, BA-MA RH 10/349.

10   OB West Ia Nr. 4858/44 geh.Kdos, den 22.6.44., T311, R25, F7029750.

11   OB West Ia Nr. 4952/44 g.Kdos, 24.6.44, T311, R25, F7029824.

12   West Ia Nr. 5228/44 g.Kdos. 2.7.44, T311, R28, F7034145, but see also OB West Ia Nr. 5152/44 g.Kdos. 30.6.44, T311, R25, F7030013 and OB West Ia Nr. 5185/44 g.Kdos, 1.7.44, T311, R28, F7034124.

13 BA-MA RH 10/334.

14 Pz.Gr. West Ia, Nr. 306/44 geh. von 10.7.1944., Nachtrag zur Tagesmeldung BA-MA RH 21-5/50.

15 Pz.Gr. West Ia, Nr. 361/44 geh. von 12.7.1944., Nachtrag zur Tagesmeldung T313, R420, F8713888.

16 Pz.Gr. West Ia, Nr. 348/44 geh. von 14.7.1944., Nachtrag zur Tagesmeldung T313, R420, F8713904.

17 Pz.Gr. West Ia Nr. (impossible to read), v. 15.7.44, Nachtrag zur Tagesmeldung 14.7, T313, R420, F8713914.

18 Pz.Gr. West Ia Nr. 388/44 g.Kdos 16.7.44, Nachtrag zur Tagesmeldung 15.7, T313, R420, F8713921.

19 Pz.Gr. West Ia, Nr. 491/44 geh. von 21.7.1944., Nachtrag zur Tagesmeldung BA-MA RH 21-5/50.

20 Pz.Gr. West Ia Nr. 665/44 g.Kdos. 31.7.44, Nachtrag zur Tagesmeldung 30.7. T313, R420, F8714049.

21 Pz.Gr. West Ia Nr. 775/44 g.Kdos. 6.8.44, Nachtrag zur Tagesmeldung 5.8, T313, R420, F8714097.

22 Pz.Gr. West Ia Nr. 846/44 g.Kdos. 9.8.44, Nachtrag zur Tagesmeldung 8.8, T313, R420, F8714139.

23 PzAOK 5 Ia Nr. 899/44 g.Kdos, 12.8.44, Nachtrag zur Tagesmeldung 11.8, T313, R420, F8714187. The battalion was at the time subordinated to 271. Inf.Div.

24 According to a report captured by British forces. See 8 Corps "G" Branch 1944 Aug, Sept Intelligence summary no 52, part II, Captured enemy document from 102nd Hvy SS Tank Battalion, Public Record Office, Kew Gardens WO file 171/287.

25 Ibid

26 Ibid

27 Ibid

28 Ibid

29 W. Tieke, *Im Feuersturm letzter Kriegsjahre* (Munin Verlag, Osnabrück 1986) p 115ff.

30 Ibid, p. 152.

31 Anlage 3 zu Gen.Kdo. II. SS-Pz.Korps Qu. Tgb.Nr. 765/44 geh. vom 3.8.44. copy found in LVIII. Pz.Korps Qu Anlagen, T314, R1497, F000430.

32 W. Tieke, *Im Feuersturm letzter Kriegsjahre* (Munin Verlag, Osnabrück 1986) p 233.

33 Ibid, p. 245.

34 Ibid, p. 275.

35 According to a report captured by British forces. See 8 Corps "G" Branch 1944 Aug, Sept Intelligence summary no 52, part II, Captured enemy document from 102nd Hvy SS Tank Battalion, Public Record Office, Kew Gardens WO file 171/287.

Panzer-Abteilung 206

Panzer-Abteilung 206 was formed in December 1943 for the *7. Armee*.[1] It was located west of Cherbourg on 5 June.[2] On 1 April 1944 the battalion had a strength of 385 men and the following armored fighting vehicles:[3] 28 Hotchkiss'; 10 Somuas; 6 B 2's; and, 2 R 35's.

On 10 June it was reported that the battalion possessed 46 captured tanks,[4] a number identical to that on 1 April. It was suggested that 10 of the battalion's Hotchkiss tanks should be exchanged with 10 Somuas from the *21. Panzer-Division*,[5] but whether this was actually done is unclear. The battalion was among the units isolated in the Cherbourg area.[6] It was subsequently destroyed and never rebuilt.[7]

---

1   G. Tessin, *Verbände und Truppen der deutschen Wehrmacht und Waffen-SS* (Mittler & Sohn, Frankfurt am Main and Biblio Verlag, Osnabrück 1966–75).

2   Lagekarte AOK 7 5.6.1944, BA-MA RH 20-7/138K.

3   Gliederungen der AOK 7, Kleinere Verbände im Ber. LXXXIV A.K., T312, R1566, F000214.

4   Im Westen vorhandene gepanzerte Kraftfahrzeuge, Stand 10.6.44, BA-MA RH 10/90.

5   Gliederungen der AOK 7, Kleinere Verbände im Ber. LXXXIV A.K., T312, R1566, F000214.

6   Kriegsgliederungen zum KTB in der Führungsabteilung AOK 7 6.6.44 – 30.6.44, T312, R1566, F000002-000025.

7   Tessin, op. cit.

Sturmpanzer-Abteilung 217

This unit was unique in Normandy, since it was the only unit equipped with the *Sturmpanzer IV*. With its short 15 cm howitzer in a box-like superstructure, the *Sturmpanzer IV* was a very specialized vehicle. The low muzzle velocity of the weapon made it unsuitable against enemy tanks, but it was quite effective against other targets.

The battalion had a TOE strength of three companies with 14 vehicles each and three *Sturmpanzer IV* in the battalion staff. This is similar to the organization of *Sturmpanzer-Abteilung 216*, first employed at the battle at Kursk 1943 and also similar to the organization of the *Tiger* battalions.

At the end of June the unit was still located in Grafenwöhr, Germany.[1] On 24 June it was intended to send the battalion to the Conde — Le Beny Bocage — Vire area in Normandy.[2] The battalion still had not arrived by 18 July.[3] It appears the battalion was never employed in Normandy as a complete unit; it also does not appear that it had its full complement of *Sturmpanzer IV's*.

On 21 July one company (probably the *2./Sturmpanzer-Abteilung 217)* had arrived in the area of operations of the *21. Panzer-Division*.[4] Two days later, the *2./Sturmpanzer-Abteilung 217* was attached to the *21. Panzer-Division*.[5] On 24 July, the company had 11 *Sturmpanzer IV's* operational and 2 in short-term repair.[6] Later, on 29 July, the company was attached to the *1. SS-Panzer-Division "Leibstandarte"*. One day later its strength stood at 9 vehicles operational and 2 in short-term repair.[7]

The first document found where the *3./Sturmpanzer-Abteilung 217* is mentioned is dated 30 July. It is stated that the company was transferring from the *II. SS-Panzer-Korps* area to the *LXXIV. Korps*.[8] The *2./Sturmpanzer-Abteilung 217* remained with the *1. SS-Panzer-Division "Leibstandarte"* and had 10 *Sturmpanzer IV's* operational on 31 July.[9] That number was unchanged on 1 August,[10] but had risen to 12 on 3 August,[11] when the company was still in support of the *"Leibstandarte"*.[12] Both strength and location were unchanged on 4 August.[13]

On 6 August the *2./Sturmpanzer-Abteilung 217* was with the *II. SS-Panzer-Korps* and had 3 *Sturmpanzer IV's* operational.[14] At the same rime, 13 *Sturmpanzer IV's* were with the *89. Infanterie-Division*.[15] Three days later 10 were operational with the 12 SS-Panzer-Division "Hitlerjugend" and just one with the *89. Infanterie-Division*[16]. This shrunk to just 5 operational *Sturmpanzer IV's* with the *"Hitlerjugend"* on 10 August.[17] On 11 August the situation remained unchanged.[18] On the same day, it was also reported the *1./Sturmpanzer-Abteilung 217* was attached to the *271. Infanterie-Division*.[19]

From that date on no mention is made of the battalion in staff reports emanating from Western Europe. This should not be interpreted as indicating that the unit did not take part in the fighting, however, since higher command echelons usually did not deal with smaller units than divisions. Furthermore, the excellent daily reports on tank strength found in *Panzergruppe West/5. Panzer-Armee* records only cover the period up to 11 August. On 4 September *Sturmpanzer-Abteilung 217* was still committed.[20]

One report referencing the battalion and dated 16 August has been found among the files of the Inspector-General of Panzer Troops. According to it the battalion had 17 operational *Sturmpanzer IV's* and 14 in short-term repair (within three weeks). The casualties from 1–15 August amounted to 10 killed in action, 33 wounded and 12 missing. The authorized manpower strength was 772 men, but it was short 69 men.[21]

The *2./Sturmpanzer-Abteilung 217* clearly took part in the battle, but the whereabouts of the other two companies is unclear. Only on 30 July is the *3./Sturmpanzer-Abteilung 217* explicitly mentioned. On 6 August *Sturmpanzer IV's* were found with both the *12. SS-Panzer-Division "Hitlerjugend"* and the *89. Infanterie-Division,* which might mean that two companies were present. However, these two divisions were quite close at the time and it is not inconceivable that they came from the same company. The total number of *Sturmpanzer IV's* with these two divisions was 16, which exceeds the strength of a company, but it is also possible that the battalion staff was in Normandy (with its three TOE-allocated *Sturmpanzer IV's*). Whatever the truth, the number of *Sturmpanzer IV's* employed was certainly small. As indicated by the table below, only 28 *Sturmpanzer IV's* were delivered before the end of the campaign in Normandy.

On 1 October, the battalion had a strength of 603 men, while casualties during September were 13 killed, 57 wounded and 53 missing.[22] Only 11 men had arrived at the battalion as replacements and 36 men had left the battalion for other reasons (non-casualties).[23] This indicates that the battalion had more than 700 men on 1 September, which means that it was far from destroyed.

The deliveries of *Sturmpanzer IV's* to the battalion were:[24]

24 May	19 *Sturmpanzer IV's*
25 June	2 *Sturmpanzer IV's*
10 July	7 *Sturmpanzer IV's*
18 August (arrived at the battalion 5 September)	10 *Sturmpanzer IV's*
16 September (arrived at the battalion 17 September)	10 *Sturmpanzer IV's*
26 September	4 *Sturmpanzer IV's*

On 1 October the battalion had 14 combat-ready *Sturmpanzer IV's,* while 5 were in short-term repair. The number in long-term repair is not known.[25]

---

1   Gen.Inp.d.Pz.Tr. Org.Abt. (III) Nr. 7557/44 geh 28.6, BA-MA RH 10/70.
2   Ob.West Ia Nr. 4927/44 geh.Kdos. 24.6.44, T311, R25, F7029822.

3   Gliederung Pz.Gr. West 18.7.44, BA-MA RH 21-5/50.

4   Pz.Gruppe West Ia Nr. 517/44 g.Kdos. v. 21.7.44., BA-MA RH 21-5/50.

5   Pz.Gr. West Ia, Nr. 557/44 geh. von 25.7.1944., Nachtrag zur Tagesmeldung 24.7., BA-MA RH 21-5/50.

6   Ibid.

7   Pz.Gr. West Ia Nr. 665/44 g.Kdos, 31.7.44, Nachtrag zur Tagesmeldung 30.7, T313, R420, F8714049

8   Pz.Gr. West Ia Nr. 665/44 g.Kdos, 31.7.44, Nachtrag zur Tagesmeldung 30.7, T313, R420, F8714049.

9   Pz.Gr. West Ia, Nr. 678/44 geh. von 1.8.1944., Nachtrag zur Tagesmeldung 31.7., BA-MA RH 21-5/50.

10 Pz.Gr. West Ia, Nr. 704/44 geh. von 2.8.1944., Nachtrag zur Tagesmeldung 1.8., T313, R420, F8714069.

11 Pz.Gr. West Ia, Nr. 734/44 geh. von 4.8.1944., Nachtrag zur Tagesmeldung 3.8., BA-MA RH 21-5/50.

12 Ibid.

13 Pz.Gr. West Ia, Nr. 758/44 geh. von 5.8.1944., Nachtrag zur Tagesmeldung 4.8., T313, R420, F8714096.

14 Pz.Gr. West Ia Nr. 801/44 g.Kdos, 7.8.44, Nachtrag zur Tagesmeldung 6.8, T313, R420, F8714118f.

15 Ibid.

16 Pz.Gr. West Ia Nr. 853/44 g.Kdos, 10.8.44, Nachtrag zur Tagesmeldung 9.8, T313, R420, F87141177.

17 Pz.Gr. West Ia Nr. 890/44 g.Kdos, 11.8.44, Nachtrag zur Tagesmeldung 10.8, T313, R420, F87141181.

18 Pz.Gr. West Ia Nr. 899/44 g.Kdos, 12.8.44, Nachtrag zur Tagesmeldung 11.8, T313, R420, F87141187.

19 PzAOK 5 Ia Nr 899/44 g.Kdos vom 12.8.44, T313, R420, F8714187.

20 Obkdo.H.Gr.B. Ia Nr. 6917/44 g.Kdos, 4.9.44, T313, R420, F8714263.

21 Report from 217. Stu.Pz.Abt. to the Generalinspekteur der Panzertruppe 16.8.44, BA-MA RH 10/219.

22 Gen.Kdo LXXXI. A.K., Zustandberichte T314, R1597, F000066

23 Ibid.

24 Lieferungen der Panzerfahrzeuge, Bd. ab Mai 1943, BA-MA RH 10/349.

25 Gen.Kdo LXXXI. A.K., Zustandberichte T314, R1597, F000066.

Panzer-Abteilung 301 (Funklenk)

This unit has sometimes erroneously been assumed to have taken part in the Normandy campaign. It was, however, not far from being committed to the battle. On 18 May the battalion was located near Avesnes.[1] It was at full strength, with four companies totaling 1,085 men.[2] Orders were issued on 3 June instructing the battalion to depart for the Eastern Front on 5 June.[3] This did not include the fourth company, which was to remain in France.[4] It was intended to use the company as a cadre for the forming of *Panzer-Abteilung 302 (Funklenk)*.[5]

The *4./Panzer-Abteilung 301 (Funklenk)* did not join *Panzer-Abteilung 302 (Funklenk)*, however. It fought with the *2. Panzer-Division* in Normandy.[6] On 1 June 1944 this company had two *Panzer III's,* six *Sturmgeschütz III's* and 36 *B IV* remote-controlled vehicles.[7] Given the strength of the entire battalion, it can be assumed that the company had 200–250 men.

---

1   Anlage zu HGr D Ia Nr. 315/44 g.Kdos, 18.5.44, T312, R1563, F000613.

2   Status report to the Inspector-General of Panzer Troops, Stand 1.6.44, BA-MA RH 10/219.

3   Abschriften KTB mit Anlagen 1.6. - 15.6.44, HGr B, BA-MA RH 19 IX/93. See also OB West Ia Nr. 4253/44 g.Kdos, 2.6.44, T311, R24, F7029065.

4   Ibid.

5   OB West Ia/Pz.Offz. Nr. 954/44 g.Kdos BA-MA RH 21-5/50.

6   See OKH/GenStdH/Org.Abt. u. Gen.Insp. d. Pz. Tr./Org II Nr. 1669/44 g.K. v. 2.7.44, BA-MA RH 10/20 and Pz.Gr. West Ia Nr. 572/44 g.Kdos., 26.7.44, Nachtrag zur Tagesmeldung 25.7, BA-MA RH 21-5/50.

7   Status report from the *2. Panzer-Division* to the Inspector-General of Panzer Troops, Stand 1.6.44, BA-MA RH 10/141.

Panzer-Abteilung 302 (Funklenk)

When the Allied forces landed in France, this battalion was still forming. It was intended to use three existing companies to form the new battalion. These were the *4./Panzer-Abteilung 301 (Funklenk)* and two separate companies, *Panzer-Kompanien 315* and *317 (Funklenk)*.[1] On 10 June the battalion had ten *Sturmgeschütz III's*.[2]

The *4./Panzer-Abteilung 301 (Funklenk)* fought with the *2. Panzer-Division* and, on 2 July, it was decided to let the company remain with the division and use *Panzer-Kompanie 316 (Funklenk)* instead.[3] At that moment, the company was with the *Panzer-Lehr-Division* at the front.[4] The battalion never fought in Normandy. It was located near Vouziers on 5 August and, even at that date, it was still not decided to commit it.[5] Eventually, in mid-August, it was sent to Warsaw.[6]

---

1   OB West Ia/Pz.Offz. Nr. 954/44 g.Kdos BA-MA RH 21-5/50.
2   Im Westen vorhandene gepanzerte Kraftfahrzeuge, Stand 10.6.44, BA-MA RH 10/90.
3   OKH/GenStdH/Org.Abt. u. Gen.Insp. d. Pz. Tr./Org II Nr. 1669/44 g.K. v. 2.7.44, BA-MA RH 10/20.
4   Ibid.
5   PzAOK 5 Ia Nr. 753/44 g.Kdos, 5.8.44, T313, R420, F8714098.
6   T. Jentz, *Panzertruppen, Vol 2* (Schiffer, Atglen 1996) p. 175.

schwere Panzer-Abteilung 503

The battalion had been employed on the Eastern Front since the winter of 1942–43. It took part in the battle at Kursk and was continually engaged from that point on. In the spring of 1944, the battalion was withdrawn to Germany for rest and refitting. It had no tanks on 1 June 1944.[1] Deliveries took place during June, however. The following shipments of Tigers were sent to the battalion:[2]

11 June: 6 *Tiger I's*
12 June: 11 *Tiger I's* and 12 *Tiger II's*
14 June: 6 *Tiger I's*
15 June: 5 *Tiger I's*
17 June: 5 *Tiger I's*

The *Tiger II* tanks were all found in the 1./schwere Panzer-Abteilung 503.[3]

Since the battalion was still in Germany, where the rail net was still in relatively good condition, the *Tigers* probably arrived within a day or two. On 12 June, *OB West* reported that the battalion would be transferred to Normandy.[4] Ten days later, the battalion was described as the best and most experienced Tiger battalion in the German Army.[5] It was reported to be in transit to *Panzergruppe West* on 28 June.[6] Two days later, two of the trains transporting the battalion had reached Dreux, while the remaining six were between Toul and Paris.[7]

All trains had reached Dreux by 5 July, where the battalion had unloaded.[8] By 10 July the battalion had arrived at the *LXXXVI. Korps* area of operations.[9] It seems, however, that at least four *Tigers* were still missing at that date, since the battalion reported 41 *Tigers* on 11 July and 45 two days later.[10] The battalion remained with the *LXXXVI. Korps* until 23 July, when it was decided to shift the battalion to the *I. SS-Panzer-Korps*.[11]

During July the battalion's casualties amounted to 26 killed, 31 wounded and 18 missing.[12] On 1 August the authorized strength of the unit was 873 officers and men, plus 90 HiWi (Eastern volunteers).[13] It reported a shortage of SO officers and men.[14] The unit was also short 64 HiWi.[15] During July the battalion had received no replacements at all.[16]

The losses suffered by the battalion were to a large extent incurred by the *3./ schwere Panzer-Abteilung 503*. On 18 July alone, that company lost 14 men killed. Subsequently, the *3. Kompanie* handed over its remaining *Tiger I* tanks to the *2./ schwere Panzer-Abteilung 503* on 20 July and its men went to Mailly-le-Camp to reequip with *Tiger II* ranks.[17] The exact number of *Tigers* lost by the battalion is unclear, but it seems that up until 27 July 33 *Tigers* were complete write-offs, for all units in Normandy.[18]

Fourteen *Tiger II's* were dispatched to the battalion from 27–29 July.[19] The tanks arrived during the first week of August. On 11 August the company left Mailly by rail. It did not arrive in time for the Falaise battle.[20]

The two companies that remained in Normandy endured the Falaise battle. It is known that the *1. Kompanie* blew up four of its *Tigers* on 18 August and a further two on 20 August.[21] Most of the other tanks were lost during the retreat due to lack of fuel, mechanical breakdowns or lack of ferries to take such heavy vehicles over rivers like the Seine.

Tank Strength of *schwere Panzer-Abteilung 503* during the Campaign:

Date	Number of tanks operational	Tanks in short-term repair	Tanks in long-term repair
11 July[22]	23	3	15
13 July[23]	32	13	0
16 July[24]	40	?	?
17 July[25]	39	1	5
18 July (evening)[26]	9	?	?
25 July[27]	20	8	?
27 July[28]	20	4	?
28 July[29]	14	?	?
29 July[30]	15	7	?
1 August[31]	13	16	?
6 August[32]	11	?	?

---

1   Lieferungen der Pz-Fahrz. Bd. ab Mai 1943, BA-MA RH 10/349.

2   Ibid.

3   A. Rubbel, *Erinnerungen an die Tiger-Abteilung 503 1942–1945* (Bassum 1990) p. 266.

4   OB West Ia Nr 4521/44 g.Kdos, 12.6.44, T311, R25, F7029499.

5   Ferngespräche und Besprechungen AOK 7 Ia, Besprechung mit Gen.Maj. Tomale 22.6.44, T312, R1566, F000313.

6   Pz.Gr. West Ia, Nr 24/44 g.Kdos, Nachtrag zur Tagesmeldung 29.6.44, BA-MA RH 21-5/50.

7   OB West Ia Nr. 5152/44 g.Kdos. 30.6.44, T311, R25, F7030013.

8   OB West Ia Nr. 5323/44 g.Kdos., 5.7.44, T311, R28, F7034222.

9   HGr B Ia Tagesmeldung 10.7.44, BA-MA RH 19 IX/9a.

10 Pz.Gr. West Ia, Nr. 361/44 geh. von 12.7.1944., Nachtrag zur Tagesmeldung 11.7., T313, R420, F8713888. and Pz.Gr. West Ia, Nr. 348/44 geh. v. 14.7.44, Nachtrag zur Tagesmeldung 13.7., T313, R420, F8713903.

11 Pz.Gr. West Ia, Nr. 535/44 geh. von 23.7.1944., Nachtrag zur Tagesmeldung 22.7., BA-MA RH 21-5/50.

12 Monthly reports from *schwere Panzer-Abteilung 503* to the Inspector-General of Armored Troops, file BA-MA RH 10/220.

13 Ibid.

14 Ibid.

15 Ibid.

16 Ibid.

17 Rubbel, op. cit. p. 284

18 HGr. B Ia, 1. Anlage zu Tgb Nr. 1281/44 geh. O.U. den 29. Juli 1944, BA-MA RH 19 IX/46. I have reasons to believe the document contins a typo, where 23 was accidentally written instead of 33.

19 Lieferungen der Pz-Fahrz. Bd. ab Mai 1943, BA-MA RH 10/349.

20 Rubbel, op. cit., p. 293ff.

21 Ibid, p. 289f

22 Pz.Gr. West Ia, Nr. 361/44 geh. von 12.7.1944., Nachtrag zur Tagesmeldung 11.7., T313, R420, F8713888.

23 Pz.Gr. West Ia, Nr. 348/44 geh. v. 14.7.44, Nachtrag zur Tagesmeldung 13.7., T313, R420, F8713903.

24 Pz.Gr. West Ia, Nr. 424/44 geh. von 17.7.1944., Nachtrag zur Tagesmeldung 16.7., BA-MA RH 21-5/50.

25 Pz.Gr. West Ia Nr. 479/44 geheim von 18.7.44, Nachtrag zur Tagesmeldung 17.7.44, BA-MA RH 21-5/50.

26 OB West Ia Nr. 5814/44 g.Kdos, 19.7.44, T78, R313, F6265849.

27 Pz.Gr. West Ia, Nr. 572/44 geh. von 26.7.1944., Nachtrag zur Tagesmeldung 25.7., BA-MA RH 21-5/50.

28 Pz.Gr. West Ia, Nr. 605/44 geh. von 27.7.1944., Nachtrag zur Tagesmeldung 28.7., BA-MA RH 21-5/50.

29 Pz.Gr. West Ia Nr. 633/44 g.Kdos, 29.7.44, Nachtrag zur Tagesmeldung 28.7, T313, R420, F8714036.

30 Pz.Gr. West Ia Nr. 647/44 g.Kdos, 30.7.44, Nachtrag zur Tagesmeldung 29.7, T313, R420, F8714042.

31 Status report to the Inspector-General of Panzer Troops, Stand 1.8.44, BA-MA RH 10/220.

32 Pz.Gr. West Ia, Nr. 801/44 geh. von 7.8.1944., Nachtrag zur Tagesmeldung 6.8., T313, R420, F8714118.

schwere Panzerjäger-Abteilung 654

Formed before the outbreak of the war, this battalion took part in the campaign in Poland in 1939, the defeat of Holland, Belgium and France in 1940 and in Operation *Barbarossa*. In 1942 it received the new 7.5 cm *Pak* 40 AT gun and, in 1943, it was equipped with the *Ferdinand* tank destroyer and was part of the *9. Armee* in the battle of Kursk.

Later it transferred its *Ferdinands* to *schwere Panzer-Jäger-Abteilung 653*. It was intended to have all three companies equipped with the new *Jagdpanther* tank destroyer. These arrived slowly, however. On 28 April eight were transported by rail to the battalion.[1] These were the only vehicles that arrived for a long time. As late as 11 June 1944 it still had only one partially equipped company with the total number of *Jagdpanthers* unchanged.[2] It was intended to send the company to Normandy.[3] On 14 June, however, trains with another 17 *Jagdpanthers* were dispatched to the battalion,[4] even though it is unclear when they arrived. Two days prior to that — 12 June 1944 — *OB West* had recommended a company with the eight available *Jagdpanthers* should be sent to *Sturmgeschütz-Lehr-Brigade 902* in the Valognes area south of Cherbourg.[5] This recommendation was overcome by events and, on 19 June, its new destination was the *Panzer-Lehr-Division*.[6] According to Ritgen, the company was attached to the division from 27–29 June.[7] After that, it was under the operational control of *Panzergruppe West*.[8]

On 1 July the unit had 25 operational vehicles,[9] indicating the dispatched trains had arrived. However, most of the vehicles were probably still at Mailly-le-Camp.

The *2./schwere Panzer-Jäger-Abteilung 654* seems to have been the first unit to arrive in Normandy, since it was reported to be present within the area of operations of *Panzergruppe West* with the *XLVII. Panzer-Korps* on 18 July, while the remainder of the battalion was said to be on its way.[10] One further company — the *3./schwere Panzer-Jäger-Abteilung 654* — must have arrived somewhat later, since the elements of the battalion at *Panzergruppe West* reported 21 *Jagdpanthers* operational, 3 in short-term repair and 1 in long term-repair on 28 July.[11] This makes for a total of 25 vehicles with the unit, a number that coincides exactly with the number dispatched, as indicated above. This means that all dispatched vehicles had arrived with the unit at the front and none had been lost.

On 1 August it was reported that the battalion had 8 operational *Jagdpanzer V's*, while 13 were in short-term repair and 3 in long-term repair.[12] Two had been total losses during July as had one *Befehlspanzer V*. Casualties during July amounted to 11 men.[13] The *1./schwere Panzerjäger-Abteilung 654* remained at Mailly-le-Camp without any *Jagdpanthers*.[14]

The final deliveries of *Jagdpanthers* to the battalion were 8 vehicles on 31 July and another 8 on 14 August.[15] The latter eight would have been hard pressed to have been employed in the battle in. Normandy, but those dispatched at the end of July may have arrived at the large tank training facility at Mailly-le-Camp, east of Paris. The *1./schwere Panzer-Jäger-Abteilung 654* was still there, and it was recommended the company be sent to Normandy on 10 August.[16]

For this unit, a copy of the war diary has survived, something which is unusual for German battalion sized units.[17] The following is based on the detailed war diary of the 654. *Jagdpanther* battalion.

When it started moving towards Normandy, the battalion had 25 *Jagdpanthers*. On 27 July, three command *Panthers* and one *Jagdpanther* arrived at the battalion. They first had to be checked by the workshops and on 29 July they were ready for action.

Marching to Normandy took its toll of the battalion. There were several air attacks, which caused losses in the battalion, but none of the *Jagdpanthers* were destroyed. However, many *Jagdpanthers* suffered mechanical breakdowns. During the march (approx. 300 kilometers) the following cases of damage was recorded: 18 final drives (a well-known problem), two engines, 2 oil coolers, 3 cooling fans, 1 torsion bar, 4 road wheels, 1 drive shaft, 4 drive sprockets, 2 idler wheels and 109 track links.

The result was that on 17 July, the battalion had 8 operational *Jagdpanthers*, 16 in short repair and 1 in long repair. Efforts by the repair and recovery services raised the operational readiness to 23 *Jagdpanther* on 30 July, 2 in long repair and 1 long repair. This includes one additional *Jagdpanther* that arrived on this day. Until 26 July, the following damage had been caused by enemy action: 1 gear box, 4 radiators, 1 oil cooler, 4 cooling fans, 6 drive sprockets, 2 final drives, and 16 road wheels.

It is unclear how many vehicles that were damaged up to this point, as single vehicles could have suffered more than one kind of damage. For example, a hit on a tank could cause damage to more than one road wheel. Before 31 July, no *Jagdpanthers* were completely lost.

The 2nd Company arrived ahead of the rest of the battalion at the front in Normandy and it reported 6 operational *Jagdpanthers* on 7 July, when it was attached to the *Panzer-Lehr* division. It was however transferred to 276th ID when *Panzer-Lehr* left its sector. When moving on July 8, four *Jagdpanthers* broke down. Two more broke down on 9 July, but four were also repaired. On 11 July, one *Jagdpanther* was penetrated in the left side armor and three crew members were wounded, but no other damage was recorded. Also, another *Jagdpanther* was penetrated (does not say from which direction). The loader was killed and the commander, driver and gunner were wounded. The crew still managed to drive the tank into safety.

At least one *Jagdpanther* was repaired by the company between 12 and 17 July.

Given the increase in operational *Jagdpanthers* from 17–29 July at least 14 must have been repaired. At least five were repaired by 2nd Company before 17 July. So far there are indications of 19 repairs. However, there were further *Jagdpanthers* damaged between 18 and 29 July. On 20 July, two were damaged by enemy artillery fire and classified as short repair. Two days later, a periscope on one *Jagdpanther* was destroyed by enemy artillery fire. On 26 July one *Jagdpanther* caught fire in the engine room, not by enemy action. Vehicle classified as short repair. Four days later, one *Jagdpanther* was damaged by artillery fire and classified as short repair.

There were at least five vehicles damaged in this period when the operational readiness rose thanks to the efforts of the mechanics. We can conclude that at least 24 had been repaired before 31 July. But this cannot possibly account for all vehicles damaged Also, it is clear that the kind of damage sustained thus far was of a kind that ought to be repaired and it can safely be assumed that more than 100% of its *Jagdpanthers* had been in repair and not a single one had been lost.

At the end of July, mounting enemy pressure would push the battalion back and from then *Jagdpanthers* would start to become complete losses. The first took place on 31 July, when the final drives of Lt. Scheiber's *Jagdpanther* were damaged. The vehicle could not be recovered due to strong enemy artillery fire and lack of towing vehicles. It was blown up by the crew on 2 August. On 31 July, another 11 *Jagdpanthers* were damaged, but all of them were short time damage.

On 1 August, the number of *Jagdpanthers* in long term repair increased from 1 to 3 and that number remained constant until August 13. From 31 July 31 to 2 August, the number of tanks in short repair shrunk by 4, suggesting at least that many were repaired. On 5 August, the number in short repair was 17, but it shrunk to 13 on 6 July, again suggesting that 4 were repaired. Indeed, one of the Kampfgruppen was notified that it could expect to receive three *Jagdpanthers* from the workshops in the night or on 6 August.

From 7 August onwards, the number of *Jagdpanther* in short repair increased. On 14 August, 17 *Jagdpanther* were in short repair, but it was noted that spare parts had to be brought up to repair them. At this point the German supply situation in general was desperate, which meant that the arrival of spare parts was not very likely. The battalion was ordered to pull out and bring its vehicles in workshops along. Thus far, seven tanks had been irretrievably lost (including one confiscated by an SS-units and whose fate was unknown).

During all of August, the following complete losses (including command tanks) were recorded, by cause (including Scheiber's *Jagdpanther* mentioned above):

Mechanical damage, tank blown up by crew: 12
Destroyed by AT fire: 2
Stuck in terrain, could not move, subsequently hit by enemy tank, burnt out: 1
Destroyed by HE or phosphorus rounds: 2
Damaged by enemy fire and blown up by crew since it could not be recovered: 2
Confiscated by SS-unit, unknown fate: 1
Lack of fuel, blown up by crew: 1
Carpet bombing at Rouen: 1

Up to 5 August we know of at least 32 cases when tanks in the battalion were repaired, which can be contrasted to 7 cases of complete losses. Obviously, this includes vehicles that suffered technical damage during the approach march, but is must also be noted that all cases of damage are not mentioned by the war diary. In August, there are a few cases noted:

4 August: Unspecified number of *Jagdpanther* damaged by artillery fire.
5 August: One *Jagdpanther* damaged during march, short term repair.
10 August: One *Jagdpanther* damaged during march, short term repair.
12 August: 1 gun barrel damaged by enemy artillery fire.
13 August: 1 case of final drive failure
14 August: 2 damaged by artillery fire.

Given the data available, exact percentage calculations are perhaps not so meaningful, but it is clear that before the battalion began to pull out, the damage received was usually of such character that it is to be expected that it will be repaired.

What is also interesting is that losses due to presence of enemy ground combat units, or in some cases artillery fire, caused the Germans to blow up many *Jagdpanthers*. In fact, more than half the losses occurred in this way, which highlights the importance of controlling the ground.

Few *Jagdpanthers* were penetrated by AT rounds and in two of the cases, the vehicles could be repaired. Furthermore, the effects of artillery fire should not be neglected. Although a HE round is not likely to destroy a heavy tank, it may well (as is evident from several instances mentioned in the war diary) cause damage to the tank and if ground units are close enough, the tank will not be recovered.

Date	Number of tanks operational	Tanks in Short-Term repair	Tanks in Long-Term repair
17 July	8	16	1
18 July	8	16	1
19 July	10	14	1
20 July	10	14	1
21 July	13	11	1
22 July	15	9	1
23 July	15	9	1
24 July	17	7	1
25 July	19	5	1
26 July	19	5	1
27 July	20	4	1

Date	Number of tanks operational	Tanks in Short-Term repair	Tanks in Long-Term repair
28 July	20	4	1
29 July	21	4	1
30 July	23 + 3 Bef.Wg	2	1
31 July	11 + 3 Bef.Wg	14	1
1 Aug	10 + 2 Bef.Wg	13	3
2 Aug	12	10	3
3 Aug	6	14	3
4 Aug	4	16	3
5 Aug	3	17	3
6 Aug	7	13	3
7 Aug	5 + 1 Bef.Wg.	13+ 1 Bef.Wg.	3
8 Aug	4 + 1 Bef.Wg.	14+ 1 Bef.Wg.	3
9 Aug	3 + 1 Bef.Wg.	15+ 1 Bef.Wg.	3
10 Aug	3 + 2 Bef.Wg.	15	3
11 Aug	3 + 2 Bef.Wg.	15	3
12 Aug	2 +1 Bef.Wg.	16	3
13 Aug	1 +1 Bef.Wg.	17	3

Casualties in July amounted to 5 killed in action, 27 wounded and 3 missing. Casualties in August amounted to 12 killed in action, 84 wounded and 11 missing.

---

1 Verteilung der Pz.-Fahrz. Bd. ab Mai 43, page 259, BA-MA RH 10/349.
2 OB West Ia, Nr 4470/44 g.Kdos. 11.6.44, T311, R25, F7029472.
3 Ibid.
4 Verteilung der Pz.-Fahrz. Bd. ab Mai 43, page 257f, BA-MA RH 10/349.
5 OB West Ia Nr 4521/44 g.Kdos, 12.6.44, T311, R25, F7029499.
6 OB West Ia Nr. 4739/44 g.Kdos, 19.6.44, T311, R25, F7029652.
7 H. Ritgen, *Die Gechichte der Panzer-Lehr-Division im Westen 1944-1945* (Motorbuch Verlag, Stuttgart 1979) pp. 145 and 317.
8 Pz.Gr. West Ia, Nr 24/44 g.Kdos, Nachtrag zur Tagesmeldung 29.6.44, BA-MA RH 21-5/50.
9 Report from 654. s.Pz.Jg.Abt. to th Generalinspekteur der Panzertruppe, 1.7.1944 BA-MA RH 10/246.
10 Gliederung Pz.Gr. West 18.7.44, BA-MA RH 21-5/50.
11 Pz.Gr. West Ia Nr. 633/44 g.Kdos, 29.7.44, Nachtrag zur Tagesmeldung 28.7, T313, R420, F8714036.
12 Report from 654. s.Pz.Jg.Abt. to th Generalinspekteur der Panzertruppe, 1.8.1944, BA-MA RH 10/246.
13 Ibid.

14 Ibid.

15 Verteilung der Pz.-Fahrz. Bd. ab Mai 43, page 256, BA-MA RH 10/349.

16 OB West Ia Nr. 6714/44 g.Kdos. 10.8.44, Fernschreiben an OKH, T78, R313, F6265974.

17 The war diary was kept by one of the veterans of the battalion and Karl-Heinz Münch has provided me with a copy of it.

Panzerjäger-Abteilung 657

The battalion had been formed in November 1943 to act as a staff for *Panzerjäger-Kompanie 612, Panzerjäger-Kompanie 613* and *Panzer-Kompanie 224.* It was located in the Netherlands.[1] It was still there on 18 May 1944.[2] The fact that the battalion had been formed from three separate companies was reflected in its equipment, which remained a hodgepodge. On 1 June 1944 it reported the following:[3]

13 combat-ready Char B2's and four in maintenance facilities
2 Somua tanks
6 4.7 cm *Pak (t)* on self-propelled chassis
9 7.5 cm *Pak 40*
6 5 cm *Pak 38*
6 8.8 cm *Pak 43/41*

It had an authorized strength of 733, but it was short 131 men. It was considered by the battalion commander to be combat ready for defensive operations.[4] Some men also seem to have remained in the Netherlands, since only 480 men accompanied the battalion when it left for Normandy on 11 June.[5] All the trains had departed by that date.[6] It took some time for the battalion to get into the line, but on 24 June it was deployed in the St. Lo area.[7]

One explanation for the long delay is that the battalion had to exchange part of its equipment. The Somuas and Char B2's were discarded and replaced by 7.5 cm Pak 40's. Fifteen such guns were on their way to the battalion but had not yet arrived on 27 June.[8]

On 12 July, the battalion was subordinated to 17. SS-Pz.Gren.Div, but detailed to cooperate with 2. SS-Pz.Div.[9]

Further information about its activities in Normandy has not been found. The battalion was disbanded on 14 October 1944.[10]

---

1   G. Tessin, *Verbände und Truppen der deutschen Wehrmacht und Waffen-SS* (Mittler & Sohn, Frankfurt am Main and Biblio Verlag, Osnabrück 1966–1975).

2   Anlage zu HGr D Ia Nr. 315/44 g.Kdos, 18.5.44, T312, R1563, F000614.

3   Status report to the Inspector-General of Panzer Troops, Stand 1.6.44, BA-MA RH 10/246.

4   Ibid.

5   Der Kommandierende General und Befehlshaber der Truppen des Heeres in den Niederlanden (Gen.Kdo. LXXXVIII. A.K.) Ia Nr. 2467/44 g.Kdos., 30.8.44, T314, R1626, F000481.

6   OB West Ia 4487/44 g.Kdos., 11.6.44, T311, R25, F7029461.

7   KTB AOK 7 Ia Anlagen 24.6.44, Stand der Aufmarschbewegungen (24.6), T312, R1565, F001298.

8   AOK 7 Ia 27.6.44, BA-MA RH 20-7/135.

9   17. *SS-Panzergrenadier-Division*. Ia Nr. 442/44 g.Kdos., 12.7.44, in M. Wind & H. Günther, Kriegstagebuch Götz von Berlichingen, Auswahl von Dokumenten.

10   Tessin, op. cit.

Panzerjäger-Abteilung 688

The battalion was formed in December 1943 in the West.[1] On 18 May 1944 it was located near Zeebrügge in Belgium.[2] The battalion had towed antitank guns and, on 1 June, it had its full complement of thirty-six 8.8 cm *Pak 43/41* guns in three companies.[3] Personnel strength amounted to 691 men and mobility was rated to be at 100%.[4] The battalion commander considered his unit to be at full combat readiness.[5]

One month later, on 1 July, the situation for the battalion was unchanged. It remained under control of the *15. Armee.*[6] Finally, on 28 July, it was decided to transfer the battalion to Normandy.[7] The unit was to be transported to Normandy by rail and, on 2 August, it was loaded on trains.[8] On 4 August the *1./Panzerjäger-Abteilung 668* arrived at the *II. SS-Panzer-Korps.*[9] Further information on the activities of the battalion has not been found. The unit was disbanded in the autumn of 1944.[10]

---

1   G. Tessin, *Verbände und Truppen der deutschen Wehrmacht und Waffen-SS* (Mittler & Sohn, Frankfurt am Main and Biblio Verlag, Osnabrück 1966–1975).
2   Anlage zu HGr D Ia Nr. 315/44 g.Kdos, 18.5.44, T312, R1563, F000613.
3   Report to the Inspector-General of Panzer Troops, Stand 1.6.44, BA-MA RH 10/247.
4   Ibid.
5   Ibid.
6   Report to the Inspector-General of Panzer Troops, Stand 1.7.44, BA-MA RH 10/247.
7   HGr B Ia Nr. 5273/44 g.Kdos v. 28.7.44, BA-MA RH 21-5/50.
8   HGr B Ia Tagesmeldung 2.8.44, BA-MA RH 19 IX/9b.
9   HGr B Ia Nr. 5572/44 g.Kdos., BA-MA RH 19 IX/9b.
10   G. Tessin, *Verbände und Truppen der deutschen Wehrmacht und Waffen-SS* (Mittler & Sohn, Frankfurt am Main and Biblio Verlag, Osnabrück 1966–1975).

Artillerie-Pak-Abteilung 1039

The battalion was formed in June 1944; it was a *bodenständig* unit (limited mobility).[1] It still remained in Germany as late as 29 June, where it was located in Saarbrücken.[2] It was sent to Normandy and, on the evening of 9 July, it had reached Lisieux.[3] On 18 July it was reported at the *LXXXVI. Korps*,[4] but it may have arrived earlier.

The battalion was equipped with 8.8 cm antitank guns and was organized into three batteries, each with nine guns.[5] It also seems that the unit was given at least limited motorization.[6] On 17 July 1944, the battalion had 27 combat-ready 8.8 cm *Pak*.[7] The battalion was involved in the British Goodwood Offensive and was reported to have knocked out 35 enemy tanks on 19 July.[8] The battalion commander was killed on that day.[9] Two days later the remnants of *Artillerie-Pak-Abteilung 1053* were absorbed by *Artillerie-Pak-Abteilung 1039*.[10]

On 24 July the battalion reported 14 combat-ready 8.8 cm antitank guns, with one 8.8 cm gun in short-term repair (less than 14 days). It also reported it had three 7.5 cm guns from *Artillerie-Pak-Abteilung 1053*.[11]

The lack of mobility probably was a severe handicap during the retreat from Normandy and on 1 September the battalion was assessed to be *zerschlagen* (combat ineffective).[12] It was subsequently disbanded.[13]

---

1   G. Tessin, *Verbände und Truppen der deutschen Wehrmacht und Waffen-SS* (Mittler & Sohn, Frankfurt am Main and Biblio Verlag, Osnabrück 1966–1975).

2   OB West Ia Nr. 5129/44 g.Kdos. 29.6.44, T311, R25, F7029994.

3   HGr B Ia Tagesmeldung 10.7.44, BA-MA RH 19 IX/9a.

4   Pz.Gr. West Ia Nr. 479/44 geheim von 18.7.44, Nachtrag zur Tagesmeldung 17.7.44, BA-MA RH 21-5/50.

5   OB West Ia/Gen.d.Art. (V.O.Art.) Nr. 1241/44 g.Kdos, T311, R25, F7029576.

6   Ibid.

7   Pz.Gr. West Ia Nr. 479/44 geheim, 18.7.44, Nachtrag zur Tagesmeldung 17.7, BA-MA RH 21-5/50.

8   OB West Ia Nr. 5129/44 g.Kdos. 29.6.44, T311, R25, F7029994.

9   Ibid.

10   PzAOK 5 Ia Nr. 517/44 g.Kdos, Nachtrag zur Tagesmeldung 21.7.44, BA-MA RH 21-5/50.

11   Pz.Gr. West Ia Nr. 557/44 geheim, 25.7.44, Nachtrag zur Tagesmeldung 24.7, BA-MA RH 21-5/50.

12   Vorläufige Zustandsmeldung der Heeresartillerie beim OB West, Stand 1.9.44, BA-MA RH 11 II/v. 4.

13   Tessin, op. cit.

Artillerie-Pak-Abteilung 1040

The battalion was formed in June 1944; it was a *bodenständig* unit (limited mobility).[1] On 14 June it was decided to move it to the area of the *348. Infanterie-Division* (near the Somme Estuary). At the time, it was organized into three batteries, each with nine 8.8 cm *Pak*. It had only 14 prime movers.[2] The unit did not arrive at the *348. Infanterie-Division* since it was re-routed. By 27 June it was located in the Paris area.[3] One battery had arrived at the *XLVII Panzer-Korps* on 10 July[4] and, three days later, the entire battalion had arrived.[5]

The lack of mobility probably was a severe handicap during the retreat from Normandy and on 1 September the battalion was assessed to be *zerschlagen* (combat ineffective).[6] It was subsequently disbanded.[7]

---

1   G. Tessin, *Verbände und Truppen der deutschen Wehrmacht und Waffen-SS* (Mittler & Sohn, Frankfurt am Main and Biblio Verlag, Osnabrück 1966–1975).
2   AOK15 O.Qu/Qu.l Nr. 1661/44 g.Kdos, 14.6.44, T312, R517, F8116491.
3   OB West Ia Nr. 5129/44 g.Kdos. 29.6.44, T311, R25, F7029994.
4   HGr B Ia Tagesmeldung 10.7.44, BA-MA RH 19 IX/9a.
5   KTB OB West Ia, entry 14.7.44, T311, R16, F7016800.
6   Vorläufige Zustandsmeldung der Heeresartillerie beim OB West, Stand 1.9.44, BA-MA RH 11 II/v. 4.
7   Tessin, op. cit.

Artillerie-Pak-Abteilung 1041

The battalion was formed in June 1944; it was a *bodenständig* unit (limited mobility).[1] On 14 June it was decided to move it into a position between the *245. Infanterie-Division* and the *17. Luftwaffenfelddivision* (both attached to the *15. Armee*).[2] At the time it was organized into three batteries, each with nine 8.8 cm *Pak*. It had only 14 prime movers.[3]

It had unloaded from trains southeast of Paris on 29 June.[4] There is only one record of its presence in Normandy. On 21 July it was reported to be under the operational control of the *2. SS-Panzer-Division "Das Reich"*.[5] It had five 8.8 cm guns in each of its three batteries.[6]

The lack of mobility probably was a severe handicap during the retreat from Normandy and on 1 September the battalion was assessed to be *zerschlagen* (combat ineffective).[7] It was subsequently disbanded.[8]

---

1   G. Tessin, *Verbände und Truppen der deutschen Wehrmacht und Waffen-SS* (Mittler & Sohn, Frankfurt am Main and Biblio Verlag, Osnabrück 1966–1975).
2   AOK 15 O.Qu/Qu.l Nr. 1661/44 g.Kdos, 14.6.44, T312, R517, F8116491.
3   Ibid.
4   OB West Ia Nr. 5129/44 g.Kdos. 29.6.44, T311, R25, F7029994.
5   Gen.Kdo. LXXXIV A.K. Ia Nr. 035/44g.Kdos 22.7.44, Taktische Gliederung der Artillerie, Stand 21.7.44, T314, R1604, F001388.
6   Ibid.
7   Vorläufige Zustandsmeldung der Heeresartillerie beim OB West, Stand 1.9.44, BA-MA RH 11 II/v. 4.
8   Tessin, op. cit.

Artillerie-Pak-Abteilung 1053

The battalion was formed as a *bodenständig* unit (limited mobility).[1] Somehow it seems that it managed to collect some vehicles because, on 14 June, it was reported it had 27 antitank guns (7.5 cm) but only 14 prime movers.[2] The battalion seems to have been in the area of the *15. Armee* on D-Day.

On 14 June it was decided to send the battalion to the area of operations of the *346. Infanterie-Division*.[3] It had arrived by 26 June.[4] On 17 July the battalion had 16 combat-ready 7.5 cm *Pak*.[5] It remained in the area of the *LXXXVI. Korps* until 18 July.[6] On that day it took heavy casualties and, on 21 July, the remnants were absorbed by *Artillerie-Pak-Abteilung 1039*.[7]

---

1 G. Tessin, *Verbände und Truppen der deutschen Wehrmacht und Waffen-SS* (Mittler & Sohn, Frankfurt am Main and Biblio Verlag, Osnabrück 1966–1975).
2 AOK 15 O.Qu/Qu.l Nr. 1661/44 g.Kdos, 14.6.44, T312, R517, F8116491.
3 AOK 15 Ia Nr. 5835/44 g.Kdos, 14.6.44, T312, R516, F8411834.
4 Gliederung AOK 7 26.6.44, T312, R1566, F000018.
5 Pz.Gr. West Ia Nr. 479/44 geh. 18.7.44, Nachtrag zur Tagesmeldung 17.7.44, BA-MA RH 21-5/50.
6 Gliederung Pz.Gr. West 18.7.44, BA-MA RH 21-5/50.
7 PzAOK 5 Ia Nr. 517/44 g.Kdos, Nachtrag zur Tagesmeldung 21.7.44, BA-MA RH 21-5/50.

Fallschirm-Sturmgeschütz-Brigade 12

In January 1944 this unit was formed as *Fallschirm-Sturmgeschütz-Abteilung 2*, but it was later redesignated as *Fallschirm-Sturmgeschütz-Brigade 12*.[1] It was intended to be a permanent part of the *11. Fallschirm -Korps*.

On 17 May the unit had an authorized strength of 31 assault guns, but it had none on hand.[2] Exactly when it received its assault guns is not clear, but the unit had arrived in the area of operations of the *II. Fallschirm-Korps* on 15 June.[3] There would have been little point in sending it to the combat area without its assault guns. Whether it had received its full complement of assault guns is not clear.

According to Blauensteiner, the brigade had six *Sturmgeschütz III's* (7.5 cm cannon) and three *Sturmhaubitze 42's* (105 cm howitzer) in each battery.[4] Whether he refers to authorized strength or actual strength is not entirely clear. The brigade was still forming and training at the beginning of June.[5]

Nevertheless, the brigade was sent to Normandy together with the *3. Fallschirm-Division*.[6] The brigade reported 11 combat-ready *Sturmgeschütze* on 27 June.[7] Four days later it remained under the operational control of the *II. Fallschirm-Korps*.[8] It still had seven *Sturmgeschütz III's* and three *Sturmhaubitze 42's* combat ready on 29 July.[9]

According to Tornau/Kurowski, the brigade had about 60% of its original manpower in its combat elements when the brigade crossed the Seine. The support elements still had about 90% strength.[10]

---

1   G. Tessin, *Verbände und Truppen der deutschen Wehrmacht und Waffen-SS* (Mittler & Sohn, Frankfurt am Main and Biblio Verlag, Osnabrück 1966–1975).

2   Gliederung II. Fs.Korps, Stand 17.5.44, BA-MA RH 20-7/136.

3   Kriegsgliederungen zum KTB der Führungsabteilung AOK 7 ab 6.6.44 bis 30.6.44, T312, R1566, F000006.

4   E. Blauensteiner, *Normandie: Vorgeschichte II. Fallschirmkorps Anfang Mai 1944 - 6. Juni 1944*, MS # B-240, p. 2.

5   Ibid.

6   Tornau & Kurowski, *Sturmartillerie* (Maximilian-Verlag, Herford 1965) p. 261.

7   AOK 7 Ia Nr. 3454/44 g.Kdos 27.6.44, T312, R25, F7029978.

8   Anlage I zu Korpsarzt II. Fallsch.Korps B Nr. 65050/45 g.Kdos vom 27.1.45, Berichtzeit 1.7 - 4.9.44, BA-MA RL 33/5.

9   AOK 7 Ia Nr. 4174/44 g.Kdos. den 2.8.44, T312, R1569, F000358f.

10 Tornau & Kurowski, *Sturmartillerie* (Maximilian-Verlag, Herford 1965) p. 261.

Sturmgeschütz-Brigade 341

This unit was formed as *Sturmgeschütz-Abteilung 341* in December 1943. It was reorganized as *Sturmgeschütz-Brigade 341* in February 1944.[1] In May 1944 the unit was located near Narbonne in southern France and it was still forming.[2] On 1 June it had 19 *Sturmgeschütz III's* and 9 *Sturmhaubitze 42's* which can be compared to its authorized strength of 45 assault guns.[3]

It remained in southern France during June and received additional assault guns. On 1 July it was at full strength, having 33 *Sturmgeschütz III's* and 12 *Sturmhaubitze 42's*.[4] Finally, on 25 July, it began moving towards Normandy.[5] One day later all trains had departed and some of the units had reached Toulose.[6]

The unit was first committed to combat in the Brecey — Avranches area on 31 July.[7] It seems that the *1./Sturmgeschütz-Brigade 341* was the first unit to see action. During its first days of operations, this battery lost 12 of its 14 assault guns.[8] It was reported on 1 August that the two committed batteries were almost destroyed, while the third battery was still close to Rennes.[9] It was further reported that five railway cars with elements of the brigade were still in Redon on 2 August.[10]

According to Tornau/Kurowski the brigade quickly received new assault guns from Paris and Tours.[11] How many the brigade received is not clear, but it was reported that on 3 August four assault guns were in the area of Nantes.[12] It is possible that these were intended for *Sturmgeschütz-Brigade 341*. Tornau/Kurowski write that the brigade was also fighting in the Pontorson — Dinan — St. Malo area. Again the fighting was costly and the brigade eventually received new assault guns in Paris.[13]

The brigade had 20 assault guns on 27 August[14] and, five days later, it reported 12 assault guns.[15] On 1 October the brigade had 544 men, four less than its TOE called for. During September casualties amounted to only 18 men, while 133 men arrived as replacements. Five men had left the brigade for other reasons than being casualties. Accordingly, the brigade must have had 434 men on 1 September.[16]

No deliveries of assault guns to the brigade have been found among the records of the Inspector-General of Panzer Troops, except 17 *Sturmgeschütz III's* and 10 *Sturmhaubitze 42's* sent to *OB West* on 31 July for further distribution.[17] These arrived on 9 August and may have ended up with *Sturmgeschütz-Brigade 341*. The assault gun deliveries indicated by Tornau/Kurowski may also have been taken from various training facilities in France (there was, for example, an assault gun school at Tours). On 1 October the brigade had 10 combat-ready assault guns and 13 in short-term repair.[18]

---

1   G. Tessin, *Verbände und Truppen der deutschen Wehrmacht und Waffen-SS* (Mittler & Sohn, Frankfurt am Main and Biblio Verlag, Osnabrück 1966–1975).
2   Anlage zu HGr D Ia Nr. 315/44 g.Kdos, 18.5.44, T312, R1563, F000614.
3   StuG-Lage der Sturmartillerie, Stand 1.6.44, BA-MA RH 11 II/v. 3.

4   StuG-Lage der Sturmartillerie, Stand 1.7.44, BA-MA RH 11 II/v. 3.

5   Tessin, op. cit.

6   OB West Ia Nr. 6074/44 g.Kdos, 26.7.44, T311, R28, F7034822.

7   Tornau & Kurowski, *Sturmartillerie* (Maximilian-Verlag, Herford 1965) p. 212.

8   Ibid.

9   Anruf Ia HGr B bei Ob West um 11.55 Uhr, 1.8.44, T311, R28, F7034997.

10 HGr B Ia Nr. 5503/44 g.Kdos., Nachtrag zur Tagesmeldung 2.8.44, BA-MA RH 19 IX/9b.

11 Tornau/Kurowski, op. cit. p. 212.

12 AOK 7 Ia Nr.4209/44 g.Kdos 4.8.44, T312, R1568, F000376.

13 Tornau/Kurowski, op. cit. p. 212.

14 Gen der Art beim Chef Gen.St.d.Heeres Ib Nr. 2610/44 g.Kdos, 27.8.44, BA-MA RH 11 II/v. 4.

15 Vorläufige Zustandsmeldung der Heeresartillerie beim OB West, Stand 1.9.44, BA-MA RH 11 II/v. 4.

16 Gen.Kdo LXXXI. A.K., Zustandberichte T314, R1597, F000064.

17 Lieferungen der Panzer-Fahrzeuge, Bd. ab Mai 1943, BA-MA RH 10/349. Seventeen *Sturmhaubitze 42's* were also sent to *OB West* on 20 August, but these did not arrive until 14 September.

18 Gen.Kdo LXXXI. A.K., Zustandberichte T314, R1597, F000064.

Sturmgeschütz-Brigade 394

This unit was raised in West Prussia in March 1944 as *Sturmgeschütz-Abteilung 394*. It was reorganized as *Sturmgeschütz-Brigade 394* on 10 June 1944.[1] The authorized strength was 548 men and, more likely than not, it was not greater than that when the unit arrived in Normandy.[2] The brigade arrived in France during the last week of April.[3] On 26 May it was moved to Azay-le-Rideau.[4] By 1 June it had not received a single assault gun.[5] It had an authorized strength: 31 assault guns.[6] During June it received its full complement of assault guns; it was reported to have 31 *Sturmgeschütz III's* (and no *Sturmhaubitze 42's*) on 1 July.[7] It still had 31 assault guns on 1 August,[8] when it was on its way to Normandy, in the area of La Flèche.[9] It was heading for Mortain.[10] On 3 August it was located near Beauchêne,[11] 16 kilometers east of Mortain. One day later one battery was engaged in combat near Vire.[12]

According to Kurowski/Tornau, the brigade succeeded in extricating only one assault gun from the Falaise pocket, but the majority of its other vehicles got out.[13] The battalion had about 350 men on 26 August.[14] Thus it seems the majority of its men succeeded in escaping. Most of its heavy equipment was left behind, however, since it was reported on 1 September that the brigade had no assault guns and it was on its was to Aachen to receive 31 new ones.[15]

1   G. Tessin, *Verbände und Truppen der deutschen Wehrmacht und Waffen-SS* (Mittler & Sohn, Frankfurt am Main and Biblio Verlag, Osnabrück 1966–1975).
2   Gen.Kdo LXXXI. A.K., Zustandberichte Stand 1.10.44 T314, R1597, F000064. The authorized number of assault guns had increased to 45.
3   AOK 1 Ia, Lagebeurteilung der 1. Armee, Woche 24. - 30.44, T312, R28, F7535702.
4   AOK 1 Ia Nr. 2870/44 geh., 3.6.44, T312, R28, F7535484.
5   BA-MA RH 10/72.
6   Ibid.
7   StuG-Lage der Sturmartillerie, Stand 1.7.44, BA-MA RH 11 II/v. 4.
8   StuG-Lage der Sturmartillerie, Stand 1.8.44, BA-MA RH 11 II/v. 4.
9   AOK 7 Ia Nr. 4151/44 g.Kdos. den 2.8.44, T312, R 1569, F000357.
10   Ibid.
11   HGr B Ia Nr. 5354/44 g.Kdos. v. 4.8.44, Stand der bewegungen 3.8., BA-MA RH 19 IX/9b.
12   AOK 7 vorg. Gef.Stand Ia Nr. 554/44 g.Kdos 4.8.44, T312, R1568, F000376.
13   F. Kurowski & G. Tornau, *Sturmartillerie* (Motorbuch Verlag, Stuttgart 1978) p. 269.
14   OB West Ia Nr. 7360/44 g.Kdos, 26.8.44, T311, R29, F7035964.
15   Vorläufige Zustandsmeldung der Heeresartillerie beim OB West, Stand 1.9.44, BA-MA RH 11 II/v. 4.

Sturmgeschütz-Abteilung 902

The battalion was formed from the school at Tours[1] and it was occasionally referred to as *Sturmgeschütz-Lehr-Abteilung 902*.[2] On 1 June the battalion had 25 *Sturmgeschütz III's* operational and six in maintenance facilities. It had no *Sturmhaubitze 42's* with the 10.5 cm gun.[3]

When the Allied forces landed, the battalion was still at Tours. Two days later *Sturmgeschütz-Abteilung 902* was placed under the operational control of the *17. SS-Panzergrenadier-Division "Götz von Berlichingen"*.[4] It seems, however, that the battalion was not committed in that division's sector. Hans Stöber, who has written a history of the division, states that *Sturmgeschütz-Abteilung 902* was on its way but never arrived at the division.[5] There is some support for this in the organizational charts of the *7. Armee*.[6] On 11 June these show that the *17. SS-Panzergrenadier-Division "Götz von Berlichingen"* was attached to the *II. Fallschirm-Korps*, while *Sturmgeschütz-Abteilung 902* was with the *LXXXIV Korps*. Two days later it is indicated that the battalion was with forces committed on the Cotentin. This is also supported by an *OB West* document which indicates that the battalion was located in the Valognes area.[7]

Given its location, the battalion was among the units likely to be surrounded if the US forces succeeded in advancing to the west coast of the Cotentin Peninsula. On 19 June the organizational listings of the *7. Armee* shows that the battalion was with *Gruppe von Schlieben*.[8] However, two days later, *Sturmgeschütz-Abteilung 902* was located near La Haye du Puits and had 13 combat-ready *Sturmgeschütz III's*.[9] On 24 Tune it was in the area of the *91. Infanterie-Division*.[10] On 27 June the *91. Infanterie-Division* was reported to have 21 combat-ready *Sturmgeschütz III's*.[11] Most likely these belonged to *Sturmgeschütz-Abteilung 902*. Evidently, the battalion managed to escape from encirclement.

On 1 July the battalion was at full strength, having 30 *Sturmgeschütz III's* combat ready and one in need of repair.[12] The losses suffered by the battalion during its first month in Normandy were slight. Until 11 July only three *Sturmgeschütz III's* were total losses, while two drivers and five vehicle commanders had been killed.[13]

The second half of July seems to have been much more costly for the battalion. On 1 August it had only one *Sturmgeschütz III* combat ready, while seven were in maintenance facilities.[14] It also had 3 combat ready *Sturmhaubitze 42's*,[15] which indicates that it had received some replacements.

At the beginning of September, the battalion had 10 assault guns and was with the *19. Armee*.[16] On 1 October the battalion had 415 men. It had received 184 men as replacements during September and suffered 34 casualties. Thus the battalion must have had 265 men on 1 September. It had 19 combat-ready assault guns and one undergoing repair on 1 October.[17]

1   G. Tessin, *Verbände und Truppen der deutschen Wehrmacht und Waffen-SS* (Mittler & Sohn, Frankfurt am Main and Biblio Verlag, Osnabrück 1966–1975).

2   See e. g. Anlage zu HGr D Ia Nr. 315/44 g.Kdos, 18.5.44, T312, R1563, F000613.

3   StuG-Lage der Sturmartillerie, Stand 1.6.44, BA-MA RH 11 II/v. 3.

4   AOK 7 Ia Tagesmeldung 8.6.44, BA-MA RH 20-7/135.

5   Hans Stöber, *Die Sturmflut und das Ende, Vol I* (Munin Verlag, Osnabrück 1976) p. 62.

6   Kriegsgliederungen zum KTB in der Führungsabteilung AOK 7 6.6.44 - 30.6.44, T312, R1566, F000002-000025.

7   OB West Ia Nr 4521/44 g.Kdos, 12.6.44, T311, R25, F7029499.

8   Gliederung AOK 7 19.6.44, T312, R1566, F000009.

9   OB West Abt. Voart, H.Qu. den 24.6.1944, T311, R25, F7029844.

10   Gliederung AOK 7 246.44, T312, R1566, F000016.

11   AOK 7 Ia Nr. 3454/44 g.Kdos 27.6.44, T312, R1565, F001377.

12   StuG-Lage der Sturmartillerie, Stand 1.7.44, BA-MA RH 11 II/v. 4.

13   Höh. Offz. f. Pz. Art. Nr. 5599/44 geh. 19.7.44, BA-MA RH 11 II/v.3.

14   StuG-Lage der Sturmartillerie, Stand 1.8.44, BA-MA RH 11 II/v. 4

15   Ibid.

16   Vorläufige Zustandsmeldung der Heeresartillerie beim OB West, Stand 1.9.44, BA-MA RH 11 II/v. 4.

17   Gen.Kdo LXXXI. A.K., Zustandberichte T314, R1597, F000062. According to the report, no personnel had left the battalion during September for other reasons than being casualties.

Sturmgeschütz-Abteilung 1348

In March 1944 it was decided to form assault gun battalions within the *326., 346.* and *348. Infanterie-Divisionen.*[1] This was probably an attempt to create mobile reserves that could be employed outside the division. The battalions were quite small though. They had only ten *Sturmgeschütze* each.[2] In effect they were nothing but the assault gun company of the antitank battalion of the respective division.

Sturmgeschütz-Abteilung 1348 had 122 men, 17 trucks, 4 cars, 4 motorcycles and 5 *Sturmgeschütze*, with a further 5 *Sturmgeschütze* to be delivered to the battalion.[3] The battalion was ordered to move to Normandy on 28 July.[4] It is known that it had arrived on 6 August.[5] Nothing further is known about the unit's actions in Normandy.

---

1   See e. g. AOK 15 Ia Nr. 2928/44 g.K, 26.3.44, T312, R516, F8114452.
2   Ibid.
3   AOK 15 Ia Nr. 2928/44 g.K. 26.3.44, T312, R516, F8114452.
4   HGr B Ia Nr. 5273/44 g.Kdos v. 28.7.44, BA-MA RH 21-5/50.
5   OB West Ia Nr. 6517/44 g.Kdos. 6.8.44, T311, R28, F7035178

Infanterie-Divisionen

2. Fallschirmjäger-Division

This division was not really engaged in the battle in Normandy. It had been badly mauled on the Eastern Front and was located at the training facility at Cologne (Wahn) on D-Day. Six days later it received orders to move to the Brest area.[1] It was far from ready for combat and it also lacked several vital components.

Fallschirmjäger-Regiment 6 was ready for action, but it had been detached to the Carentan — Lessay — La Haye du Puits area and was attached to the *91. Infanterie-Division.* This regiment is covered separately.

Most of the artillery regiment did not join the division before it was surrounded in Brest. The *I./Fallschirm-Artillerie-Regiment 6* was with the division, equipped with twelve 10.5 cm *LG 42's* (recoilless guns). The *II.* and *III./Fallschirm-Artillerie-Regiment 6* were at the artillery school at Luneville in eastern France.[2] On 24 June it was reported that the *Flak-Abteilung* was with the *II. Fallschirm-Korps* in Normandy.[3] This battalion lost most of its equipment on 28 July.[4]

Fallschirmjäger-Regimenter 2 and *7* were with the division in Brest except for the *I./Fallschirmjäger-Regiment 2,* which was forming in Germany.[5] Also present was *Fallschirm-Panzerjäger-Abteilung 2.*[6] It is unclear if these units were up to strength. It is certainly possible that some of their men had been sent away as replacements to the parachute units fighting in Normandy. The division was supposed to have a mortar battalion (*Fallschirm-Granatwerfer-Bataillon 2),* which was raised in Verdun 20 May 1944. It did not move west, but did see action in eastern France during September.[7] On 1 July it was reported that the engineer battalion was with the division. However, it only had 42% of its authorized personnel strength.[8]

All these deficiencies caused the division to be quite weak. It was reported that it had the following strength on 1 July 1944[9]:

Personnel and Equipment	Authorized	On Hand	Shortage
Officers	306	161	145
Other ranks	10,183	6,470	4,343
Heavy antitank guns	60	4	56
LG 42's	12	12	0
Mortars	108	28	80
Machine guns	739	497	242
Motorcycles	442	92	350
Passenger cars	286	20	266
Trucks	1,147	59	1,088

The low authorized strength was due to the fact that many parts of the division were located elsewhere. The strength of the division increased slowly. At the end of July, it had 162 officers and 7,389 other ranks[10]. By 5 September the garrison in Brest had lost 619 killed in action, 1,965 wounded and 2,799 missing.[11] How many of these casualties were from the *2. Fallschirmjäger-Division* is unclear.

1   W. Kammann, *Der Weg der 2. Fallschirmjäger-Division* (Schild-Verlag, München 1972) p. 82 & 89.

2   See Ubersicht über den Stand der Art. Einh., Anlage 33 zum KTB des hoheren Artilleriekommandeurs der Fallschirmtruppe, KTB Nr. 1, BA-MA RL 33/3 and Hoh. Art. Kommandeur Abt 1a, Az 11 Br. B. Nr. 797/44 geh. 18.8.44, BA-MA RL 33/3.

3   Ferngeschprache und Besprechungen AOK 7 la, Besprechung mit Chef II.Fs.Korps, 24.6.44, T312, R1566, F000322.

4   See Ziegelmann, MS # B-489, p. 4.

5   See W. Kammann, *Die Geschichte des Fallschirmjäger-Regiment 2 1939 bis 1945* (Goldhammer, Scheinfeld 1987) p. 182f and W. Dierich, *Die Verbände der Luftwaffe 1935 - 1945* (Motorbuch, Stuttgart 1976) p. 637. See also Lagekarte 7. Armee, Stand 22.6.44, BA-MA RH 20-7/138K.

6   G. Tessin, *Verbände und Truppen der deutschen Wehrmacht und Waffen-SS* (Mittler & Sohn, Frankfurt am Main and Biblio Verlag, Osnabrück 1966–1975).

7   W. Kammann, *Der Weg der 2. Fallschirmjäger-Division* (Schild-Verlag, München 1972) p. 102–105.

8   Gen.Kdo XXV. A.K. Ia Nr. 836/44 g.Kdos., 8.7.44, Zustandberichte der 343., 265., 275. und 2. Fsch.Jg.Div., Stand 1.7.44., T314, R747, F000197-000210.

9   Ibid.

10 W. Kammann, *Der Weg der 2. Fallschirmjäger-Division* (Schild-Verlag, München 1972) p. 91.

11 OB West Nachtrag zur Tagesmeldung 5.9.44, Fernschreiben an OKH, T378, R313, F6266105.

3. Fallschirmjäger-Division

The division was formed in October 1943 and sent to Brittany in February 1944. Being part of the *II. Fallschirm-Korps,* it continued to train and form its component units.[1] The manpower strength of the division stood at 15,075 on 1 March 1944.[2] Twelve weeks later, on 22 May, the division had a ration strength of 17,420.[3] The structure of the division looked like this on 22 May:[4]

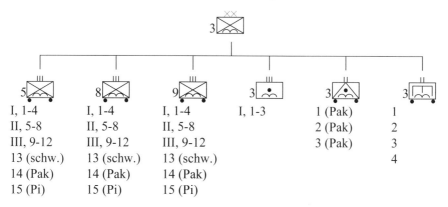

5	8	9	3	3	3
I, 1-4	I, 1-4	I, 1-4	I, 1-3	1 (Pak)	1
II, 5-8	II, 5-8	II, 5-8		2 (Pak)	2
III, 9-12	III, 9-12	III, 9-12		3 (Pak)	3
13 (schw.)	13 (schw.)	13 (schw.)			4
14 (Pak)	14 (Pak)	14 (Pak)			
15 (Pi)	15 (Pi)	15 (Pi)			

The artillery regiment had only one battalion. It was equipped with four 10.5 cm *leichte Feld-Haubitze 18s* and three 10.5 cm recoilless guns in each of the three batteries.[5] They were not motorized.[6] The *II.* and *III./Fallschirm-Artillerie-Regiment 3* were still forming in Germany; they did not see any action in Normandy.[7] The *I./Fallschirm-Artillerie-Regiment 3* had probably received its guns only recently since it was reported that the division had no artillery pieces on 1 May.[8]

The equipment of the infantry regiments was:[9]

I./Fallschirmjäger-Regiment 5	39 machine guns, 16 mortars
II./Fallschirmjäger-Regiment 5	31 machine guns, 13 mortars
III./Fallschirmjäger-Regiment 5	47 machine guns, 12 mortars
13./Fallschirmjäger-Regiment 5	10 cm recoilless rifles, number of guns unreadable
14./Fallschirmjäger-Regiment 5	2 7.5 cm antitank guns
15./Fallschirmjäger-Regiment 5	4 machine guns, 4 flamethowers
I./Fallschirmjäger-Regiment 8	42 machine guns, 13 mortars
II./Fallschirmjäger-Regiment 8	42 machine guns, 12 mortars
III./Fallschirmjäger-Regiment 8	41 machine guns, 18 mortars
13./Fallschirmjäger-Regiment 8	3 machine guns, 2 10 cm mortars
14./Fallschirmjäger-Regiment 8	9 4.2 cm antitank guns
15./Fallschirmjäger-Regiment 8	3 machine guns, 9 flamethowers

I./Fallschirmjäger-Regiment 9	35 machine guns, 13 mortars
II./Fallschirmjäger-Regiment 9	26 machine guns, 12 mortars
III./Fallschirmjäger-Regiment 9	29 machine guns, 13 mortars
13./Fallschirmjäger-Regiment 9	No heavy weapons
14./Fallschirmjäger-Regiment 9	2 7.5 cm antitank guns
15./Fallschirmjäger-Regiment 9	7 machine guns, 5 flamethowers

Fallschirm-Pionier-Bataillon 3 had 33 machine guns and 22 flame throwers.[10] Equipment of *Fallschirm-Panzerjäger-Abteilung 3* was mixed, though the three companies were similarly equipped. It seems that each company had three 7.5 cm *Pak 40's*, one medium antitank gun and four light antitank guns.[11]

A *Flak* battalion was part of the division, but it seems it had no guns.[12] It probably did not receive any guns before or during its commitment in Normandy, since *Fallschirm-Flak-Abteilung 2* of the *2. Fallschirmjäger-Division* was placed under the operational control of the *3. Fallschirmjäger-Division.*[13]

Even though the division was nominally motorized, the shortage of vehicles made it only partially motorized, despite the commandeering of vehicles. Its motorization only stood at 45% according to a report dated 22 May 1944.[14] According to the postwar estimate of the division commander, the division had no more than about 40% of its authorized vehicles.[15] Accordingly, when the division was sent to Normandy, it could motorize only one battalion in each parachute regiment.[16] Of the other components of the division only about one third could be motorized.[17]

Shortly after the Allied landings, the *3. Fallschirmjäger-Division* was sent to Normandy. On 10 June a combat group had reached Brecey-Villedieu[18] and two days later the main part of the division had assembled in the St. Lo area.[19] The entire division had arrived by 22 June.[20]

From D-Day until 12 July the division suffered 4,064 casualties.[21] By 29 July the infantry battalions assigned and attached to the division were estimated to have the following combat values:[22]

1 *stark* (strong)
2 *mittelstark (above average)*
7 *durchschnittlich (average)*
1 *abgekampft (limited combat capability)*
2 *schwach (weak)*

As the reader can see, this amounts to 13 battalions, or four more than the division actually possessed. It was quite common that battalions were temporarily placed under the operational control of other formations than the parent division. The kind of reports used in this case did not always make any distinction between organic battalions or temporarily attached.

Similarly, the division had nine light artillery batteries and fourteen heavy antitank guns.[23] The mobility was still rated 100% for the heavy weapons, but only 25% for the infantry units.[24] The explanation for the lack of mobility for the infantry is that the infantry had departed without their supply components.[25]

Many German divisions fighting in Normandy have been described as being destroyed after the battle. Often these statements are quite exaggerated. For this division, the word destroyed might, however, be more appropriate. As indicated above, the division's casualties from 6 June–12 July amounted to 4,064. During the period from 1 July–4 September, the losses were 2,561 killed in action, 7,248 wounded and 16,370 missing.[26] According to Meindl, the division was destroyed at the Mons pocket from 3–4 September,[27] which may explain the very high casualties during the period given above.

Since these casualties exceed the strength of the division, it can be concluded that either the division received replacements during the battle, or casualties suffered by temporarily subordinated units are included in the total for the division. Whatever the explanation, clearly the division suffered very serious casualties during the battle in Normandy and the subsequent retreat across northern France. Possibly, given the events at Mons in September, the retreat from Normandy may have been damaging to the division than the fighting in Normandy.

---

1   G. Tessin, *Verbände und Truppen der deutschen Wehrmacht und Waffen-SS* (Mittler & Sohn, Frankfurt am Main and Biblio Verlag, Osnabrück 1966–1975).
2   Kriegsgliederungen AOK 7, T312, R1566, F000144.
3   Gliederung 3. Fs.Div. 22.5.44. BA-MA RH 20-7/136.
4   Ibid.
5   Ibid.
6   Ibid.
7   On 7 August it was reported that these battalions were in Lüdenscheid in Germany, without any weapons. See Übersicht über den Stand der Art.Einh., Anlage 33 zum KTB des hoheren Artilleriekommandeurs der Fallschirmtruppe (BA-MA RL 33/3).
8   Übersicht der Küsten-u. Eingreifdivisionen mit Panzerbrechenden Waffen, Stand vom 1.5.44, T312, R1568, F000718.
9   Gliederung 3. Fs.Div. 22.5.44. BA-MA RH 20-7/136.
10 Ibid.
11 Gliederung 3. Fs.Div. 22.5.44. BA-MA RH 20-7/136. This source is not entirely clear about the numbers of each category of antitank guns and the information given in the text is also based on Übersicht der Küsten-u. Eingreifdivisionen mit Panzerbrechenden Waffen, Stand vom 1.5.44, T312, R1568, F000718 and Taktische Reserven panzerbrechende Waffen innerhalb der Divisionen, Stand vom 1.5.44, T312, R1568, F000695.
12 Gliederung 3. Fs.Div. 22.5.44. BA-MA RH 20-7/136.
13 Anlage I zu Korpsarzt II. Fallsch.Korps B Nr. 65050/45 g.Kdos vom 27.1.45, Berichtzeit 1.7 - 4.9.44, BA-MA RL 33/5.
14 OB West la Anlagen, Anruf OKW/WFst Gen.Major Frhr.v.Buttlar bei OB West vom 22.5.44, T311, R24, F7028756.

15 R. Schimpf, Die Kampfe der 3. Fallschirmjäger-Division bei der Invasion in Frankreich Juni/ August 1944, MS # B-020, p. 4f.

16 Ibid, p. 6.

17 Ibid.

18 OB West la 4463/44 g.Kdos., den 10.6.44., T 311, R25, F7029425.

19 OB West la 4517/44 g.Kdos, 12.6.44, T311, R25, F7029487.

20 KTB AOK 7 la, entry 22 June 1944, T312, R 1568, F000790.

21 Anlage zu O.B.der H.Gr.B "Betrachtungen zur Lage" vom 16.7. T311, R3, F7002245.

22 AOK 7 la Nr. 4174/44 g.Kdos. den 2.8.44, T312, R1569, F000358.

23 Ibid.

24 Ibid.

25 Ibid.

26 Anlage I zu Korpsarzt II. Fallsch.Korps B Nr. 65050/45 g.Kdos vom 27.1.45, Berichtzeit 1.7 - 4.9.44, BA-MA RL 33/5.

27 Meindl, II. Fallschirmkorps (21 August–3 September 1944), *MS # A-859, p. 1.*

5. Fallschirmjäger-Division

The division was formed in March 1944 and sent to Brittany in May.[1] The theoretical organization of the division was:[2]

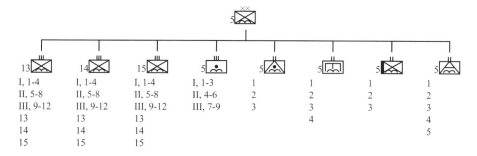

The division reported a ration strength of 12,836 men on 22 May 1944. However, most of these men must have been poorly trained and equipped. The division had an authorized strength of 17,455, but only 12,253 of these positions were manned. Many units were seriously short of equipment. *Fallschirm-Pionier-Bataillon 5* was supposed to have 738 rifles, but it had only 38. *Fallschirm-Panzerjäger-Abteilung 5* was authorized 36 7.5 cm *Pak,* but it had only three. *Fallschirmjäger-Regiment 14* had an authorization of 2,961 rifles but only had 1,162.[3]

The *Flak* battalion had all the twelve 8.8 cm *Flak* it was supposed to have. These were most likely recent arrivals, since the battalion was still forming on 15 July.[4]

These circumstances also made training more difficult. The net effect was a low combat value of the division. The verdict of von der Heydte was harsh:[5]

The 5. Fallschirmjäger-Division was of little combat value. Less than 10% of the men had jump trained, at most 20% of the officers had infantry training and combat experience. Armament and equipment incomplete; only 50% of authorized number of machine guns; one regiment without helmets, no heavy antitank weapons; not motorized.

A weakness the division suffered from was shortage of artillery. It seems that it had the *I./Fallschirm-Artillerie-Regiment 5* available when it departed for Normandy. According to the commander of the division, it traveled together with *Fallschirmjäger-Regiment 15.*[6] On 21 July the *I./Fallschirm-Artillerie-Regiment 5* was with the division and had three batteries, each with six 10.5 cm light field pieces.[7] The battalion must have lost its equipment during Operation *Cobra* because, on 1 August, it was in Luneville to receive twelve new 10.5 cm howitzers.[8] One week later the battalion was reported to be in Normandy.[9] The *II.* and *III./Fallschirm-Artillerie-Regiment 5* did not participate in the campaign in Normandy.[10]

Tessin is the only source which mentions a mortar battalion with three companies.[11] It is not mentioned at all by the commander of the division.[12] It has not been found in any documents concerning Normandy. The forming of this unit was possibly never completed.

In May 1944 the division only had 60% of its authorized manpower, only 25% of its light weapons, 23% of its heavy weapons and 9% of its motor vehicles.[13]

The low readiness posture of the division is also reflected in its piecemeal commitment in Normandy. The first unit to move to Normandy was *Fallschirmjäger-Regiment 15*. On 25 June the I./*Fallschirm-Regiment 15* had reached the vicinity of St. Lo, while the II./*Fallschirmjäger-Regiment 15* was located 5 kilometers northeast of Percy. The III./*Fallschirmjäger-Regiment 15* lagged behind and had only reached a point ten kilometers southeast of Avranches.

On 9 July it was reported that *Fallschirmjäger-Regiment 13* was located in the Villedieu — Avranches area, while *Fallschirmjäger-Regiment 14* was still in the Lamballe — Dinan area.[14] The II/*Fallschirmjäger-Regiment 13* remained in St. Malo until 14 July, when it departed for Normandy after being relieved by the *Sicherungs-Bataillon 1222*.[15]

When Operation *Cobra* was launched, the *5. Fallschirmjäger-Division* was not deployed as an organic whole. *Fallschirmjäger-Regiment 14* was attached to the *Panzer-Lehr-Division*,[16] while *Fallschirm-jäger-Regiment 15* had been sent to the *II. Fallschirm*-Korps.[17] This left the commander of the division with *Fallschirmjäger-Regiment 14, Fall-schirm-Pionier-Bataillon 5* and, probably, also an artillery battalion.

The division continued to be employed splintered like this. Thus it is almost impossible to assess its casualties. According to *OKH* estimates, which have been shown to be overly pessimistic, the division had about 4,000 men on 1 September 1944.[18] The division probably lost about 8,000 men during the fighting in Normandy, but this is just a guess.

---

1   G. Tessin, *Verbände und Truppen der deutschen Wehrmacht und Waffen-SS* (Mittler & Sohn, Frankfurt am Main and Biblio Verlag, Osnabrück 1966–1975).

2   Ibid.

3   Gliederung 5. Fs.Div. 22.5.44. BA-MA RH 20-7/136.

4   Luftflotten-Kommando 3 Ia/Flak Nr. 11457/44 g.Kdos 17.7.44, Gliederung der Flakartillerie Stand 15.7.44, BA-MA RL 7/58.

5   Von der Heydte, *Das Fallschirmjägerregiment 6 in der Normandie,* MS # B-839, p. 50.

6   G. Wilke, *Bericht über 5. Fallsch.J.Div. in der Normandie v. 6. Juni–24. Juli 44,* MS # B-820, p. 2.

7   Gen.Kdo. LXXXIV A.K. Ia Nr. 035/44g.Kdos 22.7.44, Taktische Gliederung der Artillerie, Stand 21.7.44, T314, R1604, F001388.

8   KTB des hoheres Artilleriekommandeur der Fallschirmtruppe, KTB Nr. 1, BA-MA RL 33/3.

9   Übersicht uber den Stand der Art. Einh., Anlage 33 zum KTB des höheren Artilleriekommandeurs der Fallschirmtruppe, KTN Nr. 1, BA-MA RL 33/3.

10 See KTB des höheres Artilleriekommandeur der Fallschirmtruppe, KTB Nr. 1, BA-MA RL 33/3 and Übersicht über den Stand der Art. Einh., Anlage 33 zum KTB des höheren Artilleriekommandeurs der Fallschirmtruppe, KTN Nr. 1, BA-MA RL 33/3.

11 Tessin, op. cit.

12 See G. Wilke, *Bericht über 5. Fallsch.J.Div. in der Normandie v. 6. Juni–24. Juli 44,* MS # B-820.

13 OB West Ia Anlagen, Anruf OKW/WFst Gen.Major Frhr.v.Buttlar bei OB West vom 22.5.44, T311, R24, F7028756.

14 OB West Ia Nr. 5443/44 g.Kdos, vom 9.7.44, T311, R28, F7034330.

15 KTB AOK 7 Ia, entry 14.7.44, T312, R1569, F000158.

16 Bayerlein, *Pz.Lehr Division 15–25 Juli 44,* MS # A-903, p. 6.

17 Wilke, op. cit. p. 6. Note that the author often writes June when he obviously must have meant July.

18 OKH Org.Abt. I Nr. I/19995/44 g.Kdos. 16.10.1944, T78, R432, F6403685ff.

6. Fallschirmjäger-Division

This division was formed in June 1944 and was immediately sent to the *15. Armee*.[1] Its intended organization was:[2]

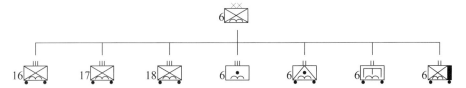

When it arrived at *15. Armee* it had a very different organization:[3]

Fallschirmjäger-Regiment 16	Three battalions, each with four companies. Also *13. Kompanie (Granatwerfer)* and *14. Kompanie (Pak)*
Fallschirmjäger-Lehr-Regiment	Three battalions, each with four companies. Also *13. Kompanie (Granatwerfer)* and *14. Kompanie (Pak)*
I./Fallschirmjäger-Artillerie-Regiment 6	three batteries, each with four 10.5 cm *leichte Feldhaubitze 18s*
schwere Werfer-Abteilung 21	four batteries with 30 cm rocket launchers
Fallschirm-Pionier-Bataillon 6	forming
Fallschirm-Luftnachrichten-Abteilung 6	two companies forming
1 Nachschub-Kompanie (mot)	?
1 Kraftfahr-Kompanie	100 ton capacity

Six weeks later, on 1 August, the division was far from complete. *Fallschirmjäger-Regiment 16* had been sent to the Eastern Front and the status of the units of the division was:[4]

Fallschirm-Panzerjäger-Abteilung 6	65% of authorized personnel strength. Seven 7.5 cm *Pak* (towed).
I./Fallschirm-Artillerie-Regiment 6	100% of authorized personnel strength Twelve 10.5 cm howitzers
Fallschirm-Pionier-Bataillon 6	66% of authorized personnel strength.
Fallschirm-Feld-Ersatz-Bataillon 6	42% of authorized personnel strength.
Fallschirmjäger-Lehr-Regiment	100% of authorized personnel strength.
schwere Werfer-Abteilung 21	100% of authorized personnel strength. 23 *Nebelwerfers*.

A *Kampfgruppe* from the division was sent to bolster German defenses against Patton's spearheads and, on 12 August, the *Kampfgruppe* was reported located in the area L'Aigle — Moulins,[6] i.e. well east of the area where elements of the 7. *Armee* were surrounded. It appears to have remained in that area until the breakout from the Falaise pocket.[7] The *Kampfgruppe* apparently consisted of *Fallschirmjäger-Lehr-Regiment, I./Fallschirm-Artillerie-Regiment 6* and *schwere Werfer-Abt. 21.*[8]

---

1   G. Tessin, *Verbände und Truppen der deutschen Wehrmacht und Waffen-SS* (Mittler & Sohn, Frankfurt am Main and Biblio Verlag, Osnabruck 1966–1975).

2   Ibid.

3   AOK 15 O.Qu/Qu.l Nr. 1687/44 g.Kdos, 17.6.44, T312, R517, F8116504.   ..

4   Anlagen zum KTB LXXXI. A.K. Ia, Gliederung 6. Fsch.-Jg.-Div., Stand vom 1.8.1944, T314, R1593, F000972.

5   The *I./Fallschirm-Artillerie-Regiment 6* was the only unit of the regiment that was combat ready. The *II./Fallschirm-Artillerie-Regiment 6* had not been raised, while the *III./Fallschirm-Artillerie-Regiment 6* was at the artillery school in Luneville. See Übersicht über den Stand der Art. Einh., Anlage 33 zum KTB des höheren Artilleriekommandeurs der Fallschirmtruppe, KTB Nr. 1, BA-MA RL 33/3. The III. Abteilung was still in Luneville on 18 August. See Höh. Art. Kommandeur Abt Ia, Az 11 Br. B. Nr. 797/44 geh. 18.8.44, BA-MA RL 33/3.

6   LXXXI. A.K. Ia Nr. 25/44 g.Kdos. 12.8.44, T314, R1592, F000511.

7   See situation maps in Anlagen zum KTB LXXXI. A.K. Ia, Lagekarten, T314, R1594, F000003ff.

8   See Anlagen zum KTB LXXXI. A.K. Ia, Gliederung 6. Fsch.-Jg.-Div., Stand vom 14.8.1944, T314, R1593, F000974. The *Fallschirmjäger-Lehr-Regiment was* also called *Fallschirmjäger-Lehr-Regiment 21.*

16. Luftwaffenfelddivision

This division was formed in December 1942. Initially it had two three-battalion infantry regiments, one antitank battalion, one artillery regiment (three battalions) and an engineer battalion. The division was moved to the Netherlands in February 1943, where it remained until the Allied invasion.[1]

In November 1943 the division was taken over by the army. It was reorganized into three two-battalion infantry regiments and a *Füsilier-Bataillon* was formed.[2] The structure of the division looked like this on 1 June 1944:[3]

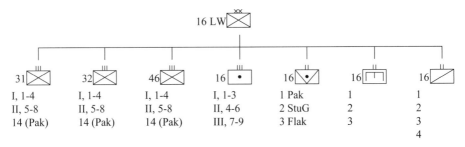

All infantry battalions had 56 machine guns and eight mortars (8 cm). The antitank company of each infantry regiment had six guns. In *Luftwaffen-Infanterie-Regiment 31* they were the 7.5 cm *Pak,* while the other two regiments had 5 cm guns. Each antitank company had three 2 cm *Flak* guns and 18 *Panzerschrecks.*[4]

Luftwaffen-Panzerjäger-Abteilung 16 had the following equipment:[5]

1.Kompanie: three 5 cm guns and six 7.5 cm guns, all of them towed (motorized)

2.Kompanie: two *Sturmgeschütz III's*

3.Kompanie: twelve 2 cm guns, all of them towed (motorized)

Luftwaffen-Artillerie-Regiment 16 had the following equipment:6

1. Batterie: No guns
2. Batterie: four 7.62 cm guns
3. Batterie: four 7.62 cm guns
4. Batterie: four 7.62 cm guns
5. Batterie: No guns
6. Batterie: four 7.62 cm guns
7. Batterie: four 12.2 cm howitzers
8. Batterie: four 12.2 cm howitzers
9. Batterie: four 12.2 cm howitzers

Luftwaffen-Pionier-Bataillon 16 had 33 machine guns and six flame-throwers.

The *Füsilier-Bataillon* was organized like the infantry battalions, except one company was equipped with bicycles. It also only had six mortars.[7]

At the end of May 1944 the division numbered 9,354 men.[8]

The division began its march to Normandy from 16–24 June.[9] Exactly how many men it brought along is unclear. One document states that the division had a strength of only 60–70 men in each company, since it left soldiers in the Netherlands to man static weapons there.[10] However, another document states the division left the Netherlands with 9,816 men, 28 artillery pieces and 32 antitank guns.[11] The latter document is dated 30 August 1944, however, more than two months after the transfer to Normandy. It is quite possible that the division initially left a considerable number of men in the Netherlands, who later joined the division in Normandy.

When the division moved to Normandy by train, it was not subject to air attack, and its losses during the march were negligible.[12] The mobility of the division was poor; it only had 57% of its authorized number of horses and the motorized components had only 50% of their vehicles.[13]

On 1 July all trains but one had unloaded.[14] One day later two battalions, the *I./Luftwaffen-Infanterie-Regiment 32* and *II./Luftwaffen-Infanterie-Regiment 46,* were already committed, while *II./Luftwaffen-Infanterie-Regiment 32* and *I./Luftwaffen-Infanterie-Regiment 46* were ready for action.[15] *Luftwaffen-Infanterie-Regiment 31* was close to the front, while the remainder of the division was still between the combat area and the marshalling area.[16]

The first major action any units from the *16. Luftwaffenfelddivision* participated in was against the British operation, *Charnwood.*

Those elements of the division that were involved in Operation *Charnwood* were badly hit. It was reported that those infantry units committed west of the Orne River suffered 75% casualties.[17] This is a high percentage, but the division probably only deployed one regiment west of the Orne, or eight companies. If, as indicated above, the companies only had a rifle strength of 60–70 men each, there were only about 500 infantry involved from the division. The infantry strength was probably somewhat higher, since reinforcements may have been brought forward during the operation.

On 9 July eight *Sturmgeschütz III's* were sent to the division.[18]

During Operation *Goodwood* the division suffered serious casualties. All commanders and staffs of infantry regiments and battalions were put out of action. Thirty-six company commanders became casualties. This made it difficult to rebuild the division and, on 23 July, Eberbach suggested that the division should be used to rebuild the *21. Panzer-Division.*[19] Evidently the infantry was used to replenish the *21. Panzer-Division,* while the rest of the division was used to form the *16. Infanterie-Division.* Casualties in July included 368 killed in action, 756 wounded and 2 496 missing.[20] The division was formally disbanded on 4 August.[21]

1   G. Tessin, *Verbände und Truppen der deutschen Wehrmacht und Waffen-SS* (Mittler & Sohn, Frankfurt am Main and Biblio Verlag, Osnabrück 1966–1975).

2   Ibid.

3   Anlagen zum KTB LXXXVIII. A.K. Ia, Gliederung 16. Lw.Felddiv., Stand T314, R1622, F000657.

4   Ibid.

5   Ibid.

6   Ibid.

7   Ibid.

8   Der Kommandierende General und Befehlshaber der Truppen des Heeres in den Niederlanden (Generalkommando LXXXVIII A.K.) Abt. Ia, Az: K95 Nr. 1495/44 g.Kdos, den 1.6.44, T314, R1622, F000651-678.

9   Der Kommandierende General und Befehlshaber der Truppen des Heeres in den Niederlanden (Gen.Kdo. LXXXVIII. A.K.) Ia Nr. 2467/44 g.Kdos., 30.8.44, T314, R1626, F000481.

10   AOK 7 Ia Nr. 1844/44 geh. 26.6.44, T312, R1565, F001339.

11   Der Kommandierende General und Befehlshaber der Truppen des Heeres in den Niederlanden (Gen.Kdo. LXXXVIII. A.K.) Ia Nr. 2467/44 g.Kdos., 30.8.44, T314, R1626, F000481.

12   Karl Sievers, *Bericht über den Einsatz der 16. Luftwaffenfelddivision in der Normandie beiderseits der Orne-Mündung vom 1.7. - 23.7.1944*, MS # A-959, p. 2f.

13   OKH Org.Abt. (I) Nr. I/6475/44 geh. 21.6.44, T78, R421, F6390305.

14   OB West Ia Nr. 5185/44 g.Kdos, 1.7.44, T311, R28, F7034124.

15   OB West Ia Nr. 5197/44 g.Kdos, 2.7.44, T311, R28, F7034134.

16   Ibid.

17   Pz.Gr. West Ia Nr. 236/444 g.Kdos., Tagesmeldung 8.7.44, T313, R420, F8713855.

18   Lieferungen der Pz.Fahrzeuge, Bd. ab Mai 1943, BA-MA RH 10/349.

19   Pz.Gr. West Ia Nr. 522/44 g.Kdos. v. 23.7.44, T313, R420, F8713976.

20   Tessin, op. cit.

21   Ibid.

77. Infanterie-Division

The division was raised in January 1944 and soon sent to the 7. *Armee* in Normandy to continue forming.[1] Of all the German infantry divisions, few had as weak an organization as the 77. *Infanterie-Division*:[2]

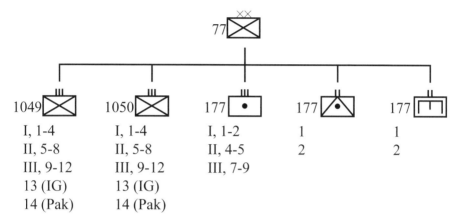

The weak organization was also reflected in its personnel strength, which stood at 8,508 on 1 March 1944.[3] One month later it was reported that the division was 588 men above its authorized strength[4] and, on 1 May, it had 8,686 officers and men[5]. At the beginning of June, it was only marginally stronger, having 9,095 officers and men plus 1,410 *HiWi* (Eastern volunteers).[6]

All infantry battalions in *Infanterie-Regiment 1050* had 40 machine guns and seven 8.1 cm mortars each. The battalions in *Infanterie-Regiment 1049* also had 40 machine guns, but the number of 8.1 cm mortars was eight.[7]

In each regiment the *14. Kompanie* was equipped with three heavy antitank guns, while the *13./Infanterie-Regiment 1049* had six Russian infantry guns and the *13./ Infanterie-Regiment 1050* had only two Russian infantry guns.[8]

The artillery regiment was very weak. The *I.* and *II./Artillerie-Regiment 177* had two batteries each, with four 10.5 cm howitzers per battery. The *III./Artillerie-Regiment 177* had three batteries, each with four towed 8.8 cm *Pak 43/41 s*. The *III./Artillerie-Regiment 177* was motorized, the remaining battalions were not.[9]

Equipment for *Panzerjäger-Abteilung 177* included one company with twelve 5 cm antitank guns and one company with twelve 7.5 cm antitank guns. Six of the lighter guns and all the heavy guns were motorized. The remaining six 5 cm guns were static and most likely did not follow the division to Normandy.[10]

The division possessed no field-replacement battalion and *Pionier-Bataillon 177* had only one of its companies equipped with heavy weapons.[11]

About 20% of the soldiers had combat experience from the Eastern Front. Another 20% were old men (up to 40 years old) from West Prussia. Men born 1925 made up 35% of the strength and the remaining men included previously injured soldiers who were no longer deemed fit enough to serve in the east.[12]

On D-Day the division was located near St. Malo[13] and, the following day, it was decided to send the *77. Infanterie-Division* to Normandy as soon as it could be relieved by the *5. Fallschirmjäger-Division.*[14] Motorized parts of the division had reached a position east of Granville 8 June[15] and, two days later, elements of the division had reached Valognes, being committed on both sides of the Merderet. Most of the division was in the area north of Coutances.[16]

It has been assumed that the *77. Infanterie-Division* was largely cut off when US forces reached the western coast of the Cotentin Peninsula and only small elements of the division succeeded in breaking out to the south.

Actually only parts of the division were ever committed that far north. Two battalions were committed north of the Utah Beach area, while one battalion was sent to the fortress area around Cherbourg.[17] Two of these battalions were subsequently transferred to St. Sauveur.[18] About 1,200 men that were cut of by the American advance broke out to the south, led by the commander of *Grenadier-Regiment 1049.*[19] Another 70 men remained in the Cherbourg area.[20]

One battalion, the I./*Grenadier-Regiment 1050,* remained in St. Malo and was later sent to join the division. On 17 June it had passed Avranches.[21] By 24 June losses amounted to (excluding parts still in Cherbourg)[22]:

34% of infantry
20% of artillery personnel
22% of engineer personnel
23% of antitank personnel

Given these percentages it seems that the division had lost from 1,800–2,000 men from 6–24 June.

On 10 July the division was reported to have a *Kampfstärke* (≈ Trench Strength) of 1,840.[23] Its artillery still comprised two battalions with 10.5 cm howitzers and one battalion with 8.8 cm guns, though only six 8.8 cm guns remained.[24]

The division remained close to the coast during July and, at the beginning of August, much of it retreated into St. Malo, where it went into captivity when the town fell in mid-August. Some elements of the division probably never went to St. Malo. According to an *OKH* document dated 16 October 1944, the division was estimated to have a strength of 3,000 on 1 September.[25] Nevertheless it was disbanded on 15 September.[26]

1   G. Tessin, *Verbände und Truppen der deutschen Wehrmacht und Waffen-SS* (Mittler & Sohn, Frankfurt am Main and Biblio Verlag, Osnabrück 1966–1975).

2   Kriegsgliederung 77.I.D., Stand 1.5.44, T312, R1566, F000223.

3   Kriegsgliederungen AOK 7, T312, R1566, F000198.

4   WFST/Op. (H)AWest Nr.004662/44 g.Kdos, den 3. Mai 1944, Fehlstellen der Divisionen im Bereich OB West, Stand 1.4.44, T77, R1421, F000237f.

5   Kriegsgliederung 77.I.D., Stand 1.5.44, T312, R1566, F000223.

6   OB West Ia Nr. 4340/44 g.Kdos, 4.6.44, T311, R24, F7029127.

7   Ibid.

8   Ibid.

9   Ibid and see also Taktische Reserven panzerbrechender Waffen innerhalb der Divisionen, Stand vom 1.5.44, T312, R1568, F000718.

10 Kriegsgliederung 77.I.D., Stand 1.5.44, T312, R1566, F000223.

11 Ibid.

12 Gefechtsbericht des Grenadier Regimentes 1050, BA-MA RH 15/441.

13 Lagekarte AOK 7 5.6.44, BA-MA RH 20-7/138K.

14 KTB AOK 7 Ia 6 Jun 1944–16 Aug 1944, entry 7.6.44, T312, R1569, F000009f.

15 OB West Ia 4432/44 g.Kdos., 8.6.44, T311, R25, F7029387.

16 KTB AOK 7 Ia 6 Jun 1944–16 Aug 1944, entry 10.6.44, T312, R1568, F000743 and OB West Ia 4517/44 g.Kdos, 12.6.44, T311, R25, F7029487.

17 HGr B Ia Nr. 3848/44 g.Kdos, 22.6.44, T311, R3, F7002297ff.

18 Ibid.

19 Ibid.

20 Ibid.

21 OB West Ia Nr. (unreadable)/44 g.Kdos, 17.6.44, T311, R25, F7029619.

22 AOK 7 Ia Nr. 3454/44 g.Kdos 27.6.44, T312, R1565, F001381.

23 KTB AOK 7 Ia, entry 10.7.44, T312, R1569, F000140.

24 Bericht über die Frontreise des Generalfeldmarschall von Kluge am 4. und 5.7.44 zum Gen.Kdo. LXXXIV. A.K. und II. Fs.Korps, T311, R28, F7034225.

25 OKH Org.Abt. I Nr. I/19995/44 g.Kdos., 16.10.44, T78, R432, F6403685. This document lists the strength of all the divisions in the west on 1 September 1944. However, it is explicitly stated that much of the data are estimates. In some cases it has been possible to check these figures against reliable data, and it is clear that the estimates given in the document are generally too low.

26 Tessin, op.cit.

84. Infanterie-Division

The division was raised in February 1944 in the area of *15. Armee* in northern France.[1] When formed it had the following organization:[2]

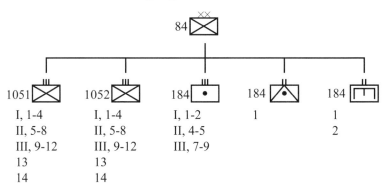

The TOE included 63 machine guns and twelve 8.1 cm mortars in each infantry battalion. The *13. Kompanie* of each infantry regiment was supposed to have two 15 cm heavy infantry guns and six 7.5 cm light infantry guns, while the *14. Kompanie* was authorized three 7.5 cm *Pak,* six machine guns and 36 *Panzerschrecks.*[3]

The single company of *Panzerjäger-Abteilung 184* was supposed to have 12 7.5 cm *Pak* and each of the two companies of *Pionier-Bataillon 184* was allotted two heavy and nine light machineguns, two 8.1 cm mortars and six flame throwers.[4]

Artillery was rather weak with only eight 10.5 cm howitzers in the *I./Artillerie-Regiment 184* and four 10.5 cm and four 15 cm howitzers in the *II./Artillerie-Regiment 184.* The *III./Artillerie-Regiment 184* battalion was supposed to have twelve 8.8 cm *Pak.*[5]

The field replacement battalion was rather weak and had only two companies.[6]

Authorized manpower strength was 8,075 officers and men and, on 1 March, the division had 6,382 personnel, a shortage of 1,708.[7] The average age of the men was 33.[8] One month later the situation had improved and the division was reported to be above authorized strength by 151 men.[9] On 20 June the division was reported to have 8,437 men plus 1,378 *HiWi* (Eastern volunteers).[10]

On 1 June the artillery regiment had four 10.5 cm *leichte Feldhaubitze 18/40's* in each of the two batteries in the *I./Artillerie-Regiment 184.* The *II./Artillerie-Regiment 184* had four 10.5 cm leichte *Feldhaubitze 18/40's* in the *4. Batterie* and four 15 cm *schwere Feldhaubitze 18's* in the *5. Batterie.* The *3.* and *6./Artillerie-Regiment 184* did not exist. The *7./Artillerie-Regiment 184* had four 8.8 cm *Flak 36's* while the *8.* and *9./Artillerie-Regiment 184* had four 8.8 cm *Flak 18's* each. All batteries — except the *1.* and *2./Artillerie-Regiment 184* — were motorized.[11]

It is possible the division exchanged its 8.8 cm *Flak* for 15 cm howitzers. A document[12] dated 22 June 1944 discusses where the 8.8 cm guns should be sent once 15 cm howitzers had arrived for the *84.* and *85. Infanterie-Divisionen.* No information on the actual arrival of the howitzers have been found.

On 12 June *Füsilier-Bataillon 84* was formed by taking elements from the two infantry regiments.[13]

It seems that the division had received its full complement of 7.5 cm antitank guns since, on 30 June, it was reported that it had 18 such guns.[14] This would correspond to 3 each in the *13. Kompanie* of the two infantry regiments and 12 in the *Panzerjäger-Kompanie.*

Late in July the division began to move to Normandy. On 3 August *Füsilier-Bataillon 84* had arrived at the *LXXXIV. Korps.*[15] Even though the division arrived late in Normandy it seems to have suffered relatively high casualties. During the Falaise pocket battle it acted as rearguard for the German units that retreated to the east.[16] The division had about 3,000 men on 22 August,[17] which would indicate that its casualties amounted to about 5,500 men.

---

1   G. Tessin, *Verbände und Truppen der deutschen Wehrmacht und Waffen-SS* (Mittler & Sohn, Frankfurt am Main and Biblio Verlag, Osnabrück 1966–1975).

2   Anlage zu AOK 15 Ia Nr. 1295/44 g.Kdos, v. 6.2.44, T312, R516, F8114596.

3   Ibid.

4   Ibid.

5   Ibid.

6   Tessin, op. cit.

7   Gen.Kdo. LXXXI. A.K. lib Nr. 272/44 geh, T314, R1590, F000826.

8   Ibid.

9   WFST/Op. (H)AWest Nr.004662/44 g.Kdos, den 3. Mai 1944, Fehlstellen der Divisionen im Bereich OB West, Stand 1.4.44, T77, R1421, F000237f.

10   OB West Ia Nr. 4772/44 g.Kdos. 20.6.44, T311, R25, F7029678.

11   Stoart AOK 15 Nr. 629/44 g.Kdos, Art.Gliederung der 15. Armee, Stand vom 1.6.44, T312, R516, F8115287ff.

12   AOK 15 Ia Nr. 6368/44 geh., 22.6.44, BA-MA RH 20-15/67.

13   Tessin, op.cit.

14   Übersicht der Ausstattung mit s.Pak u. Stu.Gesch., Stand 30.6, Anlage zu AOK 15 - 500/44 geh (Stopak), T312, R516, F8115326.

15   OB West Ia Vormittagsmeldung 3.8.44, T311, R28, F7035082.

16   See Dettling, *Bericht über die Teilnahme der 363. Inf.Div. am Feldzug in Normandie*, MS # B-163, p. 7 and also map for 19 August. The 363. ID fought to the left of 84. ID.

17   This is based on the fact that it was assessed to have a strength of 2,000 men on 1 September according to the overly pessimistic document OKH Org.Abt. I Nr. I/19995/44 g.Kdos. 16.10.1944, (T78, R432, F6403685ff). It is also compared to the *363. Infanterie-Division* which fought similar actions during the last period of the Falaise pocket.

85. Infanterie-Division

The division was raised in February 1944. It was immediately put under command of the *15. Armee* on the Channel coast.[1] The authorized organization of the division was:[2]

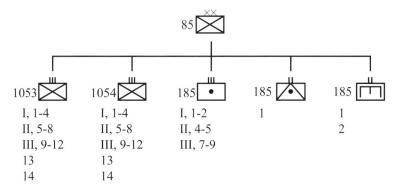

The TOE included 63 machine guns and 12 8.1 cm mortars in each infantry battalion. The *13. Kompanie* of each infantry regiment was supposed to have two 15 cm heavy infantry guns and six 7.5 cm light infantry guns, while the *14. Kompanie* was authorized three 7.5 cm *Pak*, six machine guns and 36 *Panzerschrecks*.[3]

The single company of *Panzerjäger-Abteilung 185* was supposed to have 12 7.5 cm *Pak* and each of the two companies of *Pionier-Bataillon 185* was allotted two heavy and nine light machineguns, two 8.1 cm mortars and six flame throwers.[4]

Artillery was rather weak with only eight 10.5 cm howitzers in the *I./Artillerie-Regiment 185*, four 10.5 cm and four 15 cm howitzers in the *II./Artillerie-Regiment 185*. The *III./Artillerie-Regiment 185* was supposed to have twelve heavy *Pak*.[5]

The division was relatively weak and, on 20 June, it had only 8,393 men plus 332 *HiWi* (Eastern volunteers).[6] On 1 June the artillery regiment had four 10.5 cm *leichte Feldhaubitze 18/40's* in each of the two batteries in the *I.* and *II./Artillerie-Regiment 185*. The *3.* and *8./ Artillerie-Regiment 185* did not exist. The *III./Artillerie-Regiment 185* had four 8.8 cm *Pak* guns in each of its three batteries; that battalion's batteries were motorized.[7]

It is quite possible that the 8.8 cm guns of the *III./Artillerie- Regiment 185* were replaced with 15 cm *schwere Feldhaubitzen*. This was the intention according to a report dated 22 June.[8] On 30 June the division had 18 heavy antitank guns (7.5 cm or 8.8 cm).[9] This corresponds to the authorized strength of the antitank company and the two infantry regiments.

During June, the division created a *Füsilier-Bataillon*,[10] probably by using elements from the two infantry regiments.

The *3./Panzerjäger-Abteilung 185,* equipped with 3.7 cm *Flak,* was to be raised during June by the replacement army and sent to the division.[11] If it saw action in Normandy is unclear.

At the beginning of August, the division began to move to Normandy. On 4 August *Panzerjäger-Abteilung 185* and the *III./Artillerie-Regiment 185* were on the western side of the Seine. *Grenadier-Regiment 1053,* two companies of *Füsilier-Bataillon 185, Pionier-Bataillon 185 (minus the 3. Kompanie)* and the *I./Artillerie-Regiment 185* were in the Cleres area. The rest of the division was in the area east of Neufchatel.[12]

On 10 August *Grenadier-Regiment 1053,* the *1./Pionier-Bataillon 185* and the *III./Artillerie-Regiment 185* were in action.[13] The division fought mainly on the northern shoulder of the Falaise pocket. The division probably had about 5,000 men on 22 August,[14] which would indicate that its casualties amounted to about 3,000 men.

1   G. Tessin, *Verbände und Truppen der deutschen Wehrmacht und Waffen-SS* (Mittler & Sohn, Frankfurt am Main and Biblio Verlag, Osnabrück 1966–1975).
2   Anlage zu AOK 15 Ia Nr. 1295/44 g.Kdos, v. 6.2.44, T312, R516, F8114595.
3   Ibid.
4   Ibid.
5   Ibid.
6   OB West Ia Nr. 4772/44 g.Kdos. 20.6.44, T311, R25, F7029678.
7   Stoart AOK 15 Nr. 629/44 g.Kdos, Art.Gliederung der 15. Armee, Stand vom 1.6.44, T312, R516, F8115287ff.
8   AOK 15 Ia Nr. 6368/44 geh., 22.6.44, BA-MA RH 20-15/67.
9   Übersicht der Ausstattung mit s.Pak u. Stu.Gesch., Stand 30.6, Anlage zu AOK 15 - 500/44 geh (Stopak),T312, R516, F8115326.
10 Tessin, op.cit. see units numbered 185.
11 AOK 15 Ia Nr. 5558/44 8.6.44, BA-MA RH 20-15/67.
12 OB West Ia Nr. 6436/44 g.Kdos, 4.8.44, T311, R28, F7035147.
13 OB West Ia Nr. 6724/44 g.Kdos. 10.8.44, T311, R28, F7035390.
14 This is based on the fact that it was assessed to have a strength of 3,000 men on 1 September according to the overly pessimistic document OKH Org.Abt. I Nr. 1/19995/44 g.Kdos. 16.10.1944, (T78, R432, F6403685ff).

89. Infanterie-Division

The division was raised in January 1944 in Bergen near Celle in Germany. Almost immediately it was sent to Norway to continue forming and training.[1]

In June the division was ordered to move to Western Europe and on 26 June four trains had unloaded in the Le Havre — Amiens area. A further 19 trains were on the way to that area. Other trains had not yet reached the *OB West* area.[2]

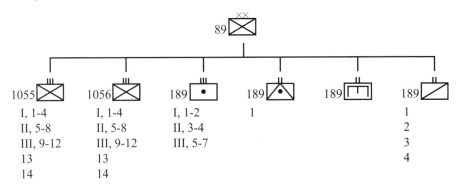

In all likelihood, the division had a personnel strength of about 8,000–8,500 men like the *84.* and *85. Infanterie-Divisionen,* which had similar organization. According to a report dated 18 July, the division had 100% mobility among its horse-drawn elements, while the motorized parts had 83% mobility.[3]

At the end of July the division was sent to Normandy and, on 3 August, it was subordinated to the *I. SS-Panzer-Korps.*[4] One day later *Grenadier-Regiment 1056* was found in the Falaise–Bretteville area together with the *III./Artillerie-Regiment 189* and *Panzerjäger-Abteilung 189. Grenadier-Regiment 1055, Füsilier-Bataillon 189* and the *II./Artillerie-Regiment 189* were near Thiberville, while the *I./Artillerie-Regiment 189* was south of Lisieux.[5]

On 6 August parts of the division were in action together with 13 *Sturmpanzer IV's* that were temporarily attached from *Sturmpanzer-Abteilung 217.*[6] The division probably lost about 4,000 men during its actions in Normandy.[7] On 25 August the division had six artillery pieces ready for action.[8]

1   G. Tessin, *Verbände und Truppen der deutschen Wehrmacht und Waffen-SS* (Mittler & Sohn, Frankfurt am Main and Biblio Verlag, Osnabruck 1966–1975).

2   OB West Ia Nr. 4858/44 geh.Kdos, den 22.6.44., T311, R25, F7029750.

3   HGr B Ia Nr. 4943/44 g.Kdos, 18.7.44, T311, R4, F7003813.

4   Pz.Gr. West Ia, Nr. 734/44 geh. von 4.8.1944., Nachtrag zur Tagesmeldung 3.8., BA-MA RH 21-5/50.

5   OB West Ia Nr. 6450/44 g.Kdos, 4.8.44, T311, R28, F7035148.

6 OB West Ia Nr. 6526/44 g.Kdos. 6.8.44, T311, R28, F7035220 and Pz.Gr. West Ia Nr. 801/44 g.Kdos, 7.8.44, Nachtrag zur Tagesmeldung 6.8, T313, R420, F8714118.

7 This is based on the fact that it was assessed to have a strength of 3,000 men on 1 September according to the overly pessimistic document prepared by OKH Org.Abt. I Nr. I/19995/44 g.Kdos. 16.10.1944, (T78, R432, F6403685ff).

8 Anlage 1 zum Gen der Art beim Chef Gen.St.d.Heeres Ib Nr. 2610/44 g.Kdos. 27.8.44, BA-MA RH 11 II/v. 4.

91. Luftlande-Division

The division was formed in January 1944 at Baumholder, Germany. It was soon moved to Reims, where it was to train for air landing operations.[1] It seems that the organization of the division was:[2]

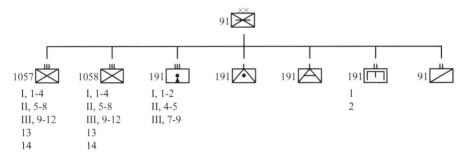

In May the *91. Luftlande-Division* was sent to Normandy. It was reported on 15 May that all rail movements were completed.[3] The division required only 32 trains,[4] which suggests it had a strength of no more than perhaps 7,000–8,000 men.

According to Tessin, *Füsilier-Bataillon 91* was formed in April 1944, but it was not included on the 7. *Armee* situation map dated 5 June 1944. It may not have been combat ready. *Fallschirmjäger- Regiment 6* was attached to the *91. Luftlande-Division* on D-Day. It seems that the division had no field replacement battalion.[5]

A particular problem for the division was that two of its artillery battalions were equipped with 10.5 cm *Gebirgs-Haubitze 40's*. This weapon, a mountain howitzer, used ammunition that was not interchangeable with the standard German 10.5 cm field howitzer. When the division arrived in Normandy it had only one basic load of ammunition for this weapon. During the fighting it received very little resupply of this ammunition and these howitzers had to be sent away and replaced with other weapons. This made the equipment of the artillery regiment very mixed.[6]

Elements of the division were engaged on D-Day, counterattacking US paratroopers on the Cotentin Peninsula. The commander of the division, Wilhelm Falley, was killed when he tried to return to his command post.

By 12 June the *91. Infanterie-Division* had lost 2,212 men killed, wounded and missing.[7] Losses continued to mount, and it was reported that the division lost 85% of its infantry from 6–24 June. During the same period, it lost 21% of the artillery manpower, 76% of its engineers and 48% of the *Panzerjäger* personnel.[8]

On 27 June the formation could no longer be regarded as a division. It had the following:[9]

Gruppe Eitner: 2 medium-strong and 1 weak battalion
Gruppe Lewendowski: 2 weak battalions

Gruppe Jäger: 1 weak *Ost-Bataillon*

Gruppe Klosterkämper: 2 medium-strength battalions (from the *243. Infanterie-Division)*

1 strong Turkish battalion

It still had considerable heavy equipment: 31 7.62 cm *Feldkanone 39s,* 1 7.5 cm *Feldkanone 17(t),* 2 10.5 cm *Gebirgs-Haubitze 40s,* 8 8.8 cm *Pak 43's,* 12 12.2 cm Russian howitzers, 7 12.5 cm Russian guns, 9 15.5 cm Russian gun-howizters, 2 8.8 cm Flak, 21 *Sturmgeschütz III's,* 10 *Pak 40's* (self-propelled), and 39 *Pak 40's* (motorized).[10] The *Sturmgeschütz III's* were most likely from *Sturmgeschütz-Abteilung 902.*

The division remained close to the coast and, on 21 July, it had the following artillery:[11]

II./Artillerie-Regiment 177: 4. Batterie (four 10.5 cm howitzers), *5. Batterie* (three 10.5 cm howitzers)

III./Artillerie-Regiment 177: 7. Batterie (three 8.8 cm *Pak), 8. Batterie* (three 8.8 cm *Pak)* and *9. Batterie* (seven 2 cm *Flak* and two 3.7 cm *Flak)*

I./Artillerie-Regiment 353: 1. Batterie (four 10.5 cm howitzers), *2. Batterie* (three 10.5 cm howitzers), *3. Batterie* (four 10.5 cm howitzers)

I./Artillerie-Regiment 265: 2. Batterie (four 7.62 cm guns), *3. Batterie* (three 7.62 cm guns), *9. Batterie* (three 12.2 cm gun-howitzers)[12]

On 23 July the division only had two infantry battalions left, and these were mere shells of themselves. The division had also detached one battalion to the *243. Infanterie-Division.*[13] The division had some other units attached to it:[14]

From the *77. Infanterie-Division:* 2 average, 1 weak and 2 combat ineffective battalions

From the *265. Infanterie-Division:* 1 combat-ineffective battalion

The division's organic artillery was detached to the *243. Infanterie- Division* (six batteries) and the *2. SS-Panzer-Division "Das Reich"* (one battery).[15]

Since the division was seriously depleted, its remaining elements were withdrawn to beef up other units. This was formally acknowledged on 10 August.[16] The casualties of the division — excluding attached units — probably amounted to about 5,000 men.

---

1 G. Tessin, *Verbände und Truppen der deutschen Wehrmacht und Waffen-SS* (Mittler & Sohn, Frankfurt am Main and Biblio Verlag, Osnabrück 1966–1975).

2 Ibid.

3 OB West Ia, Anlagen zum KTB, Meldung Gen.d.Tr.West, 15.5.44, T311, R24, F7028540.

4 OB West Ia, Anlagen zum KTB, Meldung Gen.d.Tr.West, 12.5.44, T311, R24, F7028484.

5 Tessin, op. cit.

6 See E. König, *Kämpfe in der Normandie, 91. LL Div.,* MS # B-010, p. 2f and W. Triepel, *Artl. Führer 91. Inf.Div. (18.6. - 31.7.1944),* MS # B-469, p. 1.

7 AOK 7 Ia Nr. 3116/44 g.Kdos, 15.6.44., T312, R1565, F001048.

8   AOK 7 Ia Nr. 3454/44 g.Kdos 27.6.44, T312, R1565, F001381. These figures do not include those elements that were surrounded in Cherbourg. But it was reported that only 30 men of the division were among the forces cut off at Cherbourg (HGr B Ia Nr. 3848/44 g.Kdos, 22.6.44, T311, R3, F7002297), this can hardly have affected the percentages by much.

9   AOK 7 Ia Nr. 3454/44 g.Kdos 27.6.44, T312, R1565, F001377.

10   AOK 7 Ia Nr. 3454/44 g.Kdos 27.6.44, T312, R1565, F001377.

11   Gen.Kdo. LXXXIV A.K. Ia Nr. 035/44g.Kdos 22.7.44, Taktische Glederung der Artillerie, Stand 21.7.44, T314, R1604, F001388.

12   The symbol in the original document is a gun-howitzer. However, no 12.2 cm gun-howitzer was used by the Germans. There was a 15.2 cm gun-howitzer (captured Russian) and it is possible that this is a printing error. Alternately, it could be the symbol that is wrong. If that is the case, it is most likely that the weapons were 12.2 cm howitzers. On 1 May the battery was equipped with 12.2 cm howitzers (Gliederung 265. Inf.Div. 1.5.1944, Gliederungen AOK 7, BA-MA RH 20-7/136).

13   Gen.Kdo. LXXXIV. A.K. Ia 048/44 g.Kdos. T314, R1604, F001374.

14   Ibid.

15   Ibid.

16   OKH Org.Abt. Nr. I/18681/44 g.Kdos, 10.8.44, T78, R421, F6390498.

243. Infanterie-Division

The division was formed in July 1943 in Döllersheim, Germany, and sent to Normandy in the autumn.[1] Originally it was a static division, but it had been gradually upgrading its mobility and, in May 1944, had comparatively good mobility for being a German infantry division in the west.

On 1 May 1944, the manpower strength of the division amounted to 11,529.[2] This was probably close to authorized strength, for one month earlier it was reported that the division was short 226 men.[3] The structure of the division looked like this on 1 May:[4]

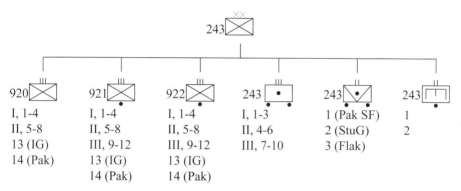

920	921	922	243	243	243
I, 1-4	I, 1-4	I, 1-4	I, 1-3	1 (Pak SF)	1
II, 5-8	II, 5-8	II, 5-8	II, 4-6	2 (StuG)	2
13 (IG)	III, 9-12	III, 9-12	III, 7-10	3 (Flak)	
14 (Pak)	13 (IG)	13 (IG)			
	14 (Pak)	14 (Pak)			

All infantry battalions had 44 light machine guns, except the *I./Infanterie-Regiment 921* which had 46 and the *I./Infanterie-Regiment 922* which had 45. The number of mortars was eight per battalion, except the *I./Infanterie-Regiment 921* which had ten. The caliber of all the mortars was 8 cm. Each infantry regiment had one infantry howitzer company with six Russian 7.62 cm infantry howitzers. Also, each regiment had one company with three 7.5 cm antitank guns. All infantry companies, except those of *Infanterie-Regiment 920,* were equipped with bicycles[5]

Equipment *of Artillerie-Regiment 243* consisted of Russian 7.62 cm guns in the *I.* and *II. Abteilungen.* The *III Abteilung* had Russian 12.2 cm howitzers in the 7.–9. *Batterien*, while the *10. Batterie* had Russian 12.2 cm guns. All batteries had four artillery pieces each. They were all motorized.[6]

Panzerjäger-Abteilung 243 had 14 *Marder 38's* and 10 *Sturmgeschütz III's.*[7] They had been sent to the division in March 1944.[8] The battalion also had a company with 12 2 cm *Flak.*[9] One platoon of these was on tracked chassis, while two were motorized.[10]

With only two companies, *Pionier-Bataillon 243* was relatively weak. It had 19 machine guns. Both companies were equipped with bicycles.[11]

The field replacement battalion had four companies. Equipment consisted of 48 machine guns and one mortar.[12]

When the Allies landed, the *243. Infanterie-Division* was deployed on the western side of the Cotentin Peninsula. Thus, it was gradually drawn into the battle. Parts of the division were encircled in Cherbourg, but also those parts not cut off had substantial casualties. Among the elements not surrounded losses amounted to 55% among the infantry, 25% in the artillery, 30–40% among antitank units and 90% of the engineers. The figures apply to the period from 6–24 June.[13]

Altogether, the division had losses of 8,189 officers and men from D-Day to 11 July.[14] The "in the trench" strength amounted to only 700 men on 10 July.[15]

On 23 July, the division was rated to have *Kampfwert V* (combat effectiveness level V) which was the lowest that could be assigned to a formation. It had only four depleted infantry battalions, eight heavy antitank guns, three *Sturmgeschütze* and nine artillery batteries left.[16]

It was decided on 10 August to rebuild the *243. Infanterie-Division* using the *182. Reserve-Infanterie-Division,* but this was never carried out. Instead, the division was disbanded on 12 September.[17]

1   G. Tessin, *Verbände und Truppen der deutschen Wehrmacht und Waffen-SS* (Mittler & Sohn, Frankfurt am Main and Biblio Verlag, Osnabrück 1966–1975).

2   Gliederung 243. Inf.Div. 1.5.44. BA-MA RH 20-7/136.

3   WFST/Op. (H)/West Nr.004662/44 g.Kdos, den 3. Mai 1944, Fehlstellen der Divisionen im Bereich OB West, Stand 1.4.44, T77, R1421, F000237f.

4   Gliederung der 243.I.D., Stand 1.5.44, T312, R1566, F000220.

5   Gliederung der 243.I.D., Stand 1.5.44, T312, R1566, F000220.

6   Ibid.

7   Ibid.

8   Lieferungen der Pz.Fahrzeuge Bd. ab Mai 1943, BA-MA RH 10/349.

9   Gliederung der 243.I.D., Stand 1.5.44, T312, R1566, F000220.

10   Ibid.

11   Ibid.

12   Ibid.

13   AOK 7 Ia Nr. 3454/44 g.Kdos 27.6.44, T312, R1565, F001381.

14   KTB OB West Ia, entry 12.7.44, T311, R16, F7016788.

15   KTB AOK 7 Ia, entry 10.7.44, T312, R1569, F000140. The sources give *Kampfstärke.*

16   Gen.Kdo. LXXXIV. A.K. Ia 048/44 g.Kdos. T314, R1604, F001375.

17   Tessin, op. cit.

265. Infanterie-Division

The division was formed in May 1943 as a static division. It was immediately sent to Brittany in France.[1] The structure of the division on 1 May 1944 was:[2]

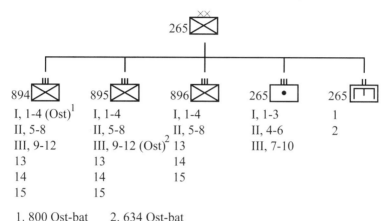

1. 800 Ost-bat   2. 634 Ost-bat

The artillery regiment had the following equipment:[3]

1./Artillerie-Regiment 265: four 7.62 cm guns
2./Artillerie-Regiment 265: four 7.62 cm guns
3./Artillerie-Regiment 265: four 7.62 cm guns
4./Artillerie-Regiment 265: four 7.62 cm guns
5./Artillerie-Regiment 265: four 7.62 cm guns
6./Artillerie-Regiment 265: four 7.62 cm guns
7./Artillerie-Regiment 265: four 12.2 cm howitzers
8./Artillerie-Regiment 265: four 12.2 cm howitzers
9./Artillerie-Regiment 265: four 12.2 cm howitzers
10./Artillerie-Regiment 265: four 12.2 cm guns

All three infantry regiments had three support companies, the *13. (schwere) Kompanie* with six 7.62 cm infantry guns, the *14. (Panzerjäger-) Kompanie* with three 7.5 cm AT guns and the *15. (Panzerjäger-) Kompanie,* which was also an antitank company, but with no organic means of transportation.[4] The division had no other anti-tank weapons and the field replacement battalion consisted of only two companies.[5]

About one quarter of the men had previous combat experience, but many of them had suffered frostbite and were not fully fit. Approximately half the soldiers came from various Landesschützverbände, i.e. units that were organized only for keeping occupied territories under control. They were obviously not first rate soldiers. The remaining quarter was made up of new recruits born 1925.[6]

Until 1 June few changes occurred. The authorized manpower strength amounted to 9,726 and it was only missing four officers. The figure included 341 HiWi (Eastern volunteers). The division had 188 motor vehicles and 117 motorcycles in running order. It also had 2,380 horses.[7]

The division formed a mobile *Kampfgruppe*. It was made up of the staff of *Infanterie-Regiment 896* plus the *III./Grenadier-Regiment 894*, */Grenadier-Regiment 895*, *13./Grenadier-Regiment 896*, *14./Grenadier-Regiment 896* and *14./Grenadier-Regiment 895*. It also included the *2., 3.* and *9. Artillerie-Batterien* under the staff of the *I./Artillerie-Regiment 265*. Finally, the *2./Pionier-Bataillon 265* was part of the *Kampfgruppe.*[8] The *Kampfgruppe* probably had a strength of about 3,500 men[9]. It had 123 light machine guns, 19 heavy machine guns, 16 8 cm mortars, 6 7.62 cm infantry howitzers, 6 7.5 cm antitank guns, 6 flame-throwers and 8 7.62 cm artillery guns and 12.2 artillery howitzers.[10]

When the Allied forces landed in Normandy, it was decided to send the *Kampfgruppe* to Normandy. It received orders to do so on 7 June and it started marching the following day.[11] On 11 June it was located west of St. Lô.[12] It was attached to 91. Division next day.[13]

At the end of June, the Kampfgruppe was transferred to 77. Inf.Div.[14] It remained with 77. Inf.Div. until 15 July, when it again was attached to 91. Inf.Div.[15] It in the sector of 91. Inf.Div. when Operation *Cobra* was launched.[16] By this time the Kampfgruppe was already seriously depleted. The rear services were pulled out, but parts were surrounded and stragglers assembled in the Fougères–Mayenne–Laval area. Eventually, remnants of the Kampfgruppe were transferred to the 18. LW-Division on 21 August.[17]

The main part of the division remained in the coastal fortresses in the Lorient area for the rest of the war. Since all its transport had been used for the mobile *Kampfgruppe*[18] it really had no other choice.

---

1   G. Tessin, *Verbände und Truppen der deutschen Wehrmacht und Waffen-SS* (Mittler & Sohn, Frankfurt am Main and Biblio Verlag, Osnabrück 1966–1975).

2   Gliederungen AOK 7, BA-MA RH 20-7/136.

3   Ibid.

4   Ibid.

5   Ibid.

6   OKH Abwicklungsstab, 29.10.44, "Taktischer Bericht für 265. Inf.Div.", BA-MA RH 15/441.

7   Gen.Kdo XXV. A.K. Ia Nr. 699/44 g.Kdos., 6.6.44, 343., 265., 275., 353I.D. und Kriegsgliederungen der Korpstruppen und Kdr. der Fest.-Stamm-Truppen XXV, Stand 1.6.44. ,T314, R747, F000004-000023.

8   Gliederungen AOK 7, BA-MA RH 20-7/136.

9   On 1 July the division — excluding the *Kampfgruppe* — had a manpower strength of 6,053. See Gen.Kdo XXV. A.K. Ia Nr. 836/44 g.Kdos., 8.7.44, Zustandberichte der 343., 265., 275. und 2. Fsch.Jg.Div., Stand 1.7.44. ,T314, R747, F000197-000210.

10 Gliederungen AOK 7, BA-MA RH 20-7/136.

11 OKH Abwicklungsstab, 29.10.44, "Taktischer Bericht für 265. Inf.Div.", BA-MA RH 15/441.

12 HGr B Ia Nr 3342/44 g.Kdos, Tagesmeldung 11.6.44, T311, R3, F7002373.

13 OKH Abwicklungsstab, 29.10.44, "Taktischer Bericht für 265. Inf.Div.", BA-MA RH 15/441.

14 OKH Abwicklungsstab, 29.10.44, "Taktischer Bericht für 265. Inf.Div.", BA-MA RH 15/441.

15 OKH Abwicklungsstab, 29.10.44, "Taktischer Bericht für 265. Inf.Div.", BA-MA RH 15/441.

16 Gen.Kdo. LXXXIV. A.K. Ia 048/44 g.Kdos. T314, R1604, F001373.

17 OKH Abwicklungsstab, 29.10.44, "Taktischer Bericht für 265. Inf.Div.", BA-MA RH 15/441.

18 HGr B Ia Nr. 4943/44 g.Kdos, 18.7.44, T311, R4, F7003813ff.

266. Infanterie-Division

The division was formed in May 1943. Two months later it was sent to Brittany in France.[1] The organization was:[2]

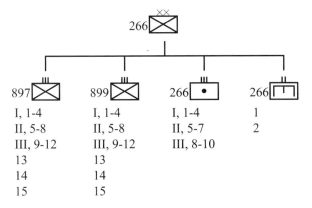

The main equipment of the artillery regiment was:[3]

1./Artillerie-Regiment 266: four 7.62 cm guns
2./Artillerie-Regiment 266: four 7.62 cm guns
3./Artillerie-Regiment 266: four 15.5 cm howitzers
4./Artillerie-Regiment 266: four 15.5 cm howitzers
5./Artillerie-Regiment 266: four 12.2 cm howitzers
6./Artillerie-Regiment 266: four 12.2 cm howitzers
7./Artillerie-Regiment 266: four 7.62 cm guns
8./Artillerie-Regiment 266: four 15.5 cm howitzers
9./Artillerie-Regiment 266: three 12.2 cm howitzers
10./Artillerie-Regiment 266: four 15.5 cm howitzers

On 1 March the division had 8,852 men.[4] Its strength probably remained close to that figure. It had 5,730 rifles on 1 March and 5,877 two months later.[5] This does not indicate a major change of manpower strength. It was also reported on 1 April the division was short of only 159 men.[6] Given the fact that it had no antitank battalion, no *Füsilier-Bataillon* and only two companies each in the engineer and field replacement battalions, a greater strength is not to be expected.

Both infantry regiments had similar support units: the *13. schwere Kompanie* with infantry howitzers, the *14.* and *15. Kompanien* with antitank guns. Most of the antitank guns lacked prime movers.[7]

A mobile *Kampfgruppe* was formed and sent to Normandy. It consisted of the staff of *Grenadier-Regiment 897,* the *I./Grenadier-Regiment 897,* the *II./Grenadier-Regiment*

897, an infantry gun company and a platoon with 7.5 cm antitank guns. An artillery battalion was also formed, consisting of the *3., 8.* and *9./Artillerie-Regiment 266.*[8]

The *Kampfgruppe* was not sent to Normandy immediately after D-Day. On 14 June it was reported that it had reached Jugon on the Brittany Peninsula,[9] which was close to its original location. It did not move quickly; six days later it was near Avranches.[10] Three days later, it had reached the combat zone.[11] During its march to Normandy, the Kampfgruppe suffered 16 casualties from air attacks and partisan attacks.[12]

Most of the time in Normandy it was employed with the *352. Infanterie-Division.*[13] The remnants of the *Kampfgruppe* were probably absorbed by the *352. Infanterie-Division* at the beginning of August.

About 5,000–6,000 men remained with the division in Brittany after the departure of the *Kampfgruppe.* The *Kampfgruppe* took all transportation means with it.[14] When US forces entered Brittany, elements of the *266. Infanterie-Division* tried to escape into the ports of the peninsula. Some of them were eventually destroyed at St. Malo; other elements made it to ports that held out for the rest of the war.[15]

---

1   G. Tessin, *Verbände und Truppen der deutschen Wehrmacht und Waffen-SS* (Mittler & Sohn, Frankfurt am Main and Biblio Verlag, Osnabrück 1966–1975).

2   Gliederungen AOK 7, BA-MA RH 20-7/136.

3   Ibid.

4   Ibid.

5   Ibid.

6   WFST/Op. (H)/West Nr.004662/44 g.Kdos, den 3. Mai 1944, Fehlstellen der Divisionen im Bereich OB West, Stand 1.4.44, T77, R1421, F000237f.

7   Gliederungen AOK 7, BA-MA RH 20-7/136.

8   OB West Ia Nr. 4797/44 g.Kdos, 20.6.44, T311, R25, F7029700.

9   HGr B Ia Nr 3489/44 g.Kdos, Tagesmeldung 14.6.44, T311, R3, F7002389f.

10 OB West Ia Nr. 4784/44 g.Kdos, 20.6.44, T311, R25, F7029690.

11 OB West Ia Nr. 4952/44 g.Kdos., 24.6.44, T311, R25, F7029824.

12 Taktischer Bericht über den Einsatz der Kampfgruppe 266. Inf.Div. (Kampfgruppe Kentner) in der Normandie, BA-MA RH 15/441.

13 See the manuscripts by Ziegelmann, MS # B-439, B-455, B-489.

14 HGr B Ia Nr. 4943/44 g.Kdos, 18.7.44, T311, R4, F7003813ff.

15 Tessin, op. cit.

271. Infanterie-Division

The division was formed in November 1943 in the Netherlands.[1] It was later moved to the Montpellier area in southern France.[2] It was brought up to strength relatively quickly and, on 1 April, it was reported to be short of only 119 men.[3] The structure of the division on 1 July was:[4]

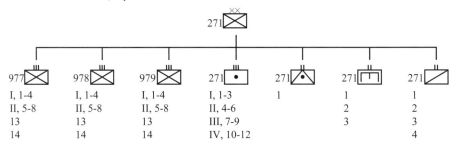

On 19 June the division had 11,617 men plus 1,004 HiWi (Eastern volunteers). It was not fully trained. Its equipment included 330 light machine guns, 72 heavy machine guns, 58 8 cm mortars, 19 7.5 cm light infantry guns, 6 15 cm heavy infantry guns, 32 10.5 cm light field pieces, 9 15 cm heavy field pieces, 22 7.5 cm *Pak*, 188 motorcycles, 158 cars, 164 trucks, 38 prime movers and 4,484 horses.[5]

The batteries of the artillery regiment had either three or four pieces. The *1., 2., 4., 5., 9., 10., 11.* and *12. Batterien* of *Artillerie-Regiment 271* had three pieces each; the remainder had four.[6]

At the end of June the division began moving to Normandy. On 1 July three trains had departed; some of them had already reached Lyon.[7] One peculiarity is that the division was actually sent first to the Rouen area, and later to Normandy. This could be interpreted as an indication that a landing in the Pas-de-Calais area was expected.[8]

During the night from 13–14 July the most advanced elements (*II./Grenadier-Regiment 979* and the *Panzerjäger-Kompanie*) reached the area north of Thury-Harcourt.[9] On 15 July it was reported that all 47 trains had departed and that 23 of them had unloaded.[10] Three days later the various elements of the division were located as follows:[11]

Livarot: *II./Grenadier-Regiment 978;3., 8.,* and *9./Artillerie-Regiment 271*
Falaise: *II./Artillerie-Regiment 271; 13.* and *14./Grenadier-Regiment 979*
Bernay: *Pionier-Bataillon 271; III./Artillerie-Regiment 271 (-)*
Brienne: *1.* and *2./Artillerie-Regiment 271*

Chartes: Main part of *IV./Artillerie-Regiment 271*
Houdan: *L/Grenadier-Regiment 978; 7./Artillerie-Regiment 271*
Rouen: *I./Grenadier-Regiment 977*

In all likelihood the combat elements of the division not included above were already in Normandy.

On 23 July *Grenadier-Regiment 979,* the *II./Grenadier-Regiment 978, Pionier-Bataillon 271* and the *3., 8., 9.* and *12./Artillerie-Regiment 271* were committed to the fighting.[12] One day later, the remainder of *Grenadier-Regiment 978* was in the front line, as were the artillery regiments (minus the *10.* and *11./Artillerie-Regiment 271).* Most of the elements not yet inserted into the frontline were in the area Livarot–St. Pierre–Mezidon.[13] Casualties in July included 206 killed in action, 569 wounded and 267 missing.[14]

At the beginning of August, the division was located south of Caen, west of the Orne. It withdrew across the Orne and, on 12 August, it was located between Thury-Harcourt and St. Germain le Vasson.[15] The division was gradually pushed back along the west side of the Caen–Argentan road.[16]

By 18 August the division started to break contact with the enemy and move to the Chambois area.[17] Late in the evening of 18 August combat elements of the division assembled northeast of Chambois.

It thus seems the division was not surrounded in the Falaise pocket; it seems to have extricated itself before the pocket closed. On 25 August the division had seven artillery howitzers serviceable.[18]

The German Army High Command estimated that the division had a strength of about 5,000 on 1 September.[19] In all cases where these estimates have been possible to compare with more accurate figures, they have been proved too low. It seems more likely the division suffered about 3,000–4,000 casualties. This would have left it with slightly more than 7,000 men.

---

1   G. Tessin, *Verbände und Truppen der deutschen Wehrmacht und Waffen-SS* (Mittler&Sohn, Frankfurt am Main and Biblio Verlag, Osnabrück 1966–1975).

2   Ibid.

3   WFST/Op. (H)/West Nr.004662/44 g.Kdos, den 3. Mai 1944, Fehlstellen der Divisionen im Bereich OB West, Stand 1.4.44, T77, R1421, F000237f.

4   Anlagen zum KTB Nr. 2 LVIII. Pz.Korps Ia, Gliederung 271. Inf.Div. 1.7.44, T314, R1496, F000963.

5   OB West Ia Nr. 4772/44 g.Kdos., T311, R25, F7029681f.

6   Anlagen zum KTB Nr. 2 LVIII. Pz.Korps Ia, Gliederung 271. Inf.Div. 1.7.44, T314, R1496, F000963.

7   OB West Ia Nr. 5185/44 g.Kdos, 1.7.44, T311, R28, F7034124.

8   *See e. g. Danhauser,* Bericht über den Einsatz der 271. Infantreie-Division in der Invasionsschlacht 1944 (Normandie - Nordfrankreich), *MS # B-256, Beilage 2* and *AOK 15 Ia Nr 6651/44 g.Kdos, 29.6.44, T312, R516, F8114748.*

9   Meldung H.Gru. B, 13.15 Uhr, H.Qu den 14.7.44, T311, R28, F7034472.

10 OB West Ia Nr. 5698/44 g.Kdos, 15.7.44, T311, R28, F7034506.

11 OB West Ia Nr. 5819/44 g.Kdos, 19.7.44, T311, R28, F7034642.

12 OB West Ia Nr. 5939/44 g.Kdos, 23.7.44, T311, R28, F7034743ff.

13 OB West Ia Nr. 5972/44 g.Kdos, 24.7.44, T311, R28, F7034777.

14 BA-MA RW 6/v. 577.

15 *Danhauser,* Einsatz der 271.I.D. in Nordfrankreich (Ab 12. August 1944), *MS # B-529, p. 2.*

16   Ibid, pp. 2–9.

17   Ibid. p. 10f.

18   Anlage 1 zum Gen der Art beim Chef Ge,St.d.Heeres Ib Nr. 2610/44 g.Kdos, BA-MA RH 11 II/v. 4.

19   OKH Org.Abt. I Nr. I/19995/44 g.Kdos., 16. Oktober 1944, Notiz Betr Errechnete bzw. Geschätzte Iststärke des Ob.West am 1.9.1944, T78, R432, F6403685-7.

272. Infanterie-Division

The origin of the *272. Infanterie-Division* was in the *216. Infanterie-Division* which had fought on the central sector of the Eastern Front since January 1942.[1] In November 1943 the division was withdrawn and sent to Western Europe to be used as cadre for the new *272. Infanterie-Division*[2] In April 1944 it was sent to the *19. Armee* in southern France, where it continued training.[3] On 1 April it was reported that the division was short only 559 men.[4] At this time the probable organization of the division was:[5]

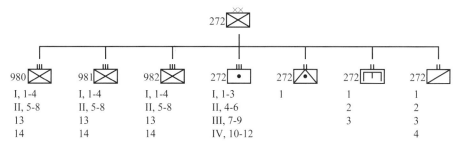

According to an organization chart for 3 August 1944,[6] minor changes had occurred. *Panzerjäger-Abteilung 272* had been expanded by *the addition of* a *Flak* company with 10 *8.8 cm Flak*, one platoon with three towed 7.5 cm antitank guns and one platoon with three self-propelled 7.5 cm antitank guns. It seems, however, that the organization chart depicts authorized organization, not the actual organization for the date indicated. There are no indications in the records that any self-propelled 7.5 cm antitank guns were sent to the division.[7] Further, all the infantry battalions are indicated to have similar equipment: 54 machine guns and 10 mortars each.[8] This is highly unlikely for a division engaged in combat.

On 19 June it was reported that the division had 11,211 men and 1,514 *HiWI* (Eastern volunteers).[9] The weapons comprised 464 light machine guns, 102 heavy machine guns, 54 medium mortars, 32 heavy mortars, 19 7.5 cm light infantry pieces, 9 15 cm heavy infantry pieces, 22 7.5 cm *Pak* and 9 15 cm howitzers. The number of 10.5 cm howitzers was 33.[10] Mobility was provided by 177 motorcycles, 105 cars, 136 trucks, 71 prime movers and 4,302 horses.[11]

Training had still not progressed enough on 19 June. Battalion exercises had only been conducted to a limited extent and further training of various specialists was required. The division was rated as useful for defensive missions.[12]

It seems that the artillery regiment did not have four guns in each battery. On 19 June, it was reported that the division had all of the nine 15 cm howitzers it was supposed to have.[13] As indicated above, the division had 33 howitzers of 10.5 cm caliber. It was reported to have a shortage of two.[14] Thus it seems that most of the light artillery batteries had four howitzers. According to the 3 August organization chart, however, all the light batteries were supposed to have only three howitzers.

On 2 July the division began to move from the Mediterranean coast to Normandy by rail.[15] It was intended to unload the division at Le Mans but, due to air attacks and damage to the rail net, several areas were used for unloading. Some of them were located as much as 200 kilometers south of Le Mans.[16] It took time to assemble the trains and load the division. On 5 July it was reported that only 18 trains had departed of the 54 needed to transport the division.[17]

During the night of 13/14 July the division began moving into the frontlines and, on 14 July, three battalions were in the main defensive line.[18] The *272. Infanterie-Division* gradually relieved the *1. SS-Panzer-Division "Leibstandarte"*.

On 16 July the following elements had entered combat: *Grenadier-Regiment 980* and the *I./Grenadier-Regiment 982*. The following elements were just behind the front, ready for action: *Füsilier-Bataillon 272* and the *2./Artillerie-Regiment 272*. In the Falaise-Argentan area were the following: *Panzerjäger-Abteilung 272* (consisting of one company), the 5. and *8./Artillerie-Regiment 272,* the *I./Grenadier-Regiment 981,* the *13./Grenadier-Regiment 982* and the *14./Grenadier-Regiment 982*. The remainder of the artillery regiment was in the Le Mans — Aleçon area, as were the *II./Grenadier-Regiment 981* and the *II./Grenadier-Regiment 982*.[19]

On 24 July it was reported that all movements of *272. Infanterie-Division* were completed.[20] The division seems to have been engaged in intensive combat soon after it arrived in Normandy. According to a telephone conversation between von Kluge and Eberbach on the evening of 17 July, the *272. Infanterie-Division* had lost 33 officers and 900 noncommissioned officers and men through 16 July.[21] Casualties in July included 242 killed in action, 951 wounded and 982 missing.[22]

At the beginning of August, the division received about 600 replacements through a march battalion and from the dissolved *16. Luftwaffenfelddivision*. The antitank battalion of the division was reinforced by elements from the *16. Luftwaffenfelddivision*.[23] This probably brought the organization to the figures indicated above for 3 August.[24]

During the night from 27/28 July the division began to be relieved. It was transferred to the east, taking over the sector of the *21. Panzer-Division* in the Troarn area.[25] As a result of that move, the *272. Infanterie-Division* was never surrounded at Falaise. It seems to have been able to withdraw from Normandy in relatively good order. This is also indicated by the fact that it was reported on 25 August that the division had 27 artillery howitzers combat ready,[26] or about 75% of its authorized strength.

In September the division was sent to Döberitz near Berlin for refitting. On 12 September elements of *Grenadier-Regiment 980* (344 officers and men) returned to the division. On that same day about 720 men from the *III.* and *IV./Artillerie-Regiment 272* were sent to Döberitz. This means that these two battalions still had more than half their personnel strength.

1 G. Tessin, *Verbände und Truppen der deutschen Wehrmacht und Waffen-SS* (Mittler & Sohn, Frankfurt am Main and Biblio Verlag, Osnabrück 1966–1975).

2 Ibid.

3 Ibid.

4 WFST/Op. (H)/West Nr.004662/44 g.Kdos, den 3. Mai 1944, Fehlstellen der Divisionen im Bereich OB West, Stand 1.4.44, T77, R1421, F000237f.

5 This has been derived from Tessin, op. cit.

6 See Anlage 1 in F.-A. Schack, *Die Kämpfe der 272. Infanterie-Division in Nord-Frankreich vom 28.7. bis 28.8.44,* MS # B-702. This Anlage is a reprint of a wartime Gliederungsbild.

7 See BA-MA RH 10/349.

8 Schack, op. cit.

9 OB West Ia Nr. 4772/44 g.Kdos., T311, R25, F7029682f.

10 Ibid.

11 Ibid.

12 Ibid.

13 Ibid.

14 Ibid.

15 F.-A. Schack, *272. Infanterie-Division, Normandie vom 5. — 26.7.1944*, MS # B-540, p. 5.

16 Ibid.

17 OB West Ia Nr. 5316/44 g.Kdos, T311, R28, F7034222.

18 Meldung HGr B 13.45 14.7.44 an OB West Ia,T311, R28, F7034472.

19 OB West Ia Nr. 5757/44 g.Kdos 16.7.44, T311, R28, F7034532.

20 BA-MA RW 6/v. 577.

21 OB West Ia Nr. 5972/44 g.Kdos, 24.7.44, T311, R28, F7034777.

22 Ferngespräch Feldmarschall v. Kluge - Gen. Eberbach 21.58 Uhr bis 22.15, 17.7.44, T311, R28, F7034568.

23 MS # B-702 (see above), p.6.

24 According to Schack (MS # B-702, p. 29), the division had a complete *Panzerjäger-Abteilung* during the latter part of the fighting in Normandy.

25 M. Jenner, *Die 216./272. Infanterie-Division* (Podzun Verlag, Bad Nauheim 1964) p 159f.

26 Anlage 1 zum Gen der Art beim Chef GenSt.d.Heeres Ib Nr. 2610/44 g.Kdos, 27.8.44, BA-MA RH 11 II/v. 4.

275. Infanterie-Division

The division was formed in November 1943 in western France.[1] It had the following structure:[2]

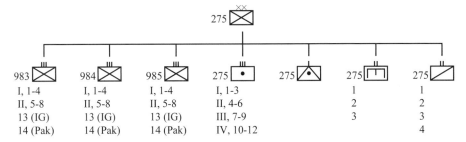

The infantry regiments had the following equipment on 1 June 1944:[3]

I./Grenadier-Regiment 983	45 machine guns, eight 8 cm mortars
II./Grenadier-Regiment 983	45 machine guns, five 8 cm mortars
13./Grenadier-Regiment 983	two heavy and two light infantry howitzers
14./Grenadier-Regiment 983	three 7.5 cm antitank guns, 34 *Panzerschrecks*
I./Grenadier-Regiment 984	42 machine guns, eight 8 cm mortars
II./Grenadier-Regiment 984	43 machine guns, eight 8 cm mortars
13./Grenadier-Regiment 984	one heavy and two light infantry howitzers
14./Grenadier-Regiment 984	three 7.5 cm antitank guns, 34 *Panzerschrecks*
I./Grenadier-Regiment 985	43 machine guns, eight 8 cm mortars
II./Grenadier-Regiment 985	43 machine guns, nine 8 cm mortars
13./Grenadier-Regiment 985	two heavy and two light infantry howitzers
14./Grenadier-Regiment 985	three 7.5 cm antitank guns, 34 *Panzerschrecks*

The *Füsilier-Bataillon* had 43 machine guns and nine 8 cm mortars. *Panzerjäger-Kompanie 275* had 11 heavy antitank guns (probably 7.5 cm).[4]

The main equipment of the artillery regiment was:[5]

1./Artillerie-Regiment 275	four 10.5 cm howitzers
2./Artillerie-Regiment 275	four 10.5 cm howitzers
3./Artillerie-Regiment 275	four 10.5 cm howitzers
4./Artillerie-Regiment 275	four 10.5 cm howitzers
5./Artillerie-Regiment 275	four 10.5 cm howitzers
6./Artillerie-Regiment 275	four 10.5 cm howitzers

7./Artillerie-Regiment 275	four 10.5 cm howitzers
8./Artillerie-Regiment 275	four 10.5 cm howitzers
9./Artillerie-Regiment 275	four 10.5 cm howitzers
10./Artillerie-Regiment 275	three 15 cm howitzers
11./Artillerie-Regiment 275	three 15 cm howitzers
12./Artillerie-Regiment 275	no guns

The division reported a strength of 11,538 men on 1 March.[6] Three months later it was reported to have 10,768 officers and men plus 1,560 *Hi Wi* (Eastern volunteers).[7]

Since the division had a shortage of transportation assets, a mobile *Kampfgruppe* was organized. This consisted of the *I./Grenadier-Regiment* 984, *II./Grenadier-Regiment 984*, one infantry howitzer platoon, one platoon with 7.5 cm antitank guns, *Pionier-Bataillon 275, Füsilier-Bataillon 275,* the *III./Artillerie-Regiment 275* and *Panzerjäger-Kompanie 275.*[8] The *Kampfgruppe* had a probable strength of about 4,100 officers and men plus close to 600 *HiWi.*[9]

When the Allies invaded it was decided to send the mobile *Kampfgruppe* to Normandy. On 8 June it had loaded on 14 trains.[10] Three days later it was reported the unit was in the area west of St. Lo.[11] The following day it was placed in support of the *352. Infanterie-Division.*[12]

On 27 June the *Kampfgruppe* was reported to have three *mittelstark* (medium-strength) battalions and one *schwach* (weak) battalion.[13]

During June this *Kampfgruppe* (also known as *Kampfgruppe Heintz*) was the only part of the *275. Infanterie-Division* committed to the fighting. On 27 June, however, it was decided the division should be sent to Normandy as soon as it could be relieved.[14]

During the night from 5/6 July, units from the *343.* and *265. Infanterie-Divisionen* began to relieve the *275. Infanterie-Division.*[15] At that point the division began to move towards the front as fast as it could given the shortage of transport. On 15 July it was reported that *Grenadier-Regiment 985* and the *I/Artillerie-Regiment 275* were located 22 kilometers southeast of Avranches. Other elements trailed behind.[16]

The *275. Infanterie-Division* counted only 7 430 officers and men on 1 July, after the departure of the Kampfgruppe.[17] On 19 July *Grenadier-Regiment 985* was near Canloy, *Grenadier-Regiment 983* was near Marigny and *Artillerie-Regiment 275* was in the Canisy–Amrigny area.[18] Six days later the last units of the division were reported to be committed.[19]

At the time of Operation *Cobra,* the 275. Infanterie-Division was not employed as a single formation. The *4.* and *6./Artillerie-Regiment 275* were with the *2. SS-Panzer-Division "Das Reich",* while one infantry battalion was with the *Panzer-Lehr-Division.*[20] This battalion was the remnants of the *Kampfgruppe* sent to Normandy previously. *Infanterie-Regiment 985* was sent to the *352. Infanterie-Division.*[21] The remainder of the artillery was placed in direct support of the *LXXXIV. Korps.*[22]

It seems that the division was never employed as an organic formation in Normandy and this makes it hard to follow its whereabouts. The reports giving its condition after the Falaise pocket are conflicting.

One report, which is consistently too pessimistic, states that the division had a strength of approximately 4,000 men on 1 September.[23] This can be compared to a report showing that the division received 5,473 replacements from 22–28 August.[24] The report also shows that no replacements arrived from 1–21 August.[25] Another report asserts that the division suffered 21,237 casualties from D-Day until 13 September.[26] This is either a typing error or else losses suffered by other units are included in the figure.

There also exists an organizational listing that shows the condition of the *275. Infanterie-Division* on 10 September 1944.[27] According to it, the infantry battalions had 2,151 men altogether. *Füsilier-Bataillon 275* had 288 men while *Pionier-Bataillon 275* had only one company with 59 men. The artillery regiment had just one battery with four guns. *Infanterie-Regiment 985* was not present. The division had not received any replacements since 29 August.[28]

It is quite likely that the missing *Infanterie-Regiment 985* had been partially absorbed by some other unit. The same could have happened to other parts of the division since it was not deployed as a complete unit. This makes it very difficult to estimate the casualties suffered.

1   G. Tessin, *Verbände und Truppen der deutschen Wehrmacht und Waffen-SS* (Mittler & Sohn, Frankfurt am Main and Biblio Verlag, Osnabrück 1966–1975).
2   Gliederungen der AOK 7, 275.I.D. Stand 1.5.44, BA-MA RH 20-7/136.
3   Gen.Kdo XXV. A.K. Ia Nr. 699/44 g.Kdos., 6.6.44, 343., 265., 275., 353.I.D. und Kriegsgliederungen der Korpstruppen und Kdr. der Fest.-Stamm-Truppen XXV, Stand 1.6.44., T314, R747, F000004-000023.
4   Ibid.
5   Ibid.
6   BA-MA RH 20-7/136.
7   OB West Ia Nr. 4352/44 g.Kdos, 4.6.44, T311, R24, F7029123.
8   OB West Ia Nr. 4797/44 g.Kdos, 20.6.44, T311, R25, F7029700.
9   On 1 July the division (excluding the *Kampfgruppe)* had a strength of 6,595 officers and men plus 983 HiWi. Its losses and replacement during June were negligible. See Gen.Kdo XXV. A.K. Ia Nr. 836/44 g.Kdos., 8.7.44, Zustandberichte der 343., 265., 275. und 2. Fsch.Jg.Div., Stand 1.7.44. ,T314, R747, F000197-000210.
10 OB West Ia 4432/44 g.Kdos, den 8.6.44, T311, R25, F7029387.
11 HGr B Ia Nr 3342/44 g.Kdos, Tagesmeldung 11.6.44, T311, R3, F7002373.
12 HGr B Ia Nr 3384/44 g.Kdos, Tagesmeldung 12.6.44, T311, R3 F7002377.
13 AOK 7 Ia Nr. 3454/44 g.Kdos., 27.6.44., T312, R1565, F001375.
14 HGr B Ia Nr. 4109/44 g.Kdos, 27.6.44, T311, R3, F7002302.
15 Ob West Ia Nr. 539/44 g.Kdos, 6.7.44, T311, R28, F7034246.
16 OB West Ia Nr. 5669/44 g.Kdos, 15.7.44, T311, R28, F7034483.

17 Anlage zu 275. I.D. Ia, Nr. 649/44, v. 4.7.44, T314, R747, 000197-210.

18 OB West Ia Nr. 5819/44 g.Kdos, 19.7.44, T311, R28, F7034643.

19 Anlagen zum KTB 21.7 - 31.7.1944, Ob West Ia, page 113, 25.7.1944, T311, R28, F7034795.

20 Gen.Kdo. LXXXIV. A.K. Ia 048/44 g.Kdos. T314, R1604, F001373.

21 See Ziegelmann, MS # B-489, p. 3. The author writes that the number of the regiment is 895, but this is probably a typing error. It must have been 985.

22 Gen.Kdo. LXXXIV A.K. Ia Nr. 035/44g.Kdos 22.7.44, Taktische Gliederung der Artillerie, Stand 21.7.44, T314, R1604, F001388.

23 OKH Org.Abt. I Nr. I/19995/44 g.Kdos. 16.10.1944, T78, R432, F6403685ff.

24 Anlagen zum KTB LXXXI. A.K., K.H.Qu., den 20.9.44, T314, R1594, F000271.

25 Ibid.

26 Anlagen zum KTB LXXXI. A.K., K.H.Qu., den 23.9.44, T314, R1594, FQ00267.

27 Gen.Kdo. LXXXI. A.K. Ia, Gliederung 275. Inf.Div., Stand 10.9.44, T314, R1563, F000980.

28 Anlagen zum KTB LXXXI. A.K., K.H.Qu., den 20.9.44, T314, R1594, F000271.

276. Infanterie-Division

The division was raised in southwestern France in November 1943.[1] It was formed by utilizing a core of soldiers from 38. and 52. Inf.Div. Many of the recruits that filled the ranks of the division belonged to the so called "Volksliste 3", which meant people that had been drafted outside the German 1939 borders.[2] The probable structure of the division was:

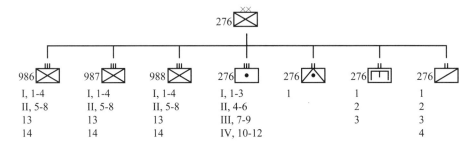

At the beginning of June the division had a manpower strength of 11,658 plus 1,704 *HiWi* (Eastern volunteers).[3] This was a considerable increase, since it only had 2,128 men on 6 January 1944.[4]

On 14 June the division received orders to transfer to Normandy.[5] Six days later one train had reached Le Mans and four had reached Tours.[6] On 23 June 23 trains had unloaded at Angers and those elements of the division that had not yet unloaded were on the way towards Domfront–Flers. The most advanced units had reached a point 20 kilometers east of Mayenne.[7] One day later it was reported that *Füsilier-Bataillon 276, Pionier-Bataillon 276* and *Nachrichten-Bataillon 276* had reached the assembly area.[8]

It was reported on 26 June that 37 trains had unloaded in the Le Mans–Angers area and a further eight were between Angers and Angouleme.[9] Two days later *Füsilier-Bataillon 276* and *Pionier-Bataillon 276* had reached Villers-Bocage.[10] On 1 July *Grenadier-Regiment 986, Füsilier-Bataillon 276* and the *I./Artillerie-Regiment 276* were committed on the right wing of the *Panzer-Lehr-Division*.[11] Five days later most of the division had arrived.[12] In the night from 6/7 July, the division took over the front previously held by the Panzer-Lehr division.[13]

Through 16 July the division had suffered about 1,000 casualties.[14] The 988. Inf. Rgt had the most losses and its soldiers were incorporated into 987. Inf.Rgt.[15] During July it fought southwest of Caen. Casualties in July included 388 killed in action, 1 851 wounded and 461 missing.[16]

The division was surrounded in the Falaise pocket, but large parts of it managed to escape. On 14 August the division commander ordered all rear services, artillery batteries without ammunition, superfluous staffs, baggage sections and other elements not immediately indispensable to withdraw out of the threatening salient.[17]

It is believed at least 4,000 men escaped due to these orders. Thus it seems that the division may have lost, at most, about 6,000 men during the battle in Normandy. This is in line with the fact that subsequently, in September, about 3 000 men from the division was used to create the new 276. Volks-Grenadier Division.[18]

1   G. Tessin, *Verbände und Truppen der deutschen Wehrmacht und Waffen-SS* (Mittler & Sohn, Frankfurt am Main and Biblio Verlag, Osnabrück 1966–1975).
2   Vorläufiger Gefechtsbericht der 276. Inf.Div. über die Kämpfe vom 1.7.-31.8.1944, BA-MA RH 15/441.
3   OB West Ia Nr. 4352/44 g.Kdos, 4.6.44, T311, R24, F7029124.
4   AOK 1 Ia Nr. 1102/44 geh. 6.1.44, T312, R28, F7535564.
5   Badinski, Bericht über Kampfeinsatz der 276. Infanterie-Division 20.6.44-20.8.44, MS # B.007, p. 6
6   OB West Ia Nr. 4784/44 g.Kdos, 20.6.44, T311, R25, F7029690.
7   OB West Ia Nr. 4879/44 g.Kdos. 23.6.44, T311, R25, F7029779.
8   HGr B Ia Nr.3978/44 g.Kdos, Nachtrag zur Tagesmeldung 24.6.44, T311, R3, F7002432.
9   OB West Ia Nr. 5027/44 g.Kdos, 26.6.44, T311, R25, F7029913.
10 OB West Ia, Nr. 5113/44 g.Kdos, 28.6.44, T311, R25, F7029978.
11 OB West Ia Nr. 5230/44 g.Kdos, 3.7.44, T311, R28, F7034151f.
12 Ob West Ia Nr. 5323/44 g.Kdos, 6.7.44, T311, R28, F7034234.
13 Vorläufiger Gefechtsbericht der 276. Inf.Div. über die Kämpfe vom 1.7.-31.8.1944, BA-MA RH 15/441.
14 Ob West Ia Nr. 5779/44 g.Kdos, 18.7.44, T311, R28, F7034577.
15 Vorläufiger Gefechtsbericht der 276. Inf.Div. über die Kämpfe vom 1.7.-31.8.1944, BA-MA RH 15/441.
16 BA-MA RW 6/v. 577.
17 Badinski, op.cit. p. 32.
18 Vorläufiger Gefechtsbericht der 276. Inf.Div. über die Kämpfe vom 1.7.-31.8.1944, BA-MA RH 15/441.

277. Infanterie-Division

The division was raised in November 1943 in Croatia. It was transferred to southern France in January 1944 to continue forming.[1] Its organization was:[2]

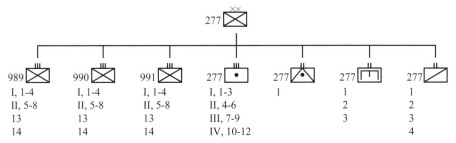

The division was largely composed of Austrians and about one third of the men were veterans from the Eastern Front.[3]

On 19 June it was reported that the division had 9,136 officers and men plus 1,513 *HiWi* (Eastern volunteers). Its equipment included 468 light machine guns, 75 heavy machine guns, 58 8 cm mortars, 19 7.5 cm light field pieces, six 15 cm heavy field pieces, 37 10.5 cm light field howitzers, nine 15 cm heavy field howitzers, 22 7.5 cm *Pak,* 173 motorcycles, 111 cars, 230 trucks, 36 prime movers and 4,618 horses.[4]

The various parts of the division had reached different levels of training. *Panzerjäger-Abteilung 277* and *Füsilier-Bataillon 277* were considered fully trained, while the artillery was sufficiently trained for defensive missions. The infantry had performed exercises as reinforced battalions, but not as complete regiments. The noncommissioned officers also needed more training.[5]

Despite not being fully trained, the division was ordered to Normandy and, on 23 June, one train had reached the area south of Angers.[6] Three days later 11 trains had unloaded in Angers, while 17 were still between Narbonne and Angers.[7] Another 24 had not yet been loaded.[8] On the morning of 2 July the division components were located:[9]

16 kilometers west of Saumur: Regimental staff and regimental units of *Grenadier-Regiment 989*

Northeast Vire: *I./Grenadier-Regiment 989*

6 kilometers east of Vire: *II./Grenadier-Regiment 989*

Chateau Gontier: *Grenadier-Regiment 990* (except the *II./Grenadier-Regiment 990*), *Pionier-Bataillon 277*

14 kilometers south southwest of Domfront: *I./Grenadier-Regiment 991*

12 kilometers northwest of Domfront: *II./Grenadier-Regiment 991*

16 kilometers south southwest of Domfront: *8. and 9 9./Artillerie-Regiment 277*

16 ilometers north northeast of Laval: *4./Artillerie-Regiment 277*

12 kilometers west northwest of Domfront: *5.* and *6./Artillerie-Regiment 277*

12 kilometers northwest of Mayenne: *3.* and *7./Artillerie-Regiment 277*

4 kilometers northwest of Anhibres le Grand: *10./Artillerie-Regiment 277*

6 kilometers northwest of Chateauneuf sur Sarthe: *11.* and *II./Artillerie-Regiment 277*

8 kilometers southwest of Anhibres le Grand: *Füsilier-Bataillon 277*

One week later the division began to take up positions in the frontline,[10] but it was not until 15 July that all rail movements were reported to be completed.[11]

The division became involved in intensive fighting starting 13 July.[12] Through 16 July the casualties amounted to 1,000 men.[13] Losses of equipment in the period from 16–18 July included: five 7.5 cm *Pak 40,* one 10.5 cm light field howitzer, 126 *MG 42's,* 21 8 cm mortars.[14] Casualties in July included 312 killed in action, 1 327 wounded and 1 161 missing.[15]

At the beginning of August, the division was facing British forces east of the Orne.[16] This meant that the division was half-way into what would eventually be the Falaise pocket. The division withdrew to the southeast.[17] It was temporarily reinforced with one company of *Jagdpanthers* and an *Artillerie-Pak-Abteilung* with 8.8 cm guns.[18] On 17 August the division was located a few kilometers southwest of Falaise.[19] Two days later the division was east of the Falaise–Argentan road, in the area north of Vorche.[20] On this day the division still had a full-strength engineer battalion, an artillery regiment at almost full strength (but with little ammunition) and an antitank battalion in relatively good shape.[21] Given the easterly location of the combat elements of the division when the Allied forces finally closed the pocket, it seems very likely that the rear services of the *277. Infanterie-Division* had already passed out of the pocket.[22]

According to the chief of staff of the division, about 2,500 men succeeded to break out of the pocket.[23] If one includes the rear services assumed to be outside of the pocket, it is probable that approximately 5,500 men remained of the division on 22 August. This would indicate that the casualties suffered during the Normandy campaign amounted to 4,000–5,000 men.

---

1   G. Tessin, *Verbände und Truppen der deutschen Wehrmacht und Waffen-SS* (Mittler & Sohn, Frankfurt am Main and Biblio Verlag, Osnabrück 1966–1975).

2   The organization has been derived from Tessin and manuscripts MS # B-009, MS # B-610 and MS # B-679.

3   A. Praun, *277. Infanterie-Division. Teilnahme am Feldzug in der Normandie,* MS # B-009, p 2f.

4   OB West Ia Nr. 4772/44 g.Kdos., T311, R25, F7029683f.

5   Ibid.

6   OB West Ia Nr. 4879/44 g.Kdos. 23.6.44, T311, R25, F7029779.

7   OB West Ia Nr. 5027/44 g.Kdos, 26.6.44, T311, R25, F7029913.

8   Ibid.

9   OB West Ia Nr. 5230/44 g.Kdos, 3.7.44, T311, R28, F7034151f.

10   Praun, op. cit. p. 4. See also H. Fürbringer, *9. SS-Panzer-Division* (Editions Heimdal, 1984) p. 307f. The *211.* Inf.Div. relieved the 9. SS-Pz.Div.

11   OB West Ia Nr. 5698/44 g.Kdos, 15.7.44, T311, R28, F7034506.

12   Praun, op.cit. p 11.

13   Ob West Ia Nr. 5779/44 g.Kdos, 18.7.44, T311, R28, F7034577.

14   HGr B Ib/Br. B Nr. 01068/44 geh 20.7.44, T311, Rl, F7000813.

15   BA-MA RW 6/v. 577.

16   Wangenheim, *Einsatz und Verwendung der 277. Inf.Div. in der Zeit vom 25.7. - 20.8.1944,* MS# B-679, p. 8.

17   Ibid, p. 13.

18   Ibid.

19   Ibid, p. 15 and Viebig, *Nordfrankreich - Einsatz und Kämpfe der 277I.D. in der Zeit vom 13.8. bis. 1.9.44,* MS # B-610, p. 7.

20   Wangenheim, op. cit. p. 19. Note that the author has spelled Vorche wrong, he writes Forche (given the German way of pronouncing "v" this is not surprising).

21   Ibid.

22   It should be noted that the *277. Infanterie-Division* fought alongside the *12. SS-Panzer-Division "Hitlerjugend",* whose rear services were not caught in the pocket.

23   Wangenheim, op. cit. p. 1.

326. Infanterie-Division

The division was raised in November 1942. It was made a static division for the occupation of France. Initially it was in southern France but, from February 1944 on, it was located in the area of operations of the *15. Armee*. During the spring it was upgraded slightly in mobility.[1] The structure of the division was:[2]

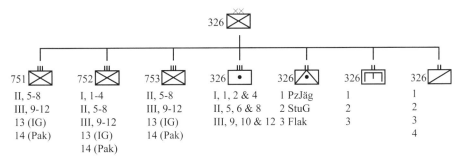

751	752	753	326	326	326	326
II, 5-8	I, 1-4	II, 5-8	I, 1, 2 & 4	1 PzJäg	1	1
III, 9-12	II, 5-8	III, 9-12	II, 5, 6 & 8	2 StuG	2	2
13 (IG)	III, 9-12	13 (IG)	III, 9, 10 & 12	3 Flak	3	3
14 (Pak)	13 (IG)	14 (Pak)				4
	14 (Pak)					

Authorized strength for the division was 11,912 and, on 1 May 1944, it was short only 93 men.[3] It seems that the infantry battalions each had 56 machine guns and eight 8 cm mortars. *Füsilier-Bataillon 326* was similarly equipped.[4]

Panzerjäger-Abteilung 326 had 14 *Marder 38s*, ten *Sturmgeschütz IIIs* and 12 light *Flak*.[5] The assault guns were often referred to as *Sturmgeschütz-Abteilung 1326*. It seems that the assault guns were organized in such a way that they could be detached for separate misions if needed.

As shown above, the artillery batteries were numbered in a peculiar way. The *1., 2.* and *4./Artillerie-Regiment 326* each had four Russian 12.2 cm howitzers; the *5., 6.* and *8./Artillerie-Regiment 326* each had four 10.5 cm *leichte Feldhaubitze 16's*; and, the *9., 10.* and *12./Artillerie-Regiment 326* each had four Russian 12.2 cm guns.[6]

On 20 June the division had a ration strength of 11,533.[7] Ten days liter it had 32 heavy *Pak* (including *Marders* and *Sturmgeschütz III's*).[8]

The division remained in the Pas-de-Calais area until mid July. It was reported on 22 July that elements of the division had crossed the Seine river.[9] One day later *Füsilier-Bataillon 326* was already in the front line and the follow-on elements were approaching.[10] The division relieved the *2. Panzer-Division*.[11]

During July the division remained in the Caumont area. Casualties in July included 126 killed in action, 463 wounded and 453 missing.[12] By mid August it was rather far to the west. The casualties suffered during its actions in Normandy probably amounted to about 6,000, but this is just an estimate.

---

1   G. Tessin, *Verbände und Truppen der deutschen Wehrmacht und Waffen-SS* (Mittler & Sohn, Frankfurt am Main and Biblio Verlag, Osnabrück 1966–1975).

2   Main source is Anlagen zum KTB LXXXII. A.K. Zustandmeldung 326. Inf.Div., Stand 1.5.44, T314, R1602, F000126. This source shows that there was an extra antitank company (numbered 15) in each infantry regiment. However, according to Tessin, these were dissolved at the beginning of June. Also the Stoart AOK 15 Nr. 629/44 g.Kdos, Art.Gliederung der 15. Armee, Stand vom 1.6.44, T312, R516, F8115287ff has been used for the artillery regiment.

3   Anlagen zum KTB LXXXII. A.K. Zustandmeldung 326. Inf.Div., Stand 1.5.44, T314, R1602, F000126.

4   Ibid.

5   Ibid.

6   Stoart AOK 15 Nr. 629/44 g.Kdos, Art.Gliederung der 15. Armee, Stand vom 1.6.44, T312, R516, F8115287ff.

7   KTB 81. A.K., Anlagen, Verpflegungs-und Gefechtstärken, Stand 20.6.44, T314, R1602, F000460.

8   Übersicht der Ausstattung mit s.Pak u. Stu.Gesch., Stand 30.6, Anlage zu AOK 15 - 500/44 geh (Stopak), T312, R516, F8115326.

9   OB West Ia Nr. 5911/44 g.Kdos, vom 22.7.44, T 311, R28, F7034717.

10 OB West Ia Nr. 5939/44 g.Kdos, 23.7.44, T311, R28, F7034743ff.

11 Pz.Gr. West Ia, Nr. 517/44 geh. von 22.7.1944., Nachtrag zur Tagesmeldung 21.7., BA-MA-RH21-5/50.

12 BA-MA RW 6/v. 577.

331. Infanterie-Division

The *331. Infanterie-Division* had been fighting on the Eastern Front since the beginning of 1942. During March 1944 it was with drawn from the east to reform. The infantry plus the equipment of the other parts of the division remained in the east and was distributed among other units. Thus, the division did not contain as many combat-experienced officers and men as could be assumed at first glance.[1]

The structure of the division was:[2]

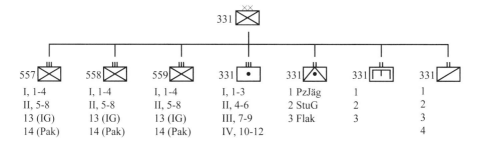

557	558	559	331	331	331	331
I, 1-4	I, 1-4	I, 1-4	I, 1-3	1 PzJäg	1	1
II, 5-8	II, 5-8	II, 5-8	II, 4-6	2 StuG	2	2
13 (IG)	13 (IG)	13 (IG)	III, 7-9	3 Flak	3	3
14 (Pak)	14 (Pak)	14 (Pak)	IV, 10-12			4

Each infantry battalion had 52 machine guns and 12 mortars. The *13. (schwere) Kompanie* of each infantry regiment had two 15 cm heavy infantry guns and four 7.5 cm light infantry guns, except the *13./Grenadier-Regiment 557* which had no 15 cm heavy guns. The *14. Kompanie* of each infantry regiment had three heavy antitank guns; in all cases these companies were at least partly motorized.[3]

On 1 May the division had an authorized strength of 12,602 but was short of 1,255 personnel.[4] At the beginning of June it was reported that the division had 10,543 men plus 1,366 *HiWi* (Eastern volunteers).[5] The artillery regiment had the following equipment on 1 June:[6]

1./Artillerie-Regiment 331	four 10.5 cm light field howitzers
2./Artillerie-Regiment 331	four 10.5 cm light field howitzers
3./Artillerie-Regiment 331	four 15 cm heavy field howitzers
4./Artillerie-Regiment 331	four 10.5 cm light field howitzers
5./Artillerie-Regiment 331	four 10.5 cm light field howitzers
6./Artillerie-Regiment 331	four 10.5 cm light field howitzers
7./Artillerie-Regiment 331	four 10.5 cm light field howitzers
8./Artillerie-Regiment 331	four 10.5 cm light field howitzers
9./Artillerie-Regiment 331	four 10.5 cm light field howitzers
10./Artillerie-Regiment 331	four French 15.5 cm howitzers
11./Artillerie-Regiment 331	four French 15.5 cm howitzers
12./Artillerie-Regiment 331	four French 15.5 cm howitzers

On 1 July the divisional antitank battalion had the following equipment:[7]

1./Panzerjäger-Abteilung 331: 14 *Marder's*
2./Panzerjäger-Abteilung 331: 10 *Sturmgeschütz III's*
3./Panzerjäger-Abteilung 331: 12 2 cm *Flak 38's*

It was reported on 18 July that the division was 100% mobile, i. e. compared to its authorized level of mobility.[8] Ten days later it was ordered that the division should be moved to *Panzergruppe West* in Normandy.[9] The division was loaded on 51 trains and, on 4 August, it had unloaded.[10]

A *Kampfgruppe* from the *331. Infanterie-Division* was in the L'Aigle — Gace area on 11 August, attached to the *LXXXI. Korps*.[11] This area is located some 20–50 kilometers east of Argentan. The US forces were operating south of that area. The rest of the division (except *Grenadier-Regiment 558*) was subsequently employed in this area.[12]

Since the US forces did not make any serious effort in the area defended by the *331. Infanterie-Division,* its casualties were slight. This is also indicated by the fact that the divisional artillery regiment was still at full strength on 25 August.[13]

The whereabouts of *Grenadier-Regiment 558* are less clear. According to Mahlmann, the divisional commander of the *353. Infanterie-Division,* a regiment — he did not remember the number of the unit — from the *331. Infanterie-Division* arrived at his division about 10–12 August.[14] The division lost about 1,500 men in Normandy by 22 August, of which more than half were incurred by *Grenadier-Regiment 558,* but this is just an estimate.[15]

---

1 G. Tessin, *Verbände und Truppen der deutschen Wehrmacht und Waffen-SS* (Mittler & Sohn, Frankfurt am Main and Biblio Verlag, Osnabrück 1966–1975).

2 Anlagen zum KTB LXXXII. A.K. Zustandmeldung 331. Inf.Div., Stand 1.5.44, T314, R1602, F000121ff and Stoart AOK 15 Nr. 629/44 g.Kdos, Art.Gliederung der 15. Armee, Stand vom 1.6.44, T312, R516, F8115287ff. Note that the 557 Gren.Rgt. had initially the number 567 (See Tessin, op. cit.).

3 Anlagen zum KTB LXXXII. A.K. Zustandmeldung 331. Inf.Div., Stand 1.5.44, T314, R1602, F000121ff.

4 Ibid.

5 OB West Ia Nr. 4325/44 g.Kdos, 5.6.44, T311, R24, F7029158.

6 Stoart AOK 15 Nr. 629/44 g.Kdos, Art.Gliederung der 15. Armee, Stand vom 1.6.44, T312, R516, F8115287ff.

7 BA-MA RH 10/242 and also BA-MA RH 10/349.

8 HGr B Ia Nr. 4943/44 g.Kdos, 18.7.44, T311, R4, F7003813.

9 HGr B Ia Nr, 5273/44 g.Kdos., 28.7.44, BA-MA RH 21-5/50.

10 OB West Ia Nr. 6435/44 g.Kdos, 4.8.44, T311, R28, F7035146.

11 HGr B Ia Nr 5961/44 g.Kdos, 11.8.44, T311, R4, F7003928.

12 See KTB LXXXI. A.K. Ia, Lagekarten, T 314, R1594, F000001ff.

13 Anlage 1 zum Gen der Art beim Chef Ge,St.d.Heeres Ib Nr. 2610/44 g.Kdos, 27.8.44, BA-MA RH 11 II/v. 4.

14 R Mahlmann, *353. Inf.Division*, MS # A-985, p 2f.

15 According to the document OKH Org.Abt. I Nr. I/19995/44 g.Kdos. 16.10.1944, T78, R432, F6403685ff, the *331. Infanterie-Division* had a strength of about 6,000 men on 1 September. This document gave estimates and, as shown in the chapter on German losses, these estimates were too pessimistic. The division must have also suffered losses between 22 August and 1 September.

343. Infanterie-Division

This division was deployed near Brest when the Allies landed in Normandy.[1] Its organization on 1 May 1944 was:[2]

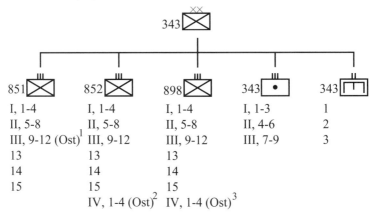

1. 285 Ost-Btl.   2. 633 Ost-Btl.   3. II./Mitte Ost-Btl.

The division had a personnel strength of 10,994.[3] All its artillery was static. The batteries had the following weapons:[4]

1./Artillerie-Regiment 343	four French 15.5 cm howitzers
2./Artillerie-Regiment 343	four French 15.5 cm howitzers
3./Artillerie-Regiment 343	four French 15.5 cm howitzers
4./Artillerie-Regiment 343	four French 15.5 cm howitzers
5./Artillerie-Regiment 343	four French 15.5 cm howitzers
6./Artillerie-Regiment 343	four French 10 cm howitzers
7./Artillerie-Regiment 343	four Russian 7.62 cm guns
8./Artillerie-Regiment 343	four Russian 7.62 cm guns
9./Artillerie-Regiment 343	four Russian 7.62 cm guns

Equipment for the infantry units was as follows:[5]

I/Infanterie-Regiment 851	56 machine guns, 12 8 cm mortars
II/Infanterie-Regiment 851	56 machine guns, 12 8 cm mortars
III/Infanterie-Regiment 851	44 machine guns, 12 8 cm mortars
13./Infanterie-Regiment 851	12 8 cm mortars
14./Infanterie-Regiment 851	static antitank guns

15./Infanterie-Regiment 851	static antitank guns
I./Infanterie-Regiment 852	56 machine guns, 12 8 cm mortars
II./Infanterie-Regiment 852	56 machine guns, 12 8 cm mortars
III./Infanterie-Regiment852	56 machine guns, 12 8 cm mortars
IV./Infanterie-Regiment 852	44 machine guns, 12 8 cm mortars
13./Infanterie-Regiment 852	12 8 cm mortars
14./Infanterie-Regiment 852	static antitank guns
15./Infanterie-Regiment 852	static antitank guns
I./Infanterie-Regiment 898	56 machine guns, 12 8 cm mortars
II./Infanterie-Regiment 898	56 machine guns, 12 8 cm mortars
III./Infanterie-Regiment898	44 machine guns, 12 8 cm mortars
13./Infanterie-Regiment 898	6 Russian 7.62 cm infantry guns
14./Infanterie-Regiment 898	static antitank guns
15./Infanterie-Regiment 898	static antitank gunsPionier-Bataillon 343

Pionier-Bataillon 343 had 29 machine guns and three flame throwers.[6]

On 1 June 1944 the division had a strength of 11,021.[7] Its mobility was poor, since it only had 86 motorcycles and 176 other motor vehicles in running order.[8] It only had 1,182 horses.[9] With only two 7.5 cm and six 5 cm antitank guns, it had marginal antitank capabilities.[10] By June the *Ost-Bataillon 285* had departed from the division.[11]

At dusk on 22 June parts of the division began to move to Normandy. These were called *Kampfgruppe Rambach* and consisted of one infantry battalion (*III./Infanterie-Regiment 898*), one engineer company *(1./Pionier-Bataillon 343),* one artillery battery *(7./Artillerie-Regiment 343)* and one antitank platoon from the *14./Infanterie-Regiment 898* with two 7.5 cm antitank guns.[12]

This force seems to have arrived at the area of operations of the *352. Infanterie-Division* from 26–28 June.[13] The infantry battalion was reported to have suffered 184 casualties by 12 July.[14] In a report dated 2 August, one light battery from the *343. Infanterie-Division* is said to have been with the *352. Infanterie-Division* on 30 July.[15] One incomplete infantry battalion (*III./Infanterie-Regiment 897* minus the *11. Kompanie)* was sent to St. Malo at the end of July.[16]

The rest of the division remained in the Brest area until US forces closed in on the city in August 1944. It was destroyed when Brest surrendered in September.

---

1   See Lagekarten AOK 7, BA-MA RH 20-7/138K.
2   Gliederungen AOK 7, BA-MA RH 20-7/136.
3   Ibid.
4   Ibid.
5   Ibid.

6 Ibid.
7 Gen.Kdo XXV. A.K. Ia Nr. 699/44 g.Kdos., 6.6.44, 343., 265., 275., 353.I.D. und Kriegsgliederungen der Korpstruppen und Kdr. der Fest.-Stamm-Truppen XXV, Stand 1.6.44., T314, R747, F000004-000023.
8 Ibid.
9 Ibid.
10 Ibid.
11 Ibid.
12 Gen.Kdo. XXV. A.K. Ia Nr. 2118/44 geh., 22.6.44, T314, R746, F000968.
13 Ziegelmann, 352. Inf.Div. in der Normandie 23.6 bis 10.7.1944, MS # B-439.
14 Anlage zu O.B.der H.Gr.B "Betrachtungen zur Lage" vom 16.7. T311, R3, F7002245.
15 AOK 7 Ia Nr. 4174/44 g.Kdos, 2.8.44, T312, R1569, F000359.
16 Gen.Kdo. XXV. A.K. Ia Nr. 909/44 geh., 29.7.44, T314, R747, F000513.

346. Infanterie-Division

Raised in Bad Hersfeld, Germany in September 1942 as a static division, it was moved to France within a month of its activation.[1] For most of 1943 it was deployed in Brittany but, in December 1943, it was withdrawn to be restructured as a more mobile unit. It was positioned near Le Havre at the end of January 1944.[2] The *I./ Infanterie-Regiment 857* left the division on 20 March 1944 to form the *Füsilier-Bataillon* of the *326. Infanterie-Division*.[3] Starting 19 April 1944, *Ost-Bataillon 630* was assigned to the division to serve as the *I./Infanterie-Regiment 857*.[4]

The division had an authorized strength of 9,816 men on 1 May 1944. Actual strength was 9,534 men. Average age of the men was 32–33, while officers on average were 37 years old.[5] On 1 June 1944 the structure of the division looked like this:[6]

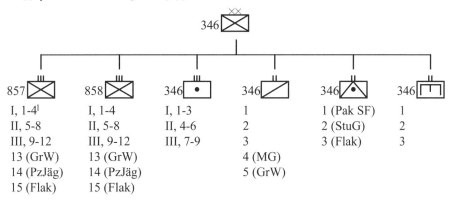

857	858	346	346	346	346
I, 1-4[1]	I, 1-4	I, 1-3	1	1 (Pak SF)	1
II, 5-8	II, 5-8	II, 4-6	2	2 (StuG)	2
III, 9-12	III, 9-12	III, 7-9	3	3 (Flak)	3
13 (GrW)	13 (GrW)		4 (MG)		
14 (PzJäg)	14 (PzJäg)		5 (GrW)		
15 (Flak)	15 (Flak)				

1. Ost.Btl. 630.

Panzerjäger-Abteilung 346 had 14 7.5 cm *Pak 40 (Sf)* in the *1. Kompanie* on 1 June, while the *3. Kompanie* had 12 2 cm *Flak 38*.[7] The *2. Kompanie* had not yet received any assault guns,[8] but ten *Sturmgeschütze III's* were dispatched to the division on 19 May.[9] These probably arrived during the first week of June. The manpower strength of the battalion was 502 men.[10]

As was the case with many other units, the artillery of the division consisted entirely of captured weapons. The artillery regiment had the following equipment:[11]

I. Abteilung: three batteries with four Russian 7.62 cm guns each
II.Abteilung: three batteries with four French 10.5 cm howitzers each
III.Abteilung: three batteries with four Russian 12.2 cm howitzers each

The artillery was not motorized.[12] Other combat elements had been made more mobile by the requisition of buses and other vehicles or by the use of bicycles.[13]

On 6 June the *346. Infanterie-Division* was ordered to move *Grenadier-Regiment 857* (except the *I./Grenadier-Regiment 857* and one platoon of the *13. Kompanie*), 1 engineer company and 1 artillery battery across the Seine as soon as possible.[14] One battalion of *Grenadier-Regiment 858* was to occupy the positions evacuated by the *II./Grenadier-Regiment 857*.[15]

The *Infanterie-Regiment 857* attacked the British positions in the Bavent–Breville area on 7 June.[16] Two days later, the first elements of *Infanterie-Regiment 858* were employed.[17] On 10 June most of the division was committed against the British bridgehead over the Orne.[18]

Casualties up to midnight on 10 June amounted to:[19]

Elements	KIA	Wounded	Missing
Infanterie-Regiment 857	36	161	49
Infanterie-Regiment 858	64	205	401
Artillerie-Regiment 346	2	8	0
Pionier-Bataillon 346	0	1	0

One man in the signals battalion was also wounded.

The division had the following strength in its combat formations on 14 June[20]:

Elements	Ration Strength	Combat Strength
Infanterie-Regiment 857	1,280	1,010
Infanterie-Regiment 858	1,030	875
Artillerie-Regiment 346	1,570	1,015
Pionier-Bataillon 346	385	310
Panzerjäger-Abteilung 346	456	265

Starting 19 June, the situation was relatively calm east of the Orne. That lasted until mid July.[21] After the Operation *Charnwood* by the British, the *346. Infanterie-Division* took over part of the sector held by the *16. Luftwaffenfelddivision*.[22] Between 10 and 17 July, minor British attacks were launched against the *346. Infanterie-Division*.[23] During these attacks, soldiers belonging to the category *Volksliste III*[24] proved unreliable and deserted.[25]

The left flank of the division was subjected to the intensive aerial bombardment preceding Operation *Goodwood* on 18 July.[26] The division successfully defended Troarn during the ground attack that followed the initial air attack.[27] After Operation *Goodwood*, the division had about 50% of its original infantry strength, while the corresponding figure for antitank components was 60%. The strength of the artillery was about 70%.[28] Casualties in July included 152 killed in action, 627 wounded and 192 missing.[29] Fortunately for the division, the period following this British operation was quite calm. It was not until 9 August, when the Allied forces were pushing towards Falaise, that the *346. Infanterie-Division* was engaged more actively. It was, however, located on the eastern flank of the British attack.[30]

The *346. Infanterie-Division* was not among the units encircled southeast of Falaise. It succeeded in withdrawing towards the Seine through the area around Lisieux.[31] According to the estimates of the chief of staff of the division, its strength after crossing the Seine was:[32]

Infantry Regiments: personnel 50%, heavy weapons 35%
Artillery Regiment: personnel 75%, guns 20%
AT battalion: 3 Assault Guns, 4 towed AT guns
Vehicles: 35%

Either the chief of staff was too pessimistic in his estimates, or the Seine crossing resulted in significant losses, particularly of heavy weapons. On 25 August it was reported that the division had 32 combat-ready artillery pieces,[33] or nearly 90% of its original strength. If these estimates are used, it can be concluded that the division must have had around 6,300 men.[34] Given its original strength, it probably suffered around 3,000–3,500 casualties from D-Day to 22 August.

Assault Gun Strength of the *346. Infanterie-Division*

Date	Combat Ready	Short-Term Repair	Long-Term Repair
18 June[35]	1	9	0
19 June[36]	4	6	0
1 July[37]	9	0	1
15 July[38]	8	1	1
19 July[39]	8	?	?
29 July[40]	7	?	?
3 Aug[41]	8	?	?
6 Aug[42]	7	?	?
8 Aug[43]	7	?	?

1   G. Tessin, *Verbände und Truppen der deutschen Wehrmacht und Waffen-SS* (Mittler & Sohn, Frankfurt am Main and Biblio Verlag, Osnabrück 1966–1975).

2   Paul Frank, *Einsatz der 346. Infanterie Division an der Invasionsfront (6.6.1944 bis 24.7.1944)*, MS # B-008, p. 1.

3   AOK 15 Ia Nr. 2773/44 g.Kdos., 20.3.44, T312, R516, F8114464.

4   Tessin, op. cit.

5   Gen.Kdo. LXXXI. A.K. Iib Nr. 398/44 geh, T314, R1590, F000849.

6   Frank, op. cit, Anlagen and Stoart AOK 15 Nr. 629/44 g.Kdos, Art.Gliederung der 15. Armee, Stand vom 1.6.44, T312, R516, F8115287ff.

7   Report to the Inspector-General of Panzer Troops, 1.6.1944, BA-MA RH 10/242.

8   Ibid.

9   Lieferungen der Pz.-Fahrz., Bd. ab Mai 1943, BA-MA RH 10/349.

10 Report to the Inspector-General of Panzer Troops, 1.6.1944, BA-MA RH 10/242. Strength refers to *Iststärke*.

11 Stoart AOK 15 Nr. 629/44 g.Kdos, Art.Gliederung der 15. Armee, Stand vom 1.6.44, T312, R516, F8115287ff.

12 Ibid.

13 Frank, op. cit. p. 2f.

14 Gen.Kdo. LXXXI. A.K. Ia Nr. 1891/44, 6.6.44, T314, R1590, F000163.

15 Ibid.

16 Lagekarten LXXXI. A.K., Kampfverlauf 7.6.44, T314, R1590, 000280.

17 Lagekarten LXXXI. A.K., Lage 9.6.44,13.00, T314, R1590, 000284.

18 Lagekarten LXXXI. A.K., Lage 10.6.44, 15.00, T314, R1590, 000286.

19 KTB Anlagen LXXXI. A.K. Ia, Gefechtsbericht v. 10.6.44, 346.I.D. Ia, 20 14.6.44, T314, R1590, F000417.

20 Gen.Kdo. LXXXI. A.K. Ia Nr. 2031/44 geh., 15.6.44, T314, R1590, F000504.

21 Frank, op. cit., pp. 15–18.

22 Ibid, p. 18.

23 Ibid, p. 18f

24 *Volksliste III* included men that were considered to be of "German race" but living in areas occupied by Germany after the outbreak of the war. See W. V. Madej, *Hitler's Dying Ground: Description and Destruction of the German Army* (Game Publishing, Allentown 1985) p. 74.

25 Frank, op.cit., p. 19.

26 Ibid, p. 21.

27 Ibid, p. 22.

28 P. Frank, *Die Kämpfe der 346. Inf.Div. (24.7.44 -15.9.44)*, MS # B-532, p. 3.

29 BA-MA RW 6/v. 577.

30 Ibid, p. 6f

31 Ibid, pp. 8–16.

32 Ibid, p. 24.

33 Anlage 1 zum Gen der Art beim Chef Ge,St.d.Heeres Ib Nr. 2610/44 g.Kdos, 33.8.44, BA-MA RH 11 II/v. 4.

34
Unit	Initial	Final
Infanterie-Regiment 857	2000	1000
Infanterie-Regiment 858	2000	1000
Artillerie-Regiment 346	1600	1200
Pionier-Bataillon 346	400	250
Panzerjäger-Abteilung 346	500	250
Füsilier-Bataillon 346	800	400
Other Parts	2200	2000
total	9500	6300

35 Gen.Kdo. 81. A.K. Ia, Tagesmedlung 18.6.44, T314, R1590, F000516.

36   Gen.Kdo. 81. A.K. Ia, 19.6.44, T314, R1590, F000513.
37   Pz.Gr. West Ia Nr. 41/44 g.Kdos, 1.7.44, T313, R420, F8713783.
38   Pz.Gr. West Ia Nr. 388/44 g.Kdos 16.7.44, Nachtrag zur Tagesmeldung 15.7, T313,   .
39   Pz.Gr. West Ia Nr. 476/44 g.Kdos, 20.7.44, Nachtrag zur Tagesmeldung 19.7, T313, R420, F8713961.
30   Pz.Gr. West Ia Nr. 647/44 g.Kdos, 30.7.44, Nachtrag zur Tagesmeldung 29.7, T313, R420, F8714042.
41   Pz.Gr. West Ia Nr. 734/44 g.Kdos, 4.8.44, Nachtrag zur Tagesmeldung 3.8, BA-MA RH 21-5/50.
42   Pz.Gr. West Ia Nr. 801/44 g.Kdos, 7.8.44, Nachtrag zur Tagesmeldung 6.8, T313, R420, F8714117.
43   Pz.Gr. West Ia Nr. 846/44 g.Kdos, 9.8.44, Nachtrag zur Tagesmeldung 8.8, T313, R420, F8714139.

352. Infanterie-Division

The division was formed on 5 November 1943 in St. Lô. The inactivated *321. Infanterie-Division* was used as cadre for the new formation.[1] On 1 February 1944 the division had a strength of 9,934.[2] One month later it had increased to 12,734 men[3]. It probably retained this strength without any considerable changes since, on 1 April, it was reported to have 494 men more than the authorized strength.[4] It also had all the weapons it was authorized.[5] This indicates that the division did not receive any major additions of men or equipment until D-Day.

Most of the recruits were born in the years 1925 and 1926. Considerable problems were experienced in training them. Shortages of ammunition meant that before March, the soldiers were only given three opportunities to fire their weapons and had thrown only two hand grenades. Training of drivers lagged behind due to shortages of fuel.[6] Starting in March training proceeded better, but it was hampered by the time spent on construction of the "Atlantic Wall". On average, a soldier spent nine hours on such work each day, while training only accounted for three hours.[7] The structure of the division looked like this on 1 May:[8]

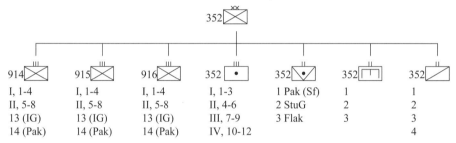

All infantry battalions had 60 light machine guns, 3 heavy machine guns and 12 8 cm mortars. *Füsilier-Bataillon 352* had identical equipment. The *1./Füsilier-Bataillon 352* had bicycles. The infantry regiments had one infantry gun company. In *Infanterie-Regimenter 914* and *915* the infantry gun company had two 15 cm and six 7.5 cm infantry howitzers. The 13./Infanterie-Regiment 916 was equipped with only two 15 cm and two 7.5 cm infantry howitzers. Each regiment had an antitank company with three 7.5 cm *Pak 40's*.[9]

The *1.* through the *9./Artillerie-Regiment 352* had four 10.5 cm howitzers each, while the *10.* through the *12./Artillerie-Regiment 352* had four 15 cm howitzers each. None of the batteries were motorized.[10] The artillery had one basic load of ammunition available.[11] For the 10.5 cm howitzers this meant 225 rounds per gun, while the 15 cm howitzers had 150 rounds each.[12] Altogether this meant 301 tons of ammunition.[13] This does not include artillery in direct support from outside the division.

Panzerjäger-Abteilung 352 had 14 *Marder 38s* and 10 *Sturmgeschütz III's*.[14] These had been received in March.[15] The battalion also had a company with nine motorized

3.7 cm Flak.[16] *Pionier-Bataillon 352* had three companies. Its equipment included 37 machine guns, 20 flame throwers and six mortars.[17] The field replacement battalion had five companies with a total of 62 machine guns, 6 8 cm mortars, 1 5 cm antitank gun, one 7.5 cm antitank gun, one 10.5 cm howitzer, one infantry howitzer and two flame throwers.[18]

Parts of *Infanterie-Regiment 916* were located close to the Omaha beaches on D-Day. One battalion from the *716. Infanterie-Division* was attached to *Infanterie-Regiment 916. Infanterie-Regiment 915* was in reserve southeast of Bayeux, while *Infanterie-Regiment 914* was deployed around Isigny.[19]

The chief of staff of the *352. Infanterie-Division,* Ziegelmann, stated in his postwar manuscript that the losses suffered by the division during 6 June amounted to about 200 killed, 500 wounded and 500 missing.[20] This is supported by wartime documents, which show that the division suffered losses exceeding 1,000 men.[21] The division remained in the area southeast of Isigny.

On 16 June it was reported that the division had about 3,000 casualties.[22] This probably included attached units. Casualties from 6–24 June amounted to 5,407 officers and men.[23] Despite these severe losses the division remained in action. Its losses mounted and, by 11 July, the division had incurred a further 2,479 casualties.[24] During the period from 1 July–25 July, the division lost 123 officers and men killed in action while 464 were wounded and 110 missing.[25]

The division was in very poor shape on 30 July, when all its battalions were classified as *abgekämpft,*[26] which meant that the unit was no longer combat capable and that the battalion had less than 100 combat-ready men left. It had four heavy antitank guns and two *Sturmgeschütz III's* combat ready, as well as four artillery batteries.[27] It also had the following units under its operational control:[28]

Three battalions from the *266. Infanterie-Division*
Two battalions from the *353. Infanterie-Division*
One battalion from the *30. Brigade*
One battalion from the *275. Infanterie-Division*
One battalion from the *343. Infanterie-Division*
One artillery battery from the *343. Infanterie-Division*
One artillery battery from *Artillerie-Abteilung "Autun"*

All of these elements were in about the same shape as the division's organic units.[29] At the beginning of August, the division was withdrawn for refitting in the area southeast of Alençon. The division only spent about a week there before US forces closed in. Elements of the division subsequently became engaged in rear-guard actions along the axis Le Mans–Dreux.[30]

The remnants of the division were merged with the *581. Volksgrenadier-Division* on 21 September 1944 to form the *352. Volksgrenadier-Division.*[31]

1   G. Tessin, *Verbände und Truppen der deutschen Wehrmacht und Waffen-SS* (Mittler & Sohn, Frankfurt am Main and Biblio Verlag, Osnabrück 1966–1975).

2   Kriegsgliederungen AOK 7, T312, R1566, F000159. Strength refers to *Kopfstärke*.

3   Kriegsgliederungen AOK 7, T312, R1566, F000197. Strength refers to *Gesamtstärke*.

4   WFST/Op. (H)AWest Nr.004662/44 g.Kdos, den 3. Mai 1944, Fehlstellen der Divisionen im Bereich OB West, Stand 1.4.44, T77, R1421, F000237f.

5   Auffrischung und Umgliederung, 14.3.44, T311, Rl, F7000461.

6   F. Ziegelmann, *Die Geschichte der 352. Infanterie-Division,* MS # B-432, p. 5.

7   Ibid, p. 8.

8   Gliederung der 352.I.D., Stand 1.5.44, T312, R1566, F000216.

9   Ibid.

10 Ibid.

11 F. Ziegelmann, *Die Geschichte der 352. Infanterie-Division,* MS # B-432, p. 12.

12 G. Donat, *Der Munitionsverbrauch im Zweiten Weltkrieg im operativen und taktischen Rahmen* (Biblio Verlag, Osnabrück 1992) Anlage 5.

13 Ibid.

14 Gliederung der 352I.D., Stand 1.5.44, T312, R1566, F000216.

15 Lieferungen der Pz.Fahrzeuge Bd. ab Mai 1943, BA-MA RH 10/349.

16 Gliederung der 352I.D., Stand 1.5.44, T312, R1566, F000216.

17 Ibid.

18 Ibid.

19 Lagekarte AOK 7, 5.6.1944, BA-MA RH 20-7/138K.

20 F. Ziegelmann, *Die Geschichte der 352. Infanterie-Division,* MS # B-432, p. 41.

21 Reisebericht Hauptmann Pickardt, 10.6.44, T311, R25, F7029436.

22 Anlagen zum KTB OB West Ia, Einzelnotizen, 16.6.44, T311, R25, F7030072

23 AOK 7 Ia Nr. 3454/44 g.Kdos 27.6.44, T312, R1565, F001381.

24 KTB OB West Ia, entry 12.7.44, T311, R16, F7016788.

25 Anlage 1 zu Korpsarzt II. Fallsch.Korps B.Nr. 65050/45 g.Kdos vom 27.1.45, Berichtzeit 1.7 - 4.9.44, p. 15, RA-MA RL 33/5.

26 AOK 7 Ia Nr. 4174/44 g.Kdos., T312, R1569, F000359.

27 Ibid.

28 Ibid.

29 Ibid.

30 Ziegelmann, MS # B-741.

31 Tessin, op. cit.

353. Infanterie-Division

The division was formed 5 November 1943 in Brittany. The inactivated *328. Infanterie-Division* was used as cadre for the new formation.[1] On 1 March 1944 the division had a strength of 14,132 men.[2] Few German infantry divisions in 1944 could match that figure. One reason for this large strength may have been the field replacement battalion, which had six companies. Another may be the fact that the strength figure refers to *Kopfstärke*, which may include men who were not really part of the division, but the division still had to feed. The structure of the division looked like this on 1 May:[3]

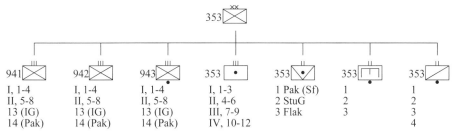

941	942	943	353	353	353	353
I, 1-4	I, 1-4	I, 1-4	I, 1-3	1 Pak (Sf)	1	1
II, 5-8	II, 5-8	II, 5-8	II, 4-6	2 StuG	2	2
13 (IG)	13 (IG)	13 (IG)	III, 7-9	3 Flak	3	3
14 (Pak)	14 (Pak)	14 (Pak)	IV, 10-12			4

The infantry battalions had the following equipment:[4]

I./Grenadier-Regiment 941: 56 machine guns, 12 mortars
II./Grenadier-Regiment 941: 56 machine guns, 12 mortars
I./Grenadier-Regiment 942: 54 machine guns, 12 mortars
II./Grenadier-Regiment 942: 50 machine guns, 12 mortars
I./Grenadier-Regiment 943: 51 machine guns, 12 mortars
II./Grenadier-Regiment 943: 51 machine guns, 12 mortars

The *14. Kompanie* of all the infantry regiments had three 7.5 cm *Pak 40s* and 36 *Panzerschrecks*. In *Grenadier-Regimenter 942* and *943,* the *13. Kompanie* had two 15 cm heavy infantry guns and five 7.5 cm light infantry guns, while the *13./Grenadier-Regiment 941* had two 15 cm heavy infantry guns and four 7.5 cm light infantry guns.[5]

Füsilier-Bataillon 353 had 63 machine guns and 12 mortars. Like the battalions of *Grenadier-Regiment 943,* it was equipped with bicycles to enhance mobility.

Panzerjäger-Abteilung 353 had 14 *Marders* and 10 *Sturmgeschütz III's.*[6] These vehicles had been sent to the division in February and March.[7]

Each artillery battery had four howitzers. The *1.* through the *9./Artillerie-Regiment 353* had 10.5 cm howitzers and the *10.* through the *12./Artillerie-Regiment 353* had 15 cm howitzers. All batteries were horse-drawn.[8]

On 1 June 1944 the division had 11,544 officers and men plus 1,786 *HiWi* (Eastern volunteers). Mobility was provided by 142 motor cycles, 573 other motor vehicles and 4,562 horses.[9]

Soon after D-Day the *353. Infanterie-Division* was ordered to move to Normandy. The division marched in two groups, a mobile and a less mobile group. On 16 June the mobile group had reached the area east of St. Lô[10] where it was employed the following day[11].

The parts of the division that moved at pedestrian pace had reached the Lamballe–Jugon area on 16 June.[12] Thus they had not yet passed Avranches. On 22 June the entire division — except the field replacement battalion — had arrived.[13]

Grenadier-Regiment 943 (except the I./*Grenadier-Regiment 943*) and *Füsilier-Bataillon 353* were almost immediately sent to the *352. Infanterie-Division* east of St. Lô.[14] They did not return until the beginning of August.[15] That group was called *Kampfgruppe Böhm.*

On 29 June the division was deployed as follows: *Kampfgruppe Böhm* still with the *352. Infanterie-Division*; the I./*Grenadier-Regimen: 941* plus elements of the artillery regiment were with the *91. Infanterie-Division*; the II./*Grenadier-Regiment 942, Pionier-Rataillon 353* plus elements of the artillery regiment were attached to the *243. Infanterie-Division,* and, the rest of the division — three infantry battalions, one or two artillery battalions and the antitank battalion — was committed in the Periers area.[16]

Five days later, the I./*Grenadier-Regiment 941* was with the *77. Infanterie-Division,* while the II./*Grenadier-Regiment 942* and the I./*Artillerie-Regiment 353* was with the *243. Infanterie-Division.* The IV./*Artillerie-Regiment 353* was placed in support of the *91. Infanterie-Division.*[17]

It was reported that the division had a *Kampfstärke* (trench strength) of 1,250 on 10 July.[18] More likely than not, this did not include the elements that were detached to other divisions. One day later the infantry battalions sent to the *91.* and *243. Infanterie-Divisionen* returned to their parent formation.[19]

During the period from 22–24 July, the division was withdrawn from the frontline and was designated as reserve for the *LXXXIV. Korps.*[20] According to the division commander's postwar manuscript, the I./*Artillerie-Regiment 353* remained with the *91. Infanterie-Division* and the IV./*Artillerie-Regiment 353* remained with the *243. Infanterie-Division.*[21] However, according to a report giving the situation on 21 July, the II., III, and IV./*Artillerie-Regiment 353* were subordinated to the division.[22] Similarly, a report concerning the status of the division on 23 July stated that it had available six light batteries and three heavy ones.[23]

The condition of the division on 23 July was reported to be: 1 *durchschnittlich* infantry battalion (mission capable), 4 *schwach* infantry battalions (weak), two infantry battalions attached to the *II. Falhchirm-Korps,* 13 7.5 cm *Pak* operational (including *Marders),* 8 *Sturmgeschütz III's* operational and three 7.5 cm *Pak* sent to the *II. Fallschirm-Korps.* Three light artillery batteries in support of the *91. Infanterie-Division.*[24]

During the last week of July, the division was encircled in the La Balaine pocket. It broke out of this rather loose pocket.[25] It remained attached to the *LXXXIV. Korps* until 18 August, when it was transferred to the area of operations of the *II. Fallschirm-Korps.*[26]

During the night of 17/18 August the division crossed the Orne River. During the following night it assembled in the Foret de Goufferns, north of Argentan. Thereafter it broke out of the so-called Falaise pocket.[27] According to an estimate by the *OKH,* the division mustered about 5,000 men on 1 September.[28] This would suggest losses of about 7,000 men in Normandy.

1 G. Tessin, *Verbände und Truppen der deutschen Wehrmacht und Waffen-SS* (Mittler & Sohn, Frankfurt am Main and Biblio Verlag, Osnabrück 1966–1975).

2 Kriegsgliederungen AOK 7, BA-MA RH 20-7/136. Strength refers to *Kopfstärke.*

3 Gliederung der 353.I.D., Stand 1.5.44, T312, R1566, F000232.

4 Ibid.

5 Ibid.

6 Ibid.

7 Lieferungen der Pz.Fahrzeuge Bd. ab Mai 1943, BA-MA RH 10/349.

8 Gliederung der 353.I.D., Stand 1.5.44, T312, R1566, F000232.

9 Gen.Kdo XXV. A.K. Ia Nr. 699/44 g.Kdos., 6.6.44, 343., 265., 275., 353.I.D. und Kriegsgliederungen der Korpstruppen und Kdr. der Fest.-Stamm-Truppen XXV, Stand 1.6.44., T314, R747, F000004-000023.

10 OB West Ia Nr. 4648/44 g.Kdos, 16.6.44, T311, R25, F7029598.

11 OB West Ia, Nr olasligt g.Kdos, 17.6.44, T311, R25, F7029619.

12 OB West Ia Nr. 4648/44 g.Kdos, 16.6.44, T311, R25, F7029598.

13 OB West Ia Nr. 4858/44 geh.Kdos, den 22.6.44., T311, R25, F7029750.

14 P. Mahlmann, *353. Inf.Division,* MS # A-983, pp. 8,11 und 14.

15 P. Mahlmann, *353. Inf.Division,* MS # A-984, p. 13.

16 P. Mahlmann, *353. Inf.Division,* MS # A-983, p 14f.

17 P. Mahlmann, *353. Inf.Division,* MS # A-983, Anlage 8.

18 KTB AOK 7 Ia, entry 10.7.44, T312, R1569, F000140.

19 P. Mahlmann, *353. Inf.Division,* MS # A-983, p 18.

20 P. Mahlmann, *353. Inf.Division,* MS # A-983, p 21.

21 Ibid.

22 Gen.Kdo. LXXXIV A.K. Ia Nr. 035/44g.Kdos 22.7.44, Taktische Gliederung der Artillerie, Stand 21.7.44, T314, R1604, F001388. Batteries 4-6 had three howitzers each, batteries 7–12 had four howitzers each. All howitzers were of the type they were originally equipped with.

23 Gen.Kdo. LXXXIV. A.K. Ia 048/44 g.Kdos. T314, R1604, F001374.

24 Gen.Kdo. LXXXIV. A.K. Ia 048/44 g.Kdos. T314, R1604, F001374.

25 P. Mahlmann, *353. Inf.Division,* MS # A-984, p 7-9.

26 See P. Mahlmann, *353. Inf.Division,* MS # A-984, p 14ff and P. Mahlmanp, *353. Inf.Division,* MS # A-985, pp. 3–7.

27 P. Mahlmann, *353. Inf.Division,* MS # A-985, p 5ff.

28 OKH Org.Abt. I Nr. I/19995/44 g.Kdos. 16.10.1944, T78, R432, F6403685ff.

363. Infanterie-Division

The division was raised in January 1944 in Poland and was sent to Denmark in April. It remained there until June.[1] The organization of the division was standard, except that it had only a single antitank company, rather than a full battalion:[2]

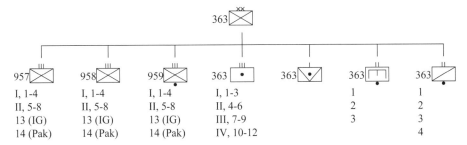

957	958	959	363	363	363	363
I, 1-4	I, 1-4	I, 1-4	I, 1-3		1	1
II, 5-8	II, 5-8	II, 5-8	II, 4-6		2	2
13 (IG)	13 (IG)	13 (IG)	III, 7-9		3	3
14 (Pak)	14 (Pak)	14 (Pak)	IV, 10-12			4

The divisional antitank company (*Panzerjäger-Kompanie 363*) was motorized and equipped with towed guns.[3] On 30 June it was reported that the division had 22 heavy antitank guns.[4] This indicates that the *Kompanie* of each infantry regiment was at full strength.

Other equipment of the division included:[5] 50 8 cm mortars, 32 12 cm mortars, one 5 cm *Pak 38*, 108 *Panzerschrecks*, 6 *leichtes Infanterie-Geschütz 18's*, 6 *schweres Infanterie-Geschütz 33's*, 37 10.5 cm *leichte Feld-Haubitze 18's* and 8 15 cm *schwere Feld-Haubitze 18's*. It had no captured weapons. Like many other divisions, it was short of vehicles.

It seems that the division had the full complement of vehicles and horses for an infantry division in 1944.[6] Given its structure, the total manpower strength of the division was probably around 11,000.

The division was moved towards Normandy incrementally. In June it was moved from Denmark to northern Belgium.[7] Then, in mid-July, it was moved to the area Amiens–Aumale–Peix, where it was located on 22 July.[8]

Using rail transport, the division was moved to the Seine and, by 26 July, 52 trains had unloaded.[9] Two days later the entire division, except *Feld-Ersatz-Bataillon 363*, had crossed the river and was marching towards the crumbling front in Normandy.[10]

On 31 July one infantry regiment, probably *Grenadier-Regiment 957*, was engaged in combat near Villedieu.[11] It seems that parts of the divisional antitank company supported this regiment.[12] During the week that followed, the division was committed near Vire. It was attached to the *LXXXIV. Korps*.[13]

The division fought withdrawal actions along the Vire–Flers–Putanges–Commeaux–Chambois axis.[14] It was among the units located furthest to the west in the so-called Falaise pocket. On the morning of 16 August, the division held positions east of Flers.[15] This was about 35 kilometers west of the Falaise–Argentan road. Three days later the division was in the Neuvy–Habloville area,[16] about 5 kilometers west of the Falaise–Argentan road. Until 19 August the German units had free routes open to the east (save for Allied air attacks). During 19 August the division, which formed part of the rear guard of the German forces in the pocket, withdrew to the area south of Trun.[17]

Generalleutnant Dettling estimated the infantry battalions of the division had a *Kampfstärke* (frontline strength) of about 120–130 men each on 20 August.[18] How many men attempted to break out from the pocket is unclear, but it seems that 2,000 men assembled on 21 August and a further 500 joined the division during the following days.[19]

1   Dettling, *Bericht über die Teilnahme der 363. Inf.Div. am Feldzug in Normandie,* MS # B-163, p. 1.

2   This has been derived from G. Tessin, *Verbände und Truppen der deutschen Wehrmacht und Waffen-SS* (Mittler & Sohn, Frankfurt am Main and Biblio Verlag, Osnabrück 1966–1975) and Dettling, op. cit. Some of the details have been possible to check against archival documents, notably AOK 15 Ia Nr. 6276/44 g.Kdos 20.6.44 (BA-MA RH 20-15/67) and Übersicht der Ausstattung mit s.Pak u. Stu.Gesch., Stand 30.6, Anlage zu AOK 15 - 500/44 geh (Stopak),T312, R516, F8115326.

3   AOK 15 Ia Nr. 6276/44 g.Kdos 20.6.44, BA-MA RH 20-15/67.

4   Übersicht der Ausstattung mit s.Pak u. Stu.Gesch., Stand 30.6, Anlage zu AOK 15 - 500/44 geh (Stopak),T312, R516, F8115326.

5   AOK 15 O.Qu. Nr. 1659/44 g.Kdos, 14.6.44, T312, R517, F8116494.

6   HGr B Ia Nr. 4943/44 g.Kdos, 18.7.44, T311, R4, F7003813.

7   AOK 15 Ia Nr. 6276/44 g.Kdos 20.6.44, BA-MA RH 20-15/67.

8   OB West Ia Nr. 5911/44 g.Kdos, vom 22.7.44, T 311, R28, F7034717.

9   OB West Ia Nr. 6074/44 g.Kdos, 26.7.44, T311, R28, F7034822.

10   OB West Ia Nr. 6123/44 g.Kdos, 28.7.44, T311, R28, F7034877.

11   See OB West Ia Abendmeldung 31.7.44, T311, R28, F7034962 and OB West Ia Nr. 6197/44 g.Kdos, 30.7.44, T311, R28, F7034938.

12   Dettling, op.cit. p.l.

13   Ibid, p. 2.

14   Ibid, p. 2–9.

15   Ibid, Anlage 5.

16   Ibid, Anlage 6.

17   Ibid, p. 8f.

18   Ibid, p. 10.

19   Ibid. p. 11.

708. Infanterie-Division

The division was raised in May 1941 as a static division and was soon sent to defend the coast of the Biscay.[1] It was organized as follows at the end of July 1944:[2]

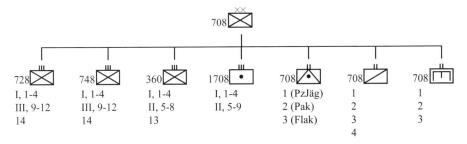

Grenadier-Regiment 360 was actually composed of Cossacks. It had been formed in April 1944 from the previous two Cossack battalions, 622 and 623.[3] Füsilier-Bataillon 708 was the former II./Infanterie-Regiment 748.[4] On 1 April it was reported that the division was 541 men below authorized strength.[5] On 4 August the division had a strength of 8,123.[6] The Cossack regiment did not move to Normandy.[7]

Equipment of the artillery batteries was:[8]

1./Artillerie-Regiment 708 four French 10.5 cm howitzers
2./Artillerie-Regiment 708 four French 10.5 cm howitzers
3./Artillerie-Regiment 708 four French 10.5 cm howitzers
4./Artillerie-Regiment 708 four French 10.5 cm howitzers
5./Artillerie-Regiment 708 four Russian 7.62 cm guns
6./Artillerie-Regiment 708 four Russian 7.62 cm guns
7./Artillerie-Regiment 708 four Russian 7.62 cm guns
8./Artillerie-Regiment 708 four Russian 12.2 cm howitzers
9./Artillerie-Regiment 708 four Russian 12.2 cm howitzers

When the division began to move towards Normandy the US forces had already broken out. This meant that the division would frequently find its approach routes to be in enemy hands.

On 2 August the division marched in several groups:[9]

I./Gruppe (towards Angers):
2./Panzerjäger-Kompanie AOK1 (a GHQ unit)
14./Grenadier-Regiment 728
One platoon of the *Flak* company

II./Gruppe (towards Niort):
Divisional staff

Nachrichten-Abteilung 708 (motorized elements)
Section from the *Flak-Kompanie*

III./Gruppe (towards Angers):
Füsilier-Bataillon 708
14./Grenadier-Regiment 748
One self-propelled platoon of the *Flak* company

IV./Gruppe (towards Niort):
Rear services

In addition, the staff of the artillery regiment plus *2., 3., 5., 6.* and *7./Artillerie-Regiment 1708* were moving out of the Royan area, as was the headquarters company of *Grenadier-Regiment 728,* the staff of I./Grenadier-Regiment 728 and the 1. and 2./Grenadier-Regiment 728.[10]

On 4 July *Füsilier-Bataillon 708* and two *Panzerjäger-Kompanien* were located between Laval and Angers. Just north of Angers were three battalions, one artillery battery and one engineer company. The division staff and rear services were south of Angers.[11]

This meant that the division's route to Normandy was soon to be cut by advancing US forces. On 5 August, the US 313th Infantry Regiment appeared outside Laval and, two days later, elements of the US 5th Armored Division reached the area south of Le Mans.[12] On 5 August combat elements of the division had reached the following positions:[13]

Laval:
Füsilier-Bataillon 708
14./Grenadier-Regiment 708

le Lion d'Angers:
1./Panzerjäger-Abteilung 708

In the area Le Mans - Sille le Guillaume - Sable sur Sarthe:
I./Grenadier-Regiment 728
III./Grenadier-Regiment 728
14./Grenadier-Regiment 728
I./Grenadier-Regiment 748
III./Grenadier-Regiment 748 14./Grenadier-Regiment 748
2./Artillerie-Regiment 1708 3 3./Artillerie-Regiment 1708
4./Artillerie-Regiment 1708
Sicherungs-Regiment 1

The rest of the division seems to have been south of the Loire.

On 7 August *Grenadier-Regiment 728, Pionier-Bataillon 708* and the *3./Artillerie-Regiment 1708* were located east of Mayenne. One battalion from *Sicherungs-Regiment 1* and the *3./Artillerie-Regiment 1708* were positioned around Evron. The *I.* and *III./Grenadier-Regiment 748, Füsilier-Bataillon 708* and the *3.* and *4./Artillerie-Regiment 1708* were deployed in St. Suzanne and southeast of the town.[14] This meant that this weak division was spread out over a sector of 40 kilometers.

It is possible large parts of *Grenadier-Regiment 748* were surrounded at Le Mans and destroyed.[15] Elements of it, under command of *Oberst* Viebahn, broke out of the encirclement.[16]

The remaining parts of the division probably never arrived in Normandy. On 6 August it was reported that 29 of the 37 trains had departed; 21 trains had unloaded.[17] On 7 August only 25 of the 37 trains needed to transport the division had unloaded.[18] Most of the artillery regiment remained in the area of the *1. Armee* during August.[19]

It seems that the division employed about 5,000 men in Normandy, while the rest remained south of the Loire and retreated towards the Vosges in eastern France. Those elements committed to the battle in Normandy — units with poor mobility employed over a vast front against a numerically superior and motorized enemy with air superiority — seem to have been largely destroyed. Losses amounted to at least 4,000, mainly in the form of prisoners.

---

1   G. Tessin, *Verbände und Truppen der deutschen Wehrmacht und Waffen-SS* (Mittler & Sohn, Frankfurt am Main and Biblio Verlag, Osnabrück 1966–1975).

2   Anlagen zum KTB LXXXI. A.K. Ia, Gliderung der 708. Inf.Div., T314, R1593, F969.

3   Ibid.

4   Ibid.

5   WFST/Op. (H)/West Nr.004662/44 g.Kdos, den 3. Mai 1944, Fehlstellen der Divisionen im Bereich OB West, Stand 1.4.44, T77, R1421, F000237f.

6   Anlagen zu KTB AOK 1 Qu, Anlage zu Gen.Kdo. LXXX. A.K. IIb 1325/44 geh. 4.8.44, T312, R29, F7537182. Strength refer to Iststärke.

7   Lagekarte OB West 21.8.44, found in K. Mehner, *Die Geheimen Tagesberichte der deutschen Wehrmachtführung im Zweiten Weltkrieg 1939–1945, Band 10* Biblio Verlag, Osnabrück 1985).

8   Anlagen zum KTB LXXXI. A.K. Ia, Gliderung der 708. Inf.Div., T314, R1593, F969.

9   See AOK 7 Ia Nr. 4151/44 g.Kdos. den 2.8.44, T312, R1569, F000357 and AOK 7 Ia Nr. 4176/44 g.Kdos. den 3.8.44, T312, R1569, F000361.

10 Ibid.

11 OB West Ia Nr. 6403/44 .Kdos,T311, R28, F7035149.

12 See M. Blumenson, *Breakout and Pursuit* (Office of the Chief of Military History, Department of the Army, Washington D.C. 1961) p. 426f.

13 KTB LXXXI. A.K. Ia, Lagekarten,T 314, R1594, F000001ff.

14 Ibid.

15 Ibid, see Lagekarte 9.8.44, 24.00.

16 See B. Gerloch, *Bericht über die Kampfe der 708. Inf.Division in der Zeit vom 10.8 - 19.8.44 in der Normandie,* MS # B-230, p. 2 and KTB LXXXI. A.K. Ia, Lagekarte 11.8.44, T 314, R1594, F000016.

17 See OB West Ia Nr. 6435/44 g.Kdos, 4.8.44, T311, R28, F7035146 and OB West Ia Nr. 6555/44 g.Kdos, 6.8.44, T311, R28, F7035219.

18 OB West Ia Nr. 6610/44 g.Kdos, 7.8.44, T311, R28, F7035267.

19 K. Hold, *Organisation und Gliederung der 1. Armee in der Zeit vom 11.8.44 - 14.2.45,* MS # B-732, Chart depicting Gliederung AOK 1 10.8 - 16.8.

709. Infanterie-Division

This division had been raised in May 1941. During the summer of that year, it was stationed in Brittany. In December 1942 it was transferred to the *LXXXIV. Korps* in Normandy. It had no combat experience before D-Day.[1] The organization of the division looked like this on 1 May 1944:[2]

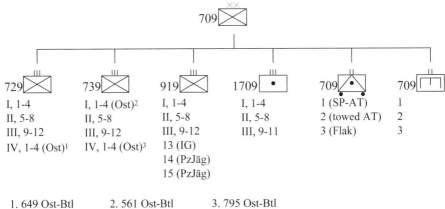

729	739	919	1709	709	709
I, 1-4	I, 1-4 (Ost)[2]	I, 1-4	I, 1-4	1 (SP-AT)	1
II, 5-8	II, 5-8	II, 5-8	II, 5-8	2 (towed AT)	2
III, 9-12	III, 9-12	III, 9-12	III, 9-11	3 (Flak)	3
IV, 1-4 (Ost)[1]	IV, 1-4 (Ost)[3]	13 (IG)			
		14 (PzJäg)			
		15 (PzJäg)			

1. 649 Ost-Btl   2. 561 Ost-Btl   3. 795 Ost-Btl

On 1 May 1944 the division had a strength of 12,320 men.[3] Since it was reported that the division was 375 men over the authorized strength on 1 April 1944,[4] it is unlikely it was given more manpower until the beginning of June. The average age of the men was 36.[5]

As organized on 1 May, *Panzerjäger-Abteilung 709* had 9 7.5 cm *Pak 40* antitank guns on tracked chassis.[6] No deliveries of *Marders* have been found in the documents covering the period from May 1943 until D-Day.[7] Either the self-propelled antitank guns were delivered before May 1943 or they are some kind of locally made conversion, possibly using captured French vehicles. *Panzerjäger-Abteilung 709* also had 12 7.5 cm *Pak 40 (mot Z)* (prime movers) and 9 3.7 cm *Flak (mot Z)*.[8]

The Artillery Regiment had the following equipment:[9]

1.Batterie: 4 Czechoslovakian 10 cm howitzers

2.Batterie: 4 Czechoslovakian 10 cm howitzers (motor drawn)

3.Batterie: 4 French 10.5 cm guns

4.Batterie: 4 French 10.5 cm guns

5.Batterie: 4 French 10.5 cm guns

6.Batterie: 4 French 15.5 cm howitzers

7.Batterie: 4 French 15.5 cm howitzers

8.Batterie: 4 French 15.5 cm howitzers

9.Batterie: 4 Russian 7.62 cm guns

10.Batterie: 4 Russian 7.62 cm guns

11.Batterie: 4 Russian 7.62 cm guns

The infantry battalions had the following equipment:[10]

I./Grenadier-Regiment 729: 46 machine guns, 4 mortars; *1. Kompanie* bicycle mounted.

II./Grenadier-Regiment 729: 46 machine guns, 4 mortars; all companies bicycle mounted.

III./Grenadier-Regiment 729: 46 machine guns, 4 mortars; *1. Kompanie* bicycle mounted.

II./Grenadier-Regiment 739: 48 machine guns; *1. Kompanie* bicycle mounted

III./Grenadier-Regiment 739: 48 machine guns; *1. Kompanie* bicycle mounted

I./Grenadier-Regiment 919: 50 machine guns, 4 flame throwers (fixed), 8 mortars (8.1 cm); *1. Kompanie* bicycle mounted

II./Grenadier-Regiment 919: 50 machine guns, 4 flame throwers (fixed), 8 mortars (8.1 cm); *1. Kompanie* bicycle mounted

III./Grenadier-Regiment 919: 50 machine guns, 4 flame throwers (fixed), 8 mortars (8.1 cm); all companies bicycle mounted

Ost-Bataillon 649: 46 machine guns, 11 mortars

Ost-Bataillon 561: 58 machine guns, 9 mortars, some 4.5 cm antitank guns (number of guns illegible)

Ost-Bataillon 795: 44 machine guns, 15 mortars

Each infantry regiment had a company with six 7.5 cm *Pak* and three 5 cm *Pak*. These were all transported by prime movers. In addition to this, *Grenadier-Regiment 919* had a company with six Russian 7.62 cm infantry howitzers (not motorized) and an extra antitank company with light, static antitank guns.[11]

The division had no field replacement battalion.[12]

Elements of the division were engaged on D-Day, defending against Allied airborne landings and also against the US 4th Infantry Division landing on Utah beach. On 16 June it was reported that the division had about 4,000 casualties.[13] This probably included attached units. The division defended Cherbourg and was destroyed when US forces liberated the city.

---

1   G. Tessin, *Verbände und Truppen der deutschen Wehrmacht und Waffen-SS* (Mittler & Sohn, Frankfurt am Main and Biblio Verlag, Osnabrück 1966–1975).
2   Gliederung der 709.I.D., Stand 1.5.44, T312, R1566, F000217.
3   Gliederung der 709.I.D., Stand 1.5.44, T312, R1566, F000217.
4   WFST/Op. (H)AVest Nr.004662/44 g.Kdos, den 3. Mai 1944, Fehlstellen der Divisionen im Bereich OB West, Stand 1.4.44, T77, R1421, F000237f.
5   HGr B la Nr. 4257/44 g.Kdos.Chefs., 3.7.44, T311, R4, F7003764.
6   Gliederung der 709.I.D., Stand 1.5.44, T312, R1566, F000217.
7   Lieferungen der Pz.Fahrzeuge Bd. ab Mai 1943, BA-MA RH 10/349.
8   Gliederung der 709.I.D., Stand 1.5.44, T312, R1566, F000217.
9   Gliederung der 709.I.D., Stand 1.5.44, T312, R1566, F000217.

10   Gliederung der 709.1.D., Stand 1.5.44, T312, R1566, F000217.
11   Gliederung der 709.1.D., Stand 1.5.44, T312, R1566, F000217.
12   Ibid.
13   Anlagen zum KTB OB West Ia, Einzelnotizen, 16.6.44, T311, R25, F7030072.

711. Infanterie-Division

The division had been formed in May 1941 as a static division and was soon attached to the *15. Armee* on the Channel coast. It remained in that area until the Allied invasion.[1] The organization of the division follows:[2]

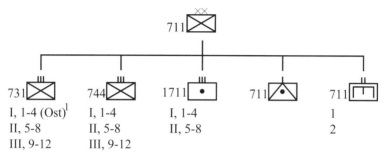

731 — I, 1-4 (Ost)[1] / II, 5-8 / III, 9-12
744 — I, 1-4 / II, 5-8 / III, 9-12
1711 — I, 1-4 / II, 5-8
711 —
711 — 1 / 2

1. 781 Ost-Btl

This was an unusually weak organization and this is reflected in its personnel strength. On 1 May 1944 it was actually over strength by 373, but still it only had 7,242 officers and men.[3] The average age of the officers was 37, while noncommissioned officers were around 31 and junior enlisted ranks at 29.[4]

Usually artillery battalions had three batteries, but the four batteries per battalion in this case did not compensate for the fact that the division had only two artillery battalions. The *I./Artillerie-Regiment 1711* was equipped with captured Russian 7.62 cm guns, while the *II./Artillerie-Regiment 1711* had captured French 15.5 cm howitzers. All batteries had four guns each.[5]

When the Allies landed the *711. Infanterie-Division* was deployed east of the Orne river. It was not heavily engaged on D-Day. The Germans did not rate the combat value of the division particularly high, since the *346. Infanterie-Division* was moved through the *711. Infanterie-Division* sector and took most of it over in order to face the British forces on the eastern side of the Orne. Consequently, the *711. Infanterie-Division* did not see much intensive action.

Even as late as 16 August one of the infantry battalions still had no combat experience.[6] Parts of the division had been temporarily attached to other formations but, generally, the division did not see much action. Consequently, it must have suffered relatively few casualties. Support for this assumption is also found in the fact that on 25 August the division still had 29 pieces of artillery operational,[7] only three less than its original number. The division probably suffered about 1,000–1,500 casualties during the battle in Normandy.

1   G. Tessin, *Verbände und Truppen der deutschen Wehrmacht und Waffen-SS* (Mittler & Sohn, Frankfurt am Main and Biblio Verlag, Osnabrück 1966–1975).

2   Derived from Tessin, MS # B-796 and Stoart AOK 15 Nr. 629/44 g.Kdos, Art.Gliederung der 15. Armee, Stand vom 1.6.44, T312, R516, F8115287ff.

3   Gen.Kdo. LXXXI. A.K. lib Nr. 398/44 geh, T314, R1590, F000849.

4   Ibid.

5   Stoart AOK 15 Nr. 629/44 g.Kdos, Art.Gliederung der 15. Armee, Stand vom 1.6.44, T312, R516, F8115287ff.

6   J. Reichert, *711. Infanteri-Division in de Zeit vom 24. Juli 44 - 15 September 44,* MS # B-796, p.4.

7   Anlage 1 zum Gen der Art beim Chef Gen.St.d.Heeres lb Nr. 2610/44 g.Kdos. 27.8.44, BA-MA RH 11 II/v. 4.

716. Infanterie-Division

The division had been raised in May 1941. It was attached to the 15. *Armee* until June 1942, when it was sent to the 7. *Armee* and the Caen area. It remained there until the Allied invasion. The division had no combat experience before D-Day.[1] The organization on 1 May 1944 was:[2]

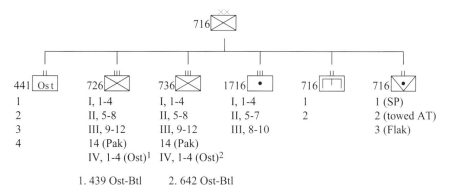

441 Ost	726	736	1716	716	716
1	I, 1-4	I, 1-4	I, 1-4	1	1 (SP)
2	II, 5-8	II, 5-8	II, 5-7	2	2 (towed AT)
3	III, 9-12	III, 9-12	III, 8-10		3 (Flak)
4	14 (Pak)	14 (Pak)			
	IV, 1-4 (Ost)[1]	IV, 1-4 (Ost)[2]			

1. 439 Ost-Btl   2. 642 Ost-Btl

The ration strength on 1 May 1944 was 7,771.[3] Among the divisions in Normandy, few were as weak as the *716. Infanterie-Division*.

As it was organized on 1 May, *Panzerjäger-Abteilung 716* had 10 heavy antitank guns on tracked chassis.[4] No deliveries of *Marders* have been found in the documents covering the period from May 1943 until D-Day.[5] Either the self-propelled antitank guns were delivered before May 1943 or they were some kind of locally made conversion, possibly using captured French vehicles. *Panzerjäger-Abteilung 716* also had eleven heavy antitank guns (not motorized). The third company was supposed to have 2 cm *Flak*, but none were present.[6] Of the antitank guns that were not on tracked chassis, two were probably 8.8 cm *Pak 43/41s* and nine were 7.5 cm *Pak 40's*.[7] The antitank guns on tracked chassis were 7.5 cm *Pak 40's*.[8]

The Artillery Regiment had the following equipment:[9]

1./Artillerie-Regiment 1716: 4 Czechoslovakian 10 cm howitzers
2./Artillerie-Regiment 1716: 4 Czechoslovakian 10 cm howitzers
3./Artillerie-Regiment 1716: 4 Czechoslovakian 10 cm howitzers
4./Artillerie-Regiment 1716: 4 French 15.5 cm howitzers
5./Artillerie-Regiment 1716: 4 Czechoslovakian 10 cm howitzers
6./Artillerie-Regiment 1716: 4 Czechoslovakian 10 cm howitzers
7./Artillerie-Regiment 1716: 4 Czechoslovakian 10 cm howitzers
8./Artillerie-Regiment 1716: 4 Czechoslovakian 10 cm howitzers
9./Artillerie-Regiment 1716: 4 Czechoslovakian 10 cm howitzers
10./Artillerie-Regiment 1716: 4 French 15.5 cm howitzers

The infantry battalions had the following equipment:[10]

I./Grenadier-Regiment 726: 48 machine guns, six 5 cm mortars, nine 8 cm mortars; *1. Kompanie* bicycle mounted.

II./Grenadier-Regiment 726: 48 machine guns, nine 5 cm mortars, six 8 cm mortars

III./Grenadier-Regiment 726: 48 machine guns, three 5 cm mortars, nine 8 cm mortars; *1. Kompanie* bicycle mounted.

Ost-Bataillon 439: 41 machine guns, 15 mortars, 1 Russian 4.5cm antitank gun

I./Grenadier-Regiment 736: 48 machine guns, five 5 cm mortars, seven 8 cm mortars; *3. Kompanie* bicycle mounted.

II./Grenadier-Regiment 736: 48 machine guns, six 5 cm mortars, six 8 cm mortars; *4. Kompanie* bicycle mounted.

III./Grenadier-Regiment 736: 48 machine guns, four 5 cm mortars, seven 8 cm mortars; *3. Kompanie* bicycle mounted.

Ost-Bataillon 642: 45 machine guns, 9 mortars

Ost-Bataillon 441: 28 machine guns, 5 mortars

Each infantry regiment had a company with nine light and medium antitank guns. These lacked prime movers.[11] The division had no field replacement battalion.

Ost-Bataillone 642 and *439* constituted the fourth battalion of the respective regiments. *Ost-Bataillon 441* was included with the division. but not as an organic part of any regiment. It seems to have been such ordinated to Grenadier-Regiment 726 for tactical purposes.

Originally the *716. Infanterie-Division* had to cover the entire sector from Carentan to the Orne Estuary. When the *352. Infanterie-Division* was inserted east of Carentan, the two divisions become slightly commingled. *Ost-Bataillon 439* remained in the Isigny area and the *III./Grenadier-Regiment 726* was located in the Grandcamp area. The *I./Grenadier-Regiment 726* was northeast of Bayeux.[12] These three battalions were under the operational control of the *352. Infanterie-Division.*[13] As it was, on 6 June elements of the *716. Infanterie-Division* were involved in the fighting on Omaha, Gold, Juno and Sword beaches. On the latter three beaches, only the *716. Infanterie-Division* provided defense until units from the *21. Panzer-Division* entered combat.

The division, already weak before D-Day, was soon depleted. By 15 June, it was decided to withdraw the division and send it to the *1. Armee* in southern France.[14] On 23 June, elements had been moved to an area 35 kilometers northwest of Le Mans.[15] However, on 29 June the following units were still involved in combat:[16]

With the *711. Infanterie-Division: 1.* and *3./Grenadier-Regiment 736,1.* and *3./Artillerie-Regiment 1716* (total of 5 officers, 39 noncommissioned officers and 239 men)

With the *346. Infanterie-Division:* Remnants of *Ost-Bataillon 642* and *Pionier-Bataillon 716* (total of 8 officers, 35 noncommissioned officers and 180 men)

With the *21. Panzer-Division: Kampfgruppe Koch, Kampfgruppe Roth,* parts of the *III./Grenadier-Regiment 736* (total of 21 officers, 151 noncommissioned officers and 586 men)

With the 352. Infanterie-Division: Parts of Ost-Bataillon 439, Grenadier-Regiment 726, the III./Artillerie-Regiment 1716 (total of 16 officers, 72 noncommissioned officers and 316 men)

On 1 July the first of the trains transporting the division departed.[17] The transfer dragged out until 20 July, when the last of the 14 trains had departed.[18] In the end the division did not transfer to the *1. Armee,* but to the *19. Armee* on the French Riviera. On 11 August the division reported a strength of 7,382 men[19].

The division suffered extensive losses in Normandy. By 11 July, the division recorded 6,261 casualties.[20] Since the division began with drawing from combat at the end of June, this is probably the complete tally of losses sustained during its commitment in Normandy.

---

1   G. Tessin, *Verbände und Truppen der deutschen Wehrmacht und Waffen-SS* (Mittler & Sohn, Frankfurt am Main and Biblio Verlag, Osnabrück 1966–1975).

2   Gliederung der 716.I.D., Stand 1.5.44, T312, R1566, F000215.

3   Gliederung der 716.I.D., Stand 1.5.44, BA-MA RH 19 IX/2.

4   Gliederung der 716.I.D., Stand 1.5.44, T312, R1566, F000215.

5   Lieferungen der Pz.Fahrzeuge Bd. ab Mai 1943, BA-MA RH 10/349.

6   Gliederung der 716.I.D., Stand 1.5.44, T312, R1566, F000215.

7   Taktische Reserven panzerbrechender Waffen innerhalb der Divisionen, Stand vom 1.5.44, T312, R1568, F000718.

8   Ibid.

9   Gliederung der 716I.D., Stand 1.5.44, T312, R1566, F000215.

10   Gliederung der 716.I.D., Stand 1.5.44, T312, R1566, F000215.

11   Gliederung der 716.I.D., Stand 1.5.44, T312, R1566, F000215.

12   Lagekarte AOK 7, 5.6.1944, BA-MA RH 20-7/138K.

13   Gliederung der 716.I.D., Stand 1.5.44, T312, R1566, F000215.

14   OB West Ia Nr. 384/44 g.Kdos Ch., 15.6.44, T311, R25, F7029588.

15   OB West Ia Nr. 4879/44 g.Kdos. 23.6.44, T311, R25, F7029779.

16   KTB AOK 7 Ia Anlagen, 29.6.44, T312, R1565, F001434.

17   OB West Ia Nr. 5185/44 g.Kdos, 1.7.44, T311, R28, F7034124.

18   OB West Ia Nr. 5862/44 g.Kdos vom 20.7.44, T311, R28, F7034667.

19   AOK 19 IIb Nr. 562/44 geh., 11.8.44, BA-MA RH 20-19/76.

20   KTB OB West Ia, entry 12.7.44, T311, R16, F7016788.

Panzer-Divisionen

1. SS-Panzer-Division "Leibstandarte"

The *1. SS-Panzer-Division "Leibstandarte"* had been fighting on the Eastern Front since the autumn of 1943 and was badly worn when it was transferred to Belgium to rest and refit in April 1944. It was far from combat ready at the beginning of June. Even though it had a strength of 19,618 on 1 June,[1] many of the men were recently arrived recruits who had to be trained. On 15 May it had reported a shortage of 4,143 men.[2] On 1 June 1,081 noncommissioned officers and men – mainly drivers and technicians – were in Germany for training.[3]

Another problem was the lack of motor transport. The division was authorized 3,887 trucks of all types, but had only 1,070 in running order and 621 in maintenance facilities.[4] It didn't have a single armored half-track operational.[5]

Due to these defects the division was not ready for combat when the Allies landed. It also had to await further deliveries of tanks. On 1 June, it had 42 *Panzer IV's*, 38 *Panthers* and 44 *Sturmgeschütz III's* operational.[6] Eight *Panzer IV's* and one *Sturmgeschütz III* were in maintenance facilities.[7] Further deliveries occurred during June:[8]

Date	Panzer IV	Panther
8 June	33	
14 June		6
17 June	20	8
18 June		8
19 June		6
29 June		6

The dates indicate when the trains departed from Germany, not when the tanks arrived at the division. No tanks were sent to the division during July and August.[9] Altogether the division employed 103 *Panzer IV's*, 72 *Panthers* and 45 *Sturmgeschütz*

*III'*s in Normandy. The structure of the division, including the elements that were not ready for combat, was (see next page):

Even though the division was not combat ready as a whole, it was decided on 8 June to send those parts that were combat ready to Normandy.[10] This decision was rescinded one day later, and the division remained in the area of the *15. Armee*.[11] Not until 17 June did the division begin loading on trains.[12]

On 22 June it was reported that the division had a full-strength *Panther* battalion which – transported on six trains – had unloaded east of Rouen.[13] The data presented above on the *Panther* deliveries to the division suggest that the division had 72 *Panthers*, including vehicles on their way to the division. The report stating that the division was at full strength is probably not correct (although with 72 *Panther*, it was at more than 90% strength). The number of trains required to move the battalion seems somewhat small for transporting a full-strength *Panther* battalion with all its vehicles.[14]

Twenty trains had unloaded west of Paris by 25 June.[15] Only parts of the division were committed to combat during June. *SS-Panzer-Grenadier-Regiment 1* (minus the *III./SS-Panzer-Grenadier-Regiment 1*) fought along National Highway 175 on the eastern flank of the British Epsom Offensive. No other elements of the division took part in the fighting during June.[16] The remainder of the division arrived gradually.[17]

The division was far from complete on 1 July. According to the status report for this date, the division had an *Iststärke* of 21,262 men.[18] This probably includes men in the replacement organizations in Germany since, according to K. G. Klietmann, the division had strength of 19,691 men on 30 June.[19] Important parts of the division also remained in Belgium. These included *SS-Werfer-Abteilung 1* (except one battery), the *III./SS-Artillerie-Regiment 1*, the *5./SS-Flak-Abteilung 1* (3.7 cm), *1./SS-Panzeraufklärungs-Abteilung 1* (*Panzerspähkompanie*) and elements of *SS-Panzer-Regiment 1*.[20] The late arrival of some of the *Panthers* had possibly delayed crew training within the armor regiment. Altogether the units left behind comprised 5,800 men.[21] Thus it seems that the division had a strength of less than 14,000 men when it arrived in Normandy. By 6 July the division, minus the elements listed above, had arrived in Normandy.[22]

On 1 July the situation concerning vehicles had improved only slightly since 1 June. The division now had 36 combat-ready *SPW* and 224 in maintenance facilities. It had 1,441 operational lorries and a further 613 in need of repairs.[23]

The *1. SS-Panzer-Division "Leibstandarte"* was in reserve south of Caen when the British Operation *Goodwood* was launched 18 July. In one report, losses suffered from 1 June until 18 July (inclusive) amounted to 1,441 officers and men.24 In another report, the casualties during July amounted to 243 killed, 747 wounded and 102 missing.25 This gives a total of 1,092, which is a figure slightly lower than those

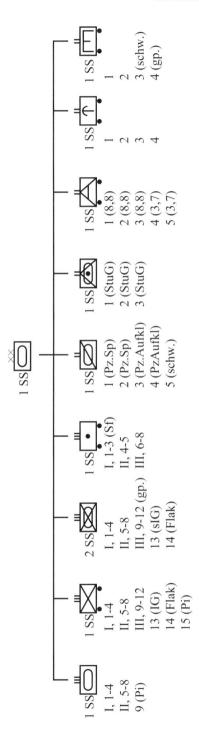

listed initially. It seems that losses were very light after 18 July and that the division may have lost about 400 men in June. By 1 August all parts of *SS-Panzer-Regiment 1* had arrived, but the *III./SS-Artillerie-Regiment 1, SS-Werfer-Abteilung 1* (minus one battery), the *5./SS-Flak-Abteilung 1* and the *1./SS-Panzeraufklärungs-Abteilung 1* still remained in Belgium.[26]

The artillery of the division was somewhat mixed. It had eight light field pieces, six heavy howitzers, four 10 cm guns, eight *Wespe* self-propelled guns, five *Hummel* self-propelled guns and five *Nebelwerfers*. Another seven pieces were in maintenance facilities.[27]

The division remained south of Caen until the night from 5/6 August, when two tank battalions, two *Panzergrenadier* battalions, one self-propelled artillery battalion, one engineer company and the *Flak* battalion began moving west to take part in the Mortain counterattack.[28]

The division broke out of the Falaise pocket, but on 22 August it was reported to have no combat-ready tanks or artillery pieces.[29]

According to Lehmann and Tiemann, the casualty reports of the *1. SS-Panzer-Division "Leibstandarte"* show losses of 3,901 officers and men killed, wounded and missing from 6 June–30 September 1944. However, since the reports are incomplete, the two authors estimate that casualties were at least 5,000. Of course, that refers to a longer period than the campaign in Normandy.[30] It seems that the estimate is very reasonable though. For much of August the division fought alongside the *2. Panzer-Division*. During the period from 1 August–30 September the *2. Panzer-Division* lost 4,559 men killed, wounded and missing.[31] The vast majority of these must have been sustained in August. The *1. SS-Panzer-Division "Leibstandarte"* probably had losses of the same magnitude. Combining this with the losses suffered before 1 August (given above), it seems that the Leibstandarte lost between 5,000 and 6,000 men during the campaign in Normandy.

The tank strength of the division varied during the campaign: (see next two pages)

Date	Panzer IV		Panther		Sturmgeschütz III	
	Combat Ready	Short-term Repair	Combat Ready	Short-term Repair	Combat Ready	Short-term Repair
1 June[1]	42	8	38	0	44	1
1 July[2]	30	73	25	38	31	14
4 July[3]	60	?	29	?	44	?
6 July[4]	59	?	31	?	39	?
8 July[5]	60	?	29	?	42	?
9 July[6]	60	?	30	?	42	?
11 July[7]	60	?	29	?	42	?
13 July[8]	58	5	29	1	42	2
14 July[9]	61	2	29	1	42	5
15 July[10]	61	8	41	5	42	3
16 July[11]	59	?	48	?	35	?
17 July[12]	59	?	46	?	35	?
18 July[13]	61	?	?	?	?	?
20 July[14]	51	8	20	28	19	13
21 July[15]	46	9	29	20	24	8
22 July[16]	41	6	24	19	29	6
23 July[17]	49	7	31	16	29	6
24 July[18]	45	7	34	13	32	3
25 July[19]	45	7	34	15	32	3
27 July[20]	33	12	36	12	22	8
28 July[21]	33	12	36	11	22	8
29 July[22]	71	8	38	9	25	6
30 July[23]	63	?	36	?	29	?
1 August[24]	61	14	40	14	23	0
5 August[25]	57	?	46	?	27	?
13 August[26]	14	?	7	?	8	?

1 BA-MA RH 10/312.
2 BA-MA RH 10/312.
3 Pz.Gr. West Ia, Nr. 197/44 geh. von 7.7.1944, Nachtrag zur Tagesmeldung., BA-MA RH 21-5/50.
4 Pz.Gr. West Ia, Nr. 217/44 geh. von 7.7.1944, Nachtrag zur Tagesmeldung 6.7., BA-MA RH 21-5/50.
5 Pz.Gr. West Ia, Nr. 268/44 geh. von 9.7.1944, Nachtrag zur Tagesmeldung 8.7., BA-MA RH 21-5/50.
6 Pz.Gr. West Ia, Nr. 306/44 geh. von 10.7.1944, Nachtrag zur Tagesmeldung 9.7., BA-MA RH 21-5/50).
7 Pz.Gr. West Ia, Nr. 361/44 geh. von 12.7.1944, Nachtrag zur Tagesmeldung 11.7., T313, R420, F8713889.
8 Pz.Gr. West Ia, Nr. 348/44 geh. v. 14.7.44, Nachtrag zur Tagesmeldung 13.7., T313, R420, F8713904.
9 Pz.Gr. West Ia Nr. Unreadable, v. 15.7.44, Nachtrag zur Tagesmeldung 14.7, T313, R420, F8713914.
10 Pz.Gr. West Ia Nr. 388/44 g.Kdos 16.7.44, Nachtrag zur Tagesmeldung 15.7, T313, R420, F8713921.
11 Pz.Gr. West Ia, Nr. 424/44 geh. von 17.7.1944, Nachtrag zur Tagesmeldung 16.7., BA-MA RH 21-5/50.
12 Pz.Gr. West Ia Nr. 479/44 geheim von 18.7.44, Nachtrag zur Tagesmeldung 17.7.44, BA-MA RH 21-5/50.
13 Pz.Gr. West Ia, Nr. 451/44 geh. von 19.7.1944, Nachtrag zur Tagesmeldung 18.7., BA-MA RH 21-5/50.
14 Pz.Gr. West Ia, Nr. 491/44 geh. von 21.7.1944., Nachtrag zur Tagesmeldung 20.7., BA-MA RH 21-5/50.
15 Pz.Gr. West Ia, Nr. 517/44 geh. von 21.7.1944., Nachtrag zur Tagesmeldung 21.7., BA-MA RH 21-5/50.
16 Pz.Gr. West Ia, Nr. 535/44 geh. von 23.7.1944., Nachtrag zur Tagesmeldung 22.7., BA-MA RH 21-5/50.
17 Pz.Gr. West Ia, Nr. 547/44 geh. von 24.7.1944., Nachtrag zur Tagesmeldung 23.7., BA-MA RH 21-5/50.
18 Pz.Gr. West Ia, Nr. 557/44 geh. von 25.7.1944., Nachtrag zur Tagesmeldung 24.7., BA-MA RH 21-5/50.
19 Pz.Gr. West Ia, Nr. 572/44 geh. von 26.7.1944., Nachtrag zur Tagesmeldung 25.7., BA-MA RH 21-5/50.
20 Pz.Gr. West Ia, Nr. 605/44 geh. von 28.7.1944., Nachtrag zur Tagesmeldung 27.7., BA-MA RH 21-5/50.
21 Pz.Gr. West Ia Nr. 633/44 g.Kdos, 29.7.44, Nachtrag zur Tagesmeldung 28.7, T313, R420, F8714036.
22 Pz.Gr. West Ia Nr. 647/44 g.Kdos, 30.7.44, Nachtrag zur Tagesmeldung 29.7, T313, R420, F8714042.
23 Pz.Gr. West Ia Nr. 665/44 g.Kdos, 31.7.44, Nachtrag zur Tagesmeldung 30.7, T313, R420, F8714049.
24 BA-MA RH 10/312.
25 Pz.Gr. West Ia Nr. 775/44 g.Kdos. 6.8.44, Nachtrag zur Tagesmeldung 5.8, T313, R420, F8714097.
26 Mittagmeldung HGr B 15.8.44, BA-MA RH 19 IX/12.

1 BA-MA RH 10/312.
2 BA-MA RH 10/112.
3 BA-MA RH 10/312.
4 BA-MA RH 10/312.
5 BA-MA RH 10/312.
6 BA-MA RH 10/312.
7 Ibid.
8 Verteilung der Panzerfahrzeuge, Bd. ab Mai 43, BA-MA RH 10/349.
9 Ibid.
10 OB West Ia 4484/44 g.Kdos v. 8.6.44., T311, R25, F7029384.
11 OB West Ia 4445/44 g.Kdos, den 9.6.44, T311, R25, F7029407.
12 R. Lehmann & R. Tiemann, *The Leibstandarte, Vol IV/1* (J. J. Fedorowicz Publishing Inc, Winnipeg 1993) p. 115.
13 OB West Ia Nr. 4858/44 geh.Kdos, den 22.6.44., T311, R25, F7029750.
14 *Schwere Panzer-Abteilung 503* was transported on eight trains (OB West Ia Nr. 5152/44 g.Kdos. 30.6.44, T311, R25, F7030013) and that unit only had 45 tanks.
15 OB West Ia Nr. 4963/44 g.Kdos, 25.6.44 (T311, R25, F7029850.
16 Lehmann & Tiemann, op. cit. pp. 121–6.
17 See OB West Ia Nr. 5227/44 g.Kdos, T311, R28, F7034143f and OB West Ia Nr. 5197/44 g.Kdos, 2.7.44, T311, R28, F7034133.
18 Status report to the Inspector-General of Panzer Troops, Stand 1.7.44, BA-MAMA RH 10/312.
19 K.G. Klietmann, *Die Waffen-SS, eine Dokumentation* (Osnabrück 1965) p. 508.
20 Status report to the Inspector-General of Panzer Troops, Stand 1.7.44, BA-MA RH 10/312.
21 Ibid.
22 Lehmann & Tiemann, op. cit. p. 115.
23 Status report to the Inspector-General of Panzer Troops, Stand 1.7.44, BA-MA RH 10/312.
24 Pz.Gr. West Ia Nr. 480/44 g.Kdos. 20.7.44, T313, R420, F8713975.
25 Status report to the Inspector-General of Panzer Troops, Stand 1.8.44, BA-MA RH 10/312.
26 Ibid.
27 Ibid.
28 KTB PzAOK 5 Ia, entry 5.8.44, T313, R420, F8713590.
29 Fernschreiben von HGr B an OB West, 22.8.44, BA-MA RH 19 IX/9b
30 Lehmann & Tiemann, op. cit. p. 228.
31 Strength report to Inspector-General of Panzer Troops, 1 October 1944, BA-MA RH 10/141.

2. Panzer-Division

The division was depleted after prolonged fighting on the Eastern Front and, during the winter of 1944, it was transferred to France for refitting. Since it had arrived in France early in 1944, the division was at full strength in most respects. It had also had time to train its replacements. By 1 April, the division was 573 men above its authorized strength.[1] For the organization of the division when it arrived in Normandy see the next page:[2]

Panzer-Regiment 3 was strong. There were 94 operational Panzer IVs in the II./ Panzer-Regiment 3, plus 2 in maintenance facilities on 31 May.[3] The *I./Panzer-Regiment 3* reported 73 *Panthers* operational and 6 in maintenance facilities on 5 June.[4] It is most likely the division received no tank replacements during the fighting in Normandy[5].

Artillerie-Regiment 74 had its full complement of self-propelled artillery: 12 *Wespe* self-propelled guns (10.5 cm howitzer on the Panzer II chassis) and 6 *Hummel* self-propelled guns (15 cm howitzers on a *Panzer III/IV* chassis).[6] Additionally, there were 26 towed artillery pieces in the regiment.[7]

A *Panzer-Division* normally only had one of its four infantry battalions mounted in *SPW's*, but this division was an exception, with the *I. Bataillon* in both *Panzer-Grenadier-Regimenter 2* and *304* equipped with them. Consequently, the division had a great number of *SPW's*. On 31 May 468 were operational and 8 were in maintenance facilities.[8]

The division had 25 *Pak 40* 7.5 cm towed antitank guns and 16 (plus 5 in maintenance facilities) *Jagdpanzer IV's*. It also had eight 8.8 cm *Flak*, that could augment the antitank capabilities.[9] *Panzerjäger-Abteilung 38* had an unusual organization. The *1. Kompanie* had 7 *Jagdpanzer IV's*, while the *2. Kompanie* had 4 and the *3. Kompanie* had 8.[10]

In terms of personnel the division was actually overstrength by 296 men and had an actual strength (Iststärke) of 16,762 on 31 May,[11] but this probably includes *Panzer-Abteilung 301 (Funklenk)* with its 1,085 men.[12] This unit was attached to the *2. Panzer-Division* at the beginning of June. By D-Day, however, it was detached with the exception of the *4. Kompanie*.[13] Thus the strength of the division was probably about 15,900 when it began to move to Normandy. The division was fully motorized.[14]

In some publications, it has been stated that a *Funklenk-Abteilung* (radio-controlled battalion) accompanied the division to Normandy. This has been attributed to either *Funklenk-Abteilung 301* or *302*. Neither of those battalions took part in the campaign, however. *Funklenk-Abteilung 301* was sent to the Eastern Front, but one company – the *4. Kompanie* – remained in the west. It followed the *2. Panzer-Division* to Normandy. For more information on these units, see the respective narratives.

When the Allies landed, the division was deployed in the area around Amiens. Two days after the invasion, von Rundstedt decided to send the division to Normandy.[15] At 0300 hours on 9 June the division received its orders to move.[16] It was decided to begin the movement at dusk.[17] However, since it was raining, it was begun at

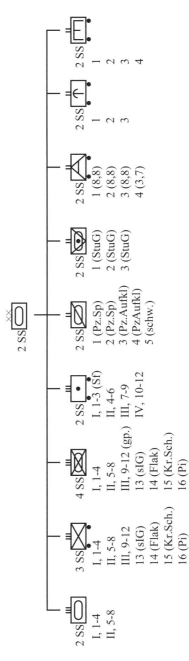

2 SS

2 SS	3 SS	4 SS	2 SS	2 SS	2 SS	2 SS	2 SS	2 SS
I, 1-4	I, 1-4	I, 1-4	I, 1-3 (Sf)	1 (Pz.Sp)	1 (StuG)	1 (8,8)	1	1
II, 5-8	II, 5-8	II, 5-8	II, 4-6	2 (Pz.Sp)	2 (StuG)	2 (8,8)	2	2
	III, 9-12	III, 9-12 (gp.)	III, 7-9	3 (Pz.Aufkl)	3 (StuG)	3 (8,8)	3	3
	13 (sIG)	13 (sIG)	IV, 10-12	4 (PzAufkl)		4 (3,7)		4
	14 (Flak)	14 (Flak)		5 (schw.)				
	15 (Kr.Sch.)	15 (Kr.Sch.)						
	16 (Pi)	16 (Pi)						

*The fourth company of 301. Fkl. Abt. was attached to 2. Pz.Div. in Normandy

1400 hours.[18] During the evening the majority of the division's wheeled elements passed through Paris.[19] The tracked units were loaded by rail, causing them to arrive later. On the morning of 11 June, the wheeled elements of the division had reached Sees-Alengon, while only 6 trains with the tracked units had departed.[20] The first elements of the division entered combat on 12 June,[21] but it was not until 20 June that all units of the division had arrived.[22] Among the late arrivals was the *Panther* battalion, which had arrived on 19 June with 52 operational vehicles and a further 20 that required minor repairs due to damage during the march.[23] The *Panzer IV* battalion arrived at the same time with about 75% of its tanks operational.[24] The *I./ Artillerie-Regiment 74* arrived with two-thirds of its *Wespe* self-propelled guns and Hummel self-propelled howitzers combat ready on 19 June.[25]

For most of June the division operated mainly in the Caumont area but, on 26 June, the British Operation *Epsom* was launched. The *I./Panzer-Regiment 3 (Panther)* was lent to support the forces resisting the British offensive. On 28 June, the battalion was credited with the destruction of 53 enemy tanks and 15 antitank guns.[26]

Casualties during June amounted to 275 killed in action, 1,021 wounded and 95 missing.[27] On 1 July the division had 85 *Panzer IV's* operational and 11 in maintenance facilities requiring short-term repairs, while the number of operational *Panthers* was 21.[28] Another 29 *Panthers* were in short-term repair,[29] while 9 were in long-term repair. Twenty had been lost during June.[30] During June, the *Panther* battalion was credited with the destruction of 89 enemy tanks and 19 antitank guns.[31]

Starting in June the organization of *Panzerjäger-Abteilung 38* changed. On 1 July it had 10 *Jagdpanzer IV's* each in the *1. And 2./Panzerjäger-Abteilung 38,* while the *3. Kompanie* had 9 towed antitank guns.[32]

On 21 July the *326. Infanterie-Division* began to relieve the *2 Panzer-Division.*[33] Four days later the division reported that it had 13 *Panthers* operational and 26 in short-term repair.[34] This did probably not include *2./Panzer-Regiment 3* which remained with the *326 Infanterie-Division* until 27 July.[35]

The division does not seem to have been involved in costly fighting during July, since it was rated as having *Kampfwert I* – meaning the unit was considered fit for any mission, offensive or defensive – on 30 July.[36] Its infantry battalions were still considered strong.[37] This is supported by a manpower return on 1 August, which shows a shortage of only 722 officers and men, plus 332 eastern volunteers.[38] Casualties in July included 170 killed in action, 663 wounded and 92 missing.[39]

The division took part in the ill-fated Mortain attack. According to the divisional history written by Franz-Joseph Strauss,[40] the division had about 60 tanks and 15 *Jagdpanzer IV's* operational when the attack was launched. The strength of its main combat units on 11 August: 820 men in *Panzer-Grenadier-Regiment 2*; 760 men in *Panzer-Grenadier-Regiment 304*; 360 men in *Panzeraufklärungs-Abteilung 2*; and 280 in *Panzer-Pionier-Bataillon 38.*[41] Even after the Mortain engagement the main combat units were still at close to half strength. On 24 August it was reported that 15 *Panthers* of the division had assembled near Meaux, east of Paris.[42]

The exact losses the division suffered during the Normandy campaign are not possible to establish. It is known that losses during June were 275 killed in action, 1,021 wounded and 95 missing.[43] Casualties during July are not known, but in the period from 1 August–30 September losses amounted to 315 killed in action, 370 wounded and 3,874 missing.[44] Given the status of the division on 30 July indicated above, it seems reasonable to assume that casualties during July were not greater than those suffered in June. If that assumption is valid, the division must have suffered casualties of about 6,000–7,000 men during the campaign. This also assumes the losses during September were small compared to August.

This contradicts many statements that the division was destroyed in Normandy. That the division was not destroyed is also evident from the fact that parts of it were still in action on 4 September.[45] Evidently it had suffered severe losses, but many divisions suffered even worse losses during the campaign, both on the German and Allied side.

	Panzer IV	
Date[44]	Combat Ready	Short-term Repair
31 May[45]	94	2
1 June[46]	?	?
19 June[47]	?	?
1 July[48]	85	11
11 August[49]	9	?

	Panther	
Date	Combat Ready	Short-term Repair
31 May	67	3
1 June	62	17*
19 June	52	20
1 July	21	29
11 August	8	?

	Jagdpanzer IV	
Date	Combat Ready	Short-term Repair
31 May	16	3
1 June	?	?
19 June	?	?
1 July	12	5
11 August	5	

* = Includes long term repair

1 WFST/Op. (H)AVest Nr.004662/44 g.Kdos, den 3. Mai 1944, Fehlstellen der Divisionen im Bereich OB West, Stand 1.4.44, T77, R1421, F000237f.

2 Strength report to Inspector-General of Panzer Troops, 31 May 1944, BA-MA RH 10/141.

3 Strength report to Inspector-General of Panzer Troops, 31 May 1944, BA-MA RH 10/141.

4 Panther Abteilungen Bestand nach Org und Gen Qu., BA-MA RH 10/70.

5 No *Panzer IVs, Sturmgeschütz III's* or *Panzerjäger* were sent to the division during June, July and August. Twenty-four *Panthers* were sent to *OB West* from 2–8 August to be distributed among the units in the west. It is not very likely that any of these arrived in time to take part in the fighting in Normandy, since 34 *Panzer IV's* that were sent on 10 August did not reach the troops until 5 September. Lieferungen der Panzerfahrzeuge, Bd. ab Mai 1943, BA-MA RH 10/349.

6 Strength report to Inspector-General of Panzer Troops, 31 May 1944, BA-MA RH 10/141.

7 Strength report to Inspector-General of Panzer Troops, 31 May 1944, BA-MA RH 10/141.

8 Strength report to Inspector-General of Panzer Troops, 31 May 1944, BA-MA RH 10/141.

9 Strength report to Inspector-General of Panzer Troops, 31 May 1944, BA-MA RH 10/141.

10 Strength report to Inspector-General of Panzer Troops, 31 May 1944, BA-MA RH 10/141.

11 Strength report to Inspector-General of Panzer Troops, 31 May 1944, BA-MA RH 10/141.

12 See narrative for 301. Fkl.Abt.

13 Ibid.

14 H. von Lüttwitz, *Einsatz der 2. Panzer-Division in der Normandie*, MS # B-257, p. 26.

15 OB West Ia Nr. 4484/44 g.Kdos, 8.6.44, T311, R25, F7029384.

16 H. von Lüttwitz, *Einsatz der 2. Panzer-Division in der Normandie*, MS # B-257, p. 5.

17 Ibid.

18 Ibid.

19 OB West Ia Nr. 4463/44 g.Kdos, 9.6.44, T311, R25, F7029425.

20 OB West Ia Nr. 4487/44 g.Kdos, 11.6.44, T311, R25, F7029461.

21 Franz-Joseph Strauß, *Geschichte der 2. (Wiener) Panzer Division* (Vowinkel, Neckargemünd 1977) page 160f.

22 OB West Ia Nr. 4748/44 g.Kdos, 20.6.44, T311, R25, F7029696.

23 AOK7 Ia Nr. 1578/44 geh. 20.6.44, T312, R1565, F0011161.

24 AOK7 Ia Nr. 1578/44 geh. 20.6.44, T312, R1565, F0011161.

25 AOK7 Ia Nr. 1578/44 geh. 20.6.44, T312, R1565, F0011161.

26 OB West Ia Nr. 5113/44 g.Kdos, 29.6.44, Fernschreiben an OKH,T78, R313, F6265719.

27 Strength report to Inspector-General of Panzer Troops, 1 July 1944, BA-MA RH 10/141.

28 Strength report to Inspector-General of Panzer Troops, 1 July 1944, BA-MA RH 10/141.

29 Strength report to Inspector-General of Panzer Troops, 1 July 1944, BA-MA RH 10/141.

30 Strength report to Inspector-General of Panzer Troops, 1 July 1944, BA-MA RH 10/141.

31 Strength report to Inspector-General of Panzer Troops, 1 July 1944, BA-MA RH 10/141.

32 Strength report to Inspector-General of Panzer Troops, 1 July 1944, BA-MA RH 10/141.

33 Pz.Gr. West Ia, Nr. 517/44 geh. von 22.7.1944., Nachtrag zur Tagesmeldung 21.7., A-MA RH 21-5/50.

34 Pz.Gr. West Ia, Nr. 572/44 geh. von 26.7.1944., Nachtrag zur Tagesmeldung 25.7., A-MA RH 21-5/50.

35 Pz.Gr. West Ia, Nr. 605/44 geh. von 28.7.1944., Nachtrag zur Tagesmeldung 27.7., BA-MA RH 21-5/50.

36 AOK 7 Ia Nr. 4174/44 g.Kdos. den 2.8.44, T312, R1569, F000359.

37 AOK 7 Ia Nr. 4174/44 g.Kdos. den 2.8.44, T312, R1569, F000359.

38 According to a report provided to me by Richard Anderson at the Dupuy Institute.

39 BA-MA RW 6/v. 577.

40 Franz-Joseph Strauss, *Geschichte der 2. (Wiener) Panzer Division* (Vowinkel, Neckargemünd 1977) page 170.

41 Mittagmeldung der HGr B, BA-MA RH 19 IX/12 and Mittagmeldung OB West la 15.8.44, T311, R29, F7035556.

42 HGr B la Nr. 6504/44 g.Kdos, 24.8.44, T311, R4, F7004039

43 Strength report to Inspector-General of Panzer Troops, 1 July 1944, BA-MA RH 10/141.

44 Strength report to Inspector-General of Panzer Troops, 1 October 1944, BA-MA RH 10/141.

45 See Obkdo. H.Gr. B, la Nr. 6917/44 g.Kdos 4.9.44 (T313, R420, F8714263). The document lists the armor units scheduled for complete withdrawal from the front to allow them to refit. Those were the *1., 2.,* and *12. SS-Panzer-Divisionen,* the three *Tiger* battalions committed to the Normandy battle and *schwere Panzerjäger-Abteilung 654.* The *2.* and *116. Panzer-Divisionen* were supposed to remain committed with parts of their formations, while the remainder of the units were to refit close behind the front. This also applied to the *9.* and *10. SS-Panzer-Divisionen* and *Sturmpanzer-Abteilung 217.*

46 Sources are analogous for the same dates for the remaining two tables.

47 BA-MA RH 10/141.

48 BA-MA RH 10/70.

49 AOK 7 la Nr. 1578/44 geh. 20.6.44, T312, R1565, F001161.

50 BA-MA RH 10/141.

51 Mittagmeldung der HGr B 11.8.44, BA-MA RH 19 IX/12.

2. SS-Panzer-Division "Das Reich"

The origin of the *2. SS-Panzer-Division "Das Reich"* was the *SS-Verfugungstruppe* (*SS-VT* = special-purpose unit) formed before the outbreak of the war. During the campaign in Poland in 1939, the *SS-VT* fought as separate regiments, but in France in 1940 it saw action as a division. It also took part in the campaign in Yugoslavia in 1941. When Operation *Barbarossa* was launched the division was part of the *2. Panzergruppe,* commanded by Heinz Guderian. *"Das Reich,"* by then a *SS-Panzer-Grenadier-Division*, played an important part in von Manstein's counteroffensive at the end of the winter of 1942-3. It was one of the spearheads in the German offensive against Kursk in July 1943. From then on, the division was almost constantly engaged on the southern sector of the Eastern Front. It gradually became more and more depleted. On 1 December 1943, the division was short 7,911 men.[1]

At the end of December 1943 elements of the division were withdrawn from the Eastern Front and, two months later, they were transported to the Bordeaux area in southern France. A *Kampfgruppe* remained on the Eastern Front, however. It was not until late April that these units also arrived in southern France.[2]

The structure of the division – officially a *SS-Panzer-Division* in January 1944 – was as shown on the opposite page.

Actually *SS-Werfer-Abteilung 102* was not an organic part of the division, but a corps unit, intended for the *II. SS-Panzer-Korps.* During the Normandy campaign, it was with the division.[3] In that capacity, it was designated as *SS-Werfer-Abteilung 2.* It seems that it left the division before 21 July.[4]

The process of rebuilding the depleted division involved training of about 9,000 new recruits.[5] The need for new equipment was urgent, particularly vehicles. On 15 May the division reported the following

Equipment	On hand	Shortage
7.5 cm *IG*	18	7
15 cm *IG*	12	0
10.5 cm *le.FH*	6	31
10 cm *K*	4	0
15 cm *s.FH*	9	9
7.5 cm *Pak 40*	21	9
2 cm *Flak*	36	14
2 cm *Flakvierling*	2	8
Motorcycles	124	1,671
Cars	374	1,237

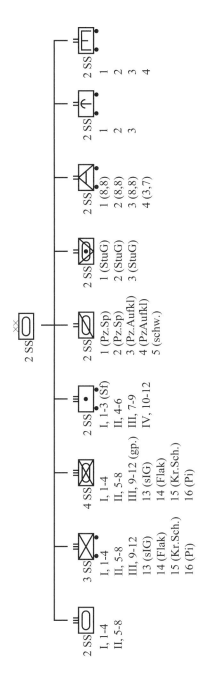

2 SS

2 SS
1
2
3
4

2 SS
1
2
3

2 SS
1 (8,8)
2 (8,8)
3 (8,8)
4 (3,7)

2 SS
1 (StuG)
2 (StuG)
3 (StuG)

2 SS
1 (Pz.Sp)
2 (Pz.Sp)
3 (Pz.Aufkl)
4 (PzAufkl)
5 (schw.)

2 SS
I, 1-3 (Sf)
II, 4-6
III, 7-9
IV, 10-12

4 SS
I, 1-4
II, 5-8
III, 9-12 (gp.)
13 (sIG)
14 (Flak)
15 (Kr.Sch.)
16 (Pi)

3 SS
I, 1-4
II, 5-8
III, 9-12
13 (sIG)
14 (Flak)
15 (Kr.Sch.)
16 (Pi)

2 SS
I, 1-4
II, 5-8

Equipment	On hand	Shortage
Trucks	1,821	1,974
Prime movers	62	320
SPW	0	326
Self-propelled antitank guns	0	26
Panzer IV	45	90
Panzer V	39	72
Sturmgeschütz III	41	4
Command Tanks	0	13

The situation had improved somewhat on 1 June. *The 2. SS-Panzer-Division "Das Reich"* had 235 combat-ready *SPW* and 14 in maintenance facilities. It had 22 towed artillery pieces and six *Wespe* and five *Hummel* self-propelled artillery pieces. The tank situation had improved somewhat. The division now had 54 *Panzer IVs*, of which 44 were combat ready, while the number of *Panthers* and *Sturmgeschütz III's* remained unchanged. The training was severely hampered, however, by the lack of ammunition and spare parts. The latter was a considerable problem for the trucks. The division only had 617 trucks in order, the remainder were in need of repairs.[7]

Further deliveries of tanks arrived at the division in June:[8]

Date	*Panzer IV*	*Panther*
24 May		8
25 May		8
27 May		8
4 June		17
16 June	24	

The dates indicate when the trains departed, not when tanks arrived at the division. Usually it took at least a week. No tanks were sent to the division during July and August, except five *Panzer IVs (Befehlswagen)* shipped on 6 July.[9] Altogether this resulted in the division employing 83 *Panzer IV's*, 80 *Panthers* and 45 *Sturmgeschütz IIIs* in Normandy.

On the morning of 7 June the division was ordered to be ready to march and civilian vehicles were commandeered to improve the mobility of the division.[10] One day later parts of the division were ordered to the Limoges–Tulle area to perform *Bandenbekampfung* (anti-partisan actions).[11] Elements of these units were involved in the massacre of civilians at Oradour and Tulle.

The division was attached to *Heeresgruppe B* on 11 June and, one day later, it was ordered to move to Normandy.[12] The elements on wheels moved by road while tanks and other full-tracked vehicles moved by rail. By 1900 hours on 13 June the division had already reached Domfront.[13] On 16 June, the wheeled elements had assembled in the Mortain area.[14] The trains with the tracked vehicles had reached Saumur-Angers and were on their way to Laval.[15] Two days later some of the tracked vehicles had reached the area west of Vire.[16] Of the *Panther* battalion, four trains were in La Fleche and two trains were south of Tours.[17] On 19 June five trains carrying the *Panther* battalion were in Le Mans.[18]

The major problem with moving the division to Normandy was not Allied air power or the French resistance. Those elements that moved by wheel marched quickly to the assembly area. Movements by rail caused greater problems. The greatest problem, however, was lack of vehicles and spare parts. Quite simply, a large part of the division did not move at all from its original area in southern France. It was not until the last days of June that the following components of the division began moving:[19]

One company of *Panzer IV's*, one company of *Panthers*, the *2./SS-Panzeraufklärungs-Abteilung 2*, the *2./SS-Panzer-Pionier-Bataillon 2*, one 3.7 cm *Flak* battery, the headquarters of *SS-Panzer-Grenadier-Regiment 3*, the *14. (Fla)/SS-Panzer-Grenadier-Regiment 3*, the *16. (Pi)/SS-Panzer-Grenadier-Regiment 3* and *SS-Feldgendarme-Kompanie 2*.

At the end of June the following elements still remained in southern France (because of lack of vehicles):[20]

The *II./SS-Panzer-Grenadier-Regiment 3*, the main part of the *Divisions-Begleit-Kompanie* (divisional escort company), part of Headquarters Company of *SS-Panzer-Grenadier-Regiment 4*, the *1./SS-Panzeraufklärungs-Abteilung 2*, one battery of *le FH18*, one battery of *s.F.H.*, the light bridging element and *SS-Panzer-Pionier-Bataillon 2* (except the *2. Kompanie*), part of *SS-Panzer-Nachrichten-Abteilung 2*, the Headquarters Battery of *SS-Sturmgeschütz-Abteilung 2* and part of the headquarters Battery and the light battery of *SS-Flak-Abteilung 2*.

On 1 July the *III./SS-Panzer-Grenadier-Regiment 3* began moving to Normandy.[21] At 18.00 on 4 July the division was located as follows:[22]

In the assembly area Torigny sur Vire–Canisy–Beaucoudray):

Divisional Staff (except the main elements of the *Divisions-Begleit-Kompanie)*
SS-Panzer-Regiment 2 (with the *I./SS-Panzer-Regiment 2*)
SS-Panzer-Grenadier-Regiment 3 (with the *I./SS-Panzer-Grenadier-Regiment 3* and the *13. Kompanie*)

SS-Panzer-Grenadier-Regiment 4 (with the *I., III., 13., 14.,* and
16./SS-Panzer-Grenadier-Regiment 4)
SS-Panzeraufklärungs-Abteilung2 (with the *2., 3., 4.* and *5./SS-Panzeraufklärungs-Abteilung 2*)
SS-Panzer-Artillerie-Regiment 2 (with the *I., II.* and *III./SS-Panzer-Artillerie-Regiment 2* minus one battery each of light and heavy howitzers)
SS-Flak-Abteilung 2 (minus one battery of 3.7 *Flak,* its supply elements and elements of the Headquarters Battery)
SS-Panzer-Pionier-Bataillon 2 (minus the *2./SS-Panzer-Pionier-Bataillon 2* and the light bridging section) *SS-Nachrichten-Abteilung 2* (except elements)
Parts of the supply, administrative, maintenance and medical services

With the *352. Infanterie-Division*:
II./SS-Panzer-Grenadier-Regiment 2 (3 companies of *Panzer IV's,* 1 battery of *Sturmgeschütz III's*)

On march from Toulouse (starting 30 June):

Headquarters of SS-Panzer-Grenadier-Regiment 3
III./*SS-Panzer-Grenadier-Regiment 3*
14./SS-Panzer-Grenadier-Regiment 3
16./SS-Panzer-Grenadier-Regiment 3
Remainder of SS-Feldgendarme-Kompanie 2
1 battery of 3.7 cm *Flak*

Still in the Toulouse area, immobile and without heavy equipment:

Main part of the *Divisions-Begleit-Kompanie*
Remainder of the headquarters Company of *SS-Panzer-Grenadier-Regiment 3*
II./SS-Panzer-Grenadier-Regiment 3
II./SS-Panzer-Grenadier-Regiment 4
1./SS-Panzeraufklärungs-Abteilung 2
1 battery of light howitzers
1 battery of heavy howitzers
The headquarters Battery of *SS-Sturmgeschütz-Abteilung 2*
Remainder of the headquarters battery and the trains of *SS-Flak-Abteilung 2*
l. Pz.Brüko (bridging element for armored vehicles)
Remainder of *SS-Panzer-Nachrichten-Abteilung 2*
Parts of the supply, administrative, maintenance and medical services

It was not until late July that the last elements began moving. On 20 July it was reported that five of the last seven trains had departed[23] and, on 26 July, six trains had finally unloaded.[24] The late arrival of many components of the division is also reflected in the personnel strength of the division. On 1 July the division had a personnel strength of 17,283 men,[25] but only 11,195 of these were among the elements sent to Normandy.[26]

The division still had a large part of its tanks in maintenance facilities on 1 July. It only had 768 trucks in running order, while the number of *SPW* operational was 227. The division had 22 towed artillery pieces and six *Wespe* and five *Hummel* self-propelled guns. Twenty-one heavy antitank guns were combat ready.[27]

During June *Kampfgruppe Weidinger* was operationally committed. It consisted of the *I./SS-Panzer-Grenadier-Regiment 3* and the *I.* and *13.-16./SS-Panzer-Grenadier-Regiment 4*. It was committed with the *9.SS-Panzer-Division "Hohenstaufen"* during the British Operation *Epsom*. The *Kampfgruppe* lost 108 killed, 408 wounded and 126 missing (through 1 July).[28]

The *2. SS-Panzer-Division "Das Reich"* was one of the few *Panzer-Divisionen* sent to the sector where American forces fought during July. During the period from 3–10 July the division (minus *Kampfgruppe Wisliceny*)[29] lost 119 men killed, 457 wounded and three missing.[30]

Altogether this means that the division suffered at least 1,221 casualties by 10 July. This can be contrasted to the fact that as late as 17 July it had received only 200 replacements.[31]

On 21 July the division had the following artillery available:[32]

I./SS-Artillerie-Regiment 2: The *1. Batterie with five Wespe and the
2.Batterie* with five *Hummel* self-propelled artillery pieces
II./SS-Artillerie-Regiment 2: The *4., 5. And 6. Batterien with four* 10.5cm howitzers each
IV./SS-Artillerie-Regiment 2: The *8. Batterie* with four 15 cm howitzers and the *10. Batterie* with four 10 cm guns
II./Artillerie-Regiment 275: The *4. Batterie* with four 10.5 cm howitzers and the *6. Batterie* with three 10.5 cm howitzers
II./Artillerie-Regiment 191: Altogether five 7.5 cm guns, four 7.5 cm light howitzers and two 15 cm heavy howitzers.

Heeres-Artillerie-Pak-Abteilung 1041 was also placed in direct support of the division with its three batteries, each equipped with five 8.8 cm antitank guns.[33]

Two days later the artillery of the division had been reduced by one battery (probably detached to support some other division). The division had one strong, one medium strong and one average battalion. One strong battalion was in transit to the division. It also had two weak battalions attached from *Fallschirmjäger-Regiment 6*, while one battalion was lent to the *Panzer-Lehr-Division*. The division was rated as having combat value I (the highest rating), but its mobility was only 60%. *Heeres-Artillerie-Pak-Abteilung 1041* was still in support of the division.[34]

The division took part in the Mortain counterattack, but it seems to have been in relatively good shape even after that engagement. Not including *SS-Panzer-Grenadier-Regiment 3, SS-Flak-Abteilung 2* and the *III./SS-Artillerie-Regiment 2,* the division had a strength of 12,817 on 9 August.[35] Why those units are not included in the report is unclear. Either no information was available, or they were subordinated to some other unit.

The division was not surrounded in Falaise; it counterattacked towards the pocket to enable the surrounded units to escape. On 4 September it was reported to be short of 7,000 men, but this report seem to have been made in haste, without a complete picture of the situation.[36] Nine days later it had 12,357 officers and men.[37] This did not include the tank regiment.[38] Thus it seems that the division was far from destroyed after the battles in Normandy. This is in stark contrast to the statement by Max Hastings that only one man in three in the division escaped from Normandy.[39] It is possible certain elements of the division suffered such a loss rate, but certainly not the division as a whole. Instead it seems that, at most, one man in three did *not* escape from Normandy in relatively good physical health.

Date	Panzer IV[40] Combat Ready	Short Term Repair
1 June[41]	44	11
1 July[42]	50	23
23 July[43]	37	?
11 Aug[44]	4	?
13 Aug[45]	5	5

Date	Panther Combat Ready	Short Term Repair
1 June	25	12
1 July	26	46
23 July	41	?
11 Aug	1	?
13 Aug	3	?

Date	Sturmgeschütz III Combat Ready	Short Term Repair
1 June	33	9
1 July	36	3
23 July	25	?
11 Aug	6	?
13 Aug	8	9

20 Aug[46]   Four operational tanks of all types
21 Aug[47]   Fifteen operational tanks of all types
28 Aug[48]   Six operational tanks of all types

---

1   Status report to the Inspector-General of Panzer Troops, Stand 1.12.43, BA-MA RH 10/313.

2   O. Weidinger, *Division Das Reich 1943-45* (Munin Verlag, Osnabrück 1982) pp. 120–9.

3   See Gliederung II. SS-Pz.Korps 1.3.44 (BA-MA RH 20-7/136). See also Weidinger, op. cit. whose descriptions of the fighting in Normandy include the *Werfer* battalion. However, he does not mention it after mid-July.

4   It is not mentioned by Gen.Kdo. LXXXIV A.K. Ia Nr. 035/44g.Kdos 22.7.44, Taktische Gliederung der Artillerie, Stand 21.7.44, T314, R1604, F001388. Neither is it mentioned by Gen.Kdo. LXXXIV. A.K. Ia 048/44 g.Kdos. T314, R1604, F001373 which gives the condition of Das Reich on 23 July.

5   Ibid, p. 130.

6   BA-MA RH 10/112

7   Status report to the Inspector-General of Panzer Troops, Stand 1.6.44, BA-MA RH 10/313.

8   Verteilung der Panzerfahrzeuge, Bd. ab Mai 43, BA-MA RH 10/349.

9   Ibid.

10 Weidinger, op. cit. p. 137.

11 Ibid, p. 138.

12 Ibid, p. 163 & 176.

13 Ibid, p. 177.

14 OB West Ia Nr. 4648/44 g.Kdos, 16.6.44, T311, R25, F7029598.

15 Ibid.

16 OB West Ia Nr. 4739/44 g.Kdos, 19.6.44, T311, R25, F7029652.

17 Ibid.

18 OB West Ia Nr. 4784/44 g.Kdos, 20.6.44, T311, R25, F7029690.

19 OB West Ia Nr. 5135/44 g.Kdos. 1.7.44, T311, R28, F7034111f.

20 Ibid.

21 OB West Ia Nr. 5157/44 g.Kdos. 23.6.44, T311, R25, F7030017.

22 HGr B Id, "Versammlung der 2. SS Pz.Div. Das Reich", Stand 4.7., 18.00 Uhr (T311, R4, F7003774)

23 OB West Ia Nr. 5862/44 g.Kdos vom 20.7.44, T311, R28, F7034667.

24 OB West Ia Nr. 6074/44 g.Kdos, 26.7.44, T311, R28, F7034822.

25 Status report to the Inspector-General of Panzer Troops, Stand 1.7.1944, BA-MA RH 10/313.

26 K.G. Klietmann, *Die Waffen-SS, eine Dokumentation* (Osnabrück 1965) p. 508.

27 Status report to the Inspector-General of Panzer Troops, Stand 1.7.1944, BA-MA RH 10/313.

28 See Weidinger, op. cit. 178-196 and 9. SS-Pz.Div. Ia/Nr. 2400/44 geh., den 2.7.1944, BA-MA RH 19 IX/3.

29 This consisted of the SS-Pz.Gren.Rgt. 3, except III. Btl. which still was on its way to the division in Normandy.

30 Weidinger, op.cit. p 217.

31 H.Gr. B Ia Nr. 4924/44 g.Kdos., 18.7.44, T311, R3, F7002570.

32 Gen.Kdo. LXXXIV A.K. Ia Nr. 035/44g.Kdos 22.7.44, Taktische Gliederung der Artillerie, Stand 21.7.44, T314, R1604, F001388.

33 Ibid.

34 Gen.Kdo. LXXXIV. A.K. Ia 048/44 g.Kdos. T314, R1604, F001373.

35 Der Reichsführer-SS Adjutantur, Kdo.Stab RF-SS Tgb.Nr. Ia/3530/44 g.Kdos den 7.9.44, Stärkemeldungen Stand vom 5.9.44, T175, R141, F2668961.

36   Status report to the Inspector-General of Panzer Troops, Stand 4.9.1944, BA-MA RH 10/313.

37   Stärkemeldungen vom 20. September 1944, T175, R141, F2668948.

38   Ibid.

39   M. Hastings, *Das Reich* (Pan, London 1983) p. 237.

40   Data for the *Panther* and the *Sturmgeschütz III* are taken from the same sources as for the *Panzer IV.*

41   Status report to the Inspector-General of Panzer Troops, Stand 1.6.1944, BA-MA RH 10/313.

42   Status report to the Inspector-General of Panzer Troops, Stand 1.7.1944, BA-MA RH 10/313.

43   Gen.Kdo. LXXXIV. A.K. Ia 048/44 g.Kdos. T314, R1604, F001373.

44   Tagesmeldung LVIII. Pz.Korps Ia an AOK 7 11.8.44, T314, R1496, F001037f.

45   Tagesmeldung LVIII. Pz.Korps Ia 13.8.44, T314, R1496, F001069.

46   Status report to the Inspector-General of Panzer Troops, Stand 1.6.1944, BA-MA RH 10/313.

47   Status report to the Inspector-General of Panzer Troops, Stand 1.7.1944, BA-MA RH 10/313.

48   Gen.Kdo. LXXXIV. A.K. Ia 048/44 g.Kdos. T314, R1604, F001373.

49   Tagesmeldung LVIII. Pz.Korps Ia an AOK 7 11.8.44, T314, R1496, F001037f.

50   Tagesmeldung LVIII. Pz.Korps Ia 13.8.44, T314, R1496, F001069.

51   Status report to the Inspector-General of Panzer Troops, Stand 1.6.1944, BA-MA RH 10/313.

52   Status report to the Inspector-General of Panzer Troops, Stand 1.7.1944, BA-MA RH 10/313.

53   Gen.Kdo. LXXXIV. A.K. Ia 048/44 g.Kdos. T314, R1604, F001373.

54   Tagesmeldung LVIII. Pz.Korps Ia an AOK 7 11.8.44, T314, R1496, F001037f.

55   Tagesmeldung LVIII. Pz.Korps Ia 13.8.44, T314, R1496, F001069.

56   OB West Ia Nr. 7050/44 g.Kdos. 20.8.44, Fernschreiben an OKH, T78, R313, F6266029.

57   HGr B Ia Nr. 6388/44 g.Kdos. 21.8.44., T311, R4, F7004565.

58   BA-MA RH 19 IX/88.

9. Panzer-Division

The *9. Panzer-Division* had been fighting on the Eastern Front until March 1944. It was transferred to southern France for refitting at the end of March.[1] The *155. Reserve-Panzer-Division* was used for this purpose. One component of the division, the reinforced *Panzer-Grenadier-Regiment 11*, remained in the east and it was not until mid-June that it returned to the division in France.[2] The organization of the division, including *Panzer-Grenadier-Regiment 11*, is given on the next page:[3]

	On hand	Shortage
Personnel	11,219	3,098
Machine Guns	475	768
8 cm mortar	67	12
12 cm mortar	4	0
15 cm *s.IG (Sf)*	0	12
10.5 cm *le.FH*	13	6
15 cm *s.FH*	14	6
10 cm *K*	4	0
7.5 cm *Pak*	13	0
2 cm *Flak*	24	17
2 cm *Flakvierling*	0	7
Flamethrower	1	19
Motorcycles	131	330
Cars	186	447
Trucks	445	1,234
RSO	6	0
Towing vehicles	11	96
SPW	221	30
Murder	9	0
Panzer IV	78	34
Panther	0	79
Sturmgeschütz III	5	26
Befehlspanzer	0	10

The *Panther* battalion belonging to the division (the *II./Panzer-Regiment 33)* was at Mailly-le-Camp to train and receive new equipment. On 20 May, this battalion had 22 combat-ready *Panthers* and two in maintenance facilities.[5]

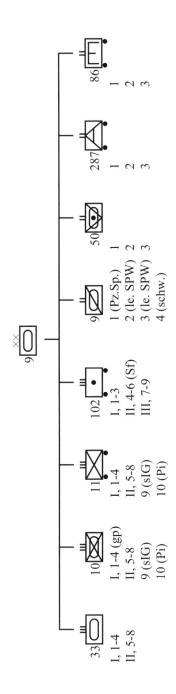

Further delivers of *Panzer IV's* and *Panthers* were:[6]

Date	Panzer IV's	Panther
15 May	4 (Befehlswagen)	
30 May		16
10 June		24
20–22 June		15

Altogether the division brought 82 *Panzer IV's* and 79 *Panthers* to Normandy. The deliveries of *Jagdpanzer IV's* for *Panzerjäger-Abteilung 50* did not take place until 20 July, when 21 vehicles were sent.[7] These were too late to arrive before the division was sent to Normandy. Rather, the battalion had to use the 9 Marders and 5 StuG indicated above.[8]

The situation for the division improved and, on 15 June, the strength of the division was (note that authorized strength had changed since 15 May):[9]

	On hand	Shortage
Personnel	14,736	
Machine Guns	823	197
8 cm mortar	68	11
15 cm *s.IG (Sf)*	6	6
10.5 cm *le.FH*	13	0
15 cm *s.FH*	8	0
10 cm *K*	4	0
Wespe	6	0
Hummel	6	0
Motorcycles	342	337
Cars	512	248
Trucks	837	968
RSO	11	0
Prime movers	19	95
SPW	264	41
Murder	9	0
Panzer V	78	0
Sturmgeschütz III	5	26
Befehlspanzer	0	10

On 1 July the division had 14,636 men. It had 284 combat-ready SPW and 12 8.8 cm *Flak*.[10]

Panzeraufklärungs-Abteilung 9 was unusual, inasmuch as it had the *Luchs* reconnaissance tank (only built in small numbers). On 1 July the battalion had 26 *Luchs*, 9 heavy armored cars, 6 light armored cars, 45 medium *SPW* and 28 light *SPW*.[11]

Given the late arrival from the Eastern Front and the fact that the division had to incorporate many new men from another formation, it was not combat ready when the Allied forces landed in Normandy. Accordingly, the 9. Panzer-Division was not ordered to move to Normandy until 27 July.[12]

When the division was ordered to move to Normandy the *II./Panzer-Regiment 33* (the *Panther* battalion) was already on its way from Mailly-le-Camp to southern France. On 24 July it was reported that nine trains with the battalion had departed and two of them had already unloaded in the Nimes–Avignon area.[13] Two days later, all 13 trains that transported the battalion had departed;[14] on 28 July eight trains had unloaded.[15]

Obviously the battalion had to retrace its movements soon after it had unloaded. Indeed the movements of the *II./Panzer-Regiment 33* are difficult to trace after it was rail loaded.

On 4 August it was reported that 12 trains with the *II./Panzer-Regiment 33*, 6 other trains with tracked elements of the division plus another 44 trains with other elements of the division had unloaded.[16] On that day elements of the division were located as follows:[17]

East of Domfront: Headquarters of *Panzer-Grenadier-Regiment 10*, Headquarters of the *I./Panzer-Grenadier-Regiment 10* and the *3./Panzer-Artillerie-Regiment 102*

West of Alençon: The *I./Panzer-Grenadier-Regiment 10*, elements of *Panzeraufklärungs-Abteilung 9* and the *I./Panzer-Regiment 33*

Trun area: The *II./Panzer-Regiment 33*

North of Angers: Parts of *Panzer-Artillerie-Regiment 102*, parts of *Panzer-Grenadier-Regimenter 10 and 11*

Tours area: elements of *Panzeraufklärungs-Abteilung 9*

According to the commander of the division, losses during the march to Normandy were insignificant, despite numerous air attacks.[18]

A problem during the operations conducted by the division was the fact that it was never employed as a complete formation. Parts of the rear services never arrived in Normandy due to the destruction of the bridges over the Loire and the enemy advance after the landing in southern France. It was not until the division had retreated to the Metz area that these units joined the division.[19]

The *Panther* battalion (the *II./Panzer-Regiment 33)* was absent from the division. This battalion was sent back and forth between various units and it seems to have made little combat contribution. It seems that it was first intended to use the *Panther* battalion in the Mortain attack, but it did not arrive in time.[20] On 9 August it was decided to send the battalion to the *I. SS-Panzer-Korps.*[21] Two days later it was on its way to the LVIII. Panzer-Korps[22] It was expected that 4 tanks would arrive on the morning of 11 August and a further 20 or the morning of 12 August. The other tanks of the battalion were unavailable due to mechanical problems suffered during all the movements.[23] On 14 August the battalion was placed under the operational control of the *116. Panzer-Division.*[24] Almost surprisingly, it remained with that division the following day.[25] The battalion had not been in combat previously; it had about 25 operational vehicles.[26] On 18 August one company (the *5./Panzer-Regiment 33)* was in the Vimoutiers area, i. e. well outside the potential encirclement area.[27] Another company (the *7./Panzer-Regiment 33)* was in the Chambois area on 19 August.[28]

On 6 August most of the division *(Panzer-Grenadier-Regimenter 10 and 11, the I./Panzer-Regiment 33 (Panzer IV), Panzeraufklärungs-Abteilung 9,* most of *Panzer-Pionier-Bataillon 86* and most of *Panzer-Artillerie-Regiment 102* was in the line Domfront–Mayenne—north of Montsurs.[29] This meant that the division was ordered to hold a front of 50 kilometers with only seven combat battalions, a task obviously impossible unless there was no enemy pressure. Some help was furnished by the fact that there were alarm units and elements from the *708. Infanterie-Division* in the area,[30] but these could not provide as much combat power as the units of the *9. Panzer-Division.*

The division continued fighting along the southern shoulder of the *7. Armee.* Much of the fighting took place in the area around Alençon. It had 15 combat-ready *Panzer IVs* on 9 August.[31]

The division was not encircled at Falaise. Already on 16 August the division was ordered to assemble in the area southwest of Paris.[32]

The division was probably in comparably good shape after the battle in Normandy. On 22 August, the division reported that it had a combat strength of 2,214 men.[33] This did not include *Panzer-Regiment 33* (most likely it was detached or else information was lacking).[34] Since a *Panzer-Division* had a combat strength of about 5,000[35] it probably had about half its combat strength left. Together with the divisional rear services, the division must have mustered about 11,000 men on *22* August. This would indicate that the division lost about 3,500 men in Normandy.

This is also supported by the fact that the division reported that it had a shortage of 1,848 men on 1 October, while losses during September amounted to 1,165. During the same time the division had received 3,164 replacements and convalescents.[36]

On the other hand, it was reported on 23 September that the division lost 7,081 men from D-Day until 13 September.[37] However, this is simply not compatible with the 1 October report. One reason for the difference is that the higher loss figure may include elements that had been sent to Germany for refitting.[38] Another explanation is that it may include losses suffered by temporarily attached units. Parts of the division whose whereabouts had been unknown may have been assumed destroyed, but showed up later with the division.[39]

1. E. Jolasse, *Einsatz der 9. Panz.Division vom 24.7. - 4.9.1944, MS # B-837*, p. 2.
2. Ibid.
3. Status Report to the Inspector-General of Panzer Troops, Stand 1.7.44, BA-MA RH 10/148.
4. BA-MA RH 10/112.
5. Panther Abteilungen Bestand nach Org und Gen Qu., BA-MA RH 10/70.
6. Lieferungen der Pz.Fahrz., Bd. ab Mai 1943, BA-MA RH 10/349.
7. Lieferungen der Pz.Fahrz., Bd. ab Mai 1943, BA-MA RH 10/349.
8. The commander of the division stated after the war that the battalion had given up its previous equipment (Jolasse, op. cit. Anlage, p. b). However, a report dated 9 August (Anlagen zum LXXXI. A.K. Ia Fernschreiben an Achilles 4, 9.8.44, T314, R1592, F000475) shows that the battalion had five combat-ready *Sturmgeschütz III's* and eight *Marders,* plus one *Marder* in short-term repair. It is possible that the battalion got its equipment back just before it left southern France. Since it had almost all these vehicles in running order, it seems not to have been engaged in intensive combat, which may be an indication of late arrival.
9. Pz.Gr. West Ia Nr, 2592/44 g.Kdos., Meldung über Stand der Neuaufstellung (Stand 15.6), H.Qu., den 21. Juni 1944 (T311, R25, F7029879f)
10. Status Report to the Inspector-General of Panzer Troops, Stand 1.7.44, BA-MA RH 10/148.
11. Ibid.
12. Ob West Ia Nr. 6097/44 g.kdos, 27.7.44, T311, R28, F7034835.
13. OB West Ia Nr. 5973/44 g.Kdos, 24.7.44, T311, R28, F7034776.
14. OB West Ia Nr. 6074/44 g.Kdos, 26.7.44, T311, R28, F7034822.
15. OB West Ia Nr. 6111/44 g.Kdos, 27.7.44, T311, R28, F7034847.
16. OB West Ia Nr. 6435/44 g.Kdos, 4.8.44, T311, R28, F7035146
17. OB West Ia Nr. 6403/44 g.Kdos, T311, R28, F7035149
18. Jolasse, op. cit. p. 4.
19. Ibid.
20. See HGr B Ia Tagesmeldung 9.8.44, BA-MA RH
21. Kurt Gätzschmann, Pz.Abt. 51 Heerestruppe - II./Pz.Rgt. 33 9. Pz.Div. 1943–45,1984.
22. Funkspruch LVIII. Pz.Korps Ia an AOK 7, T314, R1496, 001025.
23 Ibid.
24 HGr B Ia Tagesmeldung 14.8.44, BA-MA RH 19 IX/9b.
25 Kurt Gätzschmann, Pz.Abt. 51 Heerestruppe - II./Pz.Rgt. 33 9. Pz.Div. 1943–45.1984.
26 H. G. Guderian, Das letzte Kriegsjahr im Westen, Die Geschichte der 116. Pz.Div. - Windhund-Division (St. Augustin 1994) p. 92.
27 Kurt Gætzschmann, Pz.Abt. 51 Heerestruppe - II./Pz.Rgt. 33 9. Pz.Div. 1943–45.1984.
28 Kurt Gætzschmann, Pz.Abt. 51 Heerestruppe - II./Pz.Rgt. 33 9. Pz.Div. 1943–45.1984.
29 Jolasse, op.cit., p. 5.
30 Ibid.
31 Anlagen zum LXXXI. A.K. Ia Fernschreiben an Achilles 4, 9.8.44, T314, R1592, F000475.
32 Ibid, p. 9.
33 Strength refers to Gefechtstärke. Anlagen zum KTB 58. Pz.Korps, 9. Pz.Div. Ia 22.8.44, Gefechtstärken und einsatzber. Waffen, T314, R1496, F001101f.

34 Anlagen zum KTB 58. Pz.Korps, 9. Pz.Div. Ia 22.8.44, Gefechtstärken und einsatzber. Waffen, T314, R1496, F001101f.

35 At Kursk on 5 July 1943 the *3. Panzer-Division* had a combat strength (*Gefechtstärke*) of 5,170 and a ration strength of 14,141. Even the *2. SS-Panzer-Grenadier-Division "Das Reich"* at the same time had a combat strength of no more than 7,350, while ration strength was 20,659. See BA-MA RH 21-4/422. Anlage 7 zu KTB PzAOK 4 Meldungen (Beute, Verpflegungsstärken) von 1.7.1943 bis 31.12.1943 and K. Sperker: *Generaloberst Erhard Raus, ein Truppenfuhrer im Ostfeldzug.* Osnabrück 1988. Appendix: Dokumente.

36 Status Report to the Inspector-General of Panzer Troops, Stand 1.10.44, BA-MA RH 10/148.

37 LXXXI. A.K. IIa/b, 23.9.44, T314, R1594, F000267.

38 For example, *Panzer-Regiment 33* (except the *II. Abteilung*) had been sent to Germany for refitting. (LXXXI. A.K. Ia Anlagen, Befehle and Divisionen usw., Istgliederung der 9. Pz.Div. Stand 21.9.44, T314, R1592, F001005). This report shows the personnel strength as percentages of authorized strength. According to the percentages presented, the division was short of about 4,600 men. It is worth noting that the same file (Frame 000983) shows a *Gliederung* (organizational chart) giving the status of the *9. Panzer-Division* on 10 September. On this chart the division is lacking many components, such as three infantry battalions, the reconnaissance battalion and the entire *Panzer-Regiment*. All these units are present on the 21 September *Gliederung* (except for the parts of *Panzer-Regiment 33* that were in Germany).

39 Ibid.

9. SS-Panzer-Division "Hohenstaufen"

This division was created during 1943 in France. It remained in France until the spring of 1944 when it was sent to the Eastern Front. It remained there until 12 June, when it was ordered to move to Normandy.[1] The structure of the division on 1 June 1944 was:[2]

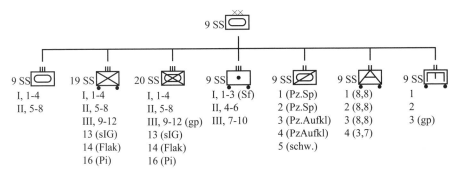

According to the report for 1 June 1944 on the condition of the division, it had certain shortages. *SS-Panzer-Grenadier-Regiment 19* had only 69% of its authorized personnel in its battalions, while *SS-Panzer-Grenadier-Regiment 20* was somewhat better off with a shortage of 21%. *SS-Panzer-Pionier-Bataillon 9* was at 71% of its authorized strength. The other units of the division were between 90 and 100% strength. The division had an authorized personnel strength of 19,855 officers and men plus 1,055 *HiWi* (Eastern volunteers). It was short 1,239 officers and men and it had only 52 *HiWi*[3] The shortage of officers was 26%, of noncommissioned officers 23%, and enlisted personnel less than 1%.[4]

Most likely the strength given above includes *SS-Panzerjäger-Abteilung 9,* which did not follow the division to Normandy. According to Klietmann, the division had a strength of 15,898 men on 30 June.[5] By that time the casualties did not exceed 1,000 so the strength given on 1 June probably includes men in replacement training organizations.

Like many *Panzer-Divisionen,* the *9. SS-Panzer-Division "Hohenstaufen"* experienced shortages of transportation means. It only had 345 operational cross-country trucks; it was authorized 1,096. This was partially covered by a surplus of conventional trucks. It had 967 operational and 199 in short-term repair compared to an authorized number of 868 trucks. Nevertheless, it had less than two thirds of its authorized transport capacity.[6]

The Panzer-Grenadier-Regimenter were equipped as follows on 1 June was:[7] (See next page)

SS-Panzer-Regiment 9 had 41 operational *Panzer IV's,* five in short-term repair and two in long-term repair.[8] It also had 38 operational *Sturmgeschütz III's* and

Formation	MG	8 cm GrW	3.7 cm le.IG (Sf)	7.5 cm Pak 40	7.5 cm le.IG	7.5 cm le.IG (Sf)	15 cm s.IG (Sf)	2 cm Flak	Flame-thrower
Panzer-Grenadier-Regiment 19									
I.	53	10		3	4				6
II.	52	11		3	4				6
III.	52	12		3	4				6
13.							6		
14.	2							11	
16.	20	2							6
Panzer-Grenadier-Regiment 20									
I.	54	12		3	4				6
II.	54	11		3	3				6
III.- (gp)	139	6	6	3	2	5			12
13.							6		
14.	2							12	
16.	20	2							4

two in workshops. *Panzer IV's* were found in the *5.* and *6./SS-Panzer-Regiment 9,* while *Sturmgeschütz III's* equipped the *7.* and *8./SS-Panzer-Regiment 9.* The *Panther* battalion — the *I./SS-Panzer-Regiment 9* — was at Mailly-le-Camp and still needed training. It had not yet trained in company- or battalion-sized formations and it needed at least four weeks of intensive training.[9] Prior to June it had not been possible for the battalion to conduct exercises on greater scale since deliveries of *Panthers* were slow. On 21 May 16 *Panthers* were sent, followed by 4 on 26 May. Another 39 were sent from 7–9 June, bringing the battalion up to its authorized strength of 79 tanks.[10]

No *Panthers, Panzer IV's* or *Sturmgeschütz III's* were sent to the division while it was in Normandy.[11]

As mentioned above, the division lacked its *Panzerjäger-Abteilung* in Normandy. The battalion had no tank destroyers. None were delivered until 29 July, when 21 were sent to the tank-destroyer battalion.[12] Given the fact that the men had to train with their new vehicles, it was not possible for the unit to join its parent formation in Normandy.

An attempt to remedy the lack of an antitank battalion was made in Normandy. A new company, called the *3 ./SS-Panzerjäger-Abteilung 9,* was formed in July, by using elements from various parts of the division. It had 12 towed 7.5 cm *Pak 40's.* Since it was formed from existing men and equipment of the division, it did not increase the division's strength, but it gave the divisional commander an additional asset.[13]

The artillery regiment had the following equipment:[14]

1./SS-Panzer-Artillerie-Regiment 9: Six *Wespe* self-propelled guns
2./SS-Panzer-Artillerie-Regiment 9: Six *Wespe* self-propelled guns
3./SS-Panzer-Artillerie-Regiment 9: Six *Hummel* self-propelled guns
4./SS-Panzer-Artillerie-Regiment 9: Four 10.5 cm howitzers (towed)
5./SS-Panzer-Artillerie-Regiment 9: Four 10.5 cm howitzers (towed)
6./SS-Panzer-Artillerie-Regiment 9: Four 10.5 cm howitzers (towed)
7./SS-Panzer-Artillerie-Regiment 9: Four 15 cm howitzers (towed)
8./SS-Panzer-Artillerie-Regiment 9: Four 15 cm howitzers (towed)
9./SS-Panzer-Artillerie-Regiment 9: Four 15 cm howitzers (towed)
10./SS-Panzer-Artillerie-Regiment 9: Four 10 cm guns (towed)

The division was part of the *II. SS-Panzer-Korps* in June and together with the *10. SS-Panzer-Division "Frundsberg"*, it was transferred to Normandy. Its movements to Normandy resembled those of *the 10. SS-Panzer-Division "Frundsberg"*.

During the later stages of the British Operation *Epsom*, the *9. SS-Panzer-Division "Hohenstaufen"* was heavily engaged. Its casualties through 1 July amounted to 1,145 killed, wounded and missing.[15] Equipment losses included: 6 *Panthers*, 16 *Panzer*

IV's, 10 *Sturmgeschütz III's,* 11 antitank guns, 1 heavy infantry gun, 6 light infantry guns, 13 mortars and 19 machine guns.[16]

On 5 July the division reported that the number of operational tanks was rising, as the workshops repaired damaged tanks. It was specifically mentioned that from the *Panther* battalion, about half the tanks were scattered along roads with minor technical problems.[17]

It seems that the division was not engaged in very intensive combat for a while, since it was reported to have suffered 1,891 casualties through 18 July.[18] On that particular day the division captured 67 enemy tanks, 56 of them destroyed and the remaining 11 in running order.[19]

As usual, the infantry suffered the vast majority of the casualties. To compensate for this *SS-Panzer-Grenadier-Regimenter 19* and *20* were combined into an ad hoc formation – *SS-Panzer-Grenadier-Regiment "H"* – on 23 July. One exception was the *SPW* battalion; the *III./SS-Panzer-Grenadier-Regiment 20* was attached to *SS-Panzer-Regiment 9* instead.[20]

SS-Panzer-Grenadier-Regiment "H" was organized into three battalions. It had rather hefty support units:[21]

13. Kompanie: 12 15 cm *sIG (Sf)*
14. Kompanie: 12 2 cm *Flak (Sf)*
15. Kompanie: 12 12 cm mortars
16. Kompanie: Combat engineers, partly equipped with *SPW*
17. Kompanie: Headquarters Company with *SPW* platoon, motorcycle platoon and scout platoon

Casualties in July included 467 killed in action, 1 628 wounded and 277 missing.[22] The division remained in the area southwest of Caen until the beginning of August. At the beginning of August the division was sent to the area northeast of Vire.[23] By 31 July the division lost (complete write-offs) 20 *Panthers,* 13 *Panzer IV's,* 14 *Sturmgeschütz III's,* 4 *SPW,* cars, 52 trucks and six prime movers.[24]

On 16 August the division was ordered to move outside the area that would eventually become known as the "Falaise pocket".[25] The elements moving by truck reached the Vimoutiers area on 18 August, while the tanks and other units moving on tracks moved by another route. Some of the tanks were commandeered by the *12. SS-Panzer-Division "Hitlerjugend".*[26]

Together with the *2. SS-Panzer-Division "Das Reich",* the division attacked from the outside of the Falaise pocket to enable surrounded units to escape.[27]

Exact casualties are impossible to establish, but given the combat actions the division participated in, it seems that it may have lost from 5,000 men killed wounded and missing.[28]

As a result, the division was in relatively good condition. This is also indicated by a report on 21 August which said that the division had 20 combat-ready tanks and 20 artillery pieces ready for action. On the other hand, the division only had 460 riflemen left.[29]

On 4 September, the division handed over eight *Panthers* and two *Panzer IV's* to the *11. Panzer-Division*.[30]

Date	Pz.Kw. IV		Panther		StuG III	
	Combat Ready	Short-term Repair	Combat Ready	Short-term Repair	Combat Ready	Short-term Repair
1 June[31]	41	5	30	4	38	2
10 June[32]			Total of 40 *Panthers*			
30 June (late)[33]	9	?	27	?	22	?
2 July[34]	10	?	19	?	19	?
3 July[35]	11	?	20	?	22	?
4 July[36]	12	?	35	?	20	?
5 July[37]	12	?	36	?	19	?
6 July[38]	?	?	37	?	?	?
7 July[39]	15	?	43	?	23	?
8 July[40]	15	10	45	8	23	7
9 July[41]	19	?	50	?	25	?
10 July[42]	20	3	50	5	27	4
12 July[43]	13	?	35	?	12	?
13 July[44]	13	?	35	?	12	?
14 July[45]	19	?	38	?	16	?
15 July[46]	19	?	41	?	22	?
16 July[47]			c:a 15 *Panther* and 20 *Stug+Pz IV*			
17 July[48]	13	?	25	?	15	?
18 July[49]	20	?	25	?	15	?
19 July[50]	22	?	24	?	17	?
20 July[51]	19	?	8 + 16*	?	16	?
21 July[52]	19	?	8 + 16*	?	19	?
24 July[53]	22	?	10	?	13	?
25 July[54]	21	?	23	?	14	?
27 July[55]	18	?	26	?	11	?
28 July[56]	22	?	26	?	22	?
29 July[57]	22	?	29	?	27	?

Date	Pz.Kw. IV		Panther		StuG III	
	Combat Ready	Short-term Repair	Combat Ready	Short-term Repair	Combat Ready	Short-term Repair
30 July[58]	22	?	29	?	27	?
31 July[59]	22	?	29	?	27	?
1 August[60]	17	?	31	?	28	?
2 August[61]	15	?	23	?	23	?
3 August[62]	7	?	18	?	9	?
5 August[63]	8	?	11	?	8	?
6 August[64]	8	?	11	?	8	?
7 August[65]	9	?	14	?	7	?
8 August[66]	9	?	12	?	6	?
9 August[67]	6	?	10	?	6	?
10 August[68]	13	?	11	?	18	?
11 August[69]	10	?	11	?	13	?
12 August[70]	10	?	13	?	15	?
13 August[71]	11	?	15	?	14	?
20 August[72]	20 operational tanks of all types					

* = Two *Panther* Companies (with 16 operational *Panthers* together)were detached to the *1. SS-Panzer-Korps.*

1   G. Tessin, *Verbände und Truppen der deutschen Wehrmacht und Waffen-SS* (Mittler & Sohn, Frankfurt am Main and Biblio Verlag, Osnabrück 1966–1975).

2   9. SS-Pz.Div. Hohenstafen, Anlage zu Ia Tgb. Nr. 547/44, BA-MA RH 10/318. Note that the *I./SS-Panzer-Regiment 9* is presented on a separate paper in the file.

3   Ibid.

4   Ibid.

5   K.G. Klietmann, *Die Waffen-SS, eine Dokumentation* (Osnabrück 1965). 509.

6   9. SS-Pz.Div. Hohenstafen, Anlage zu Ia Tgb. Nr. 547/44, 1.6.44, BA-MA RH 10/318. The division was authorized a lift capacity of 5,024 tons, but had only 2,901 tons available, plus 578 in maintenance facilities.

7   9. SS-Pz.Div. Hohenstafen, Anlage zu Ia Tgb. Nr. 547/44,1.6.44, BA-MA RH 10/318.

8   Ibid.

9   Ibid.

10   Lieferung der Pz.-Fahrzeuge Bd. ab Mai 1943, BA-MA RH 10/349.

11   Ibid.

12   Ibid.

13   H. Fürbringer, *9. SS-Panzer-Division Hohenstaufen* (Heimdal, 1984) p. 308.

14   9. SS-Pz.Div. Hohenstafen, Anlage zu Ia Tgb. Nr. 547/44,1.6.44, BA-MA RH 10/318.

15   9. SS-Pz.Div. Ia/Nr. 2400/44 geh., den 2.7.1944, BA-MA RH 19 IX/3.

16   Ibid.

17   9. SS-Pz.Div. Lagebericht 5.7.1944, BA-MA RS 3-9/2.

18 Pz.Gr. West Ia Nr. 480/44 g.Kdos. 20.7.44, T313, R420, F8713975.

19 HGr B Ib/Br. B Nr. 01087/44 geh 20.7.44, T311, Rl, F7000812.

20 H. Fürbringer, 9. *SS-Panzer-Division Hohenstaufen* (Heimdal, 1984) p. 337.

21 Ibid.

22 BA-MA RW 6/v. 577.

23 H. Fürbringer, 9. *SS-Panzer-Division Hohenstaufen* (Heimdal, 1984) p. 353ff.

24 Anlage 3 zu Gen.Kdo. II. SS-Pz.Korps Qu. Tgb.Nr. 765/44 geh. vom 3.8.44, copy found in LVIII. Pz.Korps Qu Anlagen, T314, R1497, F000430.

25 Ibid. p. 379.

26 Ibid, p 389.

27 Ibid. p. 389-391.

28 Comparisons can be made with the *1.* and *2. SS-Panzer-Divisionen.* These were committed for about the same amount of time. On 18 July the *1. SS-Panzer-Division "Leibstandarte"* had casualties almost identical to those suffered by the 9. *SS-Panzer-Division "Hohenstaufen".* The *'Leibstandarte"* was partly surrounded at Falaise, while parts of the *2. SS-Panzer-Division "Das Reich"* were surrounded in late July. No similar encirclements were endured by units from the *"Hohenstaufen.* If anything, the *"Hohenstaufen* should be expected to have suffered less casualties than those two divisions.

29 HGr B Ia Nr. 6388/44 g.Kdos. 21.8.44., T311, R4, F7004565.

30 G. W. Schrodek, *Geschichte des Panzer-Regiments 15* (Schild, München 1976) p. 309.

31 Anlage 2 zu SS-Pz.Div. "H" Ia Tgb. Nr. 597/44, 1.6.44, BA-MA RH 10/318.

32 OB West Ia, Nr 4470/44 g.Kdos. 11.6.44, T311, R25, F7029472.

33 H. Fürbringer, *9. SS-Panzer-Division Hohenstufen* (Heimdal, 1984) p. 286.

34 Pz.Gr. West Ia Nr. 86/44 3.7.44, T313, R420, F8713808.

35 9. SS-Pz.Div. Tagesmeldung 3.7.1944, BA-MA RS 3-9/2.

36 9. SS-Pz.Div. Tagesmeldung 4.7.1944, BA-MA RS 3-9/2

37 Pz.Gr. West Ia Nr. 187/44 6.7.44, T313, R420, F8713832.

38 Pz.Gr. West Ia, Nr. 217/44 geh. von 7.7.1944., Nachtrag zur Tagesmeldung 6.7., BA-MA RH 21-5/50

39 Pz.Gr. West Ia Nr. 258/44 g.Kdos. Nachtrag zur Tagesmeldung 7.7, BA-MA RH 21-5/50.

40 Pz.Gr. West Ia Nr. 258/44 g.Kdos. Nachtrag zur Tagesmeldung 7.7, BA-MA RH 21-5/50.

41 Pz.Gr. West Ia, Nr. 306/44 geh. von 10.7.1944., Nachtrag zur Tagesmeldung 9.7., BA-MA RH 21-5/50.

42 Pz.Gr. West Ia, Nr. 287/44 geh. von 11.7.1944., Nachtrag zur Tagesmeldung 10.7., T313, R420, F8713880.

43 9. SS-Pz.Div. Nachmeldung Stand 12.7, Abgegangen 14.7.1944, BA-MA RS 3-9/2.

44 Pz.Gr. West Ia, Nr. 348/44 geh. v. 14.7.44, Nachtrag zur Tagesmeldung 13.7., T313, R420, F8713904.

45 Pz.Gr. West Ia Nr. Unleserlich, v. 15.7.44, Nachtrag zur Tagesmeldung 14.7, T313, R420, F8713915.

46 9. SS-Pz.Div. Tagesmeldung 15.7.1944, BA-MA RS 3-9/2.

47 9. SS-Pz.Div. Tagesmeldung 16.7.1944, BA-MA RS 3-9/2.

48 Pz.Gr. West Ia Nr. 479/44 geheim von 18.7.44, Nachtrag zur Tagesmeldung 17.7.44, BA-MA RH 21-5/50.

49 Pz.Gr. West Ia, Nr. 451/44 geh. von 19.7.1944., Nachtrag zur Tagesmeldung 18.7., BA-MA RH 21-5/50.

50 Pz.Gr. West Ia Nr. 476/44 g.Kdos, 20.7.44, Nachtrag zur Tagesmeldung 19.7, T313, R420, F8713961

51 Pz.Gr. West Ia, Nr. 491/44 geh. von 21.7.1944., Nachtrag zur Tagesmeldung 20.7., BA-MA RH 21-5/50.

52 9. SS-Pz.Div. Tagesmeldung 21.7.1944, BA-MA RS 3-9/2.

53 9. SS-Pz.Div. Wochenmeldung 24.7.1944, BA-MA RS 3-9/2.

54 Pz.Gr. West Ia, Nr. 572/44 geh. von 26.7.1944., Nachtrag zur Tagesmeldung 25.7., BA-MA RH 21-5/50.

55 Pz.Gr. West Ia, Nr. 605/44 geh. von 28.7.1944., Nachtrag zur Tagesmeldung 27.7., BA-MA RH 21-5/50.

56 Pz.Gr. West Ia Nr. 633/44 g.Kdos, 29.7.44, Nachtrag zur Tagesmeldung 28.7, T313, R420, F8714036.

57 Pz.Gr. West Ia Nr. 647/44 g.Kdos, 30.7.44, Nachtrag zur Tagesmeldung 29.7, T313, R420, F8714042.

58 Pz.Gr. West Ia Nr. 665/44 g.Kdos, 31.7.44, Nachtrag zur Tagesmeldung 30.7, T313, R420, F8714049.

59 9. SS-Pz.Div. Tagesmeldung 31.7.1944, BA-MA RS 3-9/2.

60 Pz.Gr. West Ia Nr. 704/44 g.Kdos. 2.8.44, Nachtrag zur Tagesmeldung 1.8, T313, R420, F8714068.

61 9. SS-Pz.Div. Tagesmeldung 2.8.1944, BA-MA RS 3-9/2.

62 Pz.Gr. West Ia, Nr. 734/44 geh. von 4.8.1944., Nachtrag zur Tagesmeldung 3.8., BA-MA RH 21-5/50.

63 Pz.Gr. West Ia Nr. 775/44 g.Kdos. 6.8.44, Nachtrag zur Tagesmeldung 5.8, T313, R420, F8714097.

64 Pz.Gr. West Ia Nr. 801/44 g.Kdos, 7.8.44, Nachtrag zur Tagesmeldung 6.8, T313, R420, F8714118.

65 9. SS-Pz.Div. Tagesmeldung 7.8.1944, BA-MA RS 3-9/2.

66 9. SS-Pz.Div. Tagesmeldung 8.8.1944, BA-MA RS 3-9/2.

67 Pz.Gr. West Ia Nr. 853/44 g.Kdos. 10.8.44, Nachtrag zur Tagesmeldung 9.8, T313, R420, F87141177.

68 Pz.Gr. West Ia Nr. 890/44 g.Kdos, 11.8.44, Nachtrag zur Tagesmeldung 10.8, T313, R420, F87141181.

69 Pz.Gr. West Ia Nr. 899/44 g.Kdos, 12.8.44, Nachtrag zur Tagesmeldung 11.8, T313, R420, F87141187.

70 9. SS-Pz.Div. Wochenmeldung 12.8.1944, BA-MA RS 3-9/2.

71 Fürbringer, op. cit. p. 376.

72 OB West Ia Nr. 7050/44 g.Kdos. 20.8.44, Fernschreiben an OKH, T78, R313, F6266029.

10. SS-Panzer-Division "Frundsberg"

This division was created during 1943 in France. Initially it was named *Karl der Große* (Karl the Great = Charlemagne) but, on 3 October, it was redesignated as *Frundsberg*. It remained in France until the spring of 1944 when it was sent to the Eastern Front. It remained there until 12 June, when it was ordered to move to Normandy.[1] The structure of the division on 1 June 1944 was:[2]

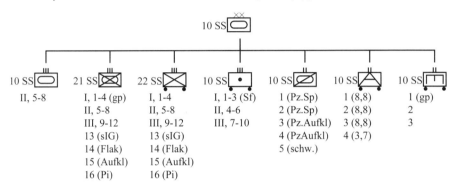

10 SS	21 SS	22 SS	10 SS	10 SS	10 SS	10 SS
II, 5-8	I, 1-4 (gp)	I, 1-4	I, 1-3 (Sf)	1 (Pz.Sp)	1 (8,8)	1 (gp)
	II, 5-8	II, 5-8	II, 4-6	2 (Pz.Sp)	2 (8,8)	2
	III, 9-12	III, 9-12	III, 7-10	3 (Pz.Aufkl)	3 (8,8)	3
	13 (sIG)	13 (sIG)		4 (PzAufkl)	4 (3,7)	
	14 (Flak)	14 (Flak)		5 (schw.)		
	15 (Aufkl)	15 (Aufkl)				
	16 (Pi)	16 (Pi)				

The *I./SS-Panzer-Regiment 10* was in France in June 1944, but it only had training vehicles and was not combat ready.[3] In fact, it did not join the division until 1945. The *II./SS-Panzer-Regiment 10* was equipped with 39 *Panzer IVs* and 38 *Sturmgeschütz III's*, if vehicles in maintenance facilities are included.[4] Thus, this division had fewer tanks and assault guns than any other *Panzer-Division* that fought in Normandy. It did not receive any replacements during its commitment there.[5] The *10. SS-Panzer-Regiment 10* also had three *Panzer III* command tanks.

SS-Panzer-Grenadier-Regimenter 21 and *22* were organized in the normal fashion, but the three battalions of *SS-Panzer-Grenadier-Regiment 21* were only at 83%, 75% and 73% of authorized strength respectively. For *SS-Panzer-Grenadier-Regiment 22* the percentages were 76%, 76% and 72%.[6]

SS-Artillerie-Regiment 10 had 11 Wespe self-propelled guns, one short of its full complement of twelve. It also had 6 Hummels, 12 10.5 cm light field pieces, 12 15 cm heavy field howitzers and four 10 cm K18s.[7]

At the time of the campaign in Normandy, *SS-Panzerjäger-Abteilung 10* was still in the process of forming. It did not become combat ready in time for the battles in Normandy. No Jagdpanzer IVs were sent to the battalion until 22 August.[8]

SS-Panzeraufklärungs-Abteilung 10 was at full strength, while *SS-Pionier-Bataillon 10* was at 88% of authorized strength.[9]

Authorized strength of the division was 17,995 (not including the *I./SS-Panzer-Regiment 10)*, but the division was short 1,984 men.[10] This gave a shortage of 11%, but as has been shown above, the shortage was greater among the infantry battalions.

Given the figures above, it could be concluded that the division had a strength of 16,011 men. However, this included *SS-Panzerjäger-Abteilung 10,* which was in the process of forming. Since it was only at 31% of authorized strength[11] it probably had no more than about 200 men, which would mean that the division had about 15,800 men. This figure also includes the field-replacement battalion. With five full-strength companies,[12] it probably had about 1,000 men. This battalion did follow the division to Normandy.[13]

Together with the *9. SS-Panzer-Division "Hohenstaufen",* the *10. SS-Panzer-Division "Frundsberg"* was ordered on 12 June 1944 to be transferred to Normandy. At that time, these divisions were located near Lvov. Since trains were available, the first elements departed late in the afternoon of 12 June.[14] On 18 June it was reported that 20 of the trains carrying the division had entered France; four of these had reached Paris.[15] Two days later 38 trains were in the area Saarbrücken — Nancy, while 13 had unloaded in Paris.[16] On 23 June, 67 trains had reached the OB West area. Of these nine had unloaded in Saarbrucken, 39 in the area around Bar-le-Duc and 21 in the Paris — Dreux area.[17]

On 24 June the following units had reached the assembly area in Normandy: divisional staff, *SS-Panzeraufklärungs-Abteilung 10, SS-Panzer-Regiment 10,* both *SS-Panzer-Grenadier-Regimenter* with three battalions each, *SS-Artillerie-Regiment 10* (minus one battalion), *SS-Pionier-Bataillon 10, SS-Flak-Abteilung 10, SS-Panzerjäger-Abteilung 10, SS-Feldersatz-Bataillon 10.*[18] One day later all the combat elements of the division, except one of the artillery battalions, had reached the assembly area. Parts of the rear services had not yet arrived.

Surprisingly, *SS-Panzerjäger-Abteilung 10* is stated to have arrived in the assembly area. This seems very unlikely since the unit had not yet received its *Jagdpanzer IV's.*[19] Neither is there anything in the daily reports on the status of the division's tanks, assault guns and antitank guns that suggest this unit would have accompanied the division to Normandy. Possibly some officers, or a small detachment from the battalion, joined the division in Normandy to get first-hand experience, but hardly the entire battalion.

Together with the II. SS-Panzer-Korps, the division was ordered to move during the night from 25/26 June to the area St. Remy–Roucamps–La Bigne–St. Symphorien–Les Buttes–Campeaux–Vire–Tinchebray.[20] On 30 June the division, minus the elements not yet sent to Normandy, numbered 13,552 men.[21]

The division first saw action in Normandy during the British Operation *Epsom.* Due to lack of fuel, only a limited number of the tanks and assault guns available could participate initially.[22] During the most intensive 36 hours (30 June–1 July) the division lost 571 men killed and wounded.[23]

Through 18 July the division lost 2,289 officers and men.[24] It had also lost 6 7.5 cm *Pak 40's,* 8 7.5 cm *leichtes Infanterie-Geschütz 18s,* 4 15 cm *schweres Infanterie-Geschütz 33's,* 18 8 cm mortars and 88 *MG 42's.*[25] By 31 July the division lost (complete write-offs)

7 *Panzer IV's*, 3 *Sturmgeschütz III's*, 11 SPW's, 57 cars, 91 trucks and 9 prime movers.[26] Casualties in July included 403 killed in action, 1 263 wounded and 470 missing.[27]

During July the division remained southwest of Caen, but in August it was sent first to the Vire area and later to the southern side of the sack that was formed around the German units west of Falaise and Argentan.

Despite this, on 14 August, the division was in relatively good shape. It had lost 12 *Panzer IV's* and 8 *Sturmgeschütz III's* since the division began moving to Normandy.[28] The *Kampfstärke,* i.e. the number of riflemen employed in the forward line and the crews of tanks and other heavy weapons employed in the direct support of the infantry, amounted to 4,136.[29]

Parts of the *10. SS-Panzer-Division "Frundsberg"* were encircled in the Falaise pocket together with the *2. Panzer-Division* and the *1. SS-Panzer-Division "Leibstandarte".*[30]

The exact losses are unknown, but given its losses up to 18 July, the *Kampfstärke* of 14 August, the outcome for divisions[31] similar in organization and the situation during the Falaise battle, a total of 5,000 casualties seems a reasonable estimate.

Panzer IV Availability for the 10. SS-Panzer-Division "Frundsberg"

Date	Combat Ready	Short-term Repair	Long-term Repair
1 June[32]	34	1	4
2 July[33]	20	?	?
6 July[34]	25	?	?
7 July[35]	27	?	?
9 July[36]	27	3	6
12 July[37]	17	6	9
13 July[38]	16	7	9
14 July[39]	16	7	9
15 July[40]	17	6	9
16 July[41]	9	?	?
17 July[42]	10	?	?
18 July[43]	12	?	?
19 July[44]	12	8	11
20 July[45]	14	?	?
21 July[46]	18	?	?
22 July[47]	14	?	?
23 July[48]	14	?	?
24 July[49]	13	9	10

Date	Combat Ready	Short-term Repair	Long-term Repair
25 July[50]	14	?	?
27 July[51]	15	?	?
28 July[52]	16	7	8
29 July[53]	17	6	8
30 July[54]	17	?	?
31 July[55]	20	?	?
2 August[56]	20	?	?
3 August[57]	20	?	?
4 August[58]	16	?	?
5 August[59]	10	?	?
6 August[60]	10	?	?
7 August[61]	5	?	p
10 August[62]	10	9	?
11 August[63]	12	8	?
12 August[64]	14	5	?
13 August[65]	11	9	?
14 August[66]	11	5	11
21 August[67]	0	?	?

Sturmgeschütz III Availability for the
10. SS-Panzer-Division "Frundsberg;"[67]

Date	Combat Ready	Short-term Repair	Long-term Repair
1 June	32	1	5
2 July	25	?	?
6 July	?	?	?
7 July	25	?	?
9 July	25	5	5
12 July	8	10	18
13 July	10	8	16
14 July	12	8	16
15 July	13	7	16
16 July	7	?	?
17 July	?	?	?
18 July	6	?	?

Date	Combat Ready	Short-term Repair	Long-term Repair
19 July	12	6	18
20 July	14	?	?
21 July	14	?	?
22 July	8	?	?
23 July	7	?	?
24 July	10	11	15
25 July	11	?	?
27 July	15	?	?
28 July	16	8	12
29 July	16	8	12
30 July	17	?	?
31 July	20	?	?
2 August	15	?	?
3 August	8	?	?
4 August	?	?	?
5 August	7	?	?
6 August	10	?	?
7 August	5	?	?
10 August	5	17	?
11 August	6	10	?
12 August	6	10	?
13 August	5	9	?
14 August	9	9	12
21 August	0	?	?

1   G. Tessin, *Verbände und Truppen der deutschen Wehrmacht und Waffen-SS* (Mittler & Sohn, Frankfurt am Main and Biblio Verlag, Osnabrück 1966–1975).
2   10. SS-Pz.Div. Frundsberg, Anlage zu la Tgb. Nr. 271/44, 1.6.44, BA-MA RH 10/319.
3   Pz. Personal-Einheiten im Bereich OB West, T311, R25, F7030050.
4   10. SS-Pz.Div. Frundsberg, Anlage zu la Tgb. Nr. 271/44,1.6.44, BA-MA RH 10/319.
5   Lieferungen der Pz.Fahrz., Bd. ab Mai 1943, BA-MA RH 10/349.
6   10. SS-Pz.Div. Frundsberg, Anlage zu la Tgb. Nr. 271/44,1.6.44, BA-MA RH 10/319.
7   Ibid.
8   Lieferungen der Pz.Fahrz., Bd. ab Mai 1943, BA-MA RH 10/349.
9   10. SS-Pz.Div. Frundsberg, Anlage zu la Tgb. Nr. 271/44,1.6.44, BA-MA RH 10/319.
10 Ibid.
11 Ibid.

12 Ibid.

13 OB West la Nr. 4963/44 g.Kdos, 25.6.1944, T311, R25, F7029849-53.

14 E. Klapdor, *Die Entscheidung* (Siek 1984) p. 215.

15 OB West la Nr. 4704/44 g.Kdos, 18.6.1944, T311, R25, F7029640-3.

16 OB West la Nr. 4784/44 g.Kdos, 20.6.44, T311, R25, F7029691.

17 OB West la Nr. 4879/44 g.Kdos. 23.6.44, T311, R25, F7029779. Note that the total trains given for the the unloading areas is 69, not 67 as stated in the document.

18 HGr B la Nr.3978/44 g.Kdos, Nachtrag zur Tagesmeldung 24.6.44, T311, R3, F7002433

19 See Lieferungen der Pz.Fahrz., Bd. ab Mai 1943, BA-MA RH 10/349.

20 HGr B la Nr. 3985/44 g.Kdos, 25.6.44, T311, R4, F7003699.

21 K.G. Klietmann, *Die Waffen-SS, eine Dokumentation* (Osnabrück 1965) p. 509.

22 E. Klapdor, Die Entscheidung (Siek 1984) p. 147.

23 Ob.West la Nr. 5223/44 geh.Kdos., 2.7.44, T311, R28, F7034140.

24 Pz.Gr. West la Nr. 480/44 g.Kdos. 20.7.44, T313, R420, F8713975.

25 HGr B Ib/Br. B Nr. 01087/44 geh 20.7.44, T311, Rl, F7000812.

26 Anlage 3 zu Gen.Kdo. II. SS-Pz.Korps Qu. Tgb.Nr. 765/44 geh. vom 3.8.44, copy found in LVIII. Pz.Korps Qu Anlagen, T314, R1497, F000430.

27 BA-MA RW 6/v. 577.

28 Compare the strength on 1 June with the strength on 14 August presented in the table on tank strengths for the *10. SS-Panzer-Division "Frundsberg"*.

29 Tagesmeldung LVIII. Pz.Korps la an AOK 7 14.8.44, T314, R1496, F001073.

30 Klapdor, op. cit. p. 370ff.

31 In particular, the *1. SS-Panzer-Division "Leibstandarte"* and the *2. Panzer-Division "Das Reich"*.

32 10. SS-Pz.Div. Frundsberg, Anlage zu la Tgb. Nr. 271/44,1.6.44, BA-MA RH 10/319.

33 Pz.Gr. West la Nr. 86/44 3.7.44, T313, R420, F8713807.

34 Pz.Gr. West la, Nr. 217/44 geh. von 7.7.1944., Nachtrag zur Tagesmeldung 6.7.. BA-MA RH 21-5/50.

35 Pz.Gr. West la Nr. 258/44 g.Kdos. Nachtrag zur Tagesmeldung 7.7, BA-MA RH 21-5/50.

36 Pz.Gr. West la, Nr. 306/44 geh. von 10.7.1944., Nachtrag zur Tagesmeldung 9.7., BA-MA RH 21-5/50.

37 Pz.Gr. West la, Nr. 335/44 geh., Nachtrag zur Tagesmeldung 12.7., T313, R420, F8713896.

38 Pz.Gr. West la, Nr. 348/44 geh. v. 14.7.44, Nachtrag zur Tagesmeldung 13.7., T313, R420, F8713904.

39 Pz.Gr. West la Nr. Unleserlich, v. 15.7.44, Nachtrag zur Tagesmeldung 14.7, T313, R420, F8713914.

40 Pz.Gr. West la Nr. 388/44 g.Kdos 16.7.44, Nachtrag zur Tagesmeldung 15.7, T313, R420, F8713921.

41 Pz.Gr. West la, Nr. 424/44 geh. von 17.7.1944., Nachtrag zur Tagesmeldung 16.7., BA-MA RH 21-5/50.

42 Pz.Gr. West la Nr. 479/44 geheim von 18.7.44, Nachtrag zur Tagesmeldung 17.7.44, BA-MA RH 21-5/50.

43 Pz.Gr. West la, Nr. 451/44 geh. von 19.7.1944., Nachtrag zur Tagesmeldung 18.7., BA-MA RH 21-5/50.

44 Pz.Gr. West la Nr. 476/44 g.Kdos, 20.7.44, Nachtrag zur Tagesmeldung 19.7, T313, R420, F8713961.

45 Pz.Gr. West la, Nr. 491/44 geh. von 21.7.1944., Nachtrag zur Tagesmeldung 20.7., BA-MA RH 21-5/50.

46 Pz.Gr. West la, Nr. 517/44 geh. von 21.7.1944., Nachtrag zur Tagesmeldung21.7., BA-MA RH 21-5/50.

47 Pz.Gr. West la, Nr. 535/44 geh. von 23.7.1944., Nachtrag zur Tagesmeldung 22.7., BA-MA RH 21-5/50.

48 Pz.Gr. West la, Nr. 535/44 geh. von 23.7.1944., Nachtrag zur Tagesmeldung 22.7., BA-MA RH 21-5/50.

49 Pz.Gr. West Ia, Nr. 557/44 geh. von 25.7.1944., Nachtrag zur Tagesmeldung 24.7., BA-MA RH 21-5/50.

50 Pz.Gr. West Ia, Nr. 572/44 geh. von 26.7.1944., Nachtrag zur Tagesmeldung 25.7., BA-MA RH 21-5/50.

51 Pz.Gr. West Ia, Nr. 605/44 geh. von 28.7.1944., Nachtrag zur Tagesmeldung 27.7., BA-MA RH 21-5/50.

52 Pz.Gr. West Ia Nr. 633/44 g.Kdos, 29.7.44, Nachtrag zur Tagesmeldung 28.7, T313, R420, F8714036.

53 Pz.Gr. West Ia Nr. 647/44 g.Kdos, 30.7.44, Nachtrag zur Tagesmeldung 29.7, T313, R420, F8714042.

54 Pz.Gr. West Ia Nr. 665/44 g.Kdos, 31.7.44, Nachtrag zur Tagesmeldung 30.7, T313, R420, F8714049.

55 Pz.Gr. West Ia, Nr. 678/44 geh. von 1.8.1944., Nachtrag zur Tagesmeldung 31.7.,BA-MA RH 21-5/50.

56 Pz.Gr. West Ia Nr. 725/44 g.Kdos. 3.8.44, Nachtrag zur Tagesmeldung 2.8, T313, R420, F8714075.

57 Pz.Gr. West Ia Nr. 734/44 g.Kdos. 4.8.44, Nachtrag zur Tagesmeldung 3.8, BA-MA RH 21-5/50.

58 Pz.Gr. West Ia Nr. 758/44 g.Kdos. 5.8.44, Nachtrag zur Tagesmeldung 4.8, T313, R420, F8714097.

59 Pz.Gr. West Ia Nr. 775/44 g.Kdos. 6.8.44, Nachtrag zur Tagesmeldung 5.8, T313, R420, F8714097.

60 Pz.Gr. West Ia Nr. 801/44 g.Kdos, 7.8.44, Nachtrag zur Tagesmeldung 6.8, T313, R420, F8714118.

61 Pz.Gr. West Ia Nr. 811/44 g.Kdos, 8.8.44, Nachtrag zur Tagesmeldung 7.8, T313, R420, F87141130.

62 Tagesmeldung LVIII. Pz.Korps Ia an AOK 7 10.8.44, T314, R1496, F001031f.

63 Tagesmeldung LVIII. Pz.Korps Ia an AOK 7 11.8.44, T314, R1496, F001037f.

64 Tagesmeldung LVIII. Pz.Korps Ia an AOK 7 12.8.44, T314, R1496, F001044.

65 Tagesmeldung LVIII. Pz.Korps Ia 13.8.44, T314, R1496, F001069.

66 LVIII. Pz.Korps Ia Nr. 48 geh. v. 14.8.44, Panzer-, Stu.Gesch.-und s.Pak-Lage 10 SS-Pz.Div.,T314, R1496, F001074.

67 HGr B Ia Nr. 6388/44 g.Kdos. 21.8.44., T311, R4, F7004565.

68 The strength figures cited here are from the same sources as listed for the previous table.

12. SS-Panzer-Division "Hitlerjugend"

At first glance, the division might have appeared to be a very strong formation on 1 June 1944. Nominally it had a strength of 20,540 men. a number that surpassed most divisions on either side of the Channel. The number is somewhat misleading, however. The following table gives the manpower situation:[1]

Personnel	Authorized Strength	Actual Strength	Difference
Officers	664	520	- 144
NCOs	4,575	2,383	- 2,192
Enlisted men	15,277	17,637	+ 2,360
Total	20,516	20,540	+ 24

The shortage of NCOs was covered by a surplus of enlisted men.[2] Another shortcoming was the fact that neither the *Panzerjäger-Abteilung* nor the *Nebelwerfer-Abteilung* were combat ready on 6 June. Neither the *SS-Panzerjäger-Abteilung 12* nor the *Nebelwerfer-Abteilung (IV./SS-Artillerie-Regiment 12)* were combat ready on 6 June.

The training of *SS-Panzerjäger-Abteilung 12* had lagged behind the remainder of the division. It had received its first *Jagdpanzer IVs* only recently. Ten such vehicles left Germany by rail on 26 April.[3] These were the first sent to the division. This was sufficient to equip one company. No further vehicles were sent to the battalion until 22 June, when a train with 11 *Jagdpanzer IVs* departed for the battalion.[4] According to Hubert Meyer, the *1./SS-Panzerjäger-Abteilung 12* joined the division on 19 July.[5] From the armored vehicle strength reports, it seems that no further tank destroyers ever joined the division in Normandy.

The *Nebelwerfer-Abteilung* lacked all prime movers, making the unit immobile. Thus, it could not immediately accompany the division to Normandy. On 12 June, the first battery of the battalion arrived,[6] but it was not until the beginning of July that the entire battalion had arrived.[7]

As a consequence of these circumstances, the division did not bring its entire strength when it arrived in Normandy. Even though elements did arrive later, these units did not compensate for casualties suffered. According to an *OB West* document dated 1 August, Sepp Dietrich, the commander of the *I. SS-Panzer-Korps,* requested the 2,000 men available in the replacement battalion be moved from Arnhem to Normandy to cover losses suffered by the division.[8] According to another document,[9] the replacement battalion was supposed to send an unspecified number of men to Normandy on 8 August, which were to be followed by another 350 men. It seems that Dietrich's wishes were at least partly granted, but perhaps too late to be of any use in the battle for Normandy. According to Meyer, parts of the division were being rebuilt at the time of the Falaise battle. This indicates the replacements sent to the division did not take part in the Normandy battle (if this is assumed to end

22 August). They may have participated in the subsequent retreat out of France.[10] (See organizational chart on the next page.)

SS-Panzer-Regiment 12 had the standard organization, i. e. the *I./SS-Panzer-Regiment 12* was equipped with *Panthers* and the *II./SS-Panzer-Regiment 12* with *Panzer IV's*. Authorized strength was 17 tanks per company in the *Panther* battalion and 22 per company in the *Panzer IV battalion*. Each battalion had four companies. Together with the tanks belonging to the battalion and regiment staffs, this gave a total of 79 *Panthers* and 101 *Panzer IV's*.

There were 91 operational *Panzer IV's* and 7 in maintenance facilities on 1 June.[11] The situation was less favorable concerning the *Panthers*. At the end of April 1944 the division had only 26 *Panthers* available.[12] Further vehicles were sent in May:[13]

16 May: 8 *Panthers*
17 May: 8 *Panthers*
22 May: 16 *Panthers* (two trains)
24 May: 8 *Panthers*

This made a total of 66 *Panthers* with the division. All of them had not arrived on 1 June; the division reported 48 combat-ready *Panthers* and 2 in maintenance facilities.[14] According to a document entitled *Im Westen vorhandene gepanzerte Kraftfahrzeuge, Stand 10.6.44* (Armored Vehicles Present in the West as of 10 June 1944),[15] the division had 66 *Panthers* on 10 June, which indicates that all the *Panzer V's* dispatched in May had arrived. An additional 13 *Panthers* were sent by train to the division on 7 June to bring the division up to full strength.[16] When these actually arrived is unclear, but given the condition of the railroads in France after the intensive aerial bombardment they had been subjected to, it may very well have taken quite some time to reach the division.

No *Panthers* were sent to the division to replace losses during the fighting in Normandy, but 17 *Panzer IVs* were dispatched on 8 July and an additional 12 on 10 August.[17] The latter did not arrive at the division until 5 September.[18]

According to Meyer, the *3./SS-Panzer-Regiment 12* was reconstituted at the beginning of July by using a delivery of 17 *Panthers*.[19] This has led to the conclusion that the 12. SS-Panzer-Division "Hitlerjugend" received more than 79 *Panthers*, if deliveries both before and during the battle in Normandy are included. This conclusion is not supported by available documents, where no mention of any such deliveries exist. In all likelihood, the 13 *Panthers* dispatched on 7 June are those that were used for this purpose. From other shipments, it is clear that a two-week delay across the damaged rail net is not inconceivable. Why Meyer states that the number of *Panthers* was 17 is not clear. One possible explanation is that he includes vehicles that had received serious damage and been sent to rear facilities for repair and then returned.

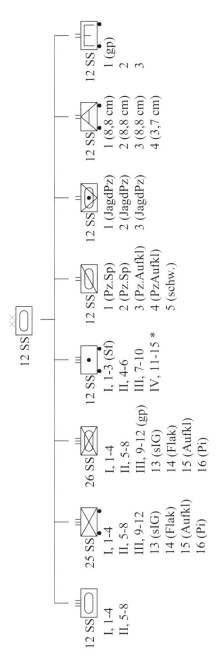

12 SS

12 SS	25 SS	26 SS	12 SS	12 SS	12 SS	12 SS	12 SS
I, 1-4	I, 1-4	I, 1-4	I, 1-3 (Sf)	1 (Pz.Sp)	1 (JagdPz)	1 (8,8 cm)	1 (gp)
II, 5-8	II, 5-8	II, 5-8	II, 4-6	2 (Pz.Sp)	2 (JagdPz)	2 (8,8 cm)	2
	III, 9-12	III, 9-12 (gp)	III, 7-10	3 (Pz.Aufkl)	3 (JagdPz)	3 (8,8 cm)	3
	13 (sIG)	13 (sIG)	IV, 11-15 *	4 (PzAufkl)		4 (3,7 cm)	
	14 (Flak)	14 (Flak)		5 (schw.)			
	15 (Aufkl)	15 (Aufkl)					
	16 (Pi)	16 (Pi)					

* = battalion had Nebelwerfer, but was not motorized.

Including tanks sent to the division while it was in Normandy, the *SS-Panzer-Division "Hitlerjugend"* employed a total of 79 *Panthers* and 115 *Panzer IV's*.

The artillery regiment was strong. The *I./SS-Artillerie-Regiment 12* had 12 *Wespe* and 6 *Hummel* self-propelled guns. The *II./SS-Artillerie-Regiment 12* had three batteries with six 10.5 cm howitzers each, while the *III./SS-Artillerie-Regiment 12* had four 15 cm howitzers in the *7.–9. Batterien* and four 10 cm guns in the *10. Batterie*. All artillery pieces but two were combat ready.[20]

One of the division's six infantry battalions was equipped with armored half tracks; that was the *III./SS-Panzer-Grenadier-Regiment 26*. Other parts of the division were at least partially equipped with *SPW's*, e.g. *SS-Pionier-Bataillon 12* and *SS-Panzeraufklärungs-Abteilung 12*. Altogether the division had 306 operational *SPW's* on 1 June and 27 were in short-term repair.[21]

On 1 June, the equipment of the infantry regiments was:[22] (See next page.)

With three *8.8* cm batteries, *SS-Flak-Abteilung 12* had 12 guns of that type, while the fourth battery had 9 3.7 cm guns.[23]

The division received its baptism of fire on 7 June, when *SS-Panzer-Grenadier-Regiment 25*, supported by tanks from the *II./SS-Panzer-Regiment 12*, counterattacked Canadian forces north of Caen. The division remained in the Caen area for the remainder of the campaign. In August, it fought along the main road from Caen to Falaise. During this extended period of combat it suffered serious losses:

Timeframe	Killed in Action	Wounded	Missing	Total
6 June–16 June[24]	405	847	165	1,417
6 June–24 June[25]				2,550
6 June–27 June[26]	878	2,116	898	3,892
6 June–11 July[27]				(4,485)
6 June–18 July[28]				6,164
6 June–22 August[29]				ca 8,000

The loss figure in brackets is questionable, since there is information available[30] which shows greater losses from 28 June to 11 July than the figures in the table would suggest. Also, the division was not involved in such costly fighting between 11 and 18 July as would be implied by the table. The figure in brackets either refers to an earlier date or it is a printing error. Perhaps it should be 5,485, which fits better with the other data in the table.

In July, casualties amounted to 463 killed in action, 1,075 wounded and 505 missing.[31]

Formation	MG	8 cm GrW	3,7cm le.IG (Sf)	7.5 cm Pak 40	7.5 cm le.IG	7.5 cm le.IG (Sf)	15 cm s.IG (Sf)	2 cm Flak	Flame throwers
I./SS-Panzer-Grenadier-Regiment 25	69	12		3	4				6
II./SS-Panzer-Grenadier-Regiment 25	69	12		3	4				6
III./SS-Panzer-Grenadier-Regiment 25	69	12		3	4				6
13./SS-Panzer-Grenadier-Regiment 25	7						6		
14./SS-Panzer-Grenadier-Regiment 25	4							2	
15./SS-Panzer-Grenadier-Regiment 25	9								
16./SS-Panzer-Grenadier-Regiment 25	22	2		3					6
I./SS-Panzer-Grenadier-Regiment 26	69	12		3	4				6
II./SS-Panzer-Grenadier-Regiment 26	69	12		3	4				6
III./SS-Panzer-Grenadier-Regiment 26 (gp)	151	6	4	4	3	2	12		12
13./SS-Panzer-Grenadier-Regiment 26	7						6		
14./SS-Panzer-Grenadier-Regiment 26	4							2	
15./SS-Panzer-Grenadier-Regiment 26 (gp)	34			3					6
16./SS-Panzer-Grenadier-Regiment 26	22	2							6

Tank losses are possible to establish up to 9 July:

Timeframe	Panzer IV	Panther
6–26 June[32]	26	15
27 June–5 July[33]	18	6
6 July–9 July[33]	7	11

Figures refer to total write-offs. Further vehicles were put out of action, but repaired.

During August the division played an important part in keeping the withdrawal routes open for many German units. The division itself did not suffer unduly. From 15 to 22 August its casualties amounted to 45 killed, 248 wounded and 655 missing.[35] One reason for the fact that casualties were relatively low during the period is that most of the division was not encircled. All the rear services were outside the area that would eventually be called the Falaise pocket.[36] Considerable parts of its combat elements were also outside the pocket before it closed.[37]

In many publications it has been said that the *12. SS-Panzer-Division "Hitlerjugend"* only had a few hundred men left after the end of the Falaise battle on 22 August. This is completely wrong. According to the very thorough research in the records of casualties suffered by the division presented by Meyer, it is clear that the division lost about 8,000 officers and men, killed, wounded and missing.[38] The casualty reports are almost complete for all the divisions units, but those few exceptions warrant the round figure of 8,000.

Given the fact that the *SS-Nebelwerfer-Abteilung*, parts of *SS-Panzerjäger-Abteilung 12* and parts of *SS-Ersatz-Bataillon 12* joined the division while it was in Normandy, it is clear that it had around 12,000 men on 22 August 1944. Even though most of its infantry were casualties, the division was far from destroyed. Certainly, its combat power was diminished drastically, but its rear services seem to have been almost intact.

During late July and the first third of August various *Kampfgruppen* were formed. These usually comprised at least part of *SS-Panzer-Regiment 12*. As a result, it is occasionally difficult to establish the actual tank strength of the division. Two of these *Kampfgruppen* were *Kampfgruppe Wünsche* and *Kampfgruppe Olboeter*. The tank strength of these groups is also given below.

The tank strength varied during the campaign according to the table on pages 320–321.

Kampfgruppe Wünsche

This ad hoc combat formation was commanded by Max Wünsche, who was the commander of *SS-Panzer-Regiment 12*. Initially, the *Kampfgruppe* consisted of the regimental staff, the *Panther* battalions of the *1.* and *12. SS-Panzer-Divisionen, schwere*

SS-Panzer-Abteilung 101 and the *III./SS-Panzer-Grenadier-Regiment 26 (SPW).*[39] Later, further tank units from the two SS-Panzer-Divisionen were added. Parts of Sturmpanzer-Abteilung 217 were also temporarily attached. During the period of its existence, it acted as a reserve southeast of Caen. Later it was dissolved, and the units returned to their parent organizations.

Panzer IV

Date	Combat Ready	Short-term Repair
31 July[40]	4	?
1 August[41]	17	?
2 August[42]	5	?
3 August[43]	5	?
4 August[44]	39	?

Panther

Date	Combat Ready	Short-term Repair
31 July	61	?
1 August	66	?
2 August	58	?
3 August	53	?
4 August	59	?

Tiger I

Date	Combat Ready	Short-term Repair
31 July	19	?
1 August	19	?
2 August	19	?
3 August	20	?
4 August	20	?

Kampfgruppe Olboeter

This was another ad hoc formation, formed from parts of the division to reinforce the II. SS-Panzer-Korps. It consisted of one company of *Panthers* (*2./SS-Panzer-Regiment 12*), one company of *Panzergrenadiere* (*10./SS-Panzer-Grenadier-Regiment 26*) and one battery of self-propelled artillery (*I./SS-Artillerie-Regiment 12*).

Date	Panther	
	Combat Ready	Short-term Repair
2 August[45]	13	?
5 August[46]	7	?
7 August[47]	7	?

1 BA-MA RH 10/321. Actual strength is *Iststärke*.

2 According to former Ia, Hubert Meyer, in a letter to me. Lieferung der Panzerfahrzeuge, Bd. ab Mai 1943, RH 10/349.

3 Lieferung der Panzerfahrzeuge, Bd. ab Mai 1943, RH 10/349.

4 See H. Meyer, *Kriegsgeschichte der 12. SS-Panzerdivision "Hitlerjugend"*, *Vol I* (Munin Verlag, Osnabrück 1982) p 281.

5 See H. Meyer, *Kriegsgeschichte der 12. SS-Panzerdivision "Hitlerjugend"*, *Vol I* (Munin Verlag, Osnabrück 1982) p 147.

6 Ibid, p.248.

9 See Ob West Ia Nr. 6291/44 g.Kdos, 1.8.44, T311, R28, F7035038.

10 KTB LXXXVIII. A.K. Ia Anlagen, Küstenverteidigungsabschnitt Bfh.d.W.SS Ia Nr. 420/44 g.Kdos, 8.8.44, T314, R1626, F0000590.

11 See, Meyer, op. cit. p. 354f.

12 BA-MA RH 10/321.

13 Deduced from Lieferung der Panzerfahrzeuge, Bd. ab Mai 1943, RH 10/349.

14 Lieferung der Panzerfahrzeuge, Bd. ab Mai 1943, RH 10/349.

15 BA-MA RH 10/321.

16 Im Westen vorhandene gepanzerte Kraftfahrzeuge, Stand 10.6.44, BA-MA RH 10/90. The document seems to give the strength on 1 June 1944, plus any deliveries that had occurred up to 10 June. It seems that any losses suffered in Normandy are not accounted for.

17 Lieferung der Panzerfahrzeuge, Bd. ab Mai 1943, RH 10/349.

18 Lieferung der Panzerfahrzeuge, Bd. ab Mai 1943, RH 10/349.

19 Lieferung der Panzerfahrzeuge, Bd. ab Mai 1943, RH 10/349.

20 H. Meyer, *Kriegsgeschichte der 12. SS-Panzerdivision "Hitlerjugend"*, *Vol I* (Munin Verlag, Osnabrück 1982) p 270.

21 BA-MA RH 10/321.

22 BA-MA RH 10/321.

23 BA-MA RH 10/321.

24 BA-MA RH 10/321.

25 Anlage zu HGr. B Ia Nr. 3725/44 g.K. O.U 16.6.44, BA-MA RH 19 IX/2.

26 Gen.Kdo. I. SS-Pz.Korps IaTgb. Nt. 880/44 g.Kdos 26.6.44, BA-MA RH 19 IX/3.

27 BA-MA RH 10/321.

28 KTB OB West Ia, entry 12.7.44, T311, R16, F7016788.

29 Pz.Gr. West Ia Nr. 480/44 g.Kdos. 20.7.44, T313, R420, F8713975. Note that the original document says the loss refers to 6-18 June, rather than 18 July.

30 See H. Meyer, *Kriegsgeschichte der 12. SS-Panzerdivision "Hitlerjugend"*, *Vol I* (Munin Verlag, Osnabrück 1982) p 355.

31 BA-MA RW 6/v. 577.

32 See H. Meyer, *Kriegsgeschichte der 12. SS-Panzerdivision "Hitlerjugend"*, *Vol I* (Munin Verlag, Osnabrück 1982) pp 229, 248, 264. The detailed information presented on these pages indicatess

a loss of 822 men in the major actions fought between 28 June and 11 July. Further casualties may have been suffered beside these major actions.

33 KTB HGr B Ia Anlagen, BA-MA RH 19 IX/3, frame 34 on Mikrofiche 1

34 Pz.Gr. West Ia Nr.268/44 geh. v. 9.7, Nachtrag zur Tagesmeldung 8.7, BA-MA RH 21-5/50.

35 Pz.Gr. West Ia, Nr. 306/44 geh. von 10.7.1944., Nachtrag zur Tagesmeldung 9.7., BA-MA RH 21-5/50.

36 Meyer, op. cit. p. 354.

37 Ibid, p. 354f.

38 Ibid.

39 Meyer, op. cit. pages 355 and 384-6.

40 H. Meyer, *Kriegsgeschichte der 12. SS-Panzerdivision "Hitlerjugend", Vol I* (Munin Verlag, Osnabrück 1982) p. 287.

41 Pz.Gr. West Ia, Nr. 678/44 geh. von 1.8.1944., Nachtrag zur Tagesmeldung 31.7., BA-MA RH 21-5/50. The data for *Panther* and *Tiger I* strength are also taken from the same sources for the corresponding dates.

42 Pz.Gr. West Ia Nr. 704/44 g.Kdos. 2.8.44, Nachtrag zur Tagesmeldung 1.8, T313, R420, F8714068.

43 Pz.Gr. West Ia Nr. 725/44 g.Kdos. 3.8.44, Nachtrag zur Tagesmeldung 2.8, T313, R420, F8714075.

44 Pz.Gr. West Ia, Nr. 734/44 geh. von 4.8.1944., Nachtrag zur Tagesmeldung 3.8., BA-MA RH 21-5/50.

45 Pz.Gr. West Ia Nr. 758/44 g.Kdos. 5.8.44, Nachtrag zur Tagesmeldung 4.8, T313, R420, F8714097.

46 Figures are from the same sources as for the *Panzer IV* table.

47 Figures are from the same sources as for the *Panzer IV* table.

48 Pz.Gr. West Ia Nr. 725/44 g.Kdos. 3.8.44, Nachtrag zur Tagesmeldung 2.8, T313, R420, F8714075.

49 Pz.Gr. West Ia Nr. 775/44 g.Kdos. 6.8.44, Nachtrag zur Tagesmeldung 5.8, T313, R420, F8714097.

50 PzAOK 5 Ia Nr. 811/44 g.Kdos, Nachtrag zur Tagesmeldung 7.8.44, v. 8.8.44, T313, R420, F8714130.

Tank Strength of the 12.SS-Panzer-Division "Hitlerjugend" During the Normany Campaign

Date	Panzer IV		Panther		Panzedager IV	
	Combat Ready	Short-term Repair	Combat Ready	Short-term Repair	Combat Ready	Short-term Repair
1 June[1]	91	7	48	2		
16 June[2]	52	?	38	?		
17 June[3]	46	?	38	?		
18 June[4]	45	?	33	?		
20 June[5]	59	?	42	?		
22 June[6]	59	?	42	?		
23 June[7]	55	?	43	?		
24 June[8]	58	?	44	?		
26 June[9]	60	12*	37	27*		
27 June[10]	32	22	24	16		
2 July[11]	32	?	24	?		
4 July[12]	37	?	24	?		
5 July[13]	30	24*	28	30*		
6 July[14]	32	?	28	?		
7 July[15]	40	?	39	?		
9 July[16]	10	27†	18	24††		
10 July[17]	19	27	18	24		
16 July[18]	21	?	18	?		
23 July[19]	37	?	21	?		
24 July[20]	37	?	21	?		
25 July[21]	37	?	21	?		
27 July[22]	39	?	22	?		
28 July[23]	39	12	22	11		
29 July[24]	39	12	22	11		
30 July[25]	39	12	22	11		
31 July[26]	39	?				
1 August[27]	39	?				

2 August[28]	39	?				
3 August[29]	39	?			10	?
5 August[30]	37	?	9	?	10	?
6 August[31]	37	?	9	?	10	?
9 August[32]	10	?	5	?		
10 August[33]	18	?	9	?	9	?
11 August[34]	17	?	7	?	5	?
15 August[35]	15 Combat-ready tanks of all types					
21 August[36]	10 Combat-ready tanks of all types					

*= Includes vehicles in long term repair.

† = Also 9 in long-term repair.

†† = Also 5 in long-term repai.

---

1 BA-MA RH 10/321.

2 Anlage zu HGr. B la Nr. 3725/44 g.K. O.U 16.6.44, BA-MA RH 19 IX/2.

3 12. SS-Pz.Div. "HJ" Tgb. Nr. 764/44 g.K. O.U.den 18.6.44, BA-MA RH 19 IX/2.

4 12. SS-Pz.Div. "HJ" Tgb. Nr. 764/44 g.K. O.U.den 18.6.44, BA-MA RH 19 IX/2.

5 12. SS-Pz.Div. "HJ" la Nr. 780/44, 21.6.44, Lagebericht fur den 20.6.44, BA-MA RH 19 IX/2.

6 12. SS-Pz.Div. Ia Nr. 734/44,22.6.44, BA-MA RH 19 IX/3.

7 KTB HGr B Ia Anlagen, BA-MA RH 19 IX/3.

8 KTB HGr B Ia Anlagen, BA-MA RH 19 IX/3.

9 KTB HGr B Ia Anlagen, BA-MA RH 19 IX/3.

10 BA-MA RH 10/321.

11 Pz.Gr. West Ia Nr. 86/44 3.7.44, T313, R420, F8713807.

12 Pz.Gr. West Ia, Nr. 197/44 geh. von 7.7.1944., Nachtrag zur Tagesmeldung., BA-MA RH 21-5/50.

13 Pz.Gr. West Ia Nr. 187/44 6.7.44, T313, R420, F8713832 gives the number of operational tanks, while the number in maintenance facilities is calculated using data on operational tanks, tanks issued (see main text) and number of total write-offs (given by Pz.Gr. West Ia Nr.268/44 geh. v. 9.7, Nachtrag zur Tagesmeldung 8.7, BA-MA RH 21-5/50).

14 Pz.Gr. West Ia, Nr. 217/44 geh. von 7.7.1944., Nachtrag zur Tagesmeldung 6.7., BA-MA RH 21-5/50.

15 Pz.Gr. West la Nr. 258/44 g.Kdos. Nachtrag zur Tagesmeldung 7.7, BA-MA RH 21-5/50.

16 Pz.Gr. West la, Nr. 306/44 geh. von 10.7.1944., Nachtrag zur Tagesmeldung 9.7., BA-MA RH 21-5/50.

17 Pz.Gr. West la, Nr. 287/44 geh. von 11.7.1944., Nachtrag zur Tagesmeldung 10.7., T313, R420, F8713880.

18 Pz.Gr. West la, Nr. 424/44 geh. von 17.7.1944., Nachtrag zur Tagesmeldung 16.7., BA-MA RH 21-5/50.

19 Pz.Gr. West la, Nr. 535/44 geh. von 23.7.1944., Nachtrag zur Tagesmeldung 22.7., BA-MA RH 21-5/50.

20 Pz.Gr. West la, Nr. 557/44 geh. von 25.7.1944., Nachtrag zur Tagesmeldung 24.7., BA-MA RH 21-5/50.

21 Pz.Gr. West la, Nr. 572/44 geh. von 26.7.1944., Nachtrag zur Tagesmeldung 25.7, BA-MA RH 21-5/50.

22 Pz.Gr. West la, Nr. 605/44 geh. von 27.7.1944, Nachtrag zur Tagesmeldung 28.7, BA-MA RH 21-5/50.

23 Pz.Gr. West la Nr. 633/44 g.Kdos, 29.7.44, Nachtrag zur Tagesmeldung 28.7, T313, R420, F8714036.

24 Pz.Gr. West la Nr. 647/44 g.Kdos, 30.7.44, Nachtrag zur Tagesmeldung 29.7, T313, R420, F8714042.

25 Pz.Gr. West la Nr. 665/44 g.Kdos, 31.7.44, Nachtrag zur Tagesmeldung 30.7, T313, R420, F8714049.

26 Pz.Gr. West la, Nr. 678/44 geh. von 1.8.1944, Nachtrag zur Tagesmeldung 31.7, BA-MA RH 21-5/50.

27 Pz.Gr. West la Nr. 704/44 g.Kdos. 2.8.44, Nachtrag zur Tagesmeldung 1.8, T313, R420, F8714068.

28 Pz.Gr. West la Nr. 725/44 g.Kdos. 3.8.44, Nachtrag zur Tagesmeldung 2.8, T313, R420, F8714075.

29 Pz.Gr. West la, Nr. 734/44 geh. von 4.8.1944, Nachtrag zur Tagesmeldung 3.8.. BA-MA RH 21-5/50.

30 Pz.Gr. West la Nr. 775/44 g.Kdos. 6.8.44, Nachtrag zur Tagesmeldung 5.8, T313, R420, F8714097.

31 Pz.Gr. West la Nr. 801/44 g.Kdos, 7.8.44, Nachtrag zur Tagesmeldung 6.8, T313, R420, F8714118.

32 Pz.Gr. West la Nr. 853/44 g.Kdos. 10.8.44, Nachtrag zur Tagesmeldung 9.8, T313, R420, F87141177.

33 Pz.Gr. West la Nr. 890/44 g.Kdos, 11.8.44, Nachtrag zur Tagesmeldung 10.8, T313, R420, F87141181.

34 Pz.Gr. West la Nr. 899/44 g.Kdos, 12.8.44, Nachtrag zur Tagesmeldung 11.8, T313, R420, F87141187.

35 KTB Pz.AOK 5 la, entry 15 .8.44, T313, F420, F8713625.

36 HGr B la Nr. 6388/44 g.Kdos. 21.8.44, T311, R4, F7004565.

17. SS-Panzer-Grenadier-Division "Götz von Berlichingen"

According to an order by Hitler dated 3 October 1943, the *17. SS-Panzer-Grenadier-Division "Götz von Berlichingen"* was to be formed, a process that was begun on 15 November.[1] The structure of the division was as illustrated on the next page:[2]

Due to its late formation the division was not fully combat ready when the Allies landed. On 1 June it was reported that one third of the men had 22 weeks of training and the remainder had 25 weeks of training.

Its manpower strength amounted to 17,321 men on 1 June, but it was short 233 officers and 1,541 noncommissioned officers, while it had a surplus of 741 privates.[3] This meant that the division was short of about 40% of its officers and NCO's, a serious disadvantage.

At the beginning of June, the division had many deficiencies. The greatest was probably the lack of vehicles. The supply services of the division lacked any means of transportation on 1 June.[4] According to a report dated 15 May concerning the situation, the division had only 257 trucks and towing vehicles of all types.[5] No deliveries of *Jagdpanzer IVs* had yet occurred, but the *3,/SS-Panzerjäger-Abteilung 17* had three self-propelled *7.62 cm Pak* and nine self-propelled *7.5 cm Pak*.[6]

By using *SS-Panzeraufklärungs-Abteilung 17*, *SS-Panzer-Abteilung 17* (consisting of *Sturmgeschütz III's*), *SS-Panzer-Grenadier-Regiment 38* and one reinforced artillery battalion (consisting of four batteries with light howitzers and one battery with heavy howitzers) a mobile Kampfgruppe was formed. Except for vehicles, the division was rather well equipped. On 1 June it had the following:[7]

Weapon System	On hand	Shortage
Machine Guns	1,008	146
8 cm mortar	99	0
7.5 cm *le.IG*	8	21
15 cm *s.IG (Sf)*	12	0
10.5 cm *le.FH*	25	0
15 cm *s.FH*	12	0
10 cm *K*	4	0
7.5 cm *Pak*	22	5
2 cm *Flak*	44	0
2 cm *Flakvierling*	7	0
3.7 cm *Flak*	9	0
8.8 cm *Flak*	12	0
Flamethrower	72	2

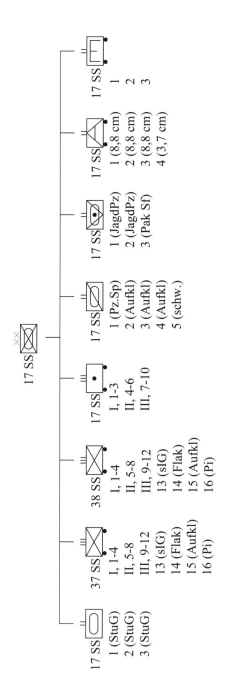

Weapon System	On hand	Shortage
Motorcycles	275	410
Cars	1,104	22
Trucks	245	1,441
RSO	2	0
Prime movers	10	245
SPW	0	0
Marder	12	0
Sturmgeschütz III	42	0
Befehlspanzer	0	3

A disadvantage was the shortage of *Panzerfäuste.* According to Stöber, the division did not receive any until mid-July and then only in insufficient quantities.[8]

The division had all 42 *Sturmgeschütz III's* it was authorized, but it lacked command vehicles. Command vehicles were not delivered to the division until 12 August when three *Panzer IV (Befehlswagen)* arrived.[9] It seems that the division received no replacements of assault guns during the campaign.

Lack of transport meant that the division could not be moved immediately to Normandy after the Allied invasion. On 6 June only route reconnaissance of roads to Normandy occurred; on 7 June the first units began to move.[10] The unit that moved fastest was *SS-Panzeraufklärungs-Abteilung 17,* which reached Balleroy (half-way between St. Lo and Bayeux) by 8 June, despite being subjected to several attacks by enemy fighter-bombers.[11] These attacks caused only slight losses.[12]

Only four of the six infantry battalions began the march to Normandy on 7 June and not even these could be fully motorized. The remaining two infantry battalions had to use bicycles for their march to Normandy. On the evening of 7 June the artillery and the *2./SS-Flak-Abteilung 17* began moving north, while the assault guns and the *Marders* were loaded on trains.[13]

The trains carrying the assault guns and antitank elements were subjected to several air attacks. One *Sturmgeschütz III* was destroyed when fuel barrels were hit; three men were killed during these attacks. The division claimed to have shot down two fighter-bomber aircraft.[14]

At about 1000 hours on 9 June the assault guns and *Marders* had unloaded between Montreuil and la Fleche. They then began marching towards Mayenne.[15]

On 10 June *SS-Panzeraufklärungs-Abteilung 17* went into action in the sector weakly held by the *352. Infanterie-Division.*[16] The same day the most advanced elements of SS-Panzer-Grenadier-Regiment 37 had reached La Chapelle (south east of St. Lo).[17]

One day later it was reported that parts of the division were in position southwest of Carentan, ready to attack in a northerly or easterly direction.[18] On 14 June it was reported that most of the division had arrived. One component that did not arrive in June was *SS-Pionier-Bataillon 17*, which remained in the Saumur area, working on crossings over the Loire river. Not until 10 July did it begin moving from Saumur to Normandy.[19] It arrived two days later.[20] The ration strength of the battalion amounted to 726 before it began the movement.[21] The divisional bridging elements remained in the Saumur area.[22] The *Flak* battalion also remained near Saumur. It was not until the end of June that it deployed to Normandy.[23] The *Flak* battalion had a strength of 657 men.[24] One battery, the *1./SS-Flak-Abteilung 17*, remained guarding the bridges at Saumur since it had no vehicles to tow its *8.8* cm guns.[25]

Since the *SS-Flak-Abteilung 17*, *SS-Pionier-Bataillon 17* and most of *SS-Panzerjäger-Abteilung 17* were missing when the division arrived in Normandy, it probably numbered no more than about 15,500 men. When they arrived, the missing elements did not compensate for the losses incurred.

The first major actions for the division were fought southwest of Carentan. On 13 June, *SS-Panzer-Grenadier-Regiment 37*, supported by assault guns, attacked the US 101st Airborne Division.[26]

Through 15 June the division lost 79 killed in action, 316 wounded and 61 missing. Twenty-four assault guns were still operational, while thirteen were in short-term repair.[27]

Casualties continued to mount and, through 24 June, they stood at 186 killed in action, 641 wounded and 72 missing.[28]

On 27 June all of the six infantry battalions deployed were still considered strong. *SS-Panzeraufklärungs-Abteilung 17*, on the other hand, was rated as weak. The division had 18 combat-ready *Sturmgeschütz III's*, 32 7.5 cm antitank guns (including self-propelled vehicles) and four *8.8* cm *Pak 43*.[29]

The divisional status report for 1 July showed losses amounting to 165 killed in action, 514 wounded and 83 missing during June. It had received 120 replacements during June. 31 StuG were operational and 6 were in short term repair. It was reported on 26 June that 12 StuG were operational.[30]

Fuel and ammunition was not available in sufficient quantities. The division was forced to husband its stores, in order to have sufficient ammunition in case a major enemy attack was launched.[31]

According to a report from 11 July, only two StuG were operational. Eleven were expected to be repaired within three days and another eight were expected to be repaired within two weeks. Seven StuG were in workshops with a repair time exceeding two week. Fourteen had been irrevocably lost.[32]

Five days later, on 16 July, it had 5 operational StuG, 5 to be repaired in three days, 10 to be repaired within 14 days and another 6 had a repair time estimated to exceed two week. This would imply that 16 had been lost.[33]

On 21 July, the division had the following artillery assigned and attached in direct support:[34]

II./SS-Artillerie-Regiment 17: six 10.5 cm light howitzers
II./SS-Artillerie-Regiment 17: nine 15 cm heavy howitzers
Artillerie-Regiment 456: 1. Batterie with four 12.2 cm guns; *2. Batterie* with two
8.8 cm guns; and, *3. Batterie* with three 15.2 cm gun-howitzers

Two days later the following status of the division was reported:[35]

Two weak battalions and five *abgekampfte* (combat ineffective) battalions
Ten heavy antitank guns
Ten *Sturmgeschütz III's*
Five light artillery batteries (three heavy batteries with the *Panzer-Lehr-Division)*
Mobility 30%
Combat value rating: IV

The division was partially surrounded in the Coutances pocket after Operation *Cobra*, but broke out with considerable loss of equipment.[36] At the beginning of August parts of the division were withdrawn for refitting, while other elements remained attached to the *2. SS-Panzer-Division "Das Reich"* and took part in the Mortain attack.[37] Later they were subordinated to the *10. SS-Panzer-Division "Frundsberg".*[38]

According to the monthly status report for 1 August 1944, the division numbered 14 017 officers and men. It had suffered losses amounting to 351 killed in action, 1 093 wounded and 1 573 missing during July. No StuG were operational, but 10 were in short term (two weeks) repair.[39]

At the end of June, 31 *Jagdpanzer IVs* were loaded on trains in Germany and sent to *SS-Panzerjäger-Abteilung 17.*[40] Except for the *3./SS-Panzerjäger-Abteilung 17*, this battalion had remained in its original location when the division began marching towards Normandy. During August, this unit began moving north. When it had reached Chateau Gontier it was ordered to move westwards to deploy between Laval and Rennes.[41] Events forced the battalion to be committed in the Laval area on 5 August.[42] After a brief action at Laval, the battalion retreated towards Sable-sur-Sarthe, but US forces had already bypassed Laval. The battalion had to fight its way east with heavy loss.[43]

Large parts of the division had been withdrawn before the pocket at Falaise was formed. This saved the division from heavy casualties during the last stages of the battle in Normandy. Nevertheless, casualties were very heavy.

On 15 September the division had a strength of 16,832 officers and men. During the first half of September the division had only 163 casualties. It had received 7,770 replacements and 153 convalescents. Thus it seems that the division had about 8,000 casualties during the campaign in Normandy and northern France.[44] Most of the replacements the division had received were probably men from *SS-Panzer-Grenadier-Brigaden 49* and *51,* which were absorbed by the division.[45]

1   G. Tessin, *Verbände und Truppen der deutschen Wehrmacht und Waffen-SS* (Mittler & Sohn, Frankfurt am Main and Biblio Verlag, Osnabrück 1966–1975).

2   BA-MA RH 10/324.

3   BA-MA RH 10/324.

4   BA-MA RH 10/324.

5   BA-MA RH 10/112.

6   BA-MA RH 10/324.

7   BA-MA RH 10/324.

8   H. Stöber, *Die Sturmflut und das Ende, Geschichte der 17. SS-Panzergrenadierdivision "Götz von Berlichingen"* (Munin, Osnabrück 1976) caption to photo opposite p. 64.

9   Lieferungen der Pz.-Fahrzeuge, Bd. ab Mai 1943, BA-MA RH 10/349.

10 H. Stöber, *Die Sturmflut und das Ende, Geschichte der 17. SS-Panzergrenadierdivision "Götz von Berlichingen"* (Munin, Osnabrück 1976) pp. 48–50.

11 Ibid.

12 Ibid.

13 Ibid.

14 Ibid, p. 51f.

15 HGr B Ia Nr. 3233/44 g.Kdos, Tagesmeldung 9.6.44, T311, R3, F7002366.

16 Stöber, op.cit. p. 49.

17 OB West Ia Notiz 10.6.44, T311, R25, F7030049.

18 HGr B Ia Nr 3342/44 g.Kdos, Tagesmeldung 11.6.44, T311, R3, F7002373.

19 KTB SS-Pi.Btl 17,10.7, T354, R156, F3800694.

20 KTB SS-Pi.Btl 17,12.7, T354, R156, F3800697.

21 KTB SS-Pi.Btl 17, 8.7, T354, R156, F3800926.

22 Stöber, op. cit. p 269.

23 Stöber, op.cit. p. 477.

24 Ibid, p. 459. Strength refers to Iststärke.

25 Ibid, p. 389.

26 See Stöber, pp. 72–79.

27 See 17. SS-Pz.Gren.Div. IaTgb. Nr. 1101/44, 20.6.44, BA-MA RH 19 IX/2 or Stöber p. 455f.

28 KTB HGr B Ia Anlagen, BA-MA RH 19 IX/3, frame 15 on Mikrofiche 1

29 AOK 7 Ia Nr. 3454/44 g.Kdos., 27.6.44., T312, R1565, F001375.

30 17. SS-Pz.Gren.Div. Ia/Op Nr 436/44, 1.7.1944, in M. Wind & H. Günther, Kriegstagebuch Götz von Berlichingen, Auswahl von Dokumenten.

31 17. SS-Pz.Gren.Div. Kdr.-Besprechung am 2.7.44, 16.00 Uhr im Div.Gef.St. in M. Wind & H. Günther, Kriegstagebuch Götz von Berlichingen, Auswahl von Dokumenten.

32 17. SS-Pz.Abt. Meldung an Division Ia, 11.7.44, in M. Wind & H. Günther, Kriegstagebuch Götz von Berlichingen, Auswahl von Dokumenten.

33 17. SS-Pz.Abt. Tagesmeldung 16.7.44, in M. Wind & H. Günther, Kriegstagebuch Götz von Berlichingen, Auswahl von Dokumenten.

34 Gen.Kdo. LXXXIV A.K. Ia Nr. 035/44g.Kdos 22.7.44, Taktische Gliederung der Artillerie, Stand 21.7.44, T314, R1604, F001388.

35 Gen.Kdo. LXXXIV. A.K. Ia 048/44 g.Kdos. T314, R1604, F001373.

36 Stöber, op.cit. pp. 243–260.

37 Stöber, op. cit., p. 282ff.

38 Ibid, p. 31 Iff.

39 17. SS-Pz.Gren.Div. Ia/Tgb Nr 483/44, 1.8.1944, in M. Wind & H. Günther, Kriegstagebuch Götz von Berlichingen, Auswahl von Dokumenten.

40 Lieferungen der Pz.-Fahrzeuge, Bd. ab Mai 1943, BA-MA RH 10/349.

41 Stöber, op. cit. p. 321.

42 Ibid, p. 326f.

43 Ibid, pp. 326–332.

44 Gliederung 17. SS-Pz.Gren.Div. "Götz von Berlichingen", Stand 15.9.44, BA-MA RS 3-17/13.

45 For information on these two brigades see Stöber, op. cit., p. 501f.

21. Panzer-Division

Of the German armor divisions that participated in the Normandy campaign, this was probably the most unique. It had no *Panther* battalion like the other *Panzer-Divisionen* – except the *10. SS-Panzer-Division "Frundsberg"*. On the other hand, it had both an assault gun battalion and an antitank battalion with towed 8.8 cm antitank guns (which were not found in the other panzer divisions). Each of its infantry regiments had one *SPW* battalion, which was also rather unusual. Another unusual feature was that it had two companies in the engineer battalion – *Pionier-Bataillon 220* – which were equipped with the *SPW*. Normally, there was only one. Finally, it had many modified captured vehicles included in its organization. The structure of the division on 1 June 1944 was as indicated in the chart on the next page:[1]

Since this was an unusual division it will be of interest to present its equipment in detail:[2]

Headquarters, *Panzer-Regiment 22*: 3 *Panzer IIIs*, 1 *Panzer III (Befehlswagen)*, 5 *Panzer IVs* (long barrel)

Headquarters, *I./Panzer-Regiment 22*: 1 *Panzer III*, 1 *Panzer III (Befehlswagen)*, 5 *Panzer IVs* (long barrel)

1./Panzer-Regiment 22: 17 *Panzer IVs* (long barrel)
2./Panzer-Regiment 22: 17 *Panzer IVs* (long barrel)
3./Panzer-Regiment 22: 17 *Panzer IVs* (long barrel)
4./Panzer-Regiment 22: 17 *Panzer IVs* (long barrel)

Headquarters, *II./Panzer-Regiment 22*: 5 *Panzer IVs* (long barrel), 3 Somuas *(Befehlswagen)*

5./Panzer-Regiment 22: 5 *Panzer IV's* (long barrel), 9 Somua
6./Panzer-Regiment 22: 5 *Panzer IV's* (long barrel), 13 Somua, 2 Hotchkiss
7./Panzer-Regiment 22: 5 *Panzer IV's* (long barrel), 13 Somua
8./Panzer-Regiment 22: 6 *Panzer IV's* (short barrel)

I./Panzergrenadier-Regiment 125 (gp): 137 machine guns, 9 3.7 cm *Pak*, 4 7.5 cm *Pak (Sf)*, 3 2 cm *Flak (Sf)*

II./Panzergrenadier-Regiment 125: 85 machine guns, three 7.5 cm *Pak (Sf)*, three 2 cm *Flak (Sf)*

Regiment units of *Panzergrenadier-Regiment 125*: 6 15 cm *IG auf Lorraine*, 4 *Reihenwerfer auf So*, 3 5 cm *Pak*, 25 machine guns

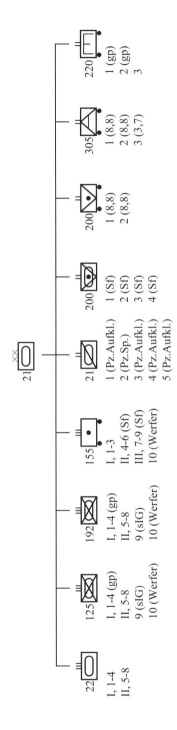

I./Panzergrenadier-Regiment 192 (gp): 104 machine guns, 9 3.7 cm *Pak*, 4 7.5 cm *Pak (Sf)*, 3 2 cm *Flak (Sf)*

II./Panzergrenadier-Regiment 192: 91 machine guns, 3 7.5 cm *Pah (Sf)*, 3 2 cm *Flak (Sf)*

Regiment units of *Panzergrenadier-Regiment 192:* 6 15 cm *IG auk Lorraine*, 4 *Reihenwerfer auf So*, 26 machine guns

1./Panzer-Artillerie-Regiment 155: 4 12.2 cm howitzers (captured Russian)
2./Panzer-Artillerie-Regiment 155: 4 12.2 cm howitzers (captured Russian)
3./Panzer-Artillerie-Regiment 155: 4 10 cm *K 18's*
4./Panzer-Artillerie-Regiment 155: 6 10.5 cm *le.FH 18 auf Lorraine*
5./Panzer-Artillerie-Regiment 155: 6 10.5 cm *le.FH 18 auf Lorraine*
6./Panzer-Artillerie-Regiment 155: 6 15 cm *s.FH 13 auf Lorraine*
7./Panzer-Artillerie-Regiment 155: 6 10.5 cm *le.FH 18 auf Lorraine*
8./Panzer-Artillerie-Regiment 155: 6 10.5 cm *le.FH 18 auf Lorraine*
9./Panzer-Artillerie-Regiment 155: 6 15 cm *s.FH 13 auf Lorraine*
10./Panzer-Artillerie-Regiment 155: 2 *Nebelwerfer (Sf) Reihenwerfer* (8.14 cm)

1./Panzeraufklärungs-Abteilung 21: 9 *Beobachtungspanzer*, 16 *mittlere SPW* (medium)
2./Panzeraufklärungs-Abteilung 21: 14 *schwere Panzerspähwagen* (six of them with 7.5 cm guns), 16 *leichte SPW* (light)
3./Panzeraufklärungs-Abteilung 21: 2 *leichte Funkpanzerwagen*, 28 *leichte SPW, 7 mittlere SPW*
4./Panzeraufklärungs-Abteilung 21: 2 *leichte Funkpanzerwagen*, 28 *leichte SPW, 7 mittlere SPW*
5./Panzeraufklärungs-Abteilung 21: 27 *mittlere SPW*

1./Sturmgeschütz-Abteilung 200: 4 7.5 cm *Pak 40 auf Ho*, 6 10.5 cm *le.FH 16 auf Ho*
2./Sturmgeschütz-Abteilung 200: 4 7.5 cm *Pak 40 auf Ho*, 6 10.5 cm *le.FH 16 auf Ho*
3./Sturmgeschütz-Abteilung 200: 4 7.5 cm *Pak 40 auf Ho*, 6 10.5 cm *le.FH 16 auf Ho*
4./Sturmgeschütz-Abteilung 200: 4 7.5 cm *Pak 40 auf Ho*, 6 10.5 cm *le.FH 16 auf Ho*

1./Panzerjäger-Abteilung 200: 12 8.8 cm *Pak (mot. Z.)*
2./Panzerjäger-Abteilung 200: 12 8.8 cm *Pak (mot. Z.)*

1./Flak-Abteilung 305: 4 8.8 cm *Flak (mot. Z.J*, 3 2 cm *Flak (gp)*
2./Flak-Abteilung 305: 4 8.8 cm *Flak (mot. Z.)*, 3 2 cm *Flak (gp)*
3./Flak-Abteilung 305: 9 2 cm *Flak (Sf)*, 2 2 cm *Flakvierling (Sf)*

1./Pionier-Bataillon 220 (gp): 1 8 cm *Granatwerfer*, 43 machine guns
2./Pionier-Bataillon 220 (gp): 1 8 cm *Granatwerfer*, 43 machine guns
3./Pionier-Bataillon (mot): 1 8 cm *Granatwerfer*, 20 machine guns

Formation	Date	Officers	Beamte	NCO's	Men	Total
Panzer-Regiment 22	1 June 1944	58	5	558	1,729	2,350
	16 June 1944	51	5	524	1,641	2,221
Panzergrenadier-Regiment 125	1 June 1944	55	3	441	1,891	2,390
	16 June 1944	45	3	359	1,484	1,891
Panzergrenadier-Regiment 192	1 June 1944	57	4	512	1,819	2,392
	16 June 1944	43	4	442	1,476	1,965
Panzer-Panzeraufklärungs-Abteilung 21	1 June 1944	20	3	289	829	1,141
	16 June 1944	20	3	255	684	962
Panzerjäger-Abteilung 200	1 June 1944	18	2	87	439	546
	16 June 1944	14	2	76	394	486
Sturmgeschütz-Abteilung 200	1 June 1944	23	1	267	620	911
	16 June 1944	20	1	247	573	841
Artillerie-Regiment 155	1 June 1944	55	6	386	1,323	1,770
	16 June 1944	47	6	336	1,106	1,495
Flak-Abteilung 305	1 June 1944	17	2	117	590	726
	16 June 1944	16	2	113	565	696
Panzer-Pionier-Bataillon 220	1 June 1944	20	4	126	735	885
	16 June 1944	18	4	118	636	776
Other Elements	1 June 1944	84	57	597	2,448	3,186
	16 June 1944	84	57	576	2,383	3,100
Total	1 June 1944	407	87	3,380	12,423	16,297
	16 June 1944	358	87	3,046	10,942	14,433

Altogether this meant that the division had 98 *Panzer IV's* (long barrel) and six obsolete *Panzer IV's* (short barrel). However, on 24 May another 14 *Panzer IV's* (long barrel) were sent to the division. They probably had not arrived by 1 June, since deliveries before 24 May comprised 98 vehicles.[3] The division also received tanks during the battle in Normandy. On 8 July 17 *Panzer IV's* were sent and, three weeks later, 3 *Panzer IV's (Befehlswagen)* were also sent.[4] Finally, on 10 August, another 10 *Panzer IV's* were dispatched to the division.[5] It is highly doubtful that the last ten arrived in time to take part in the battle.

The personnel situation for the division on 1 June and 16 June was as indicated on the opposite page.[6]

Since the division had an authorized strength of 16,925[7] it was close to full strength on 1 June. From the table on the next page it can be concluded that casualties up to 16 June amounted to 1,864. The losses mounted and, by 20 June (inclusive), 2,390 casualties had been incurred.[8] Through 24 June casualties amounted to 2,597.[9] During the entire month of June, the division lost 472 men killed in action, 1,606 wounded and 776 missing, while only 54 men had arrived to replace losses.[10] Tank losses up to 26 June included 31 Pz IV.[11]

From 6 June to 11 July the division lost 3,411 men[12] and, during the entire month of July, it lost 229 killed in action, 601 wounded and 1,019 missing.[13] These losses were covered by the arrival of 2,399 replacements and 26 convalescents.[14] This meant the division had suffered 4,703 casualties from 1 June to 31 July and received 2,479 men to cover losses. Some of the replacements received were probably infantry from the *16. Luftwaffenfelddivision.*

At the end of July the *II./Panzer-Regiment 22* was sent to Mailly-le-Camp.[15] It was still there on 18 August.[16]

During June and July the division had been fighting in the Caen area. At the end of July the division was transferred to the LXXIV. Korps.[17] It continued to fight on the northern shoulder of the salient protruding to the west. Casualties in July included 239 killed in action, 714 wounded and 996 missing.[18]

The 21. Panzer-Division was among the German divisions that suffered most during the battle in Normandy. On 1 October it had 12,097 men.[19] During September the division lost 593 men and received 1,745 replacements.[20] This indicates that the division had about 10,945 men on 1 September. That was about 3,600 less than it had on 1 August. The *II./Panzer-Regiment 22* had not returned to the division, and it probably had at least 500 men when it departed. This would indicate a loss of about 3,000 men during August and almost 8,000 for the entire campaign.

Panzer IV (long barrel) Status

Date	Combat Ready	Short-term Repair	Long-term Repair
1 June[21]	98	6	9
9 June[22]	ca 60	?	?
16 June[23]	85	?	?
17-June[24]	67	?	?
18 June[25]	65	?	?
20 June[26]	67	?	?
21 June[27]	76	?	?
1 July[28]	61	24	?
6 July[29]	67	?	?
9 July[30]	38	?	?
13 July[31]	59	?	?
14 July[32]	46	14	?
15 July[33]	47	13	?
16 July[34]	50	?	?
17 July[35]	50	?	?
22 July[36]	22	?	?
23 July[37]	18	?	?
24 July[38]	22	?	?
25 July[39]	30	?	?
27 July[40]	40	?	?
29 July[41]	41	?	?
1 August[42]	42	16	?
4 August[43]	26	?	?
6 August[44]	20	?	?
7 August[45]	19	?	?
8 August[46]	20	?	?
9 August[47]	20	?	?
10 August[48]	20	?	?
11 August[49]	20	?	?
22 August[50]	10	?	?

---

1   Status report to Inspector-General of Panzer Troops, Stand 1.6.44, BA-MA RH 10/158.
2   Ibid.

3   Lieferungen der Pz.Fahrzeuge, Bd. ab Mai 1943, BA-MA RH 10/349. Between 5 March and 24 May no *Panzer IVs* were sent to 21. Pz.Div.

4   Lieferungen der Pz.Fahrzeuge, Bd. ab Mai 1943, BA-MA RH 10/349.

5   Ibid.

6   H.Gr. B Ia Nr. 3725/44 g.K. 17.6.44, BA-MA RH 19 IX/2.

7   Status report to Inspector-General of Panzer Troops, Stand 1.6.44, BA-MA RH 10/158.

8   21. Pz.Div. Ia Nr. 1766/44, 21.6.44, BA-MA RH 19 IX/2.

9   Gen.Kdo. I. SS-Pz.Korps Ia Tgb. Nt. 880/44 g.Kdos 26.6.44, BA-MA RH 19 IX/3.

10 Status report to Inspector-General of Panzer Troops, Stand 1.7.44, BA-MA RH 10/158.

11 Gen.Kdo I. SS-Pz.Korps, Panzerlage am 26.6.44, 00.00 Uhr, T311, R278, F001376.

12 KTB OB West Ia, entry 12.7.44, T311, R16, F7016788.

13 Status report to Inspector-General of Panzer Troops, Stand 1.8.44, BA-MA RH 10/158.

14 Ibid.

15 Pz.Gr. West Ia Nr. 633/44 g.Kdos. 29.7, Nachtrag zur Tagesmeldung 28.7, T313, R420, F8714037.

16 Besprechung Oberst i.G. Koslin bei Ia/Ob.West. (Ia Gen.Kdo. LXXX A.K.) 18.8.44, T311, R29, F7035710.

17 BA-MA RW 6/v. 577.

18 See Pz.Gr. West Ia Nr. 647/44 g.Kdos, 1.8.44, Nachtrag zur Tagesmeldung 31.7, BA-RH 21-5/50.

19 Status report to Inspector-General of Panzer Troops, Stand 1.10.44, BA-MA RH 10/158.

20 Ibid.

21 BA-MA RH 10/158.

22 Reisebericht Hauptmann Pickardt, 10.6.44, T311, R25, F7029430.

23 HGr B Ia Nr. 3725/44 g.K., 17.6.44, BA-MA RH 19 IX/2.

24 21. Pz.Div. Br.B.Nr. 1755/44 g.K. 18.6.44, BA-MA RH 19 IX/2.

25 21. Pz.Div. Ia Nr. 1757/44 g.Kdos, 19.6.44, BA-MA RH 19 IX/2.

26 T311, R25, F7029701.

27 21. Pz.Div. Ia Nr. 1766/44, 21.6.44, BA-MA RH 19 IX/2.

28 BA-MA RH 10/158.

29 Pz.Gr. West Ia, Nr. 217/44 geh. von 7.7.1944., Nachtrag zur Tagesmeldung 6.7., BA-MA RH 21-5/50.

30 Pz.Gr. West Ia, Nr. 306/44 geh. von 10.7.1944., Nachtrag zur Tagesmeldung 9.7., BA-MA RH 21-5/50.

31 Pz.Gr. West Ia, Nr. 348/44 geh. v. 14.7.44, Nachtrag zur Tagesmeldung 13.7., T313, R420, F8713903.

32 Pz.Gr. West Ia Nr. Unleserlich, v. 15.7.44, Nachtrag zur Tagesmeldung 14.7, T313, R420, F8713914.

33 Pz.Gr. West Ia Nr. 388/44 g.Kdos 16.7.44, Nachtrag zur Tagesmeldung 15.7, T313, R420, F8713920.

34 Pz.Gr. West Ia, Nr. 424/44 geh. von 17.7.1944., Nachtrag zur Tagesmeldung 16.7., BA-MA RH 21-5/50.

35 Pz.Gr. West Ia, Nr. 479/44 geh. von 18.7.1944., Nachtrag zur Tagesmeldung 17.7., BA-MA RH 21-5/50.

36 Pz.Gr. West Ia, Nr. 535/44 geh. von 23.7.1944., Nachtrag zur Tagesmeldung 22.7., BA-MA RH 21-5/50.

37 Pz.Gr. West Ia, Nr. 547/44 geh. von 24.7.1944., Nachtrag zur Tagesmeldung 23.7., BA-MA RH 21-5/50.

38 Pz.Gr. West Ia, Nr. 557/44 geh. von 25.7.1944., Nachtrag zur Tagesmeldung 24.7., BA-MA RH 21-5/50.

39 Pz.Gr. West Ia, Nr. 572/44 geh. von 26.7.1944., Nachtrag zur Tagesmeldung 25.7., BA-MA RH 21-5/50.

40 Pz.Gr. West Ia, Nr. 605/44 geh. von 28.7.1944., Nachtrag zur Tagesmeldung 27.7., BA-MA RH 21-5/50.

41 Pz.Gr. West Ia Nr. 647/44 g.Kdos, 30.7.44, Nachtrag zur Tagesmeldung 29.7, T313, R420, F8714042.

42 BA-MA RH 10/158.

43 Pz.Gr. West Ia Nr. 758/44 g.Kdos. 5.8.44, Nachtrag zur Tagesmeldung 4.8, T313, R420, F8714097.

44 Pz.Gr. West Ia Nr. 801/44 g.Kdos, 7.8.44, Nachtrag zur Tagesmeldung 6.8, T313, R420, F8714118.

45 Pz.Gr. West Ia Nr. 811/44 g.Kdos, 8.8.44, Nachtrag zur Tagesmeldung 7.8, T313, R420, F87141130.

46 Pz.Gr. West Ia Nr. 846/44 g.Kdos. 9.8.44, Nachtrag zur Tagesmeldung 8.8, T313, R420, F8714139.

47 Pz.Gr. West Ia Nr. 853/44 g.Kdos, 10.8.44, Nachtrag zur Tagesmeldung 9.8, T313, R420, F87141177.

48 Pz.Gr. West Ia Nr. 890/44 g.Kdos, 11.8.44, Nachtrag zur Tagesmeldung 10.8, T313, R420, F87141181.

49 Pz.Gr. West Ia Nr. 899/44 g.Kdos, 12.8.44, Nachtrag zur Tagesmeldung 11.8, T313, R420, F87141187.

50 Fernschreiben von HGr B an OB West 22.8.44, BA-MA RH 19 IX/9b.

116. Panzer Division

The *116. Panzer-Division* was formed by merging the remnants of the *16. Panzer-Grenadier-Division* — a unit worn out after fighting or the Eastern Front — with the *179. Reserve-Panzer-Division*.[1] The 16 Panzer-Grenadier-Division did not arrive in France until April 1944. This made it impossible to create a new, fully battle-worthy division before the Allies landed. The organization of the new division was as indicated on the next page:[2]

The *Panther* battalion of the division was forming at Grafenwöhr in Germany. The *Panther* battalion of *Panzer-Grenadier-Division "Großdeutschland"* was deployed with the division in its place. The *"Großdeutschland"* battalion was sent to the Eastern Front, however, before the *116. Panzer-Division* was ordered to move to Normandy. Instead, the *Panther* battalion of the *24. Panzer-Division, the I./Panzer-Regiment 24,* followed the division to Normandy. Unfortunately, the battalion received its tanks quite late. Between 5 and 7 June, 70 *Panthers* were sent by train to the battalion.[3] Consequently, the battalion was delayed in its training program. Towards the end of June, it was reported that the battalion was still conducting platoon exercises.[4]

Including the four *Panthers* sent to *I./Panzer-Regiment 24* in January,[5] two *Panthers (Befehlswagen* = command tanks) with *Panzer-Regiment 16*[6] and the 70 sent at the beginning of June, the division had 76 *Panthers* available when it departed for Normandy. It seems that the division had 86 Panzer IV's.[7] No further tanks were sent to the division during the summer of 1944.[8] *Panzerjäger-Abteilung 228* received 21 *Jagdpanzer IV's* in July,[9] bringing it to its authorized strength.

The division also had a few extra armored vehicles. According to a report dated 8 June 1944, it had three *Panzer IV's* (short-barreled 7.5 cm main gun), seven *Panzer III's* (with the long-barreled 5 cm main gun), three *Panzer III's* (with a short-barreled main gun), six *Sturmgeschütz III's* (with the long-barreled 7.5 cm main gun) and six self-propelled 7,5 cm Pak(Sf)[10] These vehicles were not included in the authorized organization for the division, and it was planned that some of them would be issued to other formations.[11]

The manpower strength of the division improved gradually:[12]

1 April: 5,452
1 May: 12,494
15 May: 13,414
1 June: 13,621
1 July: 14,358

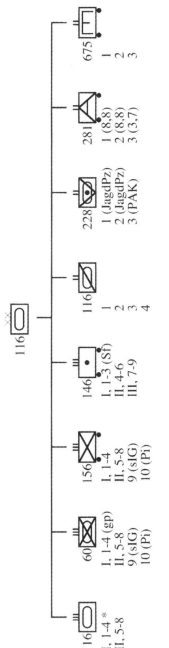

* Actually the I./24 Pz.Abt., since the divisions own Panther-Battalion was still in Germany.

Like many other armor divisions in France the *116. Panzer-Division* was short of transportation means. On 15 May it only had 342 cars, 725 trucks and 25 prime movers. It also had 163 armored troop carriers.[13] This had improved by 1 June, when it had 1,065 trucks, or almost two-thirds of the authorized strength of 1,688.[14] A major problem was the age of many of the trucks. This was aggravated by the shortage of spare parts.[15] The division was also rated as insufficiently trained.[16]

On 1 July the truck situation had only improved slightly.[17] This was only temporary though, since it was soon obliged to send some of its trucks to Normandy to alleviate the shortages within the units there.[18]

The division had 25 operational artillery pieces on 1 July. The number of armored troop carriers had increased to 243 operational and 9 in short-term repair. The division had the 13 7.5 cm *Pak* it was authorized to have.[19]

Flak-Abteilung 281 had no guns, and it did not receive any until the division had withdrawn from France.[20]

On 18 July the division had 67% mobility.[21] It was soon ordered to Normandy. On 20 July the division began crossing the Seine by ferries.[22] On 24 July the following elements had reached the assembly area:[23] *Panzer-Grenadier-Regiment 156, Panzeraufklärungs-Abteilung 16, Panzer-Grenadier-Regiment 60*, the *II./Panzer-Regiment 16* and *Panzerjäger-Abteilung 228*. The last combat units to arrive were the *I./Panzer-Regiment 24* and *Pionier-Bataillon 675*.[24] Marching always took its toll on the tanks. The following tank strengths were reported:

Panzer IV

Date	Combat Ready	Short-term Repair
25 July[25]	24	?
27 July[26]	64	15
30 July[27]	30	p
22 August[28]	4	?

Panther

Date	Combat Ready	Short-term Repair
25 July	39	?
27 July	57	17
30 July	17	?
22 August	11	?

Jagdpanzer IV & Sturmgeschütz III

Date	Combat Ready	Short-term Repair
25 July	25	?
27 July	25	?
30 July	15	?
22 August	3	?

Initially the division was in reserve southeast of Caen but, due to the American breakthrough west of St. Lo, the *116. Panzer-Division* was ordered to move to the Vire area on 28 July.[29] It reached its assembly area on 29 July

By that point the division had not seen much combat, and on 30 July, it was assessed to have *Kampfwert I* (combat capability I) the highest rating available. All its battalions were considered strong and the mobility stood at 80%.[30]

During the German Mortain counterattack, the *I./Panzer-Regiment 24* was attached to the *2. Panzer-Division.* It advanced as far as Le Mesnil-Adelee.[31]

On 11 August the division was ordered to move to the Alençon area. It remained in the Alenfon — Argentan area until 20 August.[32] The division broke out of the Falaise pocket.[33]

The following equipment situation was reported on 22 August:[34]

I./Panzer-Regiment 24: 11 operational *Panthers*
II./Panzer-Regiment 16: 4 operational *Panzer IV's*
Panzer-Grenadier-Regiment 60: two combat-ready companies
Panzer-Grenadier-Regiment 156: two battalions, combat-engineer
company and a heavy infantry-gun company without guns
Panzeraufklärungs-Abteilung 116: three reconnaissance sections, 2 *SPW* platoons,
one combat-engineer platoon
Panzerjäger-Abteilung 228: three conditionally operational assault guns
Panzer-Artillerie-Regiment 146: two *Wespe* self-propelled gunss, one *Hummel,* five
10.5 cm howitzers, five 15 cm howitzers and one 10 cm gun
Rear services: unless in need of repair fully operational

The division received 665 men as replacements during August. It also received 127 men on 6 September and another 442 six days later.[35] According to a report dated 23 September the division suffered 5,186 casualties from the Allied invasion until 13 September.[36] This seems too pessimistic, considering later reports.

According to the strength report sent to the Inspector General ot *Panzer* Troops at the beginning of October, the division had a strength of 11,875 on 1 October. During the month of September 1,998 replacements and convalescents had been received by the division. Casualties during September amounted to 677 and, at the same time, 121 men had left the division for other reasons. This would indicate a strength of 10,675 on 1 September.[37]

Compared to the strength on 1 July this would indicate a loss of 3,683 men. But since the division received 665 replacements during August, losses must have amounted to 4,348.

It does not seem very likely the division would have suffered 838 casualties between 1 and 13 September, especially since the division only suffered 677 casualties during the entire month of September. There are three probable explanations for this. The figure of 5,186 casualties may include men that had been absorbed by other units during the retreat or else stragglers who may have shown up later with the division. Another explanation is that it may include losses suffered by units temporarily attached to the division.[38]

Since the division must have suffered losses during the retreat from 22 August to 1 September not all of the 4,348 casualties indicated above may have occurred in Normandy. In all likelihood, slightly less than 4,000 were probably sustained during the battles in Normandy.

1   G. Tessin, *Verbände und Truppen der deutschen Wehrmacht und Waffen-SS* (Mittler & Sohn, Frankfurt am Main and Biblio Verlag, Osnabrück 1966–1975).

2   Status Report to the Inspector-General of Panzer Troops, 1.7.44, BA-A RH 10/163.

3   Lieferungen der Pz.Fahrzeuge, Bd. ab Mai 1943, BA-MA RH 10/349.

4   H. G. Guderian, *Das letzte Kriegsjahr im Westen, Die Geschichte der 116. Pz.Div. - Windhund-Division* (St. Augustin 1994) p.52.

5   Lieferungen der Pz.Fahrzeuge, Bd. ab Mai 1943, BA-MA RH 10/349.

6   Anlagen zum KTB LXXXI. A.K., 116. Pz.Div. Ia Nr. 304/44 geh. 8.6.44, T314, R1590, F000351.

7   According to a document labelled "Im Westen vorhandene gepanzerte Kraftfahrzeuge, Stand 10.6.44", file BA-MA RH 10/90, the division had 86 *Panzer IVs*. This document has been proved erroneous in some cases but, given its strength later in the campaign, this figure seems accurate.

8   Lieferungen der Pz.Fahrzeuge, Bd. ab Mai 1943, BA-MA RH 10/349.

9   Ibid.

10 See Anlagen zum KTB LXXXI. A.K., 116. Pz.Div. Ia Nr. 304/44 geh. 8.6.44, T314, R1590, F000351, and also Guderian, op. cit. p. 15.

11 Guderian, op. cit. p. 15.

12 Status Reports to the Inspector-General of Panzer Troops, 1.7.44, BA-MA RH 10/163 and also BA-MA RH 10/112.

13 BA-MA RH 10/112.

14 Status Report to the Inspector-General of Panzer Troops, 1.6.44, BA-MA RH 10/163.

15 Ibid.

16 Ibid.

17 Status Report to the Inspector-General of Panzer Troops, 1.6.44, BA-MA RH 10/163.

18 Guderian, op. cit. p. 55.

19 Status Report to the Inspector-General of Panzer Troops, 1.7.44, BA-MA RH 10/163.

20 Guderian, op.cit. p. 16.

21 HGr B Ia Nr. 4943/44 g.Kdos, 18.7.44, T311, R4, F7003813.

22 OB West Ia Nr. 5911/44 g.Kdos vom 22.7.44, T311, R28, F7034716.

23 OB West Ia Nr. 5970/44 g.Kdos, T311, R28, F7034778f.

24 OB West Ia Nr. 5972/44 g.Kdos, 24.7.44, T311, R28, F7034777, OB West Ia Nr. 5996/44 g.Kdos 25.7.44, T311, R28, F7034798 and OB West Ia Nr. 6068/44 g.Kdos, 26.7.44, T311, R28, F7034824.

25 Pz.Gr. West Ia, Nr. 572/44 geh. von 26.7.1944., Nachtrag zur Tagesmeldung 27.7., BA-MA RH 21-5/50. The data for the *Panther* and assault gun strength figures which follow are taken from the same sources for the corresponding dates.

26 Pz.Gr. West Ia, Nr. 605/44 geh. von 28.7.1944., Nachtrag zur Tagesmeldung 27.7., BA-MA RH 21-5/50.

27 AOK 7 Ia Nr. 4174/44 g.Kdos. den 2.8.44, T312, R1569, F000359.

28 Anlagen zum KTB LXXXI. A.K. Ia, Meldungen der Divisionen, Gliederung der 116. Panzer-Division, Stand 22.8.1944, T314, R1593, F000199.

29 Guderian, op. cit. p. 62.

30 AOK 7 Ia Nr. 4174/44 g.Kdos. den 2.8.44, T312, R1569, F000359.

31 Guderian, op. cit. p. 81.

32 See Guderian, op. cit. p. 87–103.

33 Ibid, p 103ff.

34 Anlagen zum KTB LXXXI. A.K. Ia, Meldungen der Divisionen, Gliederung der 116. Panzer-Division, Stand 22.8.1944, T314, R1593, F000199.

35 LXXXI. A.K. lib, 19.9.44, T314, R1594, F000272.

36 LXXXI. A.K. Ila/b, 23.9.44, T314, R1594, F000267.

37 Status Report to the Inspector-General of Panzer Troops, 1.10.44, BA-MA RH 10/163.

38 The document that has provided the figure 5,186 also gives suspiciously high casualties for the *9. Panzer-Division* and the *275. Infanterie-Division*. It could, of course, be argued that the higher loss figure includes losses suffered from air attack before its actions in Normandy. This seems unlikely. During June it lost only 79 men due to all causes (BA-MA RH 10/163).

Panzer-Lehr-Division

When this division arrived in Normandy, it was probably better equipped than any other German division during the war. Its organization was as indicated on the next page:[1]

It was formed from various training units and was considered to be among the best divisions in the German army. Including the attached *Panzer-Kompanie 316 (Funklenk)*, it had 99 *Panzer IV's*, 89 *Panthers*, 31 *Jagdpanzer TV's*, 10 *Sturmgeschütz IIIs*, 8 *Tigers* (five of them *Tiger II's*) on 1 June 1944. This gave a total of 237 tanks and assault guns. The division was remarkable in other aspects too. All four *Panzer-Grenadier-Bataillone* were mounted in *SPW. Panzer-Pionier-Bataillon 130* was also fully equipped with armored half tracks. Altogether, the division possessed 658 operational *SPW* and 35 in short-term repair.[2]

Each *Panzer-Grenadier-Bataillon* had 108 machine guns, six 8 cm mortars, 39 *Panzerschrecks*, 9 3.7 cm guns on *SPW* and 8 7.5 cm infantry guns on *SPW*.[3]

The artillery regiment had one battalion with 12 10.5 cm howitzers and one battalion with 15.2 cm howitzers. The *I./Panzer-Artillerie-Regiment 130* was in Germany to be equipped with Wespe and Hummel self-propelled guns. Fuel shortages delayed its march to Normandy, and by 20 June, it had reached Vire.[5] It was redesignated as the *II./Panzer-Artillerie-Regiment 130*, while the former *II. Abteilung* became the I. Abteilung.

Usually, the *Flak* battalion of a *Panzer-Division* was authorized 8 or 12 8.8 cm *Flak,* but the *Panzer-Lehr-Division* had 18.[6]

The division had a manpower strength of 14,699 on 1 June 1944.[7]

At the beginning of June, the division was deployed in the Chartres–Le Mans–Orleans area.[8] Despite the threat of Allied invasion the *Panther* battalion – the *I./Panzer-Regiment 6* which had been detached from the *3. Panzer-Division* – was loaded on trains to be sent to the Eastern Front. On 5 June the first train had reached Magdeburg in Germany while the last one was at Paris.[9] This meant that the strongest battalion of the division was missing when the Allies invaded France.

On D-Day the division received orders to march to Normandy. The *Panther* battalion was ordered to move back to France to join the division in Normandy. The journey to Normandy by the division has been described as a costly and prolonged affair due to intervention of Allied air power. It has been stated the division lost 5 tanks, 84 *SPW* and prime movers and 90 wheeled vehicles. According to Ritgen, who was the commander of the repair and maintenance company of the *Panzer IV* battalion at the time, this initial report was exaggerated.[10] The fact that the division lost 82 *SPW* and 10 prime movers during the entire month of June supports this judgement.[11]

Of greater importance than the losses were the delays. The *Panzer IV* battalion – the *II./Panzer-Regiment 130* – had only reached a wooded area north of Alençon on the

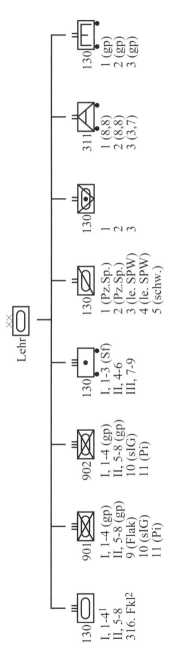

Lehr

130
I, 1-4[1]
II, 5-8
316. Fkl[2]

901
I, 1-4 (gp)
II, 5-8 (gp)
9 (Flak)
10 (sIG)
11 (Pi)

902
I, 1-4 (gp)
II, 5-8 (gp)
10 (sIG)
11 (Pi)

130
I, 1-3 (Sf)
II, 4-6
III, 7-9

130
1 (Pz.Sp.)
2 (Pz.Sp.)
3 (le. SPW)
4 (le. SPW)
5 (schw.)

130
1
2
3

311
1 (8,8)
2 (8,8)
3 (3,7)

130
1 (gp)
2 (gp)
3 (gp)

1. Actually the I./Pz.Rgt. 6
2. A Fkl.Kp.

morning of 7 June and was short of fuel.[12] The *II./Panzer-Grenadier-Regiment 902* went into action on the morning of 8 June.[13] The following day, the *II./Panzer-Regiment 130, Panzer-Grenadier-Regiment 901,* the *I./Panzer-Grenadier-Regiment 902* and *Panzerjäger-Lehr-Abteilung 130* were committed.[14] On 10 June the *Panther* battalion arrived, and it was sent into action the following day.[15]

Panzer-Kompanie 316 (Funklenk) did not bring its *Tiger II* tanks to Normandy. These vehicles were actually prototypes with technical deficiencies and it was ordered that they should be sent back to Germany. Since the rail net was damaged and the transfer of these vehicles had low priority, they remained in Chateaudun. They were subsequently blown up to avoid capture.[16]

The *Panzer-Lehr-Division* continued fighting British forces until relieved by the *276. Infanterie-Division.* This was accomplished gradually between 26 June and 5 July. June had been a month of intensive fighting for the division. Casualties during June amounted to 490 killed in action, 1,809 wounded and 673 missing.[17]

Up to 26 June, 23 *Panthers,* 19 *Pz IV* and 2 *StuG* were lost.[18]

On 8 July 11 *Panzer IV*'s were sent to the division as replacements.[19] Eight *Panthers* had been sent on 28 June.[20]

Initially the division was placed in reserve but, on 10 July, it was committed in the *LXXXIV. Korps* sector.[21]

The first action against US troops was the attack in the le Desert area on 11 July.[22] Until Operation *Cobra,* the division remained in the area west and northwest of St. Lo. On 20 July *Panzeraufklärungs-Abteilung 130* and the *II./Panzer-Grenadier-Regiment 902* were withdrawn for refitting.[23] These were placed in the Percy area.[24]

On 21 July the division had the following artillery:

1./Panzer-Artillerie-Regiment 130
  1.-3./Panzer-Artillerie-Regiment (3 *IFH* each)
II./Panzer-Artillerie-Regiment 130
  4./Panzer-Artillerie-Regiment 130 (3x *Wespe*)
  5./Panzer-Artillerie-Regiment 130 (5x *Wespe*)
  6./Panzer-Artillerie-Regiment 130 (2x *Hummel*)
III./Panzer-Artillerie-Regiment 130
  7./Panzer-Artillerie-Regiment 130 (3x 15.2 cm *H*)
  8./Panzer-Artillerie-Regiment 130 (2x *sFH*)
  9./Panzer-Artillerie-Regiment 130 (4x 10 cm *Kan*)

Flak-Abteilung 311
  1.-3./Flak-Abteilung 311 (6x 8.8 cm *Flak* each).[25]

Two days later the division had three battalions rated as *schwach* (weak) and two were rated as *abgekampft* (combat ineffective). Five other battalions were also attached to the division.[26]

During 24 and 25 July, heavy bombers targeted the positions held by the division to pave the way for the ground units attacking within the framework of Operation *Cobra*. The effects of this carpet bombing have evoked much controversy.

According to the postwar manuscript by Bayerlein, the division lost about 950 men on 24–25 July, while other units attached to the division lost another 1 200 men.[27] He also estimated that about 50% of the soldiers killed and wounded during those two days were the result of the carpet bombing.[28] However, most of the losses during these two days were probably mainly recorded as missing in action. During July, the division lost 347 men killed in action, 1,144 wounded and 1,480 missing.[29] It was explicitly stated that the majority of the missing were incurred due to the carpet bombings.

Most casualties were probably not men killed or wounded by the bombing; more likely, they were stunned soldiers who were taken prisoner when the US ground forces advanced. According to Ritgen, who commanded the *Panzer IV* battalion at the time,[30] no *Panzer IV* was hit by the bombardment since they had been withdrawn to constitute a reserve.[31] He also asserts that very few *Panthers* and tank destroyers were destroyed during the bombardment.[32]

It seems that carpet bombings did not kill or wound large numbers of soldiers. Neither does the available evidence indicate large-scale destruction of equipment. The important effect was the disruption caused and the effect on the morale of the men subjected to such an air attack. In fact, the short bombings on 24 and 25 June caused almost 900 casualties on the US side.[33] This was probably not far from the losses inflicted on the Germans.

Even before Operation *Cobra*, the *Panzer-Lehr-Division* was seriously depleted. Casualties during June and July totaled 5,943 officers and men. During the same period, 3,437 replacements and convalescents arrived at the division.[34] Consequently, it was short 2,506 men compared to 1 June 1944. Since the infantry endured the vast majority of the casualties, the division was almost deprived of riflemen. This meant that the tanks and the artillery constituted the backbone of the defense. However, these two arms suffered from serious shortages of ammunition and fuel.[35] Consequently the division and its attached units – disrupted by the bombardment – could not resist the 140,000 men assembled for Operation *Cobra*.[36]

There was a tank repair facility at Cerisy-le-Selle, where about 30 tanks had been assembled for repairs. Most of these had to be abandoned on 27 July when US forces closed in.[37] When the American units advanced towards Avranches, the division was attached to the *XXXXVII. Panzer-Korps*.[38]

On 1 August, the division had a strength of 11,018 men. It had 33 tanks and assault guns operational and a further 44 in maintenance facilities. Artillery was even scarcer. The division only had nine howitzers ready for action.[39] One reason for this was that the I./Panzer-Artillerie-Regiment 130 had been involved in ground combat with elements of the US 3rd Armored Division northwest of Marigny on

26 July.[40] The division had 391 combat-ready *SPW* and a further 54 in short-term repair.[41]

The *I./Panzer-Regiment 6* still had 89% of its authorized personnel strength. The *II./Panzer-Regiment 130* was less fortunate since it only had 63% of authorized strength.[42]

Since the division was attrited, it was decided it should be refitted. A *Kampfgruppe von Hauser was* formed from the combat-ready parts of the division on 5 August. This included a mixed artillery battalion and a weak *Panzer IV* company It was attached to the *II. Fallschirm-Korps.*[43]

The remainder of the division, including the rear services, was ordered to move to Alençon to rest and refit. These components were to receive new equipment and replacements.[44] They were attached to the *LXXXI. Korps* on 8 August.[45]

By 9 August the refitting units were located between the *9. Panzer-Division* and the *708. Infanterie-Division.* Stragglers had been returning to the division and some replacements had arrived while maintenance facilities had been able to repair some tanks and other equipment.[46]

A Kampfgruppe was formed from the refitting units. It consisted of parts of *Panzer-Grenadier-Regiment 902,* the *I./Panzer-Regiment 6, Panzer-Artillerie-Regiment 130* and *Panzeraufklärungs-Abteilung 130.* The *I./Panzer-Grenadier-Regiment 11* from the *9. Panzer-Division* was attached, as were elements of *Sicherungs-Regiment 1.* This force was committed in the sector between Joublains and Conlie.[47]

By 12 August *Kampfgruppe von Hauser* had disengaged and was moving towards Fontainebleau to rest and refit.[48] The rest of the division soon followed. On the evening of the following day Bayerlein, on his own initiative, ordered the rest of the division to follow. Early on the following day the division had already reached the area east of Argentan.[49]

A *Kampfgruppe Kuhnow* was left behind. This consisted of elements from *Panzer-Grenadier-Regiment 902,* a tank company and a howitzer battery. During the night of 16/17 August, this formation crossed the Orne river at Mesnil-Jean and joined the *12. SS-Panzer-Division "Hitlerjugend"* the following day. It broke out of the pocket by 20 August and, the following day, it assembled at Senlis, north of Paris.[50]

The main part of the division was temporarily sent into action in the Nonant-le-Pin — St. Lombard area. On 17 August, it was relieved by the *344. Infanterie-Division* and was finally moved to Fontainebleau.[51]

On 22 August the division had approximately 10 *Panzer IVs* and 10 *Panthers.*[52] The division received schnelle Abteilungen 509, 510 and 511 to use as replacements.[53]

During August, the division suffered 1,468 casualties.[54] Together with the casualties during June and July (listed above), this gave a total of 7,411 casualties during the summer of 1944.

Panzer IV

Date	Combat Ready	Short-term Repair	Long-term Repair
1 June[55]	97	2	0
18 June[56]	29	19	37
19 June[57]	24	22	37
22 June[58]	24	22	37
24 June[59]	33	9	37
26 June[60]	27	13	34
1 July[61]	36	29	10
23 July[62]	15	?	?
1 August[63]	15	7	20
9 August[64]	12	6	?

Panther

Date	Combat Ready	Short-term Repair	Long-term Repair
1 June	86	3	0
18 June	23	26	17
19 June	23	26	17
22 June	23	26	17
24 June	30	17	19
26 June	26	20	20
1 July	32	26	8
23 July	16	?	?
1 August	12	6	7
9 August	5	5	?

Sturmgeschütz III & Jagdpanzer IV

Date	Combat Ready	Short-term Repair	Long-term Repair
1 June	40	1	0
18 June	?	?	?
19 June	?	?	?
22 June	?	?	?
24 June	?	?	?
26 June	?	?	?
1 July	28	9	1

Date	Combat Ready	Short-term Repair	Long-term Repair
23 July	?	?	?
1 August	6	4	?
9 August	?	?	?

The figures for 9 August refer to those elements subordinated to the *LXXXI. Korps.*

1   BA-MA RH 10/172.

2   Ibid.

3   Ibid.

4   KTB HGr B Abt Qu., entry 10.6, T311, Rl, F7000077.

5   OB West la Nr. 4784/44 g.Kdos, 20.6.44, T311, R25, F7029691.

6   BA-MA RH 10/172.

7   Ibid.

8   H. Ritgen, *Die Gechichte der Panzer-Lehr-Division im Westen 1944-1945* (Motorbuch Verlag, Stuttgart 1979) p. 100.

9   Ibid, p. 102.

10   Ibid, p. 103–6.

11   July 1944 status report for the *Panzer-Lehr-Division* sent to Inspector-General of Panzer Troops, BA-MA RH 10/172.

12   Ritgen, op. cit. p. 106.

13   Ibid, p. 110f.

14   Ibid, p. 112.

15   Ibid, p. 134.

16   Ritgen, op. cit. p.36.

17   1 July 1944 status report for the *Panzer-Lehr-Division* sent to Inspector-General of Panzer Troops, BA-MA RH 10/172.

18   Gen.Kdo I. SS-Pz.Korps, Panzerlage am 26.6.44, 00.00 Uhr, T311, R278, F001376.

19   Lieferung der Panzerfahrzeuge, Bd. ab Mai 1943, RH 10/349.

20   Ibid.

21   Ritgen, op. cit. p . 317.

22   See the Chapter on German combat efficiency for a fuller description of this attack.

23   Ritgen, op. cit. p. 161.

24   E Bayerlein, *Pz Lehr Div 15-25 Jul44,* MS # A-903, p. 5f.

25   Gen.Kdo. LXXX3V A.K. Ia Nr. 035/44g.Kdos 22.7.44, Taktische Gliederung der Artillerie, Stand 21.7.44, T314, R1604, F001388.

26   Gen.Kdo. LXXXIV. A.K. Ia 048/44 g.Kdos. T314, R1604, F001373.

27   F. Bayerlein, *Pz Lehr Div 15-25 Jul 44,* MS # A-903, p. 5f.

28   F. Bayerlein, *Pz Lehr Div 15 - 25 Jul 44,* MS # A-902, p. 2.

29   1 August 1944 status report for the *Panzer-Lehr-Division* sent to Inspector-General of Panzer Troops, BA-MA RH 10/172.

30   Ritgen, op. cit. p. 321.

31   Ibid, p. 162–6.

32   Ibid, p. 166.

33   M. Blumenson, *Breakout and Pursuit* (Office of the Chief of Military History, Washington D.C. 1961) p. 236.

33 See 1 July and 1 August 1944 status report for the *Panzer-Lehr-Division* sent to Inspector-General of Panzer Troops, BA-MA RH 10/172.

34 See Ritgen, op. cit. p. 160 and also R. A. Hart, *Feeding mars: The Role of Logistics in the German Defeat in Normandy, 1944,* War in History 1996 3 (4).

35 Ritgen, op. cit. p 163.

36 Ibid, p. 171.

37 Ibid, p. 315.

38 1 August 1944 status report for the *Panzer-Lehr-Division* sent to Inspector-General of Panzer Troops, BA-MA RH 10/172.

39 Ritgen, op. cit. p. 168.

40 1 August 1944 status report for the *Panzer-Lehr-Division* sent to Inspector-General of Panzer Troops, BA-MA RH 10/172.

41 Ibid.

42 Ritgen, op. cit. p. 175f & 315.

43 Ibid.

44 LXXXI. A.K. Qu./Korps-Kf.-Offz./Ia Nr. 27/44 geh., 8.8.44, T314, R1592, F000471.

45 Ritgen, op. cit. p. 182f.

46 Ibid, p. 183.

47 Ibid, p. 183f.

48 Ibid, p. 184–6.

49 Ibid.

50 Ibid, p. 185.

51 Ritgen (p. 187) states that the division had about 20 *Panzer IV* and *Panther* tanks on 22 August. Two days later, 22 *Panzer IV's* arrived at the division (Ritgen p. 187). The same day it was ordered that the 32 *Panzer IV s* of the division assemble in the area near Meaux (HGr B la Nr. 6504/44 g.Kdos, 24.8.44, T311, R4, F7004039).

52 Ritgen, op.cit. p. 187.

53 Ibid, p. 318.

54 BA-MA RH 10/172. The data for the *Panther* and assault gun strength figures in the following tables are taken from the same sources for the corresponding dates.

55 Pz.Lehr Div Abt. Ia, Führerbericht fur den 18.6.44, BA-MA RH 19 IX/2.

56 Anlage zu H.Gr. B Ia Nr. 4103/44 g.Kdos 19.6.44, Pz.Lehr Ia Führerbericht, BA-MA RH 19 IX/2.

57 AOK 7 Ia Nr. 3293/44,22.6.44, BA-MA RH 19 IX/2.

58 KTB HGr B Ia Anlagen, BA-MA RH 19 IX/3, frame 19f, fiche 1.

59 KTB HGr B Ia Anlagen, BA-MA RH 19 IX/3, frame 41, fiche 1

60 BA-MA RH 10/172.

61 Gen.Kdo. LXXXIV. A.K. Ia 048/44 g.Kdos. T314, R1604, F001373.

62 BA-MA RH 10/172.

63 Anlagen zum LXXXI. A.K. Ia Fernschreiben an Achilles 4, 9.8.44, T314, R1592, F000475.

Arrival of Units in Normandy

This appendix gives the dates when the combat units arrived in Normandy. Note that the arrival may in reality have been an affair lasting several days. In those cases, either the mean between the first and last arrivals has been used or else the entries for more than one day have been used for the sub-units of the parent formation. In many cases, the available documents do not provide an exact date of arrival. In those cases, an assumption has been made. Sources are those given in the narratives for the respective units.

Date	Formation	Strength	Comments
6 June	716. Infanterie-Division	7,771	
	352. Infanterie-Division	12,734	
	91. Infanterie-Division	7,500	
	21. Panzer-Division	16,297	
	711. Infanterie-Division	1,500	Only elements
	Infanterie-Regiment 919	2,500	Reinforced; part of 709 Infanterie-Division
	Sturm-Bataillon AOK 7	1,106	
	Artillerie-Abteilung 456	500	
	Artillerie-Abteilung 457	500	
	Artillerie-Abteilung 989	500	
	I./Sturm-Werfer-Regiment 101	500	
	Panzer-Ersatz- und Aus-bildungs-Abteilung 100	664	
	Flak-Sturm-Regiment 1	3,000	Part of III. Flak-Korps
7 June	12. SS-Panzer-Division "Hitlerjugend"	17,000	
	6./Fallschirmjäger-Regiment 3	457	
	schnelle Brigade 30	1,818	

YESit v p258

	Formation	Strength	Comments
8 June	*Panzer Lehr Division*	13,099	
	Sturm-Werfer-Regiment 101	1,300	With detached elements
	243. Infanterie-Division	11,529	
	346. Infanterie-Division	9,534	
9 June	*III. Flak-Korps (-)*	9,500	With detached elements
	Artillerie-Abteilung 1151	500	
	709. Infanterie-Division	9,820	With detached elements
10 June	*SS-Aufklärungs-Abteilung 17*	800	Part of *17. SS-Panzer-Grenadier-Division "Götz von Berlichingen"*
	I./Panzer-Regiment 6	1,000	Attached to the *Panzer Lehr Division*
	Artillerie-Abteilung 992	500	
	III./Infanterie-Regiment 898	900	Reinforced; from the *343. Infanterie-Division*
11 June	*77. Infanterie-Division*	9,095	
	Fallschirmjäger-Aufklärungs-Abteilung.12	900	
	Pionier-Bataillon Angers	433	
	SS-Artillerie-Abteilung 101	600	
	7. Werfer-Brigade	3,800	
	Sturmgeschütz-Abteilung 902	450	
	Kampfgruppe 265. Infanterie-Division	3,500	
12 June	*2. Panzer-Division*	13,100	Minus some elements
	SS-Werfer-Batterie	150	Battery from *SS-Werfer-Abteilung 12 (12. SS-Panzer-Division "Hitlerjugend")*
	schwere SS-Panzer-Abteilung 101	950	
	Kampfgruppe of 275. Infanterie-Division	4,700	
	3. Fallschirmjäger-Division	17,420	
13 June	*17. SS-Panzergrenadier-Division "Götz von Berlichingen"*	16,121	Minus some elements
	12. Fallschirmjäger-Sturm-geschütz-Brigade	500	
14 June	*I./Artillerie-Abteilung Suippes*	500	

Date	Formation	Strength	Comments
15–16 June			
17 June	*353. Infanterie-Division*	1,800	Only elements
18 June	*2. Panzer-Division*	2,800	*Panzer-Regiment 3, I./Panzer-Artillerie-Regiment 74* and *4./Panzer-Abteilung 301 (Funklenk)*
	Artillerie-Abteilung 555	473	
19 June	*Artillerie-Abteilung 460*	508	
	Artillerie-Abteilung 763	500	
20 June	*II./Panzer-Artillerie-Regiment 130*	600	Part of the *Panzer-Lehr-Division*
21 June	*353. Infanterie-Division*	11,530	Minus some elements
	8. Werfer-Brigade	3,800	
	Artillerie-Abteilung Autun	500	
22 June	*Festungs-Stammtruppe*		Fortress units in
	Cherbourg	1,355	Cherbourg
	MG-Bataillon 17	632	
	Panzer-Abteilung 206	385	
23 June	*Panzerjäger-Abteilung 657*	480	
	Kampfgruppe 266.		
	Infanterie-Division	3,000	
24 June	*Artillerie-Abteilung 1192*	500	
25 June	*Artillerie-PaK-Abteilung 1053*	400	
26 June	*9. Werfer-Brigade*	3,800	
27 June	*Artillerie-Abteilung 1194*	500	
	2./schwere Panzerjäger-Abteilung 654	175	
28 June	*SS-Panzergrenadier-Regiment 1*	2,000	Minus some elements; belonged to the *1. SS-Panzer-Division "Leibstanarte"*
29 June	*10. SS-Panzer-Division "Frundsberg"*	15,800	
	9. SS-Panzer-Division "Hohenstaufen"	16,800	
	Kampfgruppe Weidinger	2,500	*Part of the 2. SS-Panzer-Division "Das Reich"*
30 June	*Artillerie-Abteilung 1198*	500	

Date	Formation	Strength	Comments
1 July	*2. SS-Panzer-Division "Das Reich"*	8,695	Minus some elements
	Artillerie-Abteilung 1193	500	
	16. Luftwaffenfelddivision	7,416	Minus some elements
2 July	*Fallschirmjäger-Regiment 15*	3,000	Reinforced; part of the *5. Fallschirmjäger-Division*
	Artillerie-Abteilung 937	500	
3 July	*schwere SS-Panzer-Abteilung 102*	950	
4 July	*1. SS-Panzer-Division "Leibstandarte"*	11,800	Minus some elements
5 July	*Artillerie-Batterie 625*	150	
	276. Infanterie-Division	13,362	
6 July	*2. SS-Panzer-Division "Das Reich"*	1600	Elements; mainly units of *SS-Panzergrenadier-Regiment 3*
7 July			
8 July	*Artillerie-Abteilung 628*	500	
9 July	*Artillerie-PaK-Abteilung 1041*	400	
10 July	*Pionier-Bataillon 600*	500	
	Schwere Panzer-Abteilung 503	950	
11 July	*277. Infanterie-Division*	9,136	
12 July	*Artillerie-PaK-Abteilung 1040*	400	
13 July	*5. Fallschirmjäger-Division*	10,500	Minus some elements
14 July	*Artillerie-PaK-Abteilung 1039*	400	
15 July	*16. Luftwaffenfelddivision*	2,400	Elements
16 July			
17 July	*272. Infanterie-Division*	11,211	
18 July			
19 July	*1./SS-Panzerjäger-Abteilung 12*	200	Part of *12. SS-Panzer-Division "Hitlerjugend"*
20 July			
21 July	*2./Sturmpanzer-Abteilung 217*	150	
	275. Infanterie-Division	8,328	Elements
22 July	*271. Infanterie-Division*	11,617	
23 July	*3./schwere Panzerjäger-Abteilung 654*	175	
24 July	*116. Panzer-Division*	14,358	

Date	Formation	Strength	Comments
25 July	2. SS-Panzer-Division "Das Reich"	4,488	The last elements of the division arrived during the last 10 days of July.
	326. Infanterie-Division	11,533	
26 July			
27 July	3./Sturmpanzer-Abteilung 217	150	
28–30 July			
31 July	Sturmgeschütz-Brigade 341	540	
1 August	363. Infanterie-Division	11,000	
2 August	266. Infanterie-Division	5,800	Minus some elements
3 August	Sturmgeschütz-Brigade 394	540	
4 August	9. Panzer-Division	13,500	Parts of the rear services never arrived in Normandy.
	SS-Panzerjäger-Abteilung 17	400	Minus some elements; part of the 17. SS-Panzergrenadier-Division "Götz von Berlichingen"
5 August	84. Infanterie-Division	8,437	
	89. Infanterie-Division	8,000	
	708. Infanterie-Division	5,000	Minus some elements
	Sturmgeschütz-Abteilung 1348	122	
6 August	Panzerjäger-Abteilung 668	691	
7 August	343. Infanterie-Division	10,394	
	2. Fallschirmjäger-Division	9,000	
8 August			
9 August	85. Infanterie-Division	8,393	
10 August	331. Infanterie-Division	11,909	
11 August			
12 August	Kampfgruppe 6. Fallschirmjäger-Division	4,000	
13–14 August			
15 August	711. Infanterie-Division	5,742	
16–22 August			

Unit Histories

There are numerous publications covering some of the German units that fought in Normandy. As could perhaps be expected, the mechanized divisions are better covered than other units. Many unit histories are written by veterans and this, of course, means that they can be biased in various way, or simply gloss over parts of the events that took place. The latter is perhaps particularly likely when it comes to war crimes. For the purposes of tracking units, their composition and fates, it is more common that the histories are not including enough detail, rather than them being wrong.

Panzer Lehr Division: There exist two histories of this division. The first published was by Franz Kurowski, *Die Panzer-Lehr-Division* (Podzun, Bad Nauheim 1964). Fifteen years later, Helmut Ritgen published *Die Gechichte der Panzer-Lehr-Division im Westen 1944–1945* (Motorbuch Verlag, Stuttgart 1979). Of these two, Ritgen's book is the preferred one. It contains much data and seems more reliable than Kurowski's. Ritgen's book is definitely recommended.

2. Panzer-Division: Franz-Joseph Strauss, *Geschichte der 2. (Wiener) Panzer Division* (Vowinkel, Neckargemünd 1977). This covers the entire war and does not contain a wealth of information on the actions in Normandy.

9. Panzer-Division: There exists a book called *68 Kriegsmonate–Weg der 9. Panzer-Division* by C. H. Hermann. It was not available to the author.

21. Panzer-Division: No published history of this unit has been found.

116. Panzer-Division: Heinz-Günther Guderian, *Das letzte Kriegsjahr im Westen* (St. Augustin 1994). A good, detailed book that has clearly used archival records plus other information that is hard to obtain for anyone who does not happen to have been chief of staff of the division. Recommended.

1. SS-Panzer-Division "Leibstandarte": R. Lehmann & R. Tiemann, *The Leibstandarte, Vol IV/1* (J. J. Fedorowicz Publishing Inc, Winnipeg 1993). This volume is not as detailed as those covering the years before 1944, but this is probably due to the availability of sources.Nevertheless, it provides good coverage of the actions fought by the *Leibstandarte* in Normandy.

2. SS-Panzer-Division "Das Reich": Otto Weidinger, *Division Das Reich 1943–45* (Munin Verlag, Osnabrück 1982). Like the corresponding volume on the

1. SS-Panzer-Division "Leibstandarte" it is not as good as the preceding volumes in the series. Still, it gives a good account of the actions in which *"Das Reich"* was involved. When reading the coverage of the massacres in Tulle and Oradour it must be kept in mind that the author, or some of his comrades, may have been directly involved in those frightful events.

9. SS-Panzer-Division "Hohenstaufen": H. Fürbringer, *9. SS-Panzer-Division* (Editions Heimdal, 1984). This book contains text in both German and French. It is very detailed and seems very reliable. Recommended.

10. SS-Panzer-Division "Frundsberg": No history of this unit has been found. However, E. Klapdor, *Die Entscheidung* (Siek 1984) contain much information on the activities of this division in Normandy. The author served with the *"Frundsberg".* This book is recommended. Also, the book *Im Feuersturm letzter Kriegsjahre* (Munin Verlag, Osnabrück 1975) by Wilhelm Tieke deals with the *II. SS-Panzer Korps* and contains information about the actions of the *10. SS-Panzer- Division.* This volume has also been published in English by J.J. Fedorowicz Publishing under the title of *In the Firestorm of the Last years of the War.*

12. SS-Panzer-Division "Hitlerjugend": Hubert Meyer, *Kriegsgeschichte der 12. SS-Panzerdivision "Hitlerjugend"* Bd. I & II. (Munin Verlag, Osnabrück 1982). The first of the two volumes covers the formation of the division and its actions in Normandy. All notes, references and appendices are found in volume two. The books are very good and clearly recommended. This title has also been published by *J.J. Fedorowicz Publishing as The History of the 12. SS-Panzerdivision "Hitlerjugend".*

17. SS-Panzergrenadier-Division "Götz von Berlichingen": H. Stöber, *Die Sturmflut und das Ende, Bd. I* (Munin Verlag, Osnabrück 1976). The layout of the book has flaws and the references are not particularlv good. However, the research is clearly of good standard and the book contain much valuable information. Thus, it is recommended.

272. Infanterie-Division: M. Jenner, *Die 216./272. niedersächsische Inanterie-Division 1939–1945* (Podzun, Bad Nauheim 1964). This is the only history of an infantry division found. It does not provide a a wealth of information on the division's actions in Normandy.

Another book that can be recommended is R. Stoves, *Die gepanzerten und motorisierten Deutschen Grossverbände 1939–45* (Podzun- Pallas-Verlag, Bad Nauheim 1986). As the title implies, the book does not only cover actions Normandy. It provide a brief description of how the units were organized and a capsule history of each armored formation covered.

Also Eric Lefèvre's *Panzers in Normandy* (Battle of Britain Prints, London 1983) is interesting, even though there are some errors in the book. For example, the author does not note that the *I./Panzer- Regiment 24* fought in Normandy, mainly with the *116. Panzer-Division.* He also states the *Panther* battalions rarely had the authorized 17 or 22 tanks per company. Although he checked the number of operational tanks on 1 June 1944, he failed to count the additional vehicles in maintenance facilities or note that deliveries of new tanks took place between 1 June and the actual transfer to Normandy.

For those interested in small-unit actions, J.J. Fedorowicz Publishing has also recently published *The Combat History of schwere Panzer-Abteilung 503* which was heretofore only available in an extremely limited edition produced by the veterans' association.

The Reliability of Casualty Reports

In 1999, the book *Deutsche militärische Verluste im Zweiten Weltkrieg* (German Military Casualties in WWII) by Rüdiger Overmans was released. It has often been used as a reference for German military losses in World War II. In his book, Overmans presents new data on overall irrecoverable losses during the war, as well as monthly figures for different theaters and other interesting information.

Overmans argues that German military reports on casualties are incomplete and unreliable. This led him to approach the matter by using a completely different method, which we will soon turn our attention to. This was a departure from the research up to that date, which mainly relied on OKH and OKW documents that were considered reliable until the end of 1944. To this was added estimates for 1945, since it has been clear that reporting during the final stages of the war has been inaccurate or incomplete. Overmans came up with a different approach.

There are of course various problems with the wartime reports compiled by OKH and OKW. For example, during catastrophic defeats, like in Belarus 1944, the system lagged behind several months. The OKH/Heeresarzt ten-day reports for the armies involved in the disaster were not brought back into sync until November 1944.[1] Similar problems occurred in other operations during the summer 1944, such as the German defeat in Normandy.

Another problem is that the German reporting system was designed to report how many soldiers were killed, wounded or missing due to enemy action. Note that the number reported as killed refers only to those who were known to have died before they arrive at medical facilities. Thus, the reporting system was never supposed to be able to answer Overmans's main question, which was how many Germans perished among those who served during the war. It must be remembered that there were many soldiers who lost their lives at the medical facilities, due to disease, in accidents or in enemy captivity. Also, some of those reported as missing were actually dead. To account for the latter problem, Overmans also makes comparisons between the sum of killed and missing as reported, and similar figures according to his sample.

According to Overmans, one consequence of the alleged too low casualty reports is that the OKH may have thought that there were more soliders on the Eastern Front than was actually the case. To support this, Overmans asserts that the German strength reports are inaccurate too. To underline this, Overmans presents data from two documents, giving the strength on the Eastern Front on 1 June 1944 as 2.55 million men and 1.85 million respectively.[2] These variations in strength reporting is interpreted by him that the OKH had vague notions about the actual strength on the Eastern Front. However, a closer scrutiny of the documents Overmans has used leads to a very different conclusion.[3]

The explanation for the discrepancey is that the reports cover different categories of units. The lower figure only refers to soldiers in divisions and brigades. The higher figure refer to soldiers in all kinds of units. Additionally, the files Overmans used contain reports on the number of troops in divisions and brigades (called *Verbände*), GHQ combat units (called *fechtende Heerestruppen*) and other GHQ units. If personnel from the latter two categories are added to the number of soldiers in divisions and brigades, there is no longer a discrepancy.

There are, of course, other methods to test the reliability of the reports. One way is to compare strength reports at two different dates with reports on the number of casualties and the replacements received, plus the convalescents returning to duty. This can be done for the period 1 July 1943 and 1 June 1944, which is a period of sustained, heavy combat.

On 1 July 1943, the Ostheer numbered (including Waffen-SS and Luftwaffe ground combat units) 3,138,000 men.[4] Until 1 June 1944, casualties 1,900,490 were suffered.[5] In the same period, the Ostheer received 1,205,030–1,227,000 replacements and convalescents that had recovered from wounds.[6] According to this, it would be expected that the Ostheer numbered 2,442,540–2,464,510 on 1 June. However, it was slightly stronger, at 2,620,000.[7] The difference is explained by unit transfers in and out of the theater, which can be estimated to a net gain of 210,000 soldiers.[8] This is slightly more than the difference to be explained, but on the other hand, soldiers may have left the theater for reasons like disease or injuries due to accidents. Nevertheless, the figures suggest that the bookkeeping was consistent.

As noted above, Overmans has used a different approach. He has relied on the records for individual servicemen kept att Deutsche Dienststelle. Specifically, he has used two sets of cards, one for confirmed dead servicemen, comprising over three million individuals, and one general set of cards, which contains those who served and have not been confirmed dead. In the latter, general set, there is a significant number of soldiers whose fate is unknown and Overmans has created a subset of about 1,100 individuals from this general set. These have been added to about 3,300 indivdual selected from the set which contains those confirmed dead.[9]

Overmans has thus used two different sets and taken a sample from each of them, then combined the two samples to create one sample. To combine two samples into one is a dangerous approach, since combining sets with different probability density functions can create a new set with a probability density function that is not representative for the overall population from which the sample originates.

This problem can easily be shown by using calculus, but I will use a numerical example to illustrate what can happen. According to Overmans's data, the share of confirmed dead declines late in the war, while the share of unknown fate increases. This is expected, as prisoners of war increased significantly in the last 12 months and also the reporting system was very strained in the same period. Hence, it is not surprising that Overmans's data shows an increasing ratio of missing vs dead.

The fact that the two sets of cards differ in their distribution over time can cause spurious results. An example can illustrate this. Assume that we have two sets of records with soldiers that have died. One set, which we can call A, contains three million names of soldiers whose death is confirmed. The other set, called B, contains names of two million soldiers whose fate is unkown but presumed dead. Assume the duration of the war was five years and in reality there were one million deaths each year, thus the death rate was constant.

To illustrate the problem more clearly, we further assume that all the confirmed deaths – i.e. individuals from set A – actually took place in the first three years, while all those whose fate is unkown but presumed dead – i.e. individuals from set B – succumbed in the final two years. This is, of course, an extreme variant, but it is chosen for pedagogical reasons.

If we obtain a representative sample consisting of 3,000 individuals from set A and 1,000 individuals from set B, we will get the following distiribution over time: from year one, we will have one third of the soldiers in the sample from set A. This means that our sample will include 1,000 soldiers that died in year one. For year two and three, we will get the same result.

For year four and five, results will be different, however. As our sample only included 1,000 individuals from set B, we will only have 500 from each year. Hence, we end up till the following distribution over time: 1,000 soldiers from each of the first three years and 500 from each of the two final years. Our sample would thus indicate that 25% of the overall losses took place in the first year and the same would apply to year two and three. In the final years, each year in the sample will contain 12.5% of the overall losses.

Given these assumptions, our sample would indicate that 25% of 5 million deaths, which is 1,25 million, took place in each of the first three years. In each of the final two years, only 625,000 deaths took place.

These calculations are quite straightforward. We can repeat them with another combination of soldiers taken from sets A and B. If we assume that we take 1,000 names from set A and 3,000 from set B – i.e. the opposite ratio – we would come up with the conclusion that in each of the first three years 417,000 deaths took places and in each of the final two years, 1,875,000 deaths took place.

We see that the distribution over time we come up with is highly sensitive to the ratio of individuals gathered from each of the two sets A and B. This means that we can conclude that Overmans's sample does not reliably portray the distribution of losses over time.

What I have described is well known in statistics, but there are more reasons to scrutinize Overmans's figures. On page 185, he presents a table and discusses its content and implications. It shows how the confidence interval vary with sample size for the confidence level 95%. The table is used to indicate that a sample of at least 4,000 individuals would be desired. It was decided to aim for a sample size of 4,300, to allow for individuals whose records are incomplete.

Unfortunately, there is not much suggesting that the full implications of this, including the information presented in the table on page 185, has been taken into account. Rather, it seems that after the sample size has been decided, the sample is used to answer many different questions, but this is problematic. For example, on page 277 there is a table showing monthly losses on the Eastern Front. To name just one example, it is said that 53,264 soldiers lost their lives on the Eastern Front in October 1943.[10]

If we return to the table Overmans used to find out the desired sample size, one can see that 53,264 is almost exactly one percent of his sample. According to the table, we find that we can say that the losses for the month is somewhere in the interval 31,000–75,000, with the 99% confidence level. Obviously, giving numbers down to the last digit can give an impression of accuracy that is not justifiable.

However, the broad interval problem is not isolated. It should be put on top of the systematic errors that follow from the improper procedure of mixing samples from two sets with different distribution over time. Also, there are further potential systematic errors.

Overmans has used a figure of 5,318,000 overall dead. This has been reached by making a sample from the general set. He has estimated the total number of individuals in the general set to 15,200,000, then obtained a sample of 7,619 individuals, of which 1,1161 or 15,2 were missing. Hence, he concluded that there were about 2.3 million soldiers in the general set that were missing presumed dead. Combining this with the sum of soldiers in the set of confirmed deaths, he arrives at an overall number of 5,318,000 individuals who lost their lives. Given the problems with the sampling shown above, one wonders how this figure has been established.

But there is one further way to check Overmans's claim that the reports give too low casualty figures. A document (Der Heeresarzt im OKH Gen.St.d.H/Gen. Qu. Az 1335 (Iib) Nr. I./01867/44 g.Kdos, 6 März 1944, BA-MA RW 6/v. 555) discusses the irrevocable losses for the army during the war up to 20 February 1944. The document shows:

Killed in action	795,698
Died due to disease, accidents, etc.	32,724
Missing	588,860
Died in medical facilities due to wounds	295,709
Died in medical facilities due to disease, accidents etc.	99,363
Sum:	1,812,354
Sum (excluding missing):	1,223,494

This can be compared to Overmans's figure for the period 1 September 1939–31 December 1943: 1.58 million men. To this can be added approximately 145,000 for the period 1 Jan–20 Feb 1944 (derived from Overmans's diagram on page 238). Overmans's total, thus, is approximately 100,000 lower than the total for dead and missing according to the document mentioned above. The issue is how many of the missing lost their lives. Essentially, there are three fates for a soldier reported as missing,: he may actually have died in combat, he may have been taken prisoner but died as PoW, or he can survive and return from captivity. According to Overmans, data for the period up to 31 August 1943 on the Eastern Front (which was responsible for the overwhelming majority of casualties up to that date), only 50,000 of those reported missing actually survived the war (page 281). Accordingly, the document cited above is actually in quite good agreement with Overmans's data. Observe that the number reported as killed in action is actually less than half the number of soldiers that actually died (if it is correct to assume that at least 63% of the missing had actually died). This also illustrates the fact that the casualty reports were not intended to answer Overmans's question, that is, how many soldiers lost their lives.

But the document also illuminates another problem. It is stated that the number of soldiers who died at medical facilities were estimates. The reporting system worked as long as the soldiers remained at the units. However, it seems that the reports from the medical facilities were not either correctly used or complete. But most of the wounded soldiers who eventually died were probably quite seriously wounded. Even if they had not died, few of them had been able to return to duty. The brutal logic of war is that they were less of a burden to the war effort as dead. It is quite possible that the percentage of wounded soldiers who died due to wounds became greater and greater during the last two years of war. First of all, motor transport and fuel became scarcer, causing the wounded soldiers to arrive later at medical facilities. Enemy air superiority may have contributed to this. It is certainly conceivable that soldiers that had been recorded as wounded at their parent unit were sent to a hospital in the rear, but during the prolonged journey they passed away. Alternatively their condition deteriorated to such an extent that they could no longer be saved.

Also, the increasing number of wounded during the last years must have strained the medical services.

There is a further way of looking at the data in the document cited above. According to the document, the number of soldiers who died is 1.54 times greater than the number who is reported as killed in action (if missing are not included). The number of soldiers reported as killed in action on the Eastern Front 22 June 1941–31 August 1943 was 559,260.[11] If it is assumed that the ratio was the same for that period, we would have 860,000 killed. To this can be added 356,939 missing, giving a total of approximately 1,220,000 killed and missing. Overmans's data for the same period shows 1,240,000 killed and missing (page 281), or an almost perfect match.[12]

In fact, Overmans's investigation does not show that the casualty reports were too low. Rather, his investigation suggests that they were very accurate, at least if the last year of the war is excluded. The reason for his claim is that he has not taken due consideration of the fact that there were many causes of deaths that the reports from the front-line units were not intended to cover. Since Overmans does not mention the wounded at all, he is actually discussing German casualties without including the majority of all casualties. To the war effort, the important part of the wounded soldiers are not those who die, but those who return to duty. The wounded cannot be divided into two categories, those who die and those who return to service. Also, there are many wounded soldiers who survive but are no longer capable of military service. It is mysterious that Overmans discusses the number of soldiers available to the Wehrmacht in 1944, by only considering those who lose their lives or were captured, but not those who were wounded.

To sum up, Overmans's investigation presents several interesting results, but his claim that the German casualty reports generally were too low is not tenable.

---

1   This example is discussed further in Niklas Zetterling & Anders Frankson, "Analyzing World War II Eastern Front Battles", *Journal of Slavic Military Studies* Vol. 11, No. 1 (March 1998), pp. 176–203.

2   Rüdiger Overmans, *Deutsche militärische Verluste im Zweiten Weltkrieg* (R. Oldenbourg Verlag, München, 1999), p. 282.

3   The documents are found at Bundesarchiv-Militärarchiv (BA-MA), Freiburg, files RH 2/1339 and RH 2/1341.

4   OKH/Gen.St.d.H./Org.Abt. Nr. I/18941/44 g.Kdos, v. 7.9.44 (National Archives, Microfilm Publication T78, Roll 414, Frame 6383114).

5   OKH/Gen.St.d.H./Org.Abt. Nr. I/18941/44 g.Kdos, v. 7.9.44 (National Archives, Microfilm Publication T78, Roll 414, Frame 6383114). The figure does not include forces in Finland. Of these about 1.3 million were wounded. Simultaneously 542,000 convalescents returned to the Eastern Front (NARA T78, R414, F6383154).

6   The figure 1,205,030 is taken from BA-MA RH 2/1343 and 1,227,000 comes from National Archives, Washington, Microfilm publication T78, Roll 414, Frame 6383154.

7   OKH/Org.Abt. Nr. I/20737/44, Notiz Betr. Iststärken, Fehlstellen und Ersatzzuführun Ostheeres von Januar bis Oktober 1944, BA-MA RH 2/1341.

8   The following divisions were sent to the Eastern Front between 1 July 1943 and 31 May 1944: 1. Pz.Div., 1. SS-Pz.Div., 2. Fallsch.Div., 9. SS-Pz.Div., 10. SS-Pz.Div., 11. SS-Pz.Gren.Div., 14. Pz.Div., 15. SS-Gren.Div., 16. Pz.Div., 19. SS-Gren.Div., 20. SS-Gren.Div., 24. Pz.Div., Feldherrnhalle, 76. Inf.Div., 100. Jäger-Div., 214. Inf.Div., 357. Inf.Div., 359. Inf.Div., 361. Inf.Div., 367. Inf.Div., 371. Inf.Div., 376. Inf.Div., 384. Inf.Div., 389. Inf.Div. Probably these numbered about 340,000 men, if assumed to be at full strength.

During the period, the following divisions were withdrawn from the Eastern Front: 1. SS-Pz. Div. (twice), 2. Fallsch.Div., 2. SS-Pz.Div., 5. Geb.Div., 6. Pz.Div., 9. Pz.Div., 11. Pz.Div., 16. Pz.Gren., 19. Pz.Div., 34. Inf.Div., 38. Inf.Div., 39. Inf.Div., 86. Inf.Div., 113. Inf.Div., 137. Inf.Div., 151. Res.Div., 216. Inf.Div., 223. Inf.Div., 250. Inf.Div., 262. Inf.Div., 321. Inf.Div., 328. Inf.Div., 330. Inf.Div., 331. Inf.Div., 333. Inf.Div., The 1. SS-Pz.Div. was withdrawn after Zitadelle, when it numbered at least 17,000. The 2. SS-Pz.Div. numbered around 9,000 when it was withdrawn, it seems that the 1. SS-Pz.Div. was of about the same strength when it was withdrawn in the spring 1944. Probably the 2. Fallsch.Div. had around 7,000 men when withdrawn. The 5. Geb.Jäg.Div. was immediately sent to the Italian front, hence it probably was reasonably strong, perhaps 9,000. The 6., 9., 11., and 19. Pz.Div. 16. Pz.Gren.Div. (according to data when they arrived in the west) seems to have had on average 7,000 men. However, both the 6. and 19. were sent late in May and are possibly still included in the 1 June strength figure for the Eastern Front. For this reason we only count them with half the indicated strength. The infantry divisions withdrawn were depleted and usually left elements (particularly infantry) to beef up units remaining on the Eastern Front. What was withdrawn were usually the staffs, rear services, signal units and some personnel from the artillery. Here we estimate these elements to have numbered, on average, 3,000 men. This would mean that around 48,000 men were withdrawn with these infantry divisions, or a total of approximately 130,000. The net increase due to transfer of units would then be 210,000.

The numbers calculated for transfer are, of course, estimates, but as we are concerned with magnitudes, rather than precis numbers down to the last digit, the suffice for the purpose.

9   Overmans (1999), pp. 151–204.

10   Overmans, p 277.

11   Der Heeresarzt b. Oberkommando des Heeres Nr. I/5846/43 g.Kdos 4.9.43, NARA T78, R414, F6383359.

12   It is worth mentioning that the document used is dated 4 September 1943. Hence, delays in reporting may have caused it to be incomplete. Also the size of Overmans's sample means that each card represents about 4,300 real cases.

Tooth-to-Tail Ratios

It has often been asserted that the Germans had a ratio between manpower employed by combat units and rear services that differed from the Allies and the Germans had a greater share of their manpower manning weapons. It has even been claimed that this is either an indicator of efficiency or a cause of superior combat effectiveness.

Exactly how the distinction between combat units and rear services should be made is not always clear. Even in an infantry regiment, there is a share of the manpower that is not supposed to directly engage the enemy. It is possible the Germans mixed in more of the rear services in their combat units than did the Allies. The German intention seems to have been that each unit should be as self-sufficient as possible. Thus, a tank regiment contained eight tank companies, but also two supply companies and a maintenance company. Additionally, there were three headquarters companies in the regiment. These contained both direct-combat units—such as reconnaissance and antiaircraft forces—and combat-support and combat-service-support forces—such as signals units and engineers. The latter two types of units do not obviously belong to the category of either combat units or rear services.

In addition to the lines blurring among different types of troops within units, intense combat can alter the ratios. Combat units suffer the majority of casualties. This may cause the actual tooth-to-tail ratio to differ from the ratio calculated on the basis of tables of organization and equipment. Since the Germans received far fewer replacements than the Allies, their tooth-to-tail relationship probably differed greatly from the intended ratio.

Even if a tooth-to-tail ratio could be properly calculated, it seems it does not necessarily say much about combat effectiveness. Of all the combat arms branches, the infantry has the greatest percentage of soldiers in actual contact with the enemy. Does this mean that the infantry is more efficient than artillery or armor? Hardly.

It is more interesting to see whether there are notable variations in the correlation between, e.g., number of tanks compared to overall manpower strength. We have seen that there were 812,000 US soldiers in Normandy on 25 July, while the corresponding figure for British and Canadian units was 640,000[1]. This can be compared to a TOE tank strength of 3,429 US tanks and 3,213 British ones.[2] Consequently, there were 237 US soldiers for each tank compared to 199 British and Canadian soldiers for each one. This can be compared to the fact that the Germans had committed almost exactly half a million men to fight in Normandy (or support the units fighting there)[3], while the number of tanks (excluding captured and obsolete models) brought to Normandy by 25 July was 1,869.[4] This results in 268 soldiers per tank, which would suggest that the German forces were slightly less tank heavy.

Similar calculations can, of course, be made for artillery. By 25 July, US units in Normandy had a TOE strength of 1,720 guns and howitzers.[5] This works out to 472 soldiers per artillery piece. For the British and Canadian forces the number of guns was 1,520[6], resulting in 421 soldiers per artillery piece. Again, the British forces were using fewer men per weapon than the Americans. In this case, however, there is an important factor to consider. The relatively light 25 pounder constituted a large part of the British artillery. Generally, heavier weapons require more men and US artillery tended to have more large-caliber weapons.

The Germans had brought 1,672 artillery pieces into the fighting in Normandy by 25 July[7]. This works out to 299 soldiers per artillery piece. Here it is worth recalling that in the American sector artillery ammunition expenditures may have been four times as high in the US forces as it was in the German forces.[8] Thus it would be rash to conclude that the higher number of guns per man in the German forces is an indication of more efficient organization. Rather, it is an indication of poor organization to have more guns than can adequately be supplied with ammunition. It seems that the Allied balance between teeth and tail was generally better in this case, however, further research is needed to clarify the issue. Nevertheless, it seems that the Germans might have done better discarding some of their artillery pieces and concentrating on getting the rest supplied. Many of the captured types presented particular problems with ammunition supply.

As shown in Chapter Four, 77% of the German manpower in Western Europe was found in divisions and 7% was employed in GHQ combat units. The remaining 16% were found in various rear and security units directly controlled by corps, army and army group headquarters. These figures can be compared to data for the Eastern Front. On 1 October 1943, the divisions comprised 1,578,000 men while the GHQ combat units accounted for 400,000 soldiers. There were 96,000 men in security units and 490,000 in non-combat GHQ units.[9] Note that these figures do not include *Waffen-SS* and *Luftwaffe* ground combat units. They do, however, include 324,000 soldiers that were sick, wounded or on home leave.

The non-combat GHQ units were composed as follows[10]:

Supply troops	82,800
Adminstration	19,400
Medical units	66,000

Veterinary units	24,300
Postal services	3,500
Signals units	101,000
Railway troops	43,900
POW supply troops	21,000
Snowplowing units	2,500
Technical troops	21,000
Military police & jurisdiction	27,000
Sentence and penal units	10,500
Propaganda units	7,500
Map and measuring units	3,000
Motor park units	34,000
Other	22,600

On the Eastern Front we find that divisions made up 62% of the manpower strength, while the percentage for GHQ combat troops was 16%. Thus divisions and GHQ combat troops accounted for 78% of the manpower, slightly lower than on the Western Front (83%). It is important to note, however, that of the 1,578,000 men employed in divisions on the Eastern Front, no less than 644,000, or 41%, belonged to supply and rear services within the divisions and the remainder, 934,000 men, were combat troops. But even this may give an inflated picture of combat troops, since the Germans had two definitions of combat troop strength, *Gefechtsstärke* and *Kampfstärke*. According to data for 1 June 1944 on the Eastern Front the latter category was 27% smaller than the former.[11] The figure of 934,000 was *Gefechtsstärke*. Hence, there is reason to suspect that the *Kampfstärke* was only about 680,000. This would indicate an even larger slice for the "non-combat" troops in the divisions.

As a result, comparisons of manpower strength must be made with great care. Perhaps it is easiest to portray the differences between organizational solutions by using the Germans as the yardstick. A German division was a largely self-sufficient organization. It could be augmented by GHQ combat units but, on average, not more than about one battalion per division. Supply, maintenance and transportation means were generally already present. The US division, by comparison, was a leaner organization. It was supported by a considerable number of GHQ units, though these need not have been subordinated to the division. The non-organic units usually doubled the combat power of the division, as a minimum. This necessitated a large supply organization at army level.

A practical example of this is the *4. Panzer-Armee* on 1 July 1943, when it stood ready to begin its attack towards Kursk. Its ten divisions had a ration strength of

190,943 officers and men. The corps troops numbered 13,184 and in formations directly under the army's command were 19,780 soldiers.[12] This can be compared to the US First Army on the eve of the battle of the Bulge. Its 14 divisions had a strength of 181,000 men, plus attachments (mainly tank, tank destroyer and antiaircraft units) of 38,500 men, giving it a total of 219,500 men. Thus, in this respect, it was quite similar in strength to the *4. Panzer-Armee*. However, the corps units numbered 49,210 men and army-level units mustered 71,571 soldiers in the US 1st Army.[13] Thus, in the US First Army, divisions accounted for 53% of the manpower, compared to 85% in the *4. Panzer-Armee*.

It could, of course, be argued that this is but two examples, from different theaters of the war and not applying to the same date. My impression though, is that they are quite representative for German and US forces and reflect the differences in organizational philosophy.

A German infantry division in 1944 was supposed to have 12,407 officers and men.[14] This can be compared to the US infantry division, which numbered 14,253 officers and men.[15] The US division was thus about 15% larger. The US infantry regiment numbered 3,258[16], while the German infantry regiment only had 1,985 officers and men[17]. Consequently, the US infantry regiment was 64% larger, a far greater difference than in size of the division.[18] All these figures are of course according to the TOE's.

---

1   See Chapter 4.
2   See Appendix 6.
3   See Chapter 4.
4   See Appendix 5.
5   Derived from S. Stanton, *Order of Battle: US Army in World War II,* Presidio Press, Novato, California 1984.
6   Derived from M. A. Beilis, *21st Army Group Order of Battle* (Malcolm A. Beilis, Cheshire 1991) and H. F. Joslen, *Orders of Battle Second World War, 1939-1945* (The London Stamp Exchange Ltd, London 1990).
7   Derived from the narratives for the units.
8   See Chapter 4.
9   OKH Org.Abt. Nr. 1/5180/43 g.Kdos, 11.11.43, T78, R414, F6383132.
10 Anlage 4 zu OKH/GenStdH/Org.Abt. (I) Nr. 1/5170/43 g.Kdos., Übersicht über die Stärken der Heeresvers.- und sonstigen Truppen im Osten (Stand 1.10.43), T78, R414, F6383134.
11 N. Zetterling & A. Frankson, Analyzing World War II Eastern Front Battles, *Journal of Slavic Military Studies,* Vol 11, no 1 (March 1998) p. 177.
12 Anlage 7 zum KTB PzAOK 4, Meldungen (Beute, Verpflegungsstärken) von 1.7.1943 bis 31.12.1943 (BA-MA RH 21-4/422).
13 Derived from T. N. Dupuy, *Hitler's Last Gamble* (Airlife, Shrewsbury 1995) appendix D and E.
14 OKH Org.Abt. document: Berechnung der Gefechts- und Kampfstärke der I.D. 44, dated 4 Oct 1944, T78, R421, F6390638.

15 S. L. Stanton, *Order of Battle US Army, World War II* (Presidio, Novato 1984) p. 15.

16 Ibid.

17 OKH Org.Abt. I Nr. 1/11924/44 geh. 8.10.44, T312, R421, F6390652.

18 The German *Füsilier-Bataillon* did reduce this difference to some extent. If it is included as part of the infantry regiment totals, the German infantry regiment was strengthend by 236 men. This would mean that US infantry regiments were 47% larger than their German equivalents.

Arrival of Panzer Units in Normandy

This appendix gives the dates when *Panzer* units arrived in Normandy, as well as their strength when they departed for Normandy. Note that the arrival may have been an affair lasting several days. In those cases, either the mean' between the first and last arrival dates has been used or else the entries for more than one day have been used for the sub-units of the parent formation. In many cases the available documents do not provide an exact date of arrival and, in those cases, an estimate has been made. Sources are those given in the narratives for the respective units. Included are units equipped with the *Panzer IV (lang), Panther, Tiger, Sturmgeschütz, Jagdpanzer IV, Jagdpanther* and *Sturmpanzer IV.* When comparing the figures in this appendix with Allied tank strengths, it must be emphasized that the figures given here refer to tanks and assault guns actually sent to Normandy. Thus, they include replacements (which were very few), but not losses. Until 27 July the Germans lost (complete write-offs) 224 *Panzer IVs,* 131 *Panther's,* 33 *Tiger's,* 3 command tanks, 60 assault guns and 45 self-propelled antitank guns.[1] The document is not entirely clear whether self-propelled antitank guns include *Jagdpanzer IVs* and *Jagdpanthers* or only *Marders* and similar vehicles.[2] In any case, this means that the number of German tanks in Normandy on 27 July was not 1,959, as indicated below, but no more than 1,518 (or even fewer if *Jagdpanzer IV's* and *Jagdpanthers* are included in the 45 self-propelled antitank guns lost). Another factor to consider is that a large percentage of the German tanks were in maintenance facilities. It seems that the Allies did not have as large a percentage in workshops.

---

1   HGr B la Anlagen, Totalausfälle an Panzern, Sturmgeschützen und Sf.-Pak in der Zeit vom 6.6. - 27.744, BA-MA RH 19 IX/46.

2   My hypothesis is that *Jagdpanzer IVs* and *Jagdpanthers* are included in assault gun totals and not self-propelled antitank guns. German classification of these vehicles, however, is not entirely consistent.

Date	Unit	Strength	Comment
6 June	352. Infanterie-Division	10 Sturmgeschutz III's	Delivery of 14 Panzer IV's shipped on 24 May assumed to have arrived.
	21. Panzer-Division	112 Panzer IV's	
		Accumulated AFV strength committed: 122	
7 June	II./SS-Panzer-Regiment 12	98 Panzer IV's	About half not ready for action at arrival.
		Accumulated AFV strength committed: 220	
8 June	I./SS-Panzer-Regiment 12	66 Panthers IV's	About half not ready for action at arrival.
	II./Panzer-Regiment 130 (Lehr)	99 Panzer IV's	
	346. Infanterie-Division	10 Sturmgeschütz III's	
	243. Infanterie-Division	10 Sturmgeschütz III's	
		Accumulated AFV strength committed: 405	
10 June	I./Panzer-Regiment 6	99 Panthers	Attached to the Panzer-Lehr-Division
		Accumulated AFV strength committed: 504	
11 June	Sturmgeschütz-Abteilung 902	31 Sturmgeschütz III's	
		Accumulated AFV strength committed: 535	
12 June	schwere SS-Pz.Abt. 101	45 Tiger Is	
		Accumulated AFV strength committed: 580	
13 June	Fallschirm-Sturmgeschütz-Brigade 12	22 Sturmgeschütz III's	Assumed to be at full strength
		9 Sturmhaubitze III's	
	SS-Panzer-Abteilung 17	42 Sturmgeschütz III's	
		Accumulated AFV strength committed: 653	

(Contd.)

Date	Unit	Strength	Comment
17 June	353. Infanterie-Division	10 Sturmgeschütz III's	
		Accumulated AFV strength committed: 663	
18 June	2. Panzer-Division	96 Panzer IVs 79 Panthers 21 Jagdpanzer IV's	Not entire division
		Accumulated AFV strength committed: 859	
21 June	12. SS-Panzer-Division "Hitlerjugend"	13 Panthers	Reinforcements sent 7 June; arrival date estimated
		Accumulated AFV strength committed: 872	
27 June	2./schwere Panzerjäger-Abteilung 654	8 Jagdpanthers	
		Accumulated AFV strength committed: 880	
29 June	10. SS-Panzer-Division "Frundsberg"	39 Panzer IV's 38 Sturmgeschütz III's	
	9. SS-Panzer-Division "Hohenstaufen"	48 Panzer IVs 79 Panthers 40 Sturmgeschütz III's	
		Accumulated AFV strength committed: 1,124	
1 July	2. SS-Panzer-Division "Das Reich"	78 Panzer IV's 80 Panthers 45 Sturmgeschütz III's	Not all elements present
	16. Luftwaffen-felddivision	2 Sturmgeschütz III's	Not all elements present
		Accumulated AFV strength committed: 1,329	

Date	Unit	Strength	Comment
3 July	schwere SS-Panzer-Abteilung 102	45 Tiger I's	Actual number probably lower.
		Accumulated AFV strength commited: 1,374	
6 July	1. SS-Panzer-Division "Leibstandarte"	103 Panzer IV's 72 Panthers 45 Sturmgeschütz III's	Not all elements present; some of the tanks arrived later.
		Accumulated AFV strength commited: 1,594	
10 July	schwere Panzer-Abteilung 503	33 Tiger I's 12 Tiger II's	
	Panzer-Lehr-Division	8 Panthers	Replacements sent 6 July; arrival date estimated
		Accumulated AFV strength commited: 1,647	
19 July	1./SS-Panzerjäger-Abteilung 12	10 Jagdpanzer IV's	
	2. SS-Panzer-Division "Das Reich"	5 Panzer IV's	Command tanks sent 6 July; arrival date estimated
		Accumulated AFV strength commited: 1,662	
20 July	12. SS-Panzer-Division "Hitlerjugend"	17 Panzer IV's	Replacements sent 8 July; arrival date estimated
	21. Panzer-Division	17 Panzer IV's	Replacements sent 8 July; arrival date estimated
	Panzer-Lehr-Division	17 Panzer IV's	Replacements sent 8 July; arrival date estimated
		Accumulated AFV strength commited: 1,707	
21 July	2./Sturmpanzer-Abteilung 217	14 Sturmpanzer IV's 8 Sturmgeschütz III's	Reinforcements sent 9 July; arrival date estimated.
	16. Luftwaffenfelddivision		
		Accumulated AFV strength committed: 1,729	

(Contd.)

Date	Unit	Strength	Comment
23 July	schwere Panzerjäger-Abteilung 654	17 Jagdpanthers	Elements of the battalion
24 July	116. Panzer-Division	Accumulated AFV strength committed: 1,746 86 Panzer IV's 21 Jagdpanzer IV's 6 Sturmgeschütz III's	Elements of the division
25 July	326. Infanterie-Division	Accumulated AFV strength committed: 1,859 10 Sturmgeschütz III's	
26 July	116. Panzer-Division	Accumulated AFV strength committed: 1,869 76 Panthers	Elements of the division
27 July	3./Sturmpanzer-Abteilung 217	Accumulated AFV strength committed: 1,945 14 Sturmpanzer IV's	
31 July	Sturmgeschütz-Brigade 341	Accumulated AFV strength committed: 1,959 33 Sturmgeschütz III's 12 Sturmgeschütz III's	
3 August	Sturmgeschütz-Brigade 394	Accumulated AFV strength committed: 2,004 31 Sturmgeschütz III's	
4 August	9. Panzer-Division	Accumulated AFV strength committed: 2,035 82 Panzer IV's 79 Panthers 5 Sturmgeschütz III's	

Date	Unit	Strength	Comment
	SS-Panzerjäger-Abteilung 17	21 Jagdpanzer IV's	Elements of the divisional antitank battalion
5 August	Sturmgeschütz-Abteilung 1348	Accumulated AFV strength commited: 2,222 10 Sturmgeschütz III's	
10 August	331. Infanterie-Division	Accumulated AFV strength commited: 2,232 10 Sturmgeschütz III's	
	21. Panzer-Division	3 Panzer IV's	Command tanks sent 29 July; arrival date estimated.
12 August	17. SS-Panzergrenadier-Division "Götz von Berlichingen"	Accumulated AFV strength commited: 2,245 3 Panzer IV's	Command tanks requested 29 July; dispatched 2 August
		Accumulated AFV strength commited: 2,248	

Further Discussion on German Casualties

In many books, the popular image of virtually wiped out German units after the Falaise battle is fostered. In Chapter Seven, the condition of the German armor divisions immediately after the battle at Falaise was discussed. It was found that the conventional wisdom of them only having a few hundred men left was wrong. Rather they had around 10,000 men or even more. This misunderstanding is the result of erroneous interpretation of a few reports made in haste. But this is not the only case of German units allegedly being wiped out. Units that were not sent to Normandy, but got involved in the retreat from France, have been similarly described. One example is the *49. Infanterie-Division,* which has been described in the following way:

> ...the division took part in the withdrawal into the Low Countries and was smashed near the Albert Canal by Montgomery's soldiers. The divisional commander, Lieutenant General Siegfried Macholz, tried to reorganize his shattered units at Hasselt, but managed to assemble only 1,500 men—mostly support troops who had no antitank guns and only one piece of artillery: a Russian 122 mm howitzer.[1]

Interestingly, there exists a report on the condition of the division on 1 October. According to the report, the division had a strength of 6,904.[2] Even more interesting is that casualties numbered 561 killed, wounded and missing during September, while replacements amounted to 342.[3] Additionally, 232 men had left the division for other reasons than being casualties.[4] Thus it can be concluded that the division had a strength of 7,355 on 1 September 1944. This can be compared to the fact that it had an authorized strength of 11,110 on 1 May[5] and on 20 June it was reported that the division had a ration strength of 10,661[6]. This is 3,306 more than on 1 September. However, a report dated 23 September stated that the division had suffered 7,960 casualties since the Allied invasion.[7] Since casualties during September were relatively light, this would suggest much greater casualties during August than the 1 September strength implies. Of course, it is possible to conclude that the division received a large number of replacements (about 4,000) during August, but this seems very unlikely. The division was first engaged in combat on 23 August.[8]

It does not seem possible it could have lost more than 7,000 men and received more than 4,000 replacements in a mere nine days.[9]

A more plausible explanation is that the division was scattered and that the higher command echelons had little knowledge about its whereabouts. As shown above, one explanation for the exaggeration of German losses is the lack of proper understanding of German reports. For example, many do not realize the Germans might have reported the number of riflemen in the division, rather than the strength of the entire division, or they may have reported *Gefechtsstärke,* rather than the entire strength of the unit. Another factor to consider is that the Germans themselves may not have had an accurate picture, at least from mid-August until late September. This becomes evident if reports from that period are compared with reports compiled in October. The latter almost invariably indicate that tbe units are in better condition, even if losses and replacements during September are considered.

---

1   S. W. Mitcham, *Hitler's Legions, German Army Order of Battle World War II* (Leo Cooper, London 1985) p. 77. I have found so many errors in this book that I have little confidence in it.

2   LXXXI. A.K., Zustandberichte 1.10.1944, T314, R1597, F000045.

3   Ibid.

4   Ibid.

5   LXXXII. A.K. Ia, Anlagen zum KTB Nr. 6, Meldung 49. Inf.Div., 1. Mai 1944, T314, R1602, F000131.

6   LXXXII. A.K. Ia, Anlagen zum KTB Nr. 6, Verpflegungs- und Gefechtsstarken 20.6.1944, T314, R1602, F000459. It should be noted that the strength on 1 October is *Iststärke.* However, the ration strength on 20 June included only the division, not attachments. Thus it differed litde from Iststärke.

7   LXXXI. A.K. IIa/b, 23.9.44, T314, R1594, F000267.

8   J. Ludewig, *Der deutsche Rückzug aus Frankreich 1944* (Rombach, Freiburg 1995) p. 143.

9   The *49. Infanterie-Division* was a low quality formation and had it been so severely mauled (losing about 70% of its manpower), the Germans would hardly have considered it worthwhile to rebuild it. It would also have been a considerable feat if the Germans had noted the depleted state of the division, taken the appropriate decisions, found the replacements and directed them to the division in a few days.

Comments on a Few Books

When the manuscript for this book was ready and sent to the publisher I encountered a book called *The GI Offensive in Europe – The Triumph of American Infantry Divisions* by Peter R. Mansoor. Since this book claims that well-led and well-trained US divisions were as good as or better than their German counterparts in Normandy, it is clearly at odds with the conclusions of this book. Thus a few comments on Mansoor's book are justified.

When discussing the performance of a force, a few things have to be kept in mind. First, performance does not exist in isolation, but must be compared to an enemy. Second, the outcome in battle is dependent on the relative resources available and how efficiently these are used. Third, a one-sided use of sources must be avoided.

Mansoor does not really make any attempt at comparing relative resources of any kind. A rare exception is the following:

> A fashionable argument in the past two decades has been that the Allies won World War II only through the sheer weight of materiel they threw at the Wehrmacht in a relatively unskilled manner. This argument is actually a restatement of the theory put forward by German officers to explain their defeat, as evidenced by wartime interrogations and post-war manuscripts prepared by the defeated. The more combat-effective German army was in the end bulldozed by less capable, but more numerous, enemies — or so the argument goes. This conclusion would have shocked the victors, especially the senior military leadership of the American army, who understood just how thin was the advantage they possessed in numerical correlation between Western Allied and German ground forces in the crucial battles fought in France and Germany in 1944 and 1945.

This is, of course, not a particularly clear statement on the numerical correlation between the opponents. But why should a researcher rely on what would be shocking to men 50 years ago when he can go to the records and find the truth?

Mansoor uses sources in a very selective manner. With one exception, all information on the German forces and their losses are taken from non-German sources. The only exception is the statement on the condition of the *Panzer-Lehr Division* after Operation *Cobra*, which is taken from Paul Carell's old and poor book *Invasion – They're Coming*. Needless to say, Carell is completely at odds with what has been found since he wrote his book. As a source it is of extremely limited value, full of exaggerations.

It is a basic error of methodology to use US sources for information on German strength and losses. Even if a figure has originated from German records, it must be ascertained whether the author has properly understood the document. An example of this is Mansoor's statement that the *3. Fallschirmjäger-Division* suffered 4,064 casualties from 11–13 July.[2] The figure 4,064 is correct, but it applies to the period 6 June–12 July. Hence it is a matter of losses suffered during a month, rather than a handful of days. Generally, his statements on German strength and losses are very vague but, in every case where they can be checked, they have proved to be wrong.

Not only is his use of sources very one-sided. Among the sources he uses he is very selective. On a few occasions, he has actually used primary German sources. These are reports on the capabilities of the US forces. Those sentences that praise the Allies are capitalised upon and regarded as reliable by Mansoor. Those sentences that criticize Allied forces are dismissed as Nazi propaganda.

Mansoor asserts that one of the most important advantages the US forces enjoyed was the vastly superior fire support. There is probably some truth to this, but Mansoor only discusses the techniques used by the US artillery. He does not mention the vast discrepancy in number of guns and artillery rounds available. Neither does he analyze German firing methods and compare them with US methods. He only cites US officers who state the Germans were inferior.

Mansoor criticizes the German replacement system and, while there were flaws with the US replacement system, he still considers the latter better.[3] He does not even discuss the fact that the major strain on the German replacement system was the casualties suffered on the Eastern Front. Given the problems with the US replacement system as described by Mansoor himself, it seems highly unlikely that the US replacement system could have coped with an additional five and a half million casualties (which was the losses suffered by the Germans on the Eastern Front from 1941–1944).[4]

Finally, it is worth mentioning his description of the attack by the *Panzer-Lehr-Division* on 11 July 1944. Mansoor writes:

> The German attack convincingly demonstrated that well-led and well-trained US divisions were as good as or better than their German counterparts in Normandy. Historians who have tried to prove otherwise have seriously underestimated the advantages conferred to the defender by the hedgerow terrain. Furthermore, the American army was the only force in Normandy that learned how to attack successfully in the bocage.[5]

Evidently, Mansoor is easily convinced. Even according to his own statements, it is clear that the *Panzer-Lehr-Division* was attacking against very poor odds. The defending US units were many times stronger than the Germans.[6]

His statement that historians have underestimated the value of defending in the Bocage is unsupported. He does not even try to present circumstantial evidence or anecdotes. If, as asserted by Mansoor, the US forces were the only ones to learn how to attack in the bocage, the British must have failed to learn this. Again, Mansoor does not provide any evidence to support his statement.

Similarly, he writes that the British and Canadian armies performed poorly during the operations to close the Falaise gap.[7] As could be expected, Mansoor does not even try to substantiate that sweeping statement. The fact that German defenses against the British were much stronger than in the American sector can very well explain the slow advance by the British, Canadian and Polish forces, although further research is needed on this question.

One of the pillars of Mansoor's argument is that US Army divisions were adept at learning from their mistakes and experiences. But this is something that must be regarded as normal. Probably every WW II army learned and made changes to its tactics, organization, training etc. The important issue is: To what extent the different armies learned. However, Mansoor only analyzes the US Army. He presents nothing of value about the German Army that shows to what extent it learned. Thus, he does not really make a comparison of the two armies and can not make a judgement on which was the better. This is actually a problem which, to a great extent, is quantitative (though there are of course qualitative aspects too), but Mansoor does not give anything that sheds light on those aspects.

To sum up, Mansoor's book has several important flaws:

1. Very one sided and tendentious use of sources, which results in several errors in basic data.
2. No methodology to account for the resources available and their effects. Indeed, he does not even try to do this.
3. The difference between evidence and what's about to be proved is blurred.
4. Many statements are presented without anything resembling proof or evidence.
5. Lack of understanding that outcome in battle is not a direct measurement of skill.

One of the books Mansoor refers to is *Draftee Division* by John Sloan Brown.[8] Of particular interest is an appendix where the calculations by Trevor Dupuy are criticized. Brown argues that the Germans were not more efficient than the US formations, rather they were less efficient, and if certain errors in Dupuy's calculations are corrected they actually show that the Germans were inferior.

Brown's argument centers around three issues:

1. The sample of formations used by Dupuy is not representative. *Panzer-* and *Panzergrenadierdivisionen* are more common in the engagements analyzed by

Dupuy than their share in the overall German forces. Thus, Brown asserts that Dupuy has compared the German elite with the Allied average.

2. Sloan Brown claims that Dupuy's formulas do not accurately reflect the inherent advantages of defense. Since most engagements studied by Dupuy show Allied forces attacking German defenders, the result is that German quality is exaggerated in Dupuys formulae.

3. Allegedly, the value of artillery and air power is exaggerated in Dupuy's model. Since the Allies presumably had greater availability of these assets, the result is an exaggeration of German prowess.

Of these points, the first has some merit. The German armor and mechanized divisions do figure quite prominently in the data presented in *Numbers, Predictions & War*.[9] If, as Brown assumes, these units received the best personnel, this would result in slightly distorted calculations. But, according to Dupuy's calculations, the German infantry divisions also had a rather consistent advantage. Hence, this can, at most, only be considered a minor factor.

According to Sloan Brown, the second point is more important than the first. However, Brown seems not to have understood how the QJM works. He argues that the values for defensive posture – which vary from 1.3 to 1.6 depending on how well the defense is prepared – are too low. However, the advantages of the defender are not only given by defensive posture in the QJM. The terrain factors have to be considered. These are multiplied with the defensive posture factors. In effect, the advantage of defense can be as high as 2.5 when these factors are considered.

But there is another method to test Brown's second point. If Dupuy's model consistently underrated the value of defense, it should be expected that the Allies fared much better in the engagements where they defended. In fact, it is not so. Of the engagements presented in *Numbers, Predictions & War*[10] there are 63 where British and US forces attack. In these, the average Combat Effectiveness Value (CEV) is 0.72 for the Allies compared to the Germans. It could thus be interpreted the Germans were 1.39 times "better". In the 14 engagements where the Allies defended against German attacks, the average Allied CEV was 0.65, yielding a German CEV superiority of 1.53. This certainly does not suggest that Dupuy has underrated the value of defensive position.

Since *Numbers, Predictions & War* was written more engagements have been researched by Dupuy and his associates. Now there are several hundred engagements which have been used to validate the QJM (and its successor, the TNDM). Of particular interest is the German Ardennes Offensive. Even in this offensive, the Germans showed a CEV superiority when attacking[11], despite the fact that their divisions had been filled with men of lower quality than was the case in 1943–44 and also received too little training.

The third point that Brown makes – that artillery and air power is overrated in QJM (or TNDM) – is either not true or not very relevant. In the 78 engagements presented in *Numbers, Predictions & War*, air power constitutes less than 10% of the Allied fire power in 69 cases. Hence, in only 12% of the cases does air power account for more than 10% of the fire power. Even if air power had been given too much weight in QJM, it can not have affected the main issue here, except to a very small extent.

Artillery is another matter. If artillery is overrated and – as assumed by Brown – the Germans had much less of it (relatively), it would substantially affect CEV calculations. Unfortunately, Brown does not try to substantiate his assumption that the Allies had much more artillery support, given an equal number of men. As is shown in Appendix 4, the Germans actually had more guns per 1,000 men than the Allies. However, the Allied guns were often better. Further, if ammunition expenditure is used as a yardstick of artillery support, the Allies probably had slightly more artillery support than the Germans, man for man. The difference is not great though. The main explanation for the greater generation of Allied firepower is simply that their forces were larger in every respect.[12] If the conditions were different in Italy is unclear, but the burden of proof in this case is Brown's. It should also be noted that the QJM does not have a supply module. Hence, it does not take into account that Allied artillery usually was better supplied with ammunition. This means that it may have overstated Allied efficiency.[13]

Two books that do not address Normandy are *German Troops on the Eastern Front and the Barbarization of Warfare* and *Hitlers Wehrmacht* by Omer Bartov. One of the most important assumptions in both these books is that the fighting on the Eastern Front was much costlier than the fighting on the Western Front, which certainly is of interest for a book on Normandy. In absolute terms, this is true of course. However, per division employed, this is not necessarily true. During the period 22 June 1941–31 May 1944 the Germans lost 4,117,087 men killed, wounded and missing on the Eastern Front.[14] This equates to 117,631 per month. Since the Germans usually had more than 117 divisions, the monthly casualty rate per division was less than 1,000. This can be compared to Normandy. The Germans suffered approximately 210,000 casualties during 2.5 months, giving an average of 84,000 per month. Given that the Germans employed 37 divisions in Normandy, this results in almost 2,300 per month, or considerably higher than the Eastern Front average.

Of course, it can be argued that there were long periods of relative inaction and that the more intensive periods resulted in higher averages. If we look at two months – July and August 1943 – on the Eastern Front, both *Heeresgruppe Süd* and *Heeresgruppe Mitte* were heavily engaged. These two army groups had 117 divisions[15] and suffered 340,949 casualties during those two months,[16] resulting in 1,457 casualties per division and month. This is still only slightly more than half the rate suffered in Normandy. It must also be considered that the Germans added divisions continuously in Normandy. Thus, the true rate per division and month must have been higher than that calculated above. In contrast, the number of divisions on the Eastern Front remained much more constant during the period in the example above.

If we look at the summer of 1944 on the Eastern Front, we find a loss rate per division higher than before. From 1 June to 31 August 1944, German casualties on the Eastern Front amounted to 826,907.[17] On 15 June, the Germans had 129 divisions on the Eastern Front.[18] This gives a monthly average of 2,137, which is still lower than in Normandy.

Needless to say, this is not the final comparison of loss rates on the Eastern and Western Fronts. It is, however, evident that it cannot be taken for granted that the fighting on the Eastern Front was more casualty intensive.[19]

It seems the loss rates were equal to or higher than on the Eastern Front not only for the Germans in Normandy. The US 4th Infantry Division, which landed on Utah beach on D-Day, suffered 22,225 casualties during the 11 months it operated in Eestern Europe.[20] Accordingly, it lost more than 2,000 men per month. However, during the operations in Normandy, the Allied units clearly suffered a higher loss rate. The 23 US divisions (including the 1st French Armored Division) that participated in the Normandy Campaign spent, on average, 53 days there.[21] Since US casualties amounted to 125,847, the divisions employed suffered on average of almost exactly 100 men per day in Normandy. This means that they lost, on average, about 3,000 men per month in Normandy.

A simplification here is the tacit assumption that all casualties were incurred by the divisions. That is not true, of course, but most casualties were suffered by the infantry, and the infantry was almost exclusively part of divisions. During the battles in White Russia and Romania during the summer 1944, matters could have been different, since large formations were cut off and destroyed. But even on the Eastern Front, most German manpower was part of divisions, hence, the difference can not have been significant.

All these precautions considered, it seems that the far greater overall casualties on the Eastern Front were the result of the much greater number of units employed and the much longer duration of the conflict, rather than bloodier combat.

Bartov's books are not only found wanting in this respect. Rather there are several other shortcomings with the basic methodology.[22] There are also problems with his methodology for certain important details.[23] Finally, it must be called into question if Bartov has understood what the documents he used actually give information on.[24]

1   P. Mansoor, *The GI Offensive in Europe—The Triumph of American Infantry Divisions* (University of Kansas Press, Lawrence 1999) p. 155.
2   Ibid, p. 156.
3   Ibid, p. 254f.

4   N. Zetterling & A. Frankson, "Analyzing WWII East Front Battles", *Journal of Slavic Military Studies 1/1998,* p. 186.

5   Mansoor, op cit. p. 155.

6   As said, even Mansoor's information shows this. For a more complete picture, see Chapter 8.

7   Mansoor, op cit. p. 170.

8   John Sloan Brown, *Draftee Division, The 88th Infantry Division in World War II* (Presidio, Novato, originally published 1986, new edition printed 1998).

9   T. N. Dupuy, *Numbers Predictions & War* (Hero Fairfax 1985). See in particular pages 234-7.

10 Ibid

11 See T.N. Dupuy et al, *Hitler's Last Gamble* (Airlife, Shresbury 1995).

12 It should be noted that the QJM (and TNDM) only considers the number of artillery pieces and their characteristics, not the amount of ammunition fired. If the model took this into account, it would probably assign the Germans a higher combat effectiveness.

13 There are further problems with Brown's arguments. For some reason, he discards all the engagements except those where US divisions faced German divisions. The British are ignored because they were "different". Corps are disregarded because they were not "standard formations". First of all, all divisions were different after some time in action, when losses had reduced them, often in an uneven fashion. Second, even the "divisional engagements" were not standard divisions pitted against each other. Usually, divisions either had elements detached or were reinforced in various ways. For example, GHQ assets could be added (in particular artillery) as could combat groups from other divisions. Brown seems to make this distinction because he does not trust the OLI system used in QJM. His method, however, does not alleviate let alone solve the problem.

14 Der Heeresarzt om OKH GenSt d H/GenQu Az 1335 c/d (lib), Personelle blutige Verluste des Feldheeres, Berichtigte Meldung für die Zeit vom 1.6.1944 bis 10.1.1945, T78, R414, F6383234.

15 KTB OKW vol III page 736. The figures refer to July 7,1943.

16 BA-MA RH 2/1343

17 Der Heeresarzt im Oberkommando des Heeres, GenStdH/Gen Qu, Az 1335 c/d (lib), Personelle blutige Verluste des Feldheeres, Berichtigte Meldung fur die Zeit vom 1.6.1944 bis 10.1.1945, T78, R414, F6383234f.

18 Derived from G. Tessin, *Verbände und Truppen der deutschen Wehrmacht und Waffen-SS* (Mittler & Sohn, Frankfurt am Main and Biblio Verlag, Osnabrück 1966–1975).

19 Since Bartov argues that the fighting on the Eastern Front was more brutal for the individual German soldier than on the Western Front, it is obviously much more interesting to consider the loss rates for the individual units than for the entire war.

20 S. L. Stanton, *Order of Battle: US Army in World War II* (Presidio Press, Novato 1984).

21 Derived from Stanton, op. cit.

22 One of the major themes in Bartov's books is that the German casualties on the Eastern Front were too great to explain combat skill, endurance and resilience by the theory of "primary group" put forward by Shils and Janowitz 50 years ago. For this purpose, it is much more important to study loss rates relative to the forces employed, rather than the absolute levels. It is quite remarkable that Bartov does not even address this issue, fundamental as it is to much of what he concludes.

23 As mentioned above, Bartov takes for granted that the high losses on the Eastern Front precluded the so called "primary group" from providing the motivation and cohesion of German units. Rather, he claims that ideology and draconian discipline provided this, thus enabling the troops to fight on despite the tremendous casualties. Since the German casualty rates on the Western Front seem to have been at least as high as on the Eastern Front, ideology can not have ranked high on the list of factors motivating the troops. Bartov argues that racism and anti-bolshevism were

among the very most important parts of the ideology that influenced the troops. This can hardly have been a strong motivating factor for those who fought on the Western Front. If draconian discipline was important for the troops continuing to fight despite heavy casualties, then one must definitely ask why the US forces in the west did not break, since they also suffered losses at an alarming rate. Even in US setbacks, like the initial phase of the German Ardennes Offensive in December 1944, US units fought tenaciously, despite suffering very severe losses (one example is the 110th Infantry Regiment).

Another problem with Bartov's methodology is that he does not regard military prowess as a complex phenomenon. Roughly, it can be seen as composed of two parts, skill and willingness to apply the skill. If either of these is missing, the outcome will not be favorable. It seems possible that draconian discipline can instill a readiness to stand and fight. However, it is probably counterproductive to the development of skill. The dominant character of the German Army was not its ability to stand and die. Rather, it was its ability to inflict casualties on its opponents. This requires skill, not least in the areas of flexible combination of fire and movement, clever use of terrain, rapid (and distributed) decision making, initiative, cooperation among various arms etc. These are not capabilities that tend to thrive in an organization dominated by draconian discipline.

It could of course be argued that the ratio between killed, wounded and missing was different on the Eastern and Western Fronts. But even if only killed and wounded are considered, the loss rates on the Eastern Front do not differ radically from the Western Front. Furthermore, it is not evident that the larger percentage of missing on the Western Front supports Bartov. First, the German units on the Eastern Front had better mobility than those on the Western Front. At the same time, the adversaries in the west were more mobile than those in the east. Hence it was easier for the Germans to retreat from difficult situations in the east. Second, the enemy air supremacy in the west may have also made it more difficult to evade the enemy, in addition to being demoralizing. A third factor to consider is that the variation in troop quality seems to have been greater on the Western Front. Low-quality units are often more prone to surrender. Fourth, soldiers lost as prisoners are especially damaging to the primary group, since they will not be returned to the unit, as some of them would if they had been wounded rather than taken prisoner. Also, it may be even more damaging to the "primary group" if it is clear that comrades defect to the enemy. Fifth, it must be kept in mind that combat power is a function both of skill and willingness to make use of the skill.

Often the situations when soldiers surrender are those which are very disadvantageous. If they have the choice of surrendering or dying, the soldiers are probably not in a situation to cause much damage to the enemy. Finally, the reader is advised to look at Chapter 8 for more information on the ratio between missing and killed/wounded among the German forces in Normandy.

24 One example is Bartov's treatment of casualties. He makes no mention at all of the fact that most losses on the Eastern Front were wounded soldiers. A considerable part of these were returned to duty with their unit. Thus, not all casualties resulted in the "destruction of primary groups". Bartov does not provide anything on this issue. Rather, he seems to assume that all casualties are lost to the unit.

Two examples will be given:

1. Bartov states (*Hitlers Army*, p. 46) that on 12 March 1943 the *18. Panzer-Division* only had 2,834 men left. However the document he refers to (note that he has given the wrong date in his note; there are no documents with that date in the file he indicates) is a report on the condition of a few of the division's components. Bartov has just added those figures together and assumed that they covered the entire division.

2. Similarly, he states (*Hitlers Army*, p. 47) that the *18. Panzer-Division* had 2,440 men, only a sixth of its original strength, on 7 April 1943. Again he has used a report that only discusses parts of the division and gives no information on the rest of it.

German Flak in the West

As mentioned in the description of the *III. Flak-Korps, Flak* was not used extensively in ground action. This is also illustrated by the deployment of *Flak* formations in France, Belgium and the Netherlands on 15 July 1944. It could be divided into three main groups, each of which is discussed below. Note that this appendix does not cover *Flak* units that were part of the ground combat units (except when detached from their normal missions). It is based on two *Luftwaffe* reports.[1]

1. III. Flak-Korps

On 15 July, this consisted of four *Flak-Sturm-Regimenter.* The fourth regiment had four battalions, while the other three had only two:

Flak-Sturm-Regiment 1 with:	*I./Flak-Regiment 1 (gemischt[2], mot)* and *II./Flak-Regiment 1 (gemischt, mot)*
Flak-Sturm-Regiment 2 with:	*I./Flak-Regiment 20 (gemischt, mot)* and *II./Flak-Regiment 52 (gemischt, mot)*
Flak-Sturm-Regiment 3 with:	*I./Flak-Regiment 22 (gemischt, mot)* and *II./Flak-Regiment 64 (gemischt, mot)*
Flak-Sturm-Regiment 4 with:	*I./Flak-Regiment 35 (gemischt, mot), I./Flak-Regiment 53(gemischt, mot), I./Flak-Regiment 141 (gemischt, mot)* and *Flak-Abteilung 996 (leicht, mot)*

These regiments provided air defense in the area where German ground combat units were in action.

The *III. Flak-Korps* also had seven battalions that were operating along the roads behind the *5. Panzer-Armee* and the *7. Armee.* These were:

Flak-Abteilung 80 (leicht, gep)
Flak-Abteilung 757 (leicht)
Flak-Abteilung 84 (leicht, SP)

Flak-Abteilung II/FASII (leicht)
Flak-Abteilung 90 (leicht, gep),
Flak-Abteilung zbV 11100 (leicht, tmot) and
Flak-Abteilung 98 (leicht, gep).

Finally, there were two *Flak-Kampfgruppen* (11700 and 13300) that were forming. The corps may have been organized differently at other dates. It was a rather flexible structure.

2. *Flaksperriegel AOK 7 and Straßenjagd*[3]

Under command of the *13. Flak-Division*, eight *Flak* battalions and two independent batteries were employed to protect the area behind the armies in Normandy and the *III. Flak-Korps.* These battalions were attached to two *Flak* regiments (note that *Flak* regiments were command and control organizations only, the actual *Flak* were guns almost invariably organized in the form of separate battalions that could be subordinated to *Flak* divisions, brigades and regiments as was deemed suitable for the situation):

Flak-Regiment 89 with:	*Flak-Abteilung 74 (leicht, mot)*
	Flak-Abteilung 78 (leicht, mot)
	Flak-Abteilung 752 (leicht)
	Flak-Abteilung 13200 (leicht)
	Flak-Abteilung 12300 (leicht, tmot)
Flak-Regiment Oberstleutnant Höhne with:	*Flak-Abteilung 958 (leicht)*
	Flak-Abteilung 959 (leicht)
	Flak-Abteilung 960 (leicht)
	4./FAS 31, 5./FAS 31

Flakregiment 89 was employed in the so-called *Flaksperriegel AOK* 7, while Hohne's three battalions and two batteries were operating to protect supply roads.

3. *Flak* employed in Point Defense

Most *Flak* was more or less immobile and used to protect certain key points, like marshalling yards, bridges, harbors, important road junctions, important industrial facilities etc. Most *Flak* battalions employed in this role were either designated *verlegbar (v)* or *ortsfest (o).* Units that were *verlegbar* could be deployed almost anywhere, but they had no organic transport. Units that were *ortsfest* not only had no organic transport, they where also dependent on other units or command echelons for deployment.

A large number of *Flak* battalions were employed in this role in France, Belgium and the Netherlands. The table below gives all the battalions on 15 July 1944. For most battalions a location is given. It seems that this is the location of the battalion headquarters. The *Flak* batteries could be located elsewhere, though most likely not far from the headquarters. Occasionally, there is no location given. Those units were most likely employed in the Paris area and are indicated as such. The type of unit could be *leicht (le.)*, *gemischt (gem.)* or *schwer (s.)*. There were also searchlight (SL) and barrage-balloon battalions. In addition to the mobility types discussed above, the battalions could also be static (bo.), motorized (mot) or makeshift motorized (b.mot.). *Flak* units could also be assigned to protect railroad transport (ETr.). According to the original document, several *Flak* battalions were designated *RAD*. The manpower of these units came from the *Reichsarbeitsdienst.* The column "Arm" indicates whether the unit belonged to the *Luftwaffe (LW)*, *Kriegsmarine* (Marine), *Fleer* (H) or *Waffen-SS*. Finally, the table also gives the regiments, brigades and divisions the battalions were supprting. Note that a battalion could be attached to a regiment that, in turn, was supporting a brigade or division.

---

1   Luftflotten-Kommando 3 Ia/Flak Nr. 11457/44 g.Kdos 17.7.44, Gliederung der Flakartillerie, Stand 15.7.44, BA-MA RL 7/58 and OKL Führungsstab Nr. 2061/44 geh, 2.8.44, Erfahrungsbericht Nr. 2 von der Invasionsfront, BA-MA RL 2 11/122.

2   *Gemischt* = mixed; *leicht* = light; *tmot* = teilmotorisiert = partly motorized; *gep = gepanzert* = armored/self-propelled. *Flaksperrriegel* = Flak blocking position; *Straßenjagd* = "road hunt."

Unit	Location	Type	Mobility	Arm	Regiment	Brigade	Division	Comment
2./VI I./Fallsch. Flak-	Amersfoort				111	19		
Regiment 11 II./Fallsch.Flak-	Paris area	gem	mot	LW	59	1		
Regiment 11 III./Fallsch.Flak	Bretigny	gern	mot	LW	11	1		
Regiment 11 I./Flak-	Villaroche	gem	mot	LW	11	1		
Regiment 14	Lajosse	gem		LW	85	5		Belonged to the
17 SS	Saumur			SS	15		13.	17. SS-Pz.Gren.Div.
F.FAS 31	Chartres	Balloon	v	LW	85	1		
102	Orange	gem	Etr	LW	95	5		
124	Cognac	s.		LW	111	12		
125	Liege	gem	v	LW	122	18		Manned by RAD crews
155	Soestuinen			LW		19		
157	Ouignicourt		v	LW		18		
175	Mont de							
168	Marsan	gem		LW	45	12		
193	Hallencourt	SL	v	LW	195	20		Manned by RAD crews
195	Le Havre	gem	o	LW	100	12	13	
196	Lapallice	gem	v	LW		12		
197	Orléans	s	o	LW		1		
	Aldernay	gem		LW				Attached to the
207	Paris area	le	ETr	LW	59	1		Channel Islands command

Unit	Location	Type	Mobility	Arm	Regiment	Brigade	Division	Comment
220	Toulon	SL	v	LW	69	5		
231	Lambazèllec	gem		Marine	III (Marine)			
242	Ch Atigneul	gem	v	LW	11	20		
246	Harlingen	gem		Marine	111	19		
252	Ostende	gem	v	LW	20		16	
253	Calais	gem	v	LW	132		16	
261	Bordeaux	gem	v	LW	45	12		Manned by RAD crews
263	Lambertsort	s	ETr	LW	117	18		
276	Le Manoir	gem	v	LW	100		13	
278	Boves	s	ETr	LW	FAS I	18		
286	Biarritz	s		Marine	45	12		
287	Tarascon	gem	mot	H	85	5		Belonged to 9. PzDiv
291	St Inglebert			H		5		Probably employed for V-1
292	Guernsey	gem	o	LW				Attached to the Channel Islands command
294	Watten							Probably employed for V-1
295	Antwerpen	gem	v	H				
308	Vieux-Rouen	SL	v	LW	20	20	16	Manned by RAD crews
314	Abbeville	gem	v	LW	195	20		
316	Paris area		bo	LW	129	20		
343	Avignon	gem	v	H	59	1		
344	Caudebec	gem	v	LW	85	5		
345	Aht	gem	v	LW	100		13	Manned by RAD crews
346	Isteres	gem	v	LW	117	18		Manned by RAD crews
347	Bordeaux	gem	v	LW	85	5		Manned by RAD crews
355	Toulon		o	LW	45	12		Manned by RAD crews
				LW	69	5		Manned by RAD crews

Unit	Location	Type	Mobility	Arm	Regiment	Brigade	Division	Comment
356	Toulouse	gem	v	LW	86	5		Attached to the Channel Islands command
364	Jersey	gem	o	LW				
369	Homeroeville	SL	v	LW	195	20		
391	Var-crossings	gem	v	LW	69	5		
402	Neuville	gem	v	LW	87	18		Manned by RAD crews
415	Zeebrügge	le	v	LW	20		16	
416	Antwerpen	s	Etr	LW	20		16	
417	Laon		v	LW	122	18		Manned by RAD crews
424	Paris area	s	ETr	LW	59	1		
428	Arnhem	s	v	LW	111	19		Manned by RAD crews
430	Brüssel	s	ETr	LW	95	18		
441	Rennes	gem	o	LW	15		13	Manned by RAD crews
442	Tours	gem	v	LW		1		
444	Paris area	s	ETr	LW	59	1		
469	Auxi le Chateau SL		v	LW	195	20		
473	Paris area	s	ETr	LW	59	1		
481	Autheor	gem	v	LW	69	5		
496	Paris area	gem	o	LW	59	1		Manned by RAD crews
I/Flak-Rgt. 501	Dijon	gem	o	LW	85	5		
501	Boulogne	gem	bo	LW	132		16	
538	Paris area	s	ETr	LW	59	1		
551	Paris area	s	v	LW	59	1		Manned by RAD crews
552	St Vincent	gem	o	LW	129	20		
553	Beauvechain	gem	o	LW	95	18		

Unit	Location	Type	Mobility	Arm	Regiment	Brigade	Division	Comment
554	Liege	gem	o	LW	95	18		
555	Dreux	gem	v	LW	100		13	
556	Marseille	s		LW	69	5		Manned by RAD crews
557	Toulouse	gem	v	LW	86	5		
559	Hesdin	SL	v	LW	195	20		
591	Nijmegen	gem	v	LW	8	19		Manned by RAD crews
592	Salon	gem	v	LW	85	5		Manned by RAD crews
593	Romilly	gem	v	LW		1		Manned by RAD crews
594	Florennes	gem	v	LW	95	18		Manned by RAD crews
595	Merignac	gem	v	LW	45	12		Manned by RAD crews
596	Nantes	gem	o	LW	15		13	Manned by RAD crews
597	Marseille		o	LW	69	5		Manned by RAD crews
598	Volkel		v	LW	8	19		Manned by RAD crews
599	Ferme de Mons		v	LW	122	18		Manned by RAD crews
600	St Trond	gem	v	LW	95	18		
607	Bayonne			Marine	45	12		
614	Brüssel	gem	v	LW	95	18		
649	Epagne	SL	v	LW	195	20		
651	Wallou-Cappel	gem	o	LW	11	20		
652	Villers	gem		LW	87	18		Manned by RAD crews
654	Champagne	gem	v	LW	87	18		
665	Rotterdam	gem	o	LW	8	19		Manned by RAD crews
667	Odenzaal	le	v	LW	111	19		
668	Volkel	le	v	LW	8	19		
671	Clos du Nord	s	v	LW	129	20		
672	Rouen	gem	o	LW	100		13	

Unit	Location	Type	Mobility	Arm	Regiment	Brigade	Division	Comment
673	Bourges	le	v	LW		1		
677	Orange	s	v	LW	85	5		
680	Vitry-Nojelle	le	v	LW	117	18		
683	Ande-Mueos	gem	v	LW	100		13	Manned by RAD crews
691	Brüssel	le		LW	95	18		
694	Laucourt	le	v	LW	FAS I	18		
703	La Villez - M	s		Marine	V (Marine)			
704	Kermoello	gem		Marine	IV (Marine)			
705	Montoie	s		Marine	V (Marine)			
708	Belle Ile M	gem		Marine	IV (Marine)			
716	Maizicourt	le	v	LW	11	20		
730	Charleroi	le		LW	95	18		
731	Nimes	le	v	LW	85	5		
741	Boquemaure	le	mot	LW	85	5		
744	Esteville	le		LW	129	20		
751		le		LW	1			
764	Bad Hoevedorp	le	v	LW	111	19		
765	Dünkirchen	le	v	LW	20		16	
780	St Jean de Luz	s	ETr	Marine	45	12		
803	Portzic	gem		Marine	III (Marine)			
804	Lanvéoc	gem		Marine	III (Marine)			
805	St Marc	gem		Marine	III (Marine)			
806	Ch Kerbletu	gem		Marine	IV (Marine)			
807	Lanester	gem		Marine	IV (Marine)			
808	Den Helder	gem		Marine	111	19		
809	Mindin	s		Marine	V (Marine)			

Unit	Location	Type	Mobility	Arm	Regiment	Brigade	Division	Comment
810	Vlissingen	gem		Marine	8	19		
811	Plougastel	gem		Marine	III (Marine)			
812	lie de Ré			Marine		12		
813	Hoek v Holland			Marine	8	19		
816	Ijmuiden	gem		Marine	111	19		
817	Kerloudon	gem		Marine	IV (Marine)			
819	Toulon			Marine	69	5		
820	St Nazaire	s		Marine	V (Marine)			
821	Paris area	le	ETr	LW	59	1		
822	Namur	le	ETr	LW	95	18		
828		le		LW		1		
831	Enschot	le	v	LW	8	19		
842	Evreux	le	v	LW	100		13	
845	Leuwarden	le	v	LW	111	19		
847	Goes	le	v	LW	8	19		
852	Feneu	le	v	LW	15		13	
859	Paris area	le	ETr	LW	59	1		
873	La Frenaye	le	v	LW	100		13	
875	Lyon bridge	le	v	LW	85	5		
877		le		LW		1		
880	Creil	le		LW	87	18		
901	Montpellier	gem	v	LW	86	5		
911	Elbeuf	le	v	LW	100		13	
912	Dinard	le	v	LW	15		13	
923	Biscarosse	le	v	LW	45	12		
932		le		LW		1		

Unit	Location	Type	Mobility	Arm	Regiment	Brigade	Division	Comment
955	Vendome	le	Etr	LW	159			
956	Roubaix	le	Etr	LW	159			
957	Vernon	le	Etr	LW	159			
958	Nancy	le	Etr	LW	159			
959	Utrecht	le	Etr	LW	159			
960	Arras	le	Etr	LW	159			
983	Perpignan	le	v	LW	86	5		
984	Bonnieres	le		LW	100		13	
997	Paris area	le	v	LW	59	1		
999	Gironde-Estuary	le	v	LW		12		
11300	Crissy	le	bmot	LW	87	18		
11400	Couvron	gem	bmot	LW	122	18		
11500	Montdidier	s		LW	FAS I	18		
11600	Remigny		bmot	LW	FAS I	18		
11800	Jodoigne		bmot	LW	95	18		
11900	La Chaussee	s	bmot	LW	87	18		
12100	Hertogenbosch	le	bmot	LW	8	19		
12200	Reilly	gem	bmot	LW	87	18		
12400	Montjavault		bmot	LW	87	18		
12500	Neuilly	gem	bmot	LW	87	18		
12600	Forges les Eaux	s	bmot	LW	129	20		
12800	Wadancourt	s	bmot	LW	87	18		
13100	Dreux			LW	100		13	
13400		s		LW	11 Fallsch	1		